Study Guide

for use with

The Economy Today

Tenth Edition

Bradley R. Schiller
American University

Prepared by
Linda Wilson
University of Texas – Arlington

Mark Maier
Glendale Community College

 McGraw-Hill Irwin

Boston   Burr Ridge, IL   Dubuque, IA   Madison, WI   New York   San Francisco   St. Louis
Bangkok   Bogotá   Caracas   Kuala Lumpur   Lisbon   London   Madrid   Mexico City
Milan   Montreal   New Delhi   Santiago   Seoul   Singapore   Sydney   Taipei   Toronto

Study Guide for use with
THE ECONOMY TODAY
Bradley R. Schiller

Published by McGraw-Hill/Irwin, an imprint of The McGraw-Hill Companies, Inc., 1221 Avenue of the Americas, New York, NY 10020. Copyright © 2006, 2003, 2000, 1997, 1994, 1991, 1989, 1986, 1983, 1980 by The McGraw-Hill Companies, Inc. All rights reserved.

1 2 3 4 5 6 7 8 9 0 QPD/QPD 0 9 8 7 6 5

ISBN 0-07-304213-7

www.mhhe.com

Table of Contents

		Preface	**v**
		Online Learning Center	**vii**
PART	**I**	**BASIC CONCEPTS**	**1**
	1.	Economics: The Core Issues	1
	2.	The U.S. Economy: A Global View	19
	3.	Supply and Demand	31
	4.	The Public Sector	51
PART	**II**	**MEASURING MACRO OUTCOMES**	**63**
	5.	National-Income Accounting	63
	6.	Unemployment	75
	7.	Inflation	89
PART	**III**	**CYCLICAL INSTABILITY**	**101**
	8.	The Business Cycle	101
	9.	Aggregate Demand	115
	10.	Self-Adjustment or Instability?	131
PART	**IV**	**FISCAL POLICY LEVERS**	**143**
	11.	Fiscal Policy	143
	12.	Deficits, Surpluses, and Debt	157
PART	**V**	**MONETARY POLICY OPTIONS**	**171**
	13.	Money and Banks	171
	14.	The Federal Reserve System	185
	15.	Monetary Policy	199
PART	**VI**	**SUPPLY-SIDE OPTIONS**	**211**
	16.	Supply-Side Policy: Short-Run Options	211
	17.	Growth and Productivity: Long-Run Possibilities	227

PART	VII	POLICY CONSTRAINTS	239
	18.	Global Macro	239
	19.	Theory and Reality	251

PART	VIII	PRODUCT MARKETS: THE BASICS	265
	20.	The Demand for Goods	265
	21.	The Costs of Production	289

PART	IX	MARKET STRUCTURE	305
	22.	The Competitive Firm	305
	23.	Competitive Markets	321
	24.	Monopoly	335
	25.	Oligopoly	349
	26.	Monopolistic Competition	363

PART	X	REGULATORY ISSUES	375
	27.	(De)Regulation of Business	375
	28.	Environmental Protection	387
	29.	The Farm Problem	403

PART	XI	FACTOR MARKETS: BASIC THEORY	413
	30.	The Labor Market	413
	31.	Labor Unions	431
	32.	Financial Markets	445

PART	XII	DISTRIBUTIONAL ISSUES	455
	33.	Taxes: Equity vs. Efficiency	455
	34.	Transfer Payments: Welfare and Social Security	469

PART	XIII	INTERNATIONAL ECONOMICS	479
	35.	International Trade	479
	36.	International Finance	493

Preface

This study guide is written to accompany *The Economy Today*, 10th edition, by Bradley R. Schiller. The overall focus of the Study Guide is to reinforce the economic principles and concepts presented in the textbook. Each section of each chapter has a particular objective.

The *Quick Review* and *Learning Objectives* sections provide brief summaries of the basic contents of the corresponding text chapters.

The *Using Key Terms* section allows students to practice using the words defined in each chapter in a crossword puzzle format.

The *True or False* and *Multiple Choice* sections help students apply economic principles in a familiar problem-solving setting. This will help greatly in the preparation for exams.

The *Problems and Applications* section lets students discover economic principles for themselves. Students not only learn the techniques that economists use, but they also discover the basis for the economic concepts they have learned.

Semester after semester, students have difficulty with the same concepts and make the same mistakes. The section called *Common Errors* addresses some of these problems, and provides an explanation using appropriate economic principles.

STUDY GUIDE

Online Learning Center

The Online Learning Center is an exciting feature of the *The Economy Today*'s 10th edition. The Student Center provides a number of ways to supplement your study efforts including Chapter Summaries, Key Terms, Multiple Choice and True or False Quizzes, Web-Based Projects, News Flashes, *New York Times* articles, DiscoverEcon, and PowerPoint slides.

A summary of each feature is provided below along with instructions on how to use it.

Chapter Summary – This is a simple summary of the material covered in the text for each chapter. To access this feature, choose the chapter number you want to work on and then click on the *Chapter Summary* link in the left-hand column.

Key Terms – This section lists the chapter's key terms, and provides a definition for each term. To access this feature, choose the chapter number you want to work on and then click on the *Key Terms* link.

Multiple Choice and True or False Quizzes – There is a 15 question multiple choice quiz and a five question true or false quiz for each chapter. Both quizzes test how well you learned the concepts covered in the chapter. After answering the multiple choice questions, you can submit the quiz for grading and send the results of the quiz to your professor by e-mail. After answering the true or false questions, you are provided with explanations of each questions answer. To access these features, choose the chapter number you want to work on and then click on the *Multiple Choice Quiz or True or False Quiz* link in the left-hand column. After answering the quiz questions, click the "Submit Answers" button to have the quiz automatically graded.

Web-based Activities – There are two interactive activities provided for each chapter. These activities allow you to explore each chapter's content through a series of questions that are tied to specific Internet links. To access this feature, choose the chapter number you want to work on and then click on the *Web-based Activities* link.

Web-based Projects – These projects are designed to help you use the Internet to explore economic questions. In these projects, you are asked a series of questions relevant to the content you are exploring in class. To find the answers, you must explore specific content located on the World Wide Web by following the links provided. These projects also have a collaborative feature that may be assigned by your professor. With this feature you collaborate with other students in your class to develop answers to specific questions together. To access this feature, simply click on the *Web-based projects* link and choose the topic relevant to the material being covered in class or the material assigned by your professor.

NewsFlashes – As up-to-date as *The Economy Today* is, it can't foretell the future. As the future becomes the present, however, Brad Schiller writes 2 page *News Flashes* describing major economic events in the news and relating them to specific text references. To access this feature, simply click on the *NewsFlashes* link and choose the topic relevant to the material being covered in class or the *NewsFlash* assigned by your professor.

New York Times **news articles** – This section contains news articles from the New York Times that are relevant to the course. To access this feature, simply click on the *New York Times News* link and choose the chapter number you want to work on.

DiscoverEcon with Paul Solman Videos – Software specifically designed to supplement Brad Schiller's *The Economy Today,* 10e was developed by Gerald Nelson at the University of Illinois, Urbana-Champaign. This software is designed to be an interactive textbook that parallels the paper textbook. The software now includes access to over 255 minutes of video created by Paul Solman, economic correspondent for *The News Hour with Jim Lehrer.* These eight to fifteen minute video segments are available via web streaming and can be linked to directly from the DiscoverEcon Video Lab. DiscoverEcon with Paul Solman videos is available with the textbook on the web. When you purchased your new textbook, you should have found an online code card sewn into the front cover of the book. Follow the instructions on the back of the code card to access DiscoverEcon and enter your unique code.

PowerPoints – Developed using Microsoft PowerPoint software, these slides are a great step-by-step review of the key points and graphs in each of the book's 36 chapters. To access this feature, choose the chapter number you want to work on and then click on the *PowerPoints* link in the left-hand column. Click on the chapter file that appears on the screen. It will take a few seconds for your computer to launch PowerPoint, but once you see the first slide, you can begin using the arrow keys to move from slide to slide within the chapter.

If you need additional help, you can click on Help Center to scroll through a list of help topics, or send your question to the webmaster via e-mail by selecting the Feedback option.

CHAPTER 1

Economics: The Core Issues

Quick Review

- Resources (land, labor, capital, and entrepreneurship) are considered scarce, even when they seem abundant, because there are not enough resources to satisfy all of society's wants.

- Because resources are limited, society must make choices about what to produce. Choosing to produce one thing means giving up the opportunity to produce something else. Economists refer to the best forgone alternative as opportunity cost.

- Economists illustrate these choices by drawing a production possibilities curve. This curve shows the combinations of goods and services a society could produce if it were operating efficiently and all of its resources were fully employed.

- The production possibilities curve appears bowed out from the origin because of the law of increasing opportunity costs, which occurs because resources are not equally well suited to the production of all goods.

- If society is inefficient in the use of its resources, it will produce inside the production possibilities curve. Additional resources and technological advances result in an outward shift of the production possibilities curve. This is known as economic growth.

- Every society confronts the problem of scarcity and must somehow answer these basic questions:
  WHAT is to be produced?
  > HOW should it be produced?
  > FOR WHOM should the output be produced?

- The United States is primarily a market-driven economy. The "invisible hand" of the market mechanism coordinates the production and consumption decisions of millions of individuals and directly affects the allocation of the economy's resources. In some economies the market mechanism is not allowed to work. Planned (or command) economies, such as North Korea, are a good example of this.

- When the market mechanism fails to provide goods and services efficiently and equitably – a situation called "market failure" – the public sector must provide assistance. However, it is possible that government intervention will make the situation even worse, which is referred to as "government failure."

1

- It is useful to break economics into two categories: microeconomics and macroeconomics. Microeconomics focuses on a specific individual, firm, industry, or government agency; macroeconomics focuses on the entire economy.

Learning Objectives

After reading Chapter 1 and doing the following exercises, you should:

1. Understand the debate concerning market allocation vs. government allocation of resources.
2. Understand that economics is the study of how to allocate society's scarce resources – land, labor, capital, and entrepreneurship.
3. Know that scarcity occurs because resources are not sufficient to satisfy all of society's wants.
4. Be able to define and illustrate opportunity costs using a production-possibilities curve.
5. Understand the law of increasing opportunity costs.
6. Be able to demonstrate efficiency, growth, unemployment, and underemployment using a production-possibilities curve.
7. Know why every economy must answer the same basic questions – WHAT, HOW, and FOR WHOM.
8. Be able to distinguish macroeconomic issues from microeconomic issues.
9. Be able to describe how the market mechanism seeks to allocate society's resources to their most valued use.
10. Be aware that there is serious debate and controversy over how the economy works.
11. Be able to discuss the tradeoffs inherent in the "peace dividend."
12. Be able to describe the mixed economy and distinguish market failure from government failure.

Using Key Terms

Fill in the puzzle on the opposite page with the appropriate terms from the list of Key Terms at the end of the chapter in the text.

Across

1. The reason there is no such thing as a "free lunch."
3. Occurs when government intervention fails to improve economic outcomes.
6. Represented by land, labor, capital, and entrepreneurship.
7. Economic study concerned with the behavior of individuals, firms, and government agencies.
11. The study of how best to allocate society's scarce resources.
14. Referred to as the "invisible hand" by Adam Smith.
16. Latin term meaning "other things remaining equal."
17. Economic policy supported by Adam Smith.

Down

2. The _____ _____ curve represents the combinations of output that can be produced with the available resources and technology.
4. The individual who brings together the resources needed to produce new or better products.
5. The study of the economy as a whole.
8. The use of both market signals and government directives to select the mix of output.
9. Illustrated in the text by the outward shift of the production-possibilities curve.
10. Occurs when the market mechanism results in the wrong mix of output.
12. Final goods used to produce other goods.
13. The idea that there are not enough resources available to satisfy all desires.
15. Every point on the production possibilities curve represents a situation of _____.

Puzzle 1.1

True or False: *Circle your choice and explain why any false statements are incorrect.*

T ~~F~~ 1. Scarcity is only a problem in the very poor countries of the world.

T F 2. Students do not pay tuition in public school, so from society's point of view, there is no opportunity cost involved in their education.

T F 3. All output combinations that lie on the production possibilities curve are characterized by efficient use of resources.

T F 4. One reason that the production possibilities curve is bowed outward is that more production means the economy is less efficient in producing output.

T F 5. If the economy is fully and efficiently employing its resources, then the only way to acquire more of one good, *ceteris paribus*, is to accept less of something else.

T F 6. The opportunity cost of a good increases as more of the good is produced because resources are not equally well-suited to the production of all goods.

T F 7. The economy achieves the greatest efficiency when it is inside the production possibilities curve.

T F 8. An economy will never be able to produce a combination of goods and services outside of its existing production possibilities curve.

T F 9. A market-driven economy is not capable of solving the problems created by pollution without intervention by government.

T F 10. Price signals direct the answers to the WHAT, HOW, and FOR WHOM decisions in a laissez-faire economy.

Multiple Choice: *Select the correct answer.*

_____ 1. Which of the following is the best description of the origin of the economic problem of scarcity?
 (a) Humans have limited wants for goods and services and resources are also limited.
 (b) Humans have limited wants for goods and services and resources are unlimited.
 (c) Humans have unlimited wants for goods and services but resources are limited.
 (d) Humans have unlimited wants for goods and services and resources are also unlimited.

_____ 2. Which of the following best describes the term "resource allocation"?
 (a) Which goods and services society will produce with available factors of production.
 (b) How society spends the income of individuals based on resource availability.
 (c) How society purchases resources, given its macroeconomic goals.
 (d) How individual market participants decide what to produce given fixed resource constraints.

_____ 3. A consequence of the economic problem of scarcity is that:
 (a) Choices have to be made about how resources are used.
 (b) There is never too much of any good or service produced.
 (c) The production of goods and services has to be controlled by the government.
 (d) The production possibilities curve is bowed outward.

4

_____ 4. Which of the following is *not* a factor of production?
  (a) A college professor.
  (b) A chalkboard used in an economics classroom.
  (c) The $10 million donated to the college by wealthy alumni.
  (d) The land on which a college is located.

_____ 5. Centrally planned economies are most likely to underestimate the value of:
  (a) Land.
  (b) Labor.
  (c) Capital.
  (d) Entrepreneurship.

_____ 6. Which of the following describes how resources are typically allocated in the U.S. economy?
  (a) By tradition.
  (b) By democratic vote.
  (c) By markets.
  (d) By government.

_____ 7. I plan on going to a $8 movie this evening instead of studying for an exam. The total opportunity cost of the movie:
  (a) Depends on how I score on the exam.
  (b) Is $8.
  (c) Is what I could have purchased with the $5 plus the study time I forgo.
  (d) Is the forgone studying I could have done in the same time.

_____ 8. The opportunity cost of installing a traffic light at a dangerous intersection is:
  (a) Negative, since it will reduce accidents.
  (b) The best possible alternative bundle of other goods or services that must be forgone in order to build and install the traffic light.
  (c) The time lost by drivers who approach the intersection when the light is red.
  (d) The cost of the stoplight plus the cost savings from a reduction in the number of accidents.

_____ 9. Which of the following events would cause the production possibilities curve to shift inward?
  (a) Immigration into a country increases.
  (b) New factories are built.
  (c) A technological breakthrough occurs.
  (d) A terrorist attack destroys roads, bridges, and factories.

_____ 10. Which of the following events would cause the production possibilities curve to shift outward?
  (a) The economy's capital stock increases.
  (b) A new, strong plastic is developed for use in building houses.
  (c) More women enter the labor force.
  (d) All of the above.

_____ 11. The slope of the production possibilities curve provides information about:
  (a) The growth of the economy.
  (b) Technological change in the economy.
  (c) Opportunity costs in the economy.
  (d) All of the above.

_____ 12. The law of increasing opportunity cost explains:
  (a) How everything becomes more expensive as the economy grows.
  (b) The shape of the production possibilities curve.
  (c) Inflation.
  (d) All of the above.

_____ 13. When an economy is producing efficiently it is:
   (a) Producing a combination of goods and services outside the production possibilities curve.
   (b) Getting the most goods and services from the available resources.
   (c) Experiencing decreasing opportunity costs.
   (d) All of the above are correct.

_____ 14. In a market economy, the answer to the WHAT to produce question is determined by:
   (a) Direct negotiations between consumers and producers.
   (b) Producer profits and sales.
   (c) Government directives.
   (d) A democratic vote of all producers.

_____ 15. In a market economy, the answer to the HOW to produce question is determined by:
   (a) Government planners.
   (b) The production possibilities curve.
   (c) The least-cost method of production.
   (d) The method of production that uses the least amount of labor.

_____ 16. The trend toward greater reliance on the market mechanism by former communist societies is evidence of:
   (a) Government failure.
   (b) Market failure.
   (c) The failure of a mixed economy.
   (d) _Ceteris paribus._

_____ 17. Which of the following are major macroeconomic goals of the economy?
   (a) Full employment.
   (b) Control of inflation.
   (c) Economic growth.
   (d) All of the above.

_____ 18. Microeconomics focuses on the performance of:
   (a) Individual consumers, firms and government agencies.
   (b) Firms only.
   (c) Government agencies only.
   (d) The economy as a whole.

_____ 19. Reread the _World View_ article "India's Economy Gets a New Jolt From Mr. Shourie." The article suggests that India has been using its resources inefficiently and operating:
   (a) On the production possibilities curve and near the middle.
   (b) Outside the production possibilities curve.
   (c) On the production possibilities curve but near one axis.
   (d) Inside the production possibilities curve.

_____ 20. Reread the _World View_ article "Food Shortages Plague North Korea." Implicitly, the article is suggesting that the maintenance of an army results in:
   (a) An opportunity cost in terms of consumer goods.
   (b) An opportunity cost in terms of investment goods only.
   (c) No opportunity cost because the army keeps the country safe.
   (d) No opportunity cost because the soldiers are being paid.

6

_____ 21. The slope of a curve at any point is given by the formula:
   (a) The change in y coordinates between two points divided by the change in their x coordinates.
   (b) The change in x coordinates between two points divided by the change in their y coordinates.
   (c) The percentage change in y coordinates between two points divided by the percentage change in their x coordinates.
   (d) The percentage change in x coordinates between two points divided by the percentage change in their y coordinates.

_____ 22. When the relationship between two variables changes:
   (a) There is movement from one point on a linear curve to another point on the same curve.
   (b) The entire curve shifts.
   (c) The labels on the axes must be changed.
   (d) The curve becomes linear.

_____ 23. A linear curve can be distinguished by:
   (a) The continuous change in its slope.
   (b) The same slope throughout the curve.
   (c) The changing relationship between the two variables.
   (d) A shift in the curve.

Problems and Applications

Exercise 1

Suppose you have only 20 hours per week to allocate to study or leisure. The following table indicates the tradeoff between leisure time (not studying) and the grade-point average achieved as a result of studying.

Table 1.1

	(a)	(b)	(c)	(d)	(e)
Leisure time (hours / week)	20	18	14.5	10	0
Grade-point average	0	1.0	2.0	3.0	4.0

1. In Figure 1.1, draw the production possibilities curve that represents the possible combinations from Table 1.1.

Figure 1.1

2. Using the information above, what is the opportunity cost of raising your grade-point average from 2.0 to 3.0? _____

3. What is the opportunity cost of raising your grade-point average from 3.0 to 4.0?

   _____

4. Why does the opportunity cost of improving your grade-point average increase?

   _____

Exercise 2

This exercise is similar to the problem at the end of Chapter 1 in the text. It provides practice in drawing and interpreting a production possibilities curve and demonstrating shifts of such a curve.

1. A production possibilities schedule showing the production alternatives between corn and lumber is presented in Table 1.2. Plot combination *A* in Figure 1.2 and label it. Do the same for combination *B*. In going from combination *A* to combination *B*, the economy has sacrificed _____ billion board feet of lumber production per year and has transferred the land to production of _____ billion bushels of corn per year. The opportunity cost of corn in terms of lumber is _____ board feet per bushel.

Table 1.2

Combination	Quantity of corn (billions of bushels per year)	Quantity of lumber (billions of board feet per year)
A	0	50
B	1	48
C	2	44
D	3	38
E	4	30
F	5	20
G	6	0

2. In answering question 1, you determined the opportunity cost of corn when the economy is initially producing only lumber (combination A). Using the information in Table 1.2, plot the rest of the production possibilities combinations in Figure 1.2 and label each of the points with the appropriate letter. Connect the points to form the production possibilities curve.

Figure 1.2

3. When Table 1.3 is completed, it should show the opportunity cost of corn at each possible combination of lumber and corn production in the economy. Opposite "1st billion bushels" insert the number of board feet per year of lumber sacrificed when the economy shifts from combination A to combination B. Complete the table for each of the remaining combinations.

Table 1.3

Corn production (billions of bushels per year)	Opportunity cost of corn in terms of lumber (billions of board feet per year)
1st billion bushels	_____
2nd billion bushels	_____
3rd billion bushels	_____
4th billion bushels	_____
5th billion bushels	_____
6th billion bushels	_____

4. In Table 1.3, as more corn is produced (as the economy moves from combination *A* toward combination *G*), the opportunity cost of corn (falls; rises; remains the same), which illustrates the law of _____.

5. Suppose that lumber companies begin to clear-cut forest areas instead of cutting them selectively. Clear-cutting improves the economy's ability to produce lumber but not corn. Table 1.4 describes such a situation. Using the information in Table 1.4, sketch the new production possibilities curve in Figure 1.2 as you did the initial production possibilities curve based on Table 1.3. For which combination does clear-cutting fail to change the amount of corn and lumber produced?

    _____

Table 1.4

Combination	Corn (billions of bushels per year)	Lumber (billions of board feet per year)
A'	0	75
B'	1	72
C'	2	66
D'	3	57
E'	4	45
F'	5	30
G'	6	0

6. After the introduction of clear-cutting most of the new production possibilities curve is (outside; inside; the same as) the earlier curve. The opportunity cost of corn has (increased; decreased) as a result of clear-cutting.

7. Study your original production possibilities curve in Figure 1.2 and decide which of the combinations shown (*U, F, O*) demonstrates each of the following. (*Hint:* Check the answers at the end of the chapter to make sure you have diagrammed the production possibilities curve in Figure 1.2 correctly.)
   (a) Society is producing at its maximum potential. Combination _____.
   (b) Society has some unemployed or underemployed resources. Combination _____.
   (c) Society cannot produce this combination at this time. Combination _____.
   (d) Society might be able to produce this combination if new resources were found or technology improved, but it cannot produce this combination currently. Combination _____.
   (e) If society produces this combination, some of society's wants will go unsatisfied unnecessarily. Combination _____.

Exercise 3

This exercise requires the understanding of scarcity, opportunity cost and production possibilities. Answer the following questions based on the information on pages 6 through 11 in the text.

_____ 1. In the U.S., the share of total output devoted to military goods:
   (a) Has remained fairly constant since 1940.
   (b) Is currently about 25 percent.
   (c) Is fairly low and results in no opportunity cost.
   (d) Is less than the share of total output devoted to military goods in Saudi Arabia.

_____ 2. According to Figure 1.1 in the text, as the mix of output moves from point *C* to point *D*:
   (a) There is an increase in the production of tanks.
   (b) There is no opportunity cost because point *D* represents the optimal mix of output.
   (c) More factors of production are available for both trucks and tanks.
   (d) All of the above are true.

_____ 3. According to the text, the North Korean army:
   (a) Is the largest in the world in terms of absolute number of personnel.
   (b) Absorbs a large share of output because North Korea is such a large country.
   (c) Absorbs approximately 16 percent of the country's resources.
   (d) All of the above are true.

_____ 4. Which of the following is the opportunity cost of maintaining an army in North Korea?
   (a) There is no opportunity cost because North Korea needs a large army to protect its citizens.
   (b) There is no opportunity cost because North Korea is producing the optimal mix of output.
   (c) Only the money spent on military equipment and salaries.
   (d) The food and other consumer goods that must be given up.

_____ 5. According to the text, Russia made the decision to reduce the size of its army, which released "... over 300,000 workers to produce civilian goods and services... As a result, Russia now has ... a lot more food." This represents:
   (a) A market economy at work.
   (b) The concept of opportunity cost.
   (c) The tradeoff between consumption and investment.
   (d) The tradeoff between food and civilian goods.

11

Exercise 4

This exercise provides practice in the use of graphs.

Use Figure 1.3 below to answer the following questions.

Figure 1.3

The slope of a line is the rate of change between two points or the vertical change divided by the horizontal change.

1. The vertical distance between the two points equals _____ .

2. The horizontal distance between the two points equals _____ .

3. The slope of the line equals _____ .

4. The slope of the line is (positive; negative) because as one variable increases the other variable (increases; decreases).

5. The line has the same slope at every point implying a (constant; changing) relationship between the two variables.

6. When the slope of a line is the same at every point, the curve is (linear; nonlinear).

Common Errors

The first statement in each "common error" below is incorrect. Each incorrect statement is followed by a corrected version and an explanation.

1. Words mean the same thing in economics that they do in our everyday conversation. WRONG!

    Words used in everyday conversation *very often* have different meanings when they are used in economics. RIGHT!

    You'll have to be very careful here. Words are used with precision in economics. You'll have difficulty if you confuse their everyday meanings with their economic meanings. For example, the term "capital" in economics means simply "final goods produced for use in the production of other goods." In everyday usage it may mean money, machines, a loan, or even the British response to the question "How are you feeling?"

2. Economic models are abstractions from the real world and are therefore useless in predicting and explaining economic behavior. WRONG!

    Economic models are abstractions from the real world and *as a result* are useful in predicting and explaining economic behavior. RIGHT!

    You must be willing to deal with abstractions if you want to get anything accomplished in economics. By using economic models based on specific assumptions, we can make reasonable judgments about what's going on around us. We try not to disregard any useful information. However, to try to include everything (such as what cereal we like for breakfast) would be fruitless. For example, the production possibilities curve is an abstraction. No economist would draw a production possibilities curve for a particular economy! But it certainly is useful in focusing on public-policy choices, such as the choice between guns and butter.

3. Because economics is a "science," all economists will arrive at the same answer to any given question. WRONG!

    Economics is a science, but there is often room for disagreement when responding to a given question. RIGHT!

    Economics is a social science, and the entire society and economy represent the economist's laboratory. Economists cannot run the type of experiments that are conducted by physical scientists. As a result, two economists may attack a given problem or question in different ways using different models. They may come up with different answers, but since there is no answer book, you cannot say which is right. The solution is, then, to do more testing, refine our models, compare results, and so on. By the way, the recent space probes have given physicists cause to reevaluate much of their theory concerning the solar system, and there is much controversy concerning what the new evidence means. But physics is still a science, as is economics!

4. Increasing opportunity cost results from increasing inefficiency. WRONG!

    Increasing opportunity cost occurs even when resources are being used at their peak efficiency. RIGHT!

    Increasing opportunity cost and inefficiency are confused because both result in a lower amount of output per unit of input. However, inefficiency results from poor utilization or underemployment of resources, while increasing opportunity cost results from the increasing difficulty of adapting resources to production as more of a good is produced. Inefficiency can be represented as a movement inward from the production possibilities curve, while increasing

13

opportunity cost can be measured in movements along the production possibilities curve. As the slope becomes steeper because of a movement down the production possibilities curve, the good on the x-axis experiences increasing opportunity cost (a steeper slope). Similarly, a movement up along the production possibilities curve represents a higher opportunity cost for the good on the y-axis – this time in the form of a flatter slope as more of the good on the y-axis is produced.

•ANSWERS•

Using Key Terms

Across

1. opportunity cost
3. government failure
6. factors of production
7. microeconomics
11. economics
14. market mechanism
16. ceteris paribus
17. laissez faire

Down

2. production possibilities
4. entrepreneurship
5. macroeconomics
8. mixed economy
9. economic growth
10. market failure
12. capital
13. scarcity
15. efficiency

True or False

1. F   All societies experience the problem of scarcity because human wants for goods and services will always exceed society's ability to produce goods and services.
2. F   Factors of production are required to produce education. These factors could have been used to produce other goods and services. The opportunity cost of education is the value of the best goods and services given up to get education.
3. T
4. F   Efficiency is maximized along a given production possibilities curve. The production possibilities curve bows outward because of the law of increasing opportunity costs, i.e., resources are not perfectly transferable from the production of one good to the production of another. Efficiency means "getting the most from what you have."
5. T
6. T
7. F   The economy achieves the greatest efficiency when it is on the curve.
8. F   An economy could produce a combination of goods and services outside its existing curve in the future if technology improves and/or the quantity of resources increase sufficiently.
9. T
10. T

14

Multiple Choice

1. c	5. d	9. d	13. b	17. d	21. a
2. a	6. c	10. d	14. b	18. a	22. b
3. a	7. c	11. c	15. c	19. d	23. b
4. c	8. b	12. b	16. a	20. a	

Problems and Applications

Exercise 1

1. **Figure 1.1 Answer**

2. 4.5 hours of leisure time
3. 10 hours of leisure time
4. Higher grades are harder to get, particularly if the class is graded on a curve, with higher grades being received by a decreasing number of students. The "law" of increasing opportunity cost is evident in the economy and in the classroom.

Exercise 2

1. 2; 1; 2

2. **Figure 1.2 Answer**

3. **Table 1.3 Answer**

Corn production (billions of bushels per year)	Opportunity cost of corn in terms of lumber (billions of board feet per year)
1st billion bushels	2
2nd billion bushels	4
3rd billion bushels	6
4th billion bushels	8
5th billion bushels	10
6th billion bushels	20

4. Rises; increasing opportunity costs
5. See Figure 1.2 answer; combination *G*
6. Outside; increased
7. a. *F* b. *U* c. *O* d. *O* e. *U*

Exercise 3

1. d
2. a
3. c
4. d
5. b

Exercise 4

1. 2
2. 4
3. Slope = vertical change ÷ horizontal change = 2 ÷ 4 = 1 ÷ 2 or 0.5
4. Positive; increases
5. Constant
6. Linear

CHAPTER 2
The U.S. Economy: A Global View

Quick Review

- The answers to the WHAT, HOW, and FOR WHOM questions in the U.S. economy are a product of both market activity and government intervention. Economic activity is assessed using economic statistics.

- The most frequently used measure of an economy's production is gross domestic product (GDP), which is the monetary value of a nation's output. Real GDP is the measure of output adjusted for inflation. GDP for the United States, at over $10 trillion, is more than one-fifth of the world's total output.

- The pattern of production in the United States has changed over the last century. At the beginning of the century farming was the dominant sector, then manufacturing, and now services. Service industries currently produce approximately 75 percent of total output.

- GDP can be classified as consumer goods, investment goods, goods purchased by the government (federal, state, and local levels) and net exports. Consumer goods represent the largest portion of U.S. output.

- Per capita GDP for the United States is nearly five times the world's average. Abundant resources, skilled management, an educated work force, and advanced technology have contributed to the high level of output. Factor mobility and capital-intensive production have resulted in high productivity. Economic freedom has also played a significant role in growth for the U.S. economy.

- Government establishes the legal rules of the game under which economic activity takes place. Government provides protection to consumers, labor and the environment through laws and regulations. Sometimes the answers to the WHAT, HOW, and FOR WHOM questions are made worse by government intervention, which is referred to as "government failure."

- Income is not distributed equally in the United States. Those in the highest income quintile receive almost half of the total U.S. income.

- In the future, society will demand different answers to the WHAT, HOW, and FOR WHOM questions as new concerns cause us to revise our priorities.

19

Learning Objectives

After reading Chapter 2 and doing the following exercises, you should:

1. Be able to explain why GDP and its components are an answer to the WHAT question.
2. Understand that factors of production differ in quantity, quality, and mobility in the United States and elsewhere.
3. Be able to trace the broad changes in industry structure in the United States from 1900 to the present.
4. Understand the role of government intervention as the economy answers the HOW question.
5. Understand that the economy's answer to the FOR WHOM question lies in the income distribution.
6. Expect that new market signals and government directives will change the answers to the WHAT, HOW, and FOR WHOM questions.

Using Key Terms

Fill in the puzzle on the opposite page with the appropriate term from the list of Key Terms at the end of the chapter in the text.

Across

1. Account for nearly half of all federal government spending but are not part of GDP.
6. One fifth of the population rank ordered by income.
9. The ability of a country to produce a good at a lower opportunity cost than another country.
10. The high level of _____ in the U.S. is the result of an abundance of capital, the use of advanced technology, and highly educated workers.
12. Goods and services bought from other countries.
13. A market situation in which the government intervenes to protect consumers from exploitation.
14. The costs or benefits of a market activity that affect a third party.
15. The resources used to produce goods and services.
16. A high ratio of capital to labor in the production process.

Down

2. Goods and services sold to other countries.
3. The sum of consumption, investment, government expenditure, and net exports.
4. The knowledge and skills possessed by the labor force.
5. An expansion of production possibilities.
7. Used to compare the average living standards in one country versus another according to the text.
8. The value of exports minus imports.
11. Expenditures for plant, machinery, and equipment.

True or False: *Circle your choice and explain why any false statements are incorrect.*

T F 1. The top 20 percent of U.S. households get nearly 20 percent of all U.S. income.

T F 2. If the economic growth rate exceeds the population growth rate, per capita GDP will increase.

T F 3. Federal government purchases of goods and services make up approximately 20 percent of GDP.

T F 4. Food stamps, medicare, and unemployment benefits are counted as government expenditures when calculating GDP.

T F 5. Technology advances allow an economy to produce more output with existing resources.

T F 6. As a percentage of GDP, output by the U.S. manufacturing sector has declined since World War II.

T F 7. Because of the outsourcing of routine jobs, the American economy is in jeopardy of falling behind other countries.

T F 8. If a business installs outdoor lighting that makes it difficult for you to sleep, this is an externality.

T F 9. In developed countries, the richest tenth of the population gets a smaller percentage of total income than the richest tenth receives in poor, developing nations.

T F 10. Income transfers are intended to alter the market's answer to the HOW question.

Multiple Choice: *Select the correct answer.*

_____ 1. The economic growth rate of the economy is best measured by:
    (a) The percentage change in the GDP between two points in time.
    (b) The percentage change in per capita GDP between two points in time.
    (c) The sum of the value of the factors of production used to produce output in a country.
    (d) A measure of output divided by a measure of population.

_____ 2. GDP per capita will decline:
    (a) Whenever the GDP falls.
    (b) If the percentage change in per capita GDP rises.
    (c) If the rate of population growth exceeds the rate of economic growth.
    (d) If factor growth exceeds economic growth.

_____ 3. The best measure of total output produced by an economy is:
    (a) Net domestic product.
    (b) Net exports.
    (c) GDP per capita.
    (d) Gross domestic product.

_____ 4. Which of the following countries annually produces the most output?
    (a) Japan.
    (b) United States.
    (c) China.
    (d) Canada.

_____ 5. Since 1900 the change in the importance of different sectors in the U.S. economy is best characterized as relative:
- (a) Growth in the farming share of output.
- (b) Growth in the manufacturing share of output.
- (c) Growth in the service share of output.
- (d) Decline in the service share of output.

_____ 6. As the United States economy relies more and more heavily on the production of services rather than goods:
- (a) GDP will decrease since there will be less "real" production.
- (b) International trade will become more difficult.
- (c) Mass unemployment will result.
- (d) None of the above are likely to occur.

_____ 7. Which of the following has contributed to the increase in international trade in the United States since the 1920s?
- (a) Reduced trade barriers.
- (b) Improved communication systems.
- (c) The growing share of services in U.S. production.
- (d) All of the above.

_____ 8. Most of the United States GDP is used by:
- (a) Consumers.
- (b) Federal, state and local governments.
- (c) Businesses.
- (d) Foreign individuals and businesses.

_____ 9. Investment plays a role in:
- (a) Both maintaining and expanding production possibilities.
- (b) Maintaining production possibilities but not expanding them.
- (c) Expanding production possibilities but not maintaining them.
- (d) Reducing the inequitable distribution of income.

_____ 10. Which of the following are included in the GDP?
- (a) Social security benefits.
- (b) Net exports.
- (c) Imports.
- (d) Welfare checks.

_____ 11. Which of the following explains the low productivity of workers in poor, developing countries?
- (a) Labor intensity of their production processes.
- (b) The low factor mobility.
- (c) The low quality of labor as a result of poor education.
- (d) All of the above.

_____ 12. An increase in the level of human capital in an economy, _ceteris paribus_, will have the following effect on the economy's production possibilities curve.
- (a) Shift the curve inward.
- (b) Result in a movement from inside the curve to a point on the curve.
- (c) Shift the curve outward.
- (d) Result in a movement along the curve.

_____ 13. The primary way to distinguish among corporations, partnerships, and proprietorships is through:
- (a) Their ownership characteristics.
- (b) The size of firms.
- (c) The market share of leading firms.
- (d) The number of firms in each classification.

_____ 14. Which of the following would *not* be a common government activity in the U.S. economy?
- (a) Control over most of the resources or factors of production.
- (b) The regulation of water pollution.
- (c) Enforcing child labor laws.
- (d) Requiring producers to label the contents of baby food.

_____ 15. When the production of a good creates external costs:
- (a) Profits for the producer of the good will be lower.
- (b) Production of the good will be lower.
- (c) Society's collective well-being will be lower.
- (d) The level of environment pollution will be lower.

_____ 16. When monopolies exist:
- (a) Prices tend to be lower than in a competitive market.
- (b) Production tends to be higher than in a competitive market.
- (c) Quantity of output tends to be less than in a competitive market.
- (d) All of the above can occur.

_____ 17. When the government intervenes in the marketplace because of market failure:
- (a) Society is always better off.
- (b) The production possibilities curve will always shift outward.
- (c) Society may be worse off.
- (d) Society will always be worse off.

_____ 18. Which of the following statements about the way markets allocate resources is most accurate from society's perspective?
- (a) The market always allocates resources in the best way.
- (b) The market may allocate resources in a way that is not in society's best interest.
- (c) Resource allocation by markets may not be perfect, but it is always better than when the government allocates resources.
- (d) Markets often fail to allocate resources properly, so we must rely on governments to determine the proper use of our resources.

_____ 19. Inequalities in income caused by market forces:
- (a) Are always undesirable.
- (b) Can provide incentives and rewards for achievements.
- (c) Cannot be addressed by government action.
- (d) Do not exist.

_____ 20. According to the *World View* article in the text titled "Income Share of the Rich," income inequality is greatest in:
- (a) Nicaragua.
- (b) Mexico.
- (c) The United States.
- (d) Sweden.

Problems and Applications

Exercise 1

Each year an economic report on the state of the U.S. economy is prepared, called *The Economic Report of the President*. It summarizes the essential features of the economy's performance and describes the policy initiatives that are likely to be undertaken. This exercise uses the kind of information that is developed in this publication. (Your answers may not be exactly the same as the answers in this book due to rounding.)

1. Table 2.1 shows the real GDP and the nominal GDP for the years 1996–2003.

Table 2.1
Real GDP and nominal GDP, 1996–2003

Year	Real GDP (in billions of dollars per year)	Nominal GDP (in billions of dollars per year)	Percentage growth in real GDP	Percentage growth in nominal GDP	U.S. population (in millions)	Real GDP per capita
1996	8,328.9	7,816.9	------------	-----------	271.1	_____
1997	8,703.5	8,304.3	_____	_____	274.4	_____
1998	9,066.9	8,747.0	_____	_____	277.5	_____
1999	9,470.3	9,268.4	_____	_____	280.7	_____
2000	9,817.0	9,817.0	_____	_____	283.7	_____
2001	9,890.7	10,128.0	_____	_____	286.6	_____
2002	10,074.8	10,487.0	_____	_____	289.5	_____
2003	10,381.3	11,004.0	_____	_____	292.3	_____

2. From the information in Table 2.1, calculate the percentage growth in nominal and real GDP for each of the years 1997–2003 and insert your answers in the appropriate columns.
   Use the following formula:

$$\text{Percentage growth in real GDP} = \frac{\text{real GDP}_t - \text{real GDP}_{t-1}}{\text{real GDP}_{t-1}} \times 100\%$$

   where: t = current year
   $t - 1$ = previous year

   For example, for 1997 real GDP grew by the following percentage:

$$\frac{\text{real GDP}_t - \text{real GDP}_{t-1}}{\text{real GDP}_{t-1}} = \frac{\$8,703.5 - \$8,328.9}{\$8,328.9} \times 100\% = 4.497\% \text{ or } 4.5\%$$

3. T   F   When nominal GDP grows, real GDP must also grow.

4. By what nominal-dollar amount did nominal GDP grow from 1996 to 2003? $_____

5. By what constant-dollar amount did real GDP grow from 1996 to 2003? $_____

6. The U.S. population for the years 1996–2003 is presented in column 6 of Table 2.1. Calculate the real GDP per capita in column 7.

7. T   F   When real GDP rises, real GDP per capita must also rise.

Exercise 2

This problem is designed to help you understand the mix of output in the United States.

1. First calculate the level of GDP, then calculate the percentage of total output accounted for by each of the expenditure categories in Table 2.2 for 2003. (Your answers may not be exactly the same as the answers in this book due to rounding.)

Table 2.2
U.S. national-income aggregates, 2003 (billions of dollars per year)

Expenditure categories		Percentage of total output
Consumption goods and services	$7,761	_____
Investment goods	1,666	_____
Exports	1,046	_____
Imports	1,544	_____
Federal government purchases	752	_____
State and local government purchases	1,323	_____
GDP	_____	

2. Which of the categories is the largest percentage of total output? _____

3. Which of the categories is the second largest percentage of total output? _____

4. Are net exports positive or negative in Table 2.2 above? _____

5. T   F   When net exports are negative, an economy uses more goods and services than it produces.

Exercise 3

This exercise focuses on the growth rates for GDP, population, and per capita GDP.

Refer to Table 2.1 in the text to answer questions 1-5.

1. Which country had the greatest increase in per capita GDP during this time period? _____

2. Which country had the greatest decline in per capita GDP during this time period? _____

3. In Nigeria, the growth rate of GDP during this time period was _____ percent and the growth rate of population was _____ percent. When the population growth rate is greater than the GDP growth rate, then per capita GDP must (increase; decrease).

4. In general, the population in high-income countries grew more (rapidly; slowly) than the population in low-income countries, which made it easier to raise living standards or per capita GDP.

5. T   F   During this time period, France and Japan had the same growth rate for population, but France had a higher growth rate for GDP, which resulted in a greater increase in per capita GDP for France than for Japan.

Common Errors

The first statement in each "common error" below is incorrect. Each incorrect statement is followed by a corrected version and an explanation.

1. A higher GDP means an increase in the standard of living. WRONG!

    A high per capita GDP is an imperfect measure of the standard of living. RIGHT!

    Many developing countries experience a rise in GDP, but their population grows faster. This means that there is actually less income per person and the standard of living falls! The growth in population must be taken into account in measuring the standard of living, which is the reason that the per capita GDP, not just the GDP, is used. However, even the per capita GDP measure fails to take into account the distribution of income.

2. Investors make an economic investment when they invest in the stock market. WRONG!

    Economic investment occurs only with the *tangible* creation or maintenance of capital goods. RIGHT!

    A distinction must be made between financial investment and economic investment. Common usage usually refers to financial investment, in which individuals purchase a financial security backed by a financial institution. Such an activity is called saving, which is the alternative to immediate consumption. Such saving may eventually be used by financial corporations to make loans that will eventually lead to economic investment. But economists have found that there are a lot of things that can happen to saving before it turns into tangible production of capital goods. Therefore economists analyze saving and investment separately.

3. As the United States imports more, consumption rises and therefore so does the GDP. WRONG!

    Imports replace the consumption of goods produced in the United States and reduce the GDP. RIGHT!

    The GDP is the sum of consumption, investment, government purchases, and *net exports*. Net exports are computed by *subtracting* imports from exports. So, let's look at the GDP as an equation:

    GDP = consumption + investment + government purchases + exports - imports

    Greater imports mean a lower GDP, if nothing else changes! Consumption of foreign goods is not the concept of U.S. consumption used by economists. Economists focus on the output that is actually produced in the United States, not all of the expenditures that consumers make.

4. Export goods are not included in the GDP because they are not consumed by Americans. WRONG!

    Export goods are produced in the United States and therefore are included in the GDP. RIGHT!

    The GDP is the sum of consumption, investment, government purchases, and *net exports*. Once again the equation appears as follows:

    GDP = consumption + investment + government purchases + exports - imports

    Larger exports mean a higher GDP! The GDP focuses on the output of the economy and our use of resources to produce that output, regardless of who consumes it.

•ANSWERS•

Using Key Terms

Across

1. income transfers
6. income quintile
9. comparative advantage
10. productivity
12. imports
13. monopoly
14. externalities
15. factors of production
16. capital intensive

Down

2. exports
3. gross domestic product
4. human capital
5. economic growth
7. per capita GDP
8. net exports
11. investment

True or False

1. F The top 20 percent of U.S. households receive nearly 50 percent of all U.S. income.
2. T
3. F Federal government purchases of goods and services only make up approximately 7 percent of GDP.
4. F These are income transfers and are not included in GDP. No good or service is directly provided in exchange for these payments.
5. T
6. T
7. F The outsourcing of routine tasks allows American workers to focus on higher-value jobs and the overall economy is better off.
8. T
9. T
10. F Income transfers alter the market's answer to the FOR WHOM question.

Multiple Choice

1.	a	5.	c	9.	a	13.	a	17.	c
2.	c	6.	d	10.	b	14.	a	18.	b
3.	d	7.	d	11.	d	15.	c	19.	b
4.	b	8.	a	12.	c	16.	c	20.	a

Problems and Applications

Exercise 1

1. Table 2.1 Answer

Year	Real GDP (in billions of dollars per year)	Nominal GDP (in billions of dollars per year)	Percentage growth in real GDP	Percentage growth in nominal GDP	U.S. population (in millions)	Real GDP per capita
1996	8,328.9	7,816.9	----	----	271.1	30,723
1997	8,703.5	8,304.3	4.5	6.2	274.4	31,718
1998	9,066.9	8,747.0	4.2	5.3	277.5	32,674
1999	9,470.3	9,268.4	4.4	6.0	280.7	33,738
2000	9,817.0	9,817.0	3.7	5.9	283.7	34,603
2001	9,890.7	10,128.0	0.8	3.2	286.6	34,510
2002	10,074.8	10,487.0	1.9	3.5	289.5	34,801
2003	10,381.3	11,004.0	3.0	4.9	292.3	35,516

2. See Table 2.1 answer; columns 4 and 5
3. F
4. $3,187.1 billion

5. $2,052.4 billion
6. See Table 2.1 answer; column 7
7. F

Exercise 2

1. Table 2.2 Answer

Expenditure categories		Percentage of total output
Consumption goods and services	$7,761	70.5
Investment goods	1,666	15.1
Exports	1,046	9.5
Imports	1,544	14.0
Federal government purchases	752	6.8
State and local government purchases	1,323	12.0
GDP	11,004	

2. Consumption goods and services
3. Investment goods

4. Negative
5. T

Exercise 3

1. China
2. Haiti
3. 2.4; 2.8; decrease
4. Slowly
5. T

CHAPTER 3
Supply and Demand

Quick Review

- Participation in the market by consumers, businesses, and government is motivated by the desire to maximize something: utility for consumers, profits for businesses, and general welfare for the government.

- Interactions in the marketplace involve either the factor market where factors of production are bought and sold, or the product market where goods and services are bought and sold.

- The demand curve represents buyer behavior. It slopes downward and to the right, showing that buyers are willing and able to purchase greater quantities at lower prices, *ceteris paribus*. The supply curve represents producer behavior. It slopes upward and to the right, indicating that producers are willing and able to produce greater quantities at higher prices, *ceteris paribus*.

- Movements along a demand curve result from a change in price and are referred to as a "change in quantity demanded." Shifts in a demand curve result from a change in a nonprice determinant—tastes, income, other goods, expectations, the number of buyers—and are referred to as a "change in demand."

- Movements along a supply curve result from a change in price and are referred to as a "change in quantity supplied." Shifts in a supply curve result from a change in a nonprice determinant—technology, factor costs, other goods, taxes and subsidies, expectations, the number of sellers—and are referred to as a "change in supply."

- Market demand and market supply summarize the intentions of all those participating on one side of the market or the other.

- Equilibrium price and quantity are established at the intersection of the supply and demand curves. At any price other than the equilibrium price, disequilibrium will occur.

- Price ceilings are set below the equilibrium price and result in shortages; price floors are set above the equilibrium price and result in surpluses. In either case, the market does not clear.

- The market mechanism relies on the forces of demand and supply to establish market outcomes (prices and quantities) in both product and factor markets. The market mechanism thus can be used to answer the WHAT, HOW, and FOR WHOM questions.

Learning Objectives

After reading Chapter 3 and doing the following exercises, you should:

1. Know the basic questions in economics and how the U.S. economy answers the questions.
2. Be able to describe the motivations of participants in the product and resource markets.
3. Understand how a demand schedule represents demand and how a supply schedule represents supply.
4. Be able to define, graph, and interpret supply and demand curves.
5. Know the nonprice determinants of both supply and demand and the direction they shift the curves.
6. Know what causes movements along demand and supply curves.
7. Understand how market-demand and market-supply curves are derived from individual demand and supply curves.
8. Know how equilibrium is established and why markets move toward equilibrium.
9. Understand the consequences of price ceilings and price floors.
10. Understand how the market mechanism provides the answer to the WHAT, HOW, and FOR WHOM questions.

Using Key Terms

Fill in the puzzle on the opposite page with the appropriate term from the list of Key Terms at the end of the chapter in the text.

Across

4. The result of the price ceiling on electricity set by the California legislature according to the text.
7. The price at which the quantity demanded equals the quantity supplied of a good.
9. A lower limit set for the price of a good.
10. The willingness and ability to sell various quantities of a good at alternative prices.
13. The willingness and ability to buy a particular good at some price.
15. The assumption by economists that nothing else changes.
18. Where businesses purchase the factors of production.
19. The use of market price and sales to signal desired output.
20. Refers to the inverse relationship between price and quantity.

Down

1. Occurs because of a change in one of the determinants such as income or tastes.
2. Put in place by the California legislature to control the retail price of electricity according to the text.
3. A curve depicting the quantities of a good a consumer is willing and able to buy at alternative prices in a given time period, *ceteris paribus*.
4. The sum of all producers' sales intentions.
5. A table showing the quantities of a good a consumer is willing and able to buy at alternative prices in a given time period, *ceteris paribus*.
6. Where goods and services are exchanged.
8. Goods frequently consumed in combination.
11. The amount by which the quantity supplied exceeds the quantity demanded at a given price.
12. Goods that can be used in place of each other.
14. The quantity of a good supplied in a given time period increases as its price increases, *ceteris paribus*.
16. The value of the most desired forgone alternative.
17. The sum of individual demands.

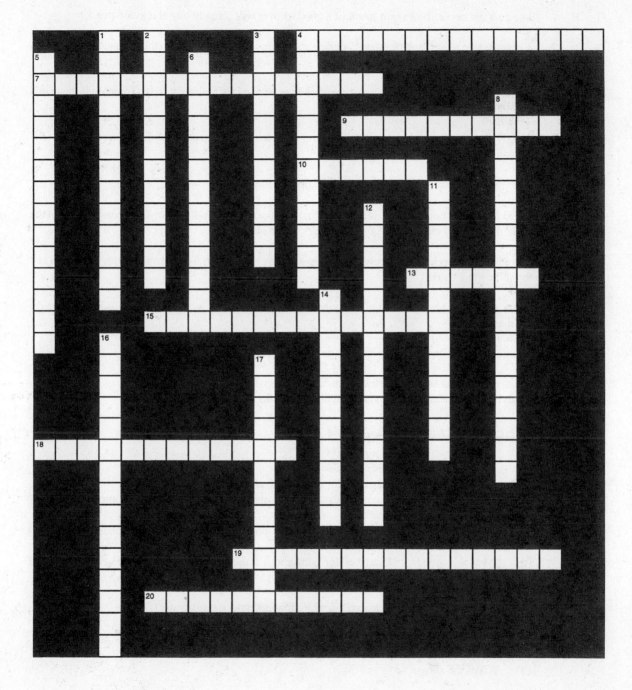

True or False: *Circle your choice and explain why any false statements are incorrect.*

T   F   1.   The demand curve shows how much of a good a buyer will actually buy at a given price.

T   F   2.   A change in one of the determinants of demand causes a movement along the demand curve for the good.

T   F   3.   An increase in the price of one good can cause the demand for another good to increase if the goods are substitutes.

T   F   4.   Supply curves reflect the potential behavior of the sellers or producers of a good or service, not of the buyers.

T   F   5.   The "law of supply" has nothing to do with opportunity costs.

T   F   6.   When the number of suppliers in a market changes, the market supply curve also changes, even if the individual supply curves of original suppliers do not shift.

T   F   7.   The equilibrium price can be determined through the process of trial and error by both the buyers and the sellers in a market.

T   F   8.   There are never shortages or surpluses when the price in a market is equal to the equilibrium price for the market.

T   F   9.   The government can eliminate a shortage by putting a price ceiling in place.

T   F   10.   When economists say that the market mechanism provides an "optimal" allocation of resources they mean that all consumer desires are satisfied and business profits are maximized.

Multiple Choice: *Select the correct answer.*

_____   1.   The goals of the principal actors in the economy are:
  (a)   Income for consumers, profits for businesses, and taxes for government.
  (b)   Goods and services for consumers, scarce resources for businesses, and resources not used by businesses for government.
  (c)   Satisfaction from purchases for consumers, profits for businesses, and general welfare for government.
  (d)   Available goods and services for consumers, scarce resources for businesses, and general welfare for government.

_____   2.   Which of the following helps to explain why economic interaction occurs?
  (a)   Limited ability to produce what we need.
  (b)   Constraints on time, energy, and resources.
  (c)   The gains possible from specialization.
  (d)   All of the above.

_____   3.   Consumers:
  (a)   Provide dollars to the product market.
  (b)   Receive dollars from the product market.
  (c)   Provide dollars to the factor market.
  (d)   Receive goods and services from the factor market.

____ 4. The law of demand states that:
   (a) As price falls, quantity demanded falls, *ceteris paribus*.
   (b) As price falls, quantity demanded increases, *ceteris paribus*.
   (c) As price falls, demand falls, *ceteris paribus*.
   (d) As price falls, demand increases, *ceteris paribus*.

____ 5. Which of the following must be held constant according to the *ceteris paribus* assumption in defining a demand schedule?
   (a) The price of the good itself.
   (b) Expectations of sellers.
   (c) Income.
   (d) Technology.

____ 6. The quantity of a good that a consumer is willing to buy depends on:
   (a) The price of the good.
   (b) The consumer's income.
   (c) The opportunity cost of purchasing that good.
   d) All of the above.

____ 7. Jon's demand schedule for donuts indicates:
   (a) How much he likes donuts.
   (b) His opportunity cost of buying donuts.
   (c) Why he likes donuts.
   (d) How many donuts he will actually buy.

____ 8. According to the law of supply, a supply curve:
   (a) Has a negative slope.
   (b) Has a positive slope.
   (c) Is a horizontal, or flat, line.
   (d) Will always be less than the demand curve.

____ 9. When a seller sells a good, *ceteris paribus*:
   (a) There is no change in supply or the quantity supplied.
   (b) The supply curve shifts to the left, but quantity supplied remains the same.
   (c) The quantity supplied of the good falls, but supply remains unchanged.
   (d) The supply curve shifts to the left, and the quantity supplied falls.

____ 10. If corn and wheat are alternative pursuits for a farmer, a change in the supply of corn will take place:
   (a) When the price of corn changes.
   (b) When the price of wheat changes.
   (c) When the demand for corn changes.
   (d) When consumers want to buy more corn at the same price.

____ 11. Suppose the equilibrium price for skateboards increases and the equilibrium quantity increases. We can conclude that there has been:
   (a) An increase in demand for skateboards.
   (b) A decrease in demand for skateboards.
   (c) A decrease in the supply of skateboards.
   (d) An increase in the supply of skateboards.

_____ 12. To calculate market supply we:
   (a)   Add the quantities supplied for each individual supply schedule horizontally.
   (b)   Add the quantities supplied for each individual supply schedule vertically.
   (c)   Find the average quantity supplied at each price.
   (d)   Find the difference between the quantity supplied and the quantity demanded at each price.

_____ 13. In the market for web design services, an increase in the number of people with web designing skills will cause:
   (a)   An increase in the equilibrium price and a decrease in the equilibrium quantity.
   (b)   A decrease in the equilibrium price and an increase in the equilibrium quantity.
   (c)   An increase in the equilibrium price and an increase in the equilibrium quantity.
   (d)   A decrease in the equilibrium price and a decrease in the equilibrium quantity.

_____ 14. In a market, the equilibrium price is determined by:
   (a)   What buyers are willing and able to purchase.
   (b)   What sellers are willing and able to offer for sale.
   (c)   Both demand and supply.
   (d)   The government.

_____ 15. A leftward shift in a demand curve and a leftward shift in a supply curve both result in a:
   (a)   Lower equilibrium quantity.
   (b)   Higher equilibrium quantity.
   (c)   Lower equilibrium price.
   (d)   Higher equilibrium price.

_____ 16. If the number of consumers in a market decreases, this will cause:
   (a)   An increase in the equilibrium price and a decrease in the equilibrium quantity.
   (b)   A decrease in the equilibrium price and an increase in the equilibrium quantity.
   (c)   An increase in the equilibrium price and an increase in the equilibrium quantity.
   (d)   A decrease in the equilibrium price and a decrease in the equilibrium quantity.

_____ 17. In a market economy, the people who receive the goods and services produced are the people who:
   (a)   Need the goods and services.
   (b)   Want the goods and services the most.
   (c)   Have the most political power.
   (d)   Are willing and able to pay the market price.

_____ 18. When economists talk about "optimal outcomes" in the marketplace, they mean that:
   (a)   The allocation of resources by the market is perfect.
   (b)   All consumer desires are satisfied and business profits are maximized.
   (c)   The allocation of resources by the market is likely to be the best possible, given scarce resources and income constraints.
   (d)   Everyone who wants a good or service can get it.

_____ 19. When effective price ceilings are set for a market, the quantity supplied will be:
   (a)   Less than the equilibrium quantity, and price will be less than the equilibrium price.
   (b)   Less than the equilibrium quantity, and price will be greater than the equilibrium price.
   (c)   Greater than the equilibrium quantity, and price will be less than the equilibrium price.
   (d)   Greater than the equilibrium quantity, and price will be greater than the equilibrium price.

_____ 20. One *In the News* article in the text is titled "Prices Soar as Cold Snap Shreds Iceberg Lettuce Supply."
This article best illustrates the concept that:
(a) An increase in the price of lettuce causes the supply of lettuce to decrease.
(b) A decrease in the supply of lettuce causes the price of lettuce to increase.
(c) A decrease in the quantity supplied of lettuce causes the price of lettuce to increase.
(d) An increase in the demand for lettuce causes the price of lettuce to decrease.

Problems and Applications

Exercise 1

This exercise provides practice in graphing demand and supply curves for individual buyers and sellers as well
as graphing market demand and market supply curves.

1. Suppose you are willing and able to buy 20 gallons of gasoline per week if the price is $1 per gallon,
but if the price is $3 per gallon you are willing and able to buy only the bare minimum of 10 gallons.
Complete the demand schedule in Table 3.1.

Table 3.1
Your demand schedule for gasoline

Price (dollars per gallon)	Quantity (gallons per week)
$1	_____
3	_____

2. Use the demand schedule in Table 3.1 to draw the demand curve in Figure 3.1. Assume the
demand curve is a straight line.

Figure 3.1
Your demand curve for gasoline

If you have drawn your demand curve correctly, it should go through point *A*.

37

3. Suppose that 999 other people in your town have demand curves for gasoline that are just like yours in Figure 3.1. Fill out the town's market-demand schedule in Table 3.2 at each price. (Remember to include your own quantity demanded along with everyone else's at each price.)

Table 3.2
Market-demand schedule for gasoline in your town

Price (dollars per gallon)	Quantity (gallons per week)
$1	_____
3	_____

4. Using the market-demand schedule in Table 3.2, draw the market-demand curve for gasoline for your town in Figure 3.2. Assume that the curve is a straight line, and label it *D*.

Figure 3.2
Market supply and demand curves for gasoline in your town

If you have drawn the demand curve correctly, it should pass through point *A*.

5. Suppose the friendly neighborhood gas station is willing to sell 250 gallons of gasoline per week at $1 per gallon and 1,250 gallons per week at $3 per gallon. Fill in the supply schedule for this gas station in Table 3.3.

Table 3.3
Supply schedule for neighborhood gas station

Price (dollars per gallon)	Quantity (gallons per week)
$1	_____
3	_____

38

6. Graph the supply curve for the gas station in Figure 3.3 using the information in Table 3.3. Assume that the supply curve is a straight line.

Figure 3.3
Supply curve for neighborhood gas station

If you have drawn the supply curve correctly, it should pass through point *A*.

7. Suppose that 19 other gas stations in your town have the same supply schedule as your neighborhood gas station (Table 3.3). Fill out the market-supply schedule for gasoline of the 20 gas stations in your town in Table 3.4.

Table 3.4
Market supply schedule for gasoline in your town

Price (dollars per gallon)	Quantity (gallons per week)
$1	_____
3	_____

8. Using the market supply schedule in Table 3.4, draw the market supply curve for gasoline for your town in Figure 3.2. Assume that the market supply curve is a straight line. If you have drawn the curve correctly, it should pass through point *A*. Label the supply curve *S*.

9. The equilibrium price for gasoline for your town's 20 gas stations and 1,000 buyers of gasoline (see Figure 3.2) is:
    (a)   Above $2.
    (b)   Exactly $2.
    (c)   Below $2.

10. At the equilibrium price:
    (a)   The quantity demanded equals the quantity supplied.
    (b)   There is a surplus.
    (c)   There is a shortage.
    (d)   There is an excess of inventory.

Exercise 2

This exercise shows the market mechanics at work in shifting market-demand curves.

1. In Figure 3.4, the supply (S_1) and demand (D_1) curves for gasoline as they might appear in your town are presented. The equilibrium price and quantity are:
    (a) $3 per gallon and 20,000 gallons.
    (b) $2 per gallon and 20,000 gallons.
    (c) $1 per gallon and 15,000 gallons.
    (d) $2 per gallon and 15,000 gallons.

Figure 3.4
Market demand and supply curves for gasoline in your town

2. Assume that one-half of the people in your town move away. Because of this, suppose that the remaining buyers are willing and able to buy only half as much gasoline at each price as was bought before. Draw the new demand curve in Figure 3.4 and label it D_2.

3. When the number of buyers in a market changes, the market demand curve for goods and services shifts and there is a change in (demand, quantity demanded).

4. When half of the buyers move from your town and the demand curve shifts, the new equilibrium price:
    (a)   Is above the old equilibrium price.
    (b)   Is below the old equilibrium price.
    (c)   Remains the same as the old equilibrium price.
    (*Hint:* See the second demand curve, D_2, in Figure 3.4.)

40

5. Given the new demand curve, if the market price remains at the old equilibrium price of $2 then:
   - (a) The quantity demanded will equal the quantity supplied.
   - (b) A shortage of gasoline will occur.
   - (c) A surplus of gasoline will occur.

6. When there is a surplus in a market:
   - (a) Buyers do not wish to buy as much as sellers want to sell.
   - (b) Sellers are likely to offer discounts to eliminate expensive excess inventories.
   - (c) Buyers who cannot buy commodities at the current market price are likely to make offers to buy at lower prices that sellers will now accept.
   - (d) All the above.

7. When there is a leftward shift of the market-demand curve, market forces should push:
   - (a) Market prices upward and market quantity downward.
   - (b) Market prices upward and market quantity upward.
   - (c) Market prices downward and market quantity downward.
   - (d) Market prices downward and market quantity upward.

8. Whenever there is a rightward shift of the market demand curve, market forces should push:
   - (a) Market prices upward and market quantity upward.
   - (b) Market prices upward and market quantity downward.
   - (c) Market prices downward and market quantity upward.
   - (d) Market prices downward and market quantity downward.

Exercise 3

This exercise gives practice in computing market demand and market supply curves using the demand and supply curves of individuals in a market. It is similar to a problem for chapter 3 in the text.

1. Table 3.5 shows the weekly demand and supply schedules for various individuals. Fill in the total market quantity that these individuals demand and supply.

Table 3.5
Individual demand and supply schedules

Price	$4	$3	$2	$1
Buyers				
Albert's quantity demanded	1	3	4	6
Bailey's quantity demanded	2	2	3	3
Peyton's quantity demanded	2	2.5	3	3.5
Total market quantity demanded	___	___	___	___
Sellers				
Allison's quantity supplied	5	3	2	0
Natali's quantity supplied	6	5	4	3
Narcel's quantity supplied	5	4	3	2
Emilio's quantity supplied	4	3	1	0
Total market quantity supplied	___	___	___	___

Use the data in Table 3.5 to answer questions 2-4.

2. Construct and label market-supply and market-demand curves in Figure 3.5.

3. Identify the equilibrium point and label it *EQ* in Figure 3.5.

4. What is true about the relationship between quantity demanded and quantity supplied at a price of $1 in Figure 3.5? _____

Figure 3.5
Market-supply and market-demand curves for buyers and sellers

Exercise 4

This exercise provides examples of events that would shift demand or supply curves. It is similar to a problem at the end of the chapter in the text.

Figure 3.6
Shifts of curves

Choose the letter of the appropriate diagram in Figure 3.6 that best describes the shift that would occur in each of the following situations. The shifts are occurring in the market for U.S. defense goods. (*Hint:* Ask yourself if the change first affects buyers or the sellers. Refer to the nonprice determinants for demand and supply listed in the text if necessary.)

_____ 1. Because of increased protectionism for steel, U.S. steel producers are able to raise the price of specialty steel, which is a key resource in the production of defense goods.

_____ 2. A new process for creating microchips is developed that reduces the cost of materials needed to produce nuclear submarines.

_____ 3. As a result of worldwide terrorist threats, new buyers enter the market to purchase defense goods.

_____ 4. A country that previously bought U.S. defense goods enters into a peace agreement.

_____ 5. Because of heightened concerns about national security, additional firms enter into the production of defense weapons.

Exercise 5

The media often provide information about supply and demand shifts. This exercise uses one of the articles in the text to show the kind of information to look for.

Reread the *In the News* article entitled "Prices Soar as Cold Snap Shreds Iceberg Lettuce Supply." Then answer the following questions:

1. Which of the four diagrams in Figure 3.6 in the previous exercise best represents the shift in the market for lettuce?   a   b   c   d   (circle one)

2. The change in the lettuce market is referred to as a:
   (a) Change in quantity supplied.
   (b) Change in supply.
   (c) Change in quantity demanded.
   (d) Change in demand.

3. What is the expected change in equilibrium price and quantity in the lettuce market?
   _____

Common Errors

The first statement in each "common error" below is incorrect. Each incorrect statement is followed by a corrected version and an explanation.

1. If a large number of people petition the government in order to get something, then there is a large demand for that item. WRONG!

   If a large number of people desire a commodity *and have the ability to pay for it,* then there is a large demand for that item. RIGHT!

   People want something, but there is no "demand" for it unless they are able to pay for it. Economists use the word "demand" in a way that is quite different from normal usage. People who want (desire; have preferences, a taste, or liking for) a commodity are seen as going to a market to purchase the commodity with money. "Demand" does not mean claiming the right to something when a person does not have the ability to buy it.

2. Market price is the same thing as equilibrium price. WRONG!

   The market price moves by trial and error (via the market mechanism) toward the equilibrium price. RIGHT!

   When demand and supply curves shift, the market is temporarily out of equilibrium. The price may move along a demand or supply curve toward the new equilibrium.

3. Since the quantity bought must equal the quantity sold, every market is always in equilibrium by definition. WRONG!

   Although the quantity bought equals the quantity sold, there may be shortages or surpluses. RIGHT!

   Although the quantity actually bought does equal the quantity actually sold, there may still be buyers who are willing and able to buy more of the good at the market price (market shortages exist) or sellers who are willing and able to sell more of the good at the market price (market surpluses exist). If the market price is above the equilibrium price, there will be queues of goods (inventories). Prices will be lowered by sellers toward the equilibrium price. If the market price is below the equilibrium price, there will be queues of buyers (shortages). Prices will be bid up by buyers toward the equilibrium price.

4. The intersection of supply and demand curves determines how much of a good or service will actually be exchanged and the actual price of the exchange. WRONG!

   The intersection of supply and demand curves represents an efficient outcome where the existing intentions of both buyers and sellers are compatible. RIGHT!

   Many institutional interferences may prevent the market from ever reaching the equilibrium point, where supply and demand curves intersect. All that can be said is that, given a market where prices and output are free to change, market forces will tend to move the economy *toward* equilibrium.

5. A change in price changes the demand for goods by consumers. WRONG!

   A change in price changes the quantity demanded by consumers in a given time period. RIGHT!

   Economists differentiate the terms "quantity demanded" and "demand." A change in the quantity demanded usually refers to a movement along the demand curve as a result of a change in price. A change in demand refers to a shift of the demand curve as a result of a change in incomes, tastes, prices or availability of other goods, or expectations.

6. A change in price changes the supply of goods produced by a firm. WRONG!

   A change in price changes the quantity supplied of a good by a firm in a given time period. RIGHT!

   Economists differentiate the terms "quantity supplied" and "supply." A change in the quantity supplied usually refers to a movement along a supply curve as a result of a change in price or production rate. A change in supply refers to a shift of the supply curve as a result of a change in technology, prices of resources, number of sellers, other goods, expectations, or taxes.

•ANSWERS•

Using Key Terms

Across

4. market shortage
7. equilibrium price
9. price floor
10. supply
13. demand
15. ceteris paribus
18. factor market
19. market mechanism
20. law of demand

Down

1. shift in demand
2. price ceiling
3. demand curve
4. market supply
5. demand schedule
6. product market
8. complementary goods
11. market surplus
12. substitute goods
14. law of supply
16. opportunity cost
17. market demand

True or False

1. F The demand curve indicates how much a buyer would like to buy and is able to pay for. How much is actually bought also depends on supply.
2. F A change in one of the determinants of demand results in a shift in the demand curve.
3. T
4. T
5. F The quantity of a good that a producer is willing and able to produce and offer for sale at any price depends on the value of the alternative goods that could have been produced with those same resources, i.e., the opportunity costs.
6. T
7. T
8. T
9. F If left alone the market will reach an equilibrium, but a price ceiling will cause a shortage.
10. F An optimal outcome does not mean that all consumer desires are satisfied and business profits are maximized. It simply means that the market outcome is likely to be the best possible given scarce resources and income constraints.

Multiple Choice

1. c	5. c	9. a	13. b	17. d
2. d	6. d	10. b	14. c	18. c
3. a	7. b	11. a	15. a	19. a
4. b	8. b	12. a	16. d	20. b

Problems and Applications

Exercise 1

1. **Table 3.1 Answer**

p	q
$1	20
3	10

2. **Figure 3.1 Answer**

3. **Table 3.2 Answer**

p	q
$1	20,000
3	10,000

4. See Figure 3.2 Answer, curve D.

Figure 3.2 Answer

5. ## Table 3.3 Answer

p	q
$1	250
3	1,250

6. ## Figure 3.3 Answer

7. ## Table 3.4 Answer

p	q
$1	5,000
3	25,000

8. See Figure 3.2 Answer, curve S.

9. b

10. a

Exercise 2

1. d

3. demand
4. b
5. c
6. d
7. c
8. a

2. **Figure 3.4 Answer**

Exercise 3

1. **Table 3.5 Answer**

Price	$4	$3	$2	$1
Buyers Total market quantity demanded	5	7.5	10	12.5
Sellers Total market quantity supplied	20	15	10	5

48

2. **Figure 3.5 Answer**

3. See point *EQ* in Figure 3.5.
4. The quantity demanded is greater than the quantity supplied or there is a shortage of 7.5 units (12.5 minus 5.)

Exercise 4

1. a
2. b
3. d
4. c
5. b

Exercise 5

1. a
2. b
3. An increase in equilibrium price and a decrease in equilibrium quantity.

CHAPTER 4
The Public Sector

Quick Review

- Market failure occurs when the market mechanism causes the economy to produce a combination of goods different from the optimal mix of output or results in an inequitable distribution of income. Market failure may prompt the government to intervene.

- There are four specific sources of market failure at the micro level: public goods, externalities, market power, and equity.

- Private goods can be consumed exclusively by those who pay for the goods, but public goods cannot. Public goods, such as national defense, can be consumed jointly by everyone no matter who pays. Because the link between paying and receiving is broken, everyone seeks to be a "free rider" and benefit from purchases made by others. As a result, the market underproduces public goods, and government intervention is necessary to provide these goods.

- Externalities are costs (or benefits) of a market transaction borne by a third party. Externalities cause a divergence between social costs and private costs and lead to suboptimal market outcomes. In the case of externalities such as pollution, which impose costs on society, too much of the polluting good is produced. If the externality produces benefits, too little of the good will be produced by the market alone. Regulations and emission fees are used to reduce the external costs associated with externalities.

- Market power allows producers to ignore the signals generated in the marketplace and produce a suboptimal mix of output. Antitrust policy and laws seek to prevent or restrict concentrations of market power.

- The market mechanism tends to allocate output to those with the most income. The government responds with a system of taxes and transfer payments to ensure a more equitable distribution of income and output.

- Markets may also fail at the macro level. In this case, the problems include unacceptable levels of unemployment, inflation, and economic growth. Government intervention is then necessary to achieve society's goals.

- State and local government activity exceeds that of the federal government and has grown much more rapidly in recent decades. Federal expenditures are supported mainly by personal income taxes and Social Security taxes. State and local governments rely most heavily on sales taxes and property taxes, respectively.

- Government intervention that does not improve economic outcomes is referred to as government failure.

Learning Objectives

After reading Chapter 4 and doing the following exercises, you should:

1. Understand that market failure can occur and as a result the government may decide to intervene.
2. Be able to describe the communal nature of public goods and the free-rider dilemma.
3. Know the nature of externalities and how they influence the decisions of producers and consumers.
4. Use the concepts of social cost and private cost to explain the problems associated with externalities.
5. Understand the policy options that can be used to address the problems associated with externalities.
6. Understand how antitrust activity attempts to combat monopoly power.
7. Be familiar with some fundamental antitrust laws.
8. Understand that inequity in income distribution is an example of market failure with respect to the FOR WHOM question.
9. Understand the concept of macro failure.
10. Understand the recent trend in terms of spending at the federal level vs. the state and local levels.
11. Know where government revenues come from and the difference between the different tax structures.
12. Understand that government failure can occur.

Using Key Terms

Fill in the puzzle on the opposite page with the appropriate term from the list of Key Terms at the end of the chapter in the text.

Across

1. The most desired goods and services that are given up in order to obtain something else.
5. An increase in the average level of prices.
8. Referred to as the "invisible hand."
10. The idea that government intervention fails to improve economic outcomes.
14. An industry in which a single firm achieves economies of scale over the entire range of output.
17. A tax system in which tax rates fall as incomes rise.
19. A form of government intervention to address the FOR WHOM question.
20. Theory that emphasizes the role of self-interest in public decision making.
21. The ability to alter the market price of a good or service.
22. The fee paid for the use of a public-sector good or service.
23. A tax system in which the tax rate stays the same as income rises.

Down

2. The most desirable combination of output attainable with existing resources, technology, and social values.
3. Occurs when people are willing to work but are unable to find jobs.
4. The market failure that occurs because of secondhand smoke.
6. A tax system in which tax rates rise as incomes rise.
7. For a _____ _____, consumption by one person excludes consumption by others.
9. Federal grants to state and local governments for specific purposes.
11. An imperfection in the market mechanism that prevents optimal outcomes.
12. Only one producer in an industry.
13. A good or service that society believes everyone is entitled to a minimal quantity of, such as food.
15. Can be consumed jointly.
16. One who does not pay but still enjoys the benefits.
18. The legislation used to prevent or break up concentrations of market power such as Microsoft.

Puzzle 4.1

True or False: *Circle your choice and explain why any false statements are incorrect.*

T F   1. Market failure implies that the forces of supply and demand have not led to the best point on the production-possibilities curve.

T F   2. Government intervention is not necessary when the market mix of output equals the optimal mix of output.

T F   3. The existence of public goods and externalities causes resource misallocations.

T F   4. Police protection is an example of a service that involves the free-rider problem.

T F   5. If you burn garbage in your backyard and the smoke damages a neighbor's health, the damage is considered an externality.

T F   6. Markets will overproduce goods that yield external benefits and underproduce goods that yield external costs.

T F   7. Market power creates a flawed response to an accurate price signal.

T F   8. Monopolies will tend to overproduce goods and charge a higher than competitive price.

T F   9. The federal government in the U.S. economy has grown in both relative and absolute terms since the 1950s.

T F 10. When the government intervenes in the economy, the market mix of goods and services is always improved.

Multiple Choice: *Select the correct answer.*

_____ 1. In a market economy, producers will produce the goods and services:
  (a) That consumers desire the most.
  (b) That consumers need the most.
  (c) That consumers demand.
  (d) That optimize consumer utility.

_____ 2. Market failure includes:
  (a) Externalities.
  (b) Market power.
  (c) Inequity in the distribution of goods and services.
  (d) All of the above.

_____ 3. Market failure suggests that the market mechanism, left alone, will:
  (a) Produce too many public goods and too few private goods.
  (b) Produce too many private goods and too few public goods.
  (c) Produce the optimal mix of output.
  (d) Result in too few resources being allocated to private goods.

_____ 4. The market will sometimes fail to produce society's optimum output because:
   (a) Producers do not always measure the same benefits and costs as society.
   (b) Producers will not produce certain types of important goods and services that cannot be kept from consumers who do not pay.
   (c) When producers have market power, they will tend to underproduce goods and services.
   (d) All of the above are correct.

_____ 5. When the market fails, which of the following is true?
   (a) The mix of goods and services is inside the production-possibilities curve.
   (b) Government intervention will improve the mix of goods and services.
   (c) The mix of goods and services is at the wrong point on the production-possibilities curve.
   (d) All of the above could be true.

_____ 6. Which of the following is most likely a public good?
   (a) Roads.
   (b) A hamburger.
   (c) An automobile.
   (d) Vegetables from a farmer's market.

_____ 7. When public goods are marketed like private goods:
   (a) Public goods are underproduced.
   (b) Many consumers want to buy the goods.
   (c) Public goods are overproduced.
   (d) Government failure results.

_____ 8. For which of the following goods and services is the government likely to encourage production because of the existence of external benefits?
   (a) Education.
   (b) Health services for the poor.
   (c) A neighborhood renovation project.
   (d) All of the above.

_____ 9. The federal government's role in antitrust enforcement is justified by considerations of:
   (a) Equity in the distribution of goods and services.
   (b) Public goods and externalities.
   (c) Underproduction by firms with market power.
   (d) Macro failure.

_____ 10. The development of market power by a firm is considered to be a market failure because firms with market power:
   (a) Produce more and charge a lower price than what is socially optimal.
   (b) Tend to ignore external costs.
   (c) Produce less and charge a higher price than what is socially optimal.
   (d) Do not respond to consumer demand.

_____ 11. Transfer payments are an appropriate mechanism for correcting:
   (a) Market power.
   (b) Government failure.
   (c) Inflation.
   (d) Inequity in the distribution of goods and services.

_____ 12. Social demand is equal to
  (a) Private demand plus market demand.
  (b) Market demand plus external benefits.
  (c) Private demand.
  (d) Market demand minus external benefits.

_____ 13. The primary function of taxes is to:
  (a) Transfer command over resources from the private sector to the public sector.
  (b) Increase the purchasing power of the private sector.
  (c) Increase private saving.
  (d) Make it possible to sell bonds to finance the U.S. budget deficit.

_____ 14. Government intervention in the market:
  (a) Involves an opportunity cost.
  (b) Never involves an opportunity cost because only market activities result in other goods and services being given up.
  (c) Does not involve an opportunity cost if market outcomes are improved.
  (d) Results in the "free-rider dilemma."

_____ 15. The largest single source of revenue for the federal government is:
  (a) Borrowing (selling government bonds).
  (b) Social security taxes.
  (c) The corporate profits tax.
  (d) The personal income tax.

_____ 16. Which of the following can be classified as a regressive tax?
  (a) The federal corporate income tax.
  (b) The federal personal income tax.
  (c) The state sales tax.
  (d) All of the above.

_____ 17. Which of the following is an example of a progressive tax?
  (a) The excise tax on distilled spirits.
  (b) The federal tax on gasoline.
  (c) The federal personal income tax.
  (d) All of the above.

_____ 18. States receive most of their tax revenues from:
  (a) Sales taxes.
  (b) State income taxes.
  (c) Property taxes.
  (d) User charges.

_____ 19. Reread the article in the text titled "Napster Gets Napped." According to the article an item is a public good if:
  (a) The government produces the good.
  (b) Consumers can be excluded from consumption.
  (c) Consumers must meet certain criteria to consume the good.
  (d) Consumers cannot be excluded from consumption.

_____ 20. Which of the following would *not* support the theory of public choice?

(a) The governor of the state vetoes a highway bill even though the highway would enhance the value of property he owns.

(b) The local mayor campaigns in favor of a bond issue for the construction of sewer lines that will raise the value of his property.

(c) The local police chief fails to give the mayor a speeding ticket because the mayor might fire him.

(d) A college president asks the board of regents to allow her to remain in office so she can bolster her retirement income, even though she has reached the mandatory retirement age.

Problems and Applications

Exercise 1

Assume point A represents the optimal mix of output in Figure 4.1. Determine which letter best represents the following situations. Then answer questions 4-7.

Figure 4.1

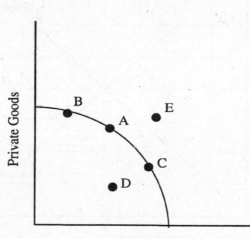

_____ 1. Government failure at the micro level that results in an overproduction of public goods.

_____ 2. Macro failure in the marketplace that results in the unemployment of resources.

_____ 3. The free-rider dilemma.

4. The market mechanism tends to _____ public goods and _____ private goods.

5. T   F   In terms of the production possibilities curve, microeconomic failures (such as public goods, externalities, and market power) imply that society is at the wrong point on the curve and macroeconomic failures imply that society is inside the curve.

6. Market failures justify government _____.

7. If government involvement fails to improve market outcomes then there is _____
   _____.

Exercise 2

This exercise examines the difference between internal and external costs and the impact on the demand curve.

The market-demand and market-supply curves for a particular good are drawn in Figure 4.2. Assume that the consumption of the good generates external costs equal to $2 per unit.

1. Draw the social demand curve in Figure 4.2 and label it.

Figure 4.2

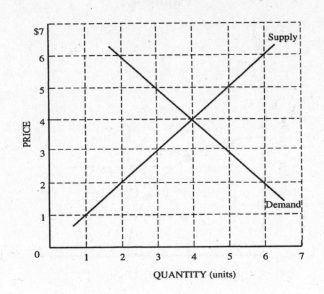

2. Market equilibrium occurs at a price of _____ and a quantity of _____ units in Figure 4.3.

3. The socially optimal level of production occurs at a price of _____ and a quantity of _____ units.

4. External costs cause the market to produce (more, less) of a good than is optimal.

5. T   F   The social demand curve will always be greater than the market demand curve if external costs are generated.

58

Exercise 3

This exercise focuses on the changes in public-sector spending in the U.S.

Refer to Figure 4.4 in the text titled "Government Growth" to answer questions 1-4.

1. The large increase in total government purchases between 1940 and 1945 was the result of an increase in (only federal; both state and local and federal) government spending.

2. Compared to the level of federal spending in 1960, the level of federal spending for 2000 is (greater; less; the same).

3. Compared to the level of state and local spending in 1960, the level of state and local spending for 2000 is (greater; less; the same).

4. The decrease in total government purchases during the 1990s was primarily due to the decrease in (federal; state and local) purchases.

Exercise 4

This exercise examines progressive, regressive, and proportional tax structures.

Suppose Table 4.1 describes the incomes and taxes for individuals in the countries of Zebot and Dobler.

1. Calculate the following in Table 4.1:
   a. The percentage of income paid in taxes at each income level for the people of Zebot (column 3).
   b. The percentage of income paid in taxes at each income level for the people of Dobler (column 5).

Table 4.1 Taxes on income in the countries of Zebot and Dobler

(1) Income	(2) Taxes paid in Zebot	(3) Tax rate	(4) Taxes paid in Dobler	(5) Tax rate
$10,000	$2,000	_____%	$1,000	_____%
40,000	6,400	_____	6,000	_____
75,000	10,500	_____	15,000	_____
125,000	12,500	_____	27,500	_____

2. In Zebot, is the income tax progressive, regressive, or proportional? _____

3. In Dobler, is the income tax progressive, regressive, or proportional? _____

4. Which of the following is the most logical approach if a society wishes to redistribute income to the poor?
   (a) A regressive tax structure.
   (b) A progressive tax structure.
   (c) A proportional tax structure.

5. T   F   A proportional tax structure means that the tax rate is constant regardless of income level.

Common Errors

The first statement in the "common error" below is incorrect. The incorrect statement is followed by a corrected version and an explanation.

1. Fire protection, police protection, education, and other services can be produced more efficiently by the private sector than by the public sector. WRONG!

   The public sector can produce many services more efficiently than the private sector. RIGHT!

   The existence of externalities and the free-rider problem force society to produce some goods and services through public-sector expenditures. Many of the goods and services we take for granted (such as education) would not be produced in sufficient quantities if left to the private sector. And can you imagine trying to provide for your own defense against foreign countries?

2. A public good is only produced by the government sector. WRONG!

   A public good is one whose consumption by one person does not prevent consumption by others. RIGHT!

   A public good can be produced by the private sector or the public sector. The source of production is not what makes it a public good. It is a public good because consumption is not exclusive. The government does provide many of the public goods such as national defense.

•ANSWERS•

Using Key Terms

Across
1. opportunity cost
5. inflation
8. market mechanism
10. government failure
14. natural monopoly
17. regressive tax
19. transfer payments
20. public choice
21. market power
22. user charge
23. proportional tax

Down
2. optimal mix of output
3. unemployment
4. externalities
6. progressive tax
7. private good
9. categorical grants
11. market failure
12. monopoly
13. merit good
15. public good
16. free rider
18. antitrust

True or False

1. T
2. F   Even in this case, equity considerations may necessitate government intervention.
3. T
4. T
5. T
6. F   Markets will underproduce goods that yield external benefits and overproduce goods that yield external costs.
7. T
8. F   Monopolies will tend to underproduce goods and are therefore able to charge a higher price.
9. F   The federal government has grown in absolute terms since the 1950s but its relative share of production has declined, i.e., it has grown more slowly than the private sector.
10. F   Sometimes government intervention worsens the market mix of goods and services. This is an example of "government failure."

Multiple Choice

1. c	5. d	9. c	13. a	17. c
2. d	6. a	10. c	14. a	18. a
3. b	7. a	11. d	15. d	19. d
4. d	8. d	12. b	16. c	20. a

Problems and Applications

Exercise 1

1. c
2. d
3. b
4. Underproduce; overproduce
5. T
6. Intervention
7. Government failure

Exercise 2

1. See Figure 4.2 answer.

Figure 4.2 Answer

2. $4.00, 4 units
3. $3.00, 3 units
4. More
5. F   The social demand curve is less than the market demand curve if external costs are generated.

Exercise 3

1. Only federal
2. Less
3. Greater
4. Federal

Exercise 4

1. See Table 4.1 Answer.

Table 4.1 Answer

(1) Income	(2) Taxes paid in Zebot	(3) Tax rate	(4) Taxes paid in Dobler	(5) Tax rate
$10,000	$2,000	20.0 %	$1,000	10.0 %
40,000	6,400	16.0	6,000	15.0
75,000	10,500	14.0	15,000	20.0
125,000	12,500	10.0	27,500	22.0

2. Regressive. With greater income, a lower percentage of income goes to taxes (from 20% to 10% in column 3).
3. Progressive. With greater income, a higher percentage of income goes to taxes (from 10% to 22% in column 5).
4. b   (A progressive tax is the most logical choice if society wants to redistribute income to the poor.)
5. T

CHAPTER 5

National-Income Accounting

Quick Review

- National-income accounting is used to measure a nation's economic activity. It provides information about the strength of an economy and can be used to evaluate economic policy.

- The most often used economic aggregate is gross domestic product (GDP)—the total market value of all final goods and services produced within a nation's borders during a year. Only transactions involving goods and services that are sold for final consumption are included. Intermediate goods are not included in GDP in order to avoid double counting.

- GDP focuses on goods and services produced within a country's borders, while gross national product (GNP) focuses on goods and services produced by a country's factors of production, regardless of where the factors are located. GDP per capita is the average GDP per person.

- GDP is not a perfect measure of a country's output because nonmarket activities and unreported income are not captured in this statistic.

- The standard of living is based on real goods and services, so a distinction is made between real GDP and nominal GDP. Nominal GDP is measured in current dollars and can increase because prices go up, because quantities go up, or both. Real GDP is measured in constant dollars and is used for comparing the output of different economies and changes in the output of a single economy over time.

- GDP can be calculated as the sum of all expenditures by the market participants—consumption, investment, government expenditures, and net exports.

- Depreciation is the value of capital that is consumed in the production process. The net domestic product (NDP) is calculated as GDP minus depreciation and is a good measure of the future production possibilities for an economy.

- NDP minus indirect business taxes plus net foreign factor income results in national income (NI). NI reflects the payments to the factors of production used to produce the nation's output. In order to determine how much of the income earned is actually received, personal income (PI) and disposable income (DI) are calculated. DI represents the dollars consumers have available to spend after personal taxes are taken out.

- Expenditures made by one market participant become income for another market participant. This income is then spent again and the circular flow continues.

Learning Objectives

After reading Chapter 5 and doing the following exercises, you should:

1. Know the purposes of national-income accounting.
2. Understand the significance of GDP as a measure of output.
3. Understand the difference between GDP and GNP and the meaning of GDP per capita.
4. Be able to explain the measurement problems associated with GDP.
5. Know the difference between real GDP and nominal GDP and be able to calculate each.
6. Understand the importance of NDP and depreciation.
7. Know the definitions and how to calculate the various national-income aggregates.
8. Understand the circular flow nature of the economy.

Using Key Terms

Fill in the puzzle on the opposite page with the appropriate term from the list of Key Terms at the end of the chapter in the text.

Across

1. Calculated as nominal GDP divided by the price index.
3. Equal to GDP minus depreciation and indirect business taxes.
4. Total investment expenditure in a given time period.
9. Alternative combinations of goods and services that can be produced with the available resources and technology.
10. The increase in the market value of a product that takes place at each stage of the production process.
11. Equal to disposable income minus consumption.
13. The reduction in the value of plant and equipment.
16. The amount of output that can be consumed without reducing a country's capital stock.
18. The income received by households before the payment of taxes.
19. After-tax income of households.
20. Used as a measure of the relative standard of living.

Down

2. The total market value of all final goods and services produced within a nation's borders in a given time period.
3. The measurement of aggregate economic activity.
5. Persistent increases in the price level.
6. Goods purchased for use as input in further stages of production.
7. The value of final output produced in a given period, measured in the prices of that period (current prices).
8. Expenditures on new plant, equipment and structures plus changes in inventories.
12. Gross investment minus depreciation.
14. Goods and services purchased from other countries.
15. The basis for indexing price changes.
16. Equal to exports minus imports.
17. Goods and services sold to other countries.

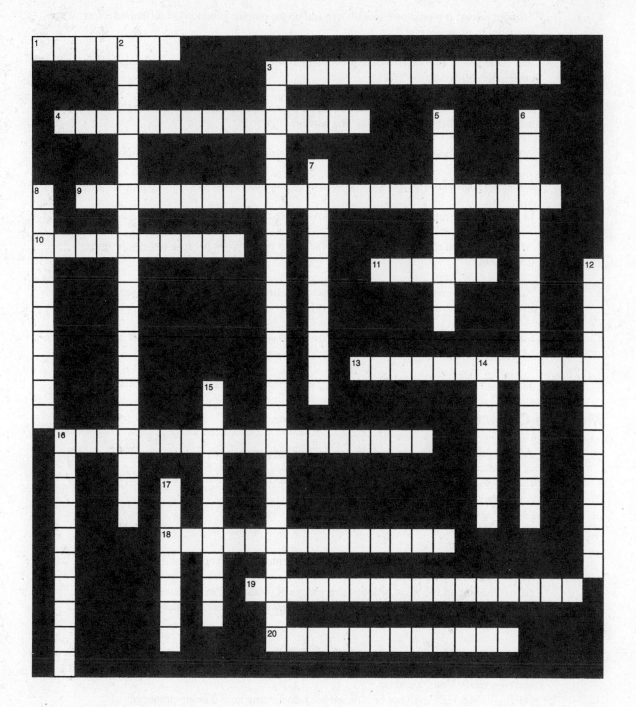

True or False: *Circle your choice and explain why any false statements are incorrect.*

T F 1. Without prices, it would be impossible to add up the outputs produced in different sectors of the economy in a meaningful way.

T F 2. The value added approach to GDP prevents intermediate goods from being counted more than once in the calculation.

T F 3. If everyone who currently does their own housework switches to a maid service that reports their income, U.S. GDP will increase, *ceteris paribus*.

T F 4. Per capita GDP provides information about the distribution of GDP within a country.

T F 5. If real per capita GDP increases, everyone in the nation is better off.

T F 6. In a period of rising prices, real GDP will rise more rapidly than nominal GDP.

T F 7. NDP provides information about future production possibilities because it measures gross investment.

T F 8. According to the expenditures approach to calculating GDP, GDP equals Consumption + Gross Investment + Government Expenditures + (Exports - Imports).

T F 9. State and local government expenditures on goods and services are *not* included in GDP because to do so would result in double counting.

T F 10. The total value of market incomes must equal the total value of final output, or GDP.

Multiple Choice: *Select the correct answer.*

_____ 1. A basic function of the national-income accounting system is to:
  (a) Identify economic problems.
  (b) Evaluate economic policy.
  (c) Provide a framework for policy.
  (d) All of the above.

_____ 2. GDP can be found by:
  (a) Adding up the spending by business, government, households, and foreigners, and subtracting imports.
  (b) Adding up the value added at every stage of production in the economy.
  (c) Adding up all the receipts of households, government, and business.
  (d) All of the above.

_____ 3. Suppose that a friend of yours claims that he is helping the economy by throwing trash on the street rather than in trash cans because the extra expenditures necessary to clean up the streets will increase GDP. Your friend is:
  (a) Wrong. GDP will not be affected because nothing new is being produced.
  (b) Right. GDP will increase because the dollars spent to clean up the trash will increase government spending, *ceteris paribus*.
  (c) Wrong. GDP will not be affected because this is not a socially desirable use of resources and will therefore not be included in GDP.
  (d) Wrong. GDP will not be affected because the economy is no better off than before the littering occurred.

4. If the real GDP is $7,500 billion in 2005 and the population is 280 million, then per capita real GDP is closest to:
   (a) $140,000 per person.
   (b) $21,000 per person.
   (c) $26,786 per person.
   (d) $3,733 per person.

5. A housewife takes over the job of a deceased family member in running the family business and hires help to clean house and baby-sit. As a result, the GDP of the economy, *ceteris paribus:*
   (a) Remains unchanged, since the amount of productive activity remains unchanged.
   (b) Rises by the amount paid to house cleaners and baby-sitters.
   (c) Falls by the amount of household work left undone by the house cleaners and baby-sitters.
   (d) Falls by the amount of income generated previously by the deceased family member.

6. The underground economy exists because:
   (a) People wish to avoid taxes.
   (b) Illegal activities are often highly profitable.
   (c) It is difficult to trace transactions in the underground economy.
   (d) All of the above are reasons.

7. A manufacturer sells assembled Palm Pilots for $250 each. If the manufacturer pays $100 for the components in each Palm Pilot, the value added to each Palm Pilot by the manufacturing process is equal to:
   (a) $250.
   (b) $100.
   (c) $350.
   (d) $150.

8. Which of the following is *not* a final good or service?
   (a) A printing press purchased by a publishing company.
   (h) Automobile tires purchased by an auto manufacturing company.
   (c) Gasoline purchased for personal use by a car owner.
   (d) The preparation of your tax return by a CPA.

9. The difference between real GDP and nominal GDP is that:
   (a) Nominal GDP is the value of output measured in constant prices.
   (b) Real GDP is the value of output measured in constant prices.
   (c) Real GDP is the value of output measured in current prices.
   (d) Real GDP can give a distorted view of economic activity because of price level changes.

10. Real GDP measures changes in:
    (a) Prices.
    (b) Production.
    (c) Prices and production.
    (d) Wages.

11. Suppose that the total market value of all the final goods and services produced in the country of GDPLAND is $24 billion in 2003 (measured in 2003 prices) and $27 billion in the year 2004 (measured in 2004 prices). Which of the following statements is definitely correct?
    (a) Production increased in GDPLAND between 2003 and 2004.
    (b) Average price levels increased in GDPLAND between 2003 and 2004.
    (c) Nominal GDP increased in GDPLAND between 2003 and 2004.
    (d) All of these statements are definitely correct.

_____ 12. If depreciation exceeds gross investment, then:
   (a)   Net investment exceeds depreciation.
   (b)   Gross investment is negative.
   (c)   The difference between GDP and NDP is smaller than gross investment.
   (d)   The nation's capital stock is being depleted.

_____ 13. The stock of capital in the United States can grow only if:
   (a)   Depreciation is positive.
   (b)   Gross investment minus depreciation is positive.
   (c)   GDP minus NDP is positive.
   (d)   All of the above.

_____ 14. An increase in business inventories during some time period, _ceteris paribus_, will:
   (a)   Decrease GDP during that period.
   (b)   Increase GDP during that period.
   (c)   Not affect GDP during that period but will increase GDP in later periods when the inventory is sold.
   (d)   Never affect GDP because changes in inventories are not included in the calculation of GDP.

_____ 15. Which of the following types of government spending is included in the calculation of GDP?
   (a)   Federal government spending only.
   (b)   Federal, state and local government spending for any purpose.
   (c)   Federal, state and local government spending on goods and services only.
   (d)   Federal, state and local spending on transfer payments only.

_____ 16. In calculating GDP:
   (a)   Imports are subtracted from exports because they represent the value of production and resources absorbed in foreign economies.
   (b)   Imports are added to exports because both represent purchases of final goods.
   (c)   Imports are subtracted from exports to obtain gross exports.
   (d)   Imports are subtracted from exports and included in gross investment.

_____ 17. _DI_ is the most practical way to:
   (a)   Measure how much income households can spend and save.
   (b)   Measure how much output can be consumed on a sustainable basis.
   (c)   Make international comparisons of the standard of living.
   (d)   Analyze the growth rate of the economy over time.

_____ 18. Net exports are equal to:
   (a)   Exports plus imports.
   (b)   Imports minus exports.
   (c)   Exports minus imports.
   (d)   Exports plus imports minus depreciation.

_____ 19. The value of total output must equal the value of total income in an economy because:
   (a)   One person's expenditures on goods and services is another person's income.
   (b)   Income earned is spent on goods and services, which creates additional production.
   (c)   Of the circular nature of the economy.
   (d)   All of the above are reasons.

_____ 20. The social well-being of a country:
   (a)   Is best measured by per capita GDP.
   (b)   Always increases when real GDP increases.
   (c)   Decreases when real GDP decreases.
   (d)   Is measured by more than changes in real GDP.

Problems and Applications

Exercise 1

This exercise demonstrates the concept of value added. It is similar to a problem in the text.

Assume that orange juice production involves the following steps.

Step 1: A juice company grows its own oranges to reduce costs.
Step 2: The juice company sells a jug of orange juice to the grocery store for $1.85.
Step 3: The grocery store sells the jug of juice to the consumer for $3.25.

1. The value added from step 1 to step 2 is equal to _____.

2. The value added from step 2 to step 3 is equal to _____.

3. If the juice company bought the oranges from a farmer, the oranges would be considered a (an) (intermediate; final) good.

4. What is the total contribution to GDP because of the production of one jug of orange juice? _____

Exercise 2

This exercise demonstrates how to calculate real GDP and emphasizes the difference between nominal and real GDP.

Table 5.1 GDP Data

	Nominal GDP (billions of dollars per year)	Price index	Real GDP (billions of dollars per year)
Year 1	$3,400	100	_____
Year 2	$3,500	103	_____
Year 3	$3,700	111	_____
Year 4	$4,000	120	_____

1. Calculate real GDP in Table 5.1. Use the formula:

$$\text{Real GDP} = \frac{\text{Nominal GDP}}{\text{Price index}} \times 100$$

2. According to Table 5.1, in which year is the real level of output greatest? _____

3. The measurement of goods and services produced, without the impact of price level changes, is referred to as _____.

4. The best measure of physical changes in output in Figure 5.1 above is (nominal; real) GDP.

5. In Figure 5.1 in the text, nominal GDP rises more rapidly than real GDP because nominal GDP includes _____.

69

Exercise 3

This exercise provides practice in calculating GDP and other national income accounts. (The chart below can be referred to as you work through this exercise.)

Flow chart 5.1

Add items in this column to get the next account	National income account	Subtract items in this column to get the next account
	GDP	
		Depreciation
	NDP	
Net Foreign Factor Income		
	NI	
Transfer Payments Net Interest		Indirect Business Taxes Corporate Taxes Retained Earnings Social Security Taxes
	PI	
		Personal Income Taxes
	DI	
		Consumption
	Saving	

Table 5.2 National Income Data

Consumption	$300 billion
Depreciation	10 billion
Exports	30 billion
Corporate Taxes	15 billion
Personal Income Taxes	60 billion
Gross Investment	30 billion
Indirect Business Taxes	5 billion
Retained Earnings	10 billion
Imports	35 billion
Government Purchases	80 billion
Social Security Taxes	15 billion
Transfer Payments	30 billion
Net Interest	5 billion
Net Foreign Factor Income	2 billion

Use the information in Table 5.2 to make the following calculations.

1. GDP _____

2. NDP _____

3. NI _____

4. PI   _____

5. DI   _____

6. Savings   _____

7. Net investment _____

8. Which of the accounts above is equal to the total income earned by the factors of production? _____.

9. Which of the accounts above is the best indicator of future production possibilities? _____

Common Errors

The first statement in each "common error" below is incorrect. Each incorrect statement is followed by a corrected version and an explanation.

1. Income and output are two entirely different things. WRONG!

   Income and output are two sides of the same coin. RIGHT!

   This is fundamental. Every time a dollar's worth of final spending takes place, the seller must receive a dollar's worth of income. It could not be otherwise. Remember, profits are used as a balancing item. Don't confuse the term "income" with the term "profit." Profits can be negative, whereas output for the economy cannot.

2. Comparisons of per capita GDP between countries tell you which population is better off. WRONG!

   Comparisons of per capita GDP between countries are only indicators of which population is better off. RIGHT!

   Simple comparisons of per capita GDP ignore how the GDP is distributed. A country with a very high per capita GDP that is unequally distributed may well provide a standard of living that is below that of another country with a lower per capita GDP, which is more equally distributed. There are other problems with comparisons of per capita GDP between countries because of exchange-rate distortions, differences in mix of output in two countries, and how the economy is organized. GDP per capita is an indicator only of the amount of goods and services each person could have, not what each person does have.

3. Value added is a measure of a firm's profit. WRONG!

   Value added includes all factor payments to land, labor, and capital in addition to the residual (profit) that goes to the entrepreneur for taking risks. RIGHT!

   In computing value added, a firm subtracts *from* total revenue the cost of items sold to the firm. There are additional cost items that normally would be subtracted to calculate "profit," which are not subtracted in the computation of value added. Those items include the cost of capital, land, and labor. When value added for all economic units is combined, the total of payments to capital (interest), land (rent), labor (wages), and risk taking (profits) will equal the total gross domestic product.

•ANSWERS•

Using Key Terms

Across

1. real GDP
3. national income
4. gross investment
9. production possibilities
10. value added
11. saving
13. depreciation
16. net domestic product
18. personal income
19. disposable income
20. GDP per capita

Down

2. gross domestic product
3. national income accounting
5. inflation
6. intermediate goods
7. nominal GDP
8. investment
12. net investment
14. imports
15. base period
16. net exports
17. exports

True or False

1. T
2. T
3. T
4. F   GDP per capita is simply a statistical average and tells us nothing about the way GDP is distributed.
5. F   Real per capita GDP is an average. When real per capita GDP rises, the living standard for the country as a whole increases. Some individuals are better off, but some individuals could be worse off.
6. F   Nominal GDP is affected by inflation and will increase faster than real GDP. Real GDP is not affected by changing price levels.
7. F   NDP provides information about future growth potential because it measures net investment.
8. T
9. F   State and local government expenditures on goods and services are included in GDP. These expenditures measure additional production beyond the goods and services the federal government consumes so there is no double counting.
10. T

72

Multiple Choice

1. d	5. b	9. b	13. b	17. a
2. d	6. d	10. b	14. b	18. c
3. b	7. d	11. c	15. c	19. d
4. c	8. b	12. d	16. a	20. d

Problems and Applications

Exercise 1

1. $1.85
2. $1.40
3. Intermediate
4. $3.25

Exercise 2

1.

Table 5.1 Answer

	Nominal GDP (billions of dollars per year)	Price index	Real GDP (billions of dollars per year)
Year 1	$3,400	100	$3,400
Year 2	$3,500	103	$3,398
Year 3	$3,700	111	$3,333
Year 4	$4,000	120	$3,333

2. Year 1
3. Real GDP
4. Real
5. An increase in the price level or inflation

Exercise 3

1. $405 billion
2. $395 billion
3. $397 billion
4. $387 billion
5. $327 billion
6. $27 billion
7. $20 billion
8. NI
9. NDP

CHAPTER 6

Unemployment

Quick Review

- The labor force is defined as those who are working for pay and those who are looking for work. Only about half of the U.S. population is included in the labor force.

- Since labor is one of the four factors of production, an increase in the size of the labor force causes an increase in the production possibilities curve and can result in economic growth.

- The institutional production possibilities curve allows for limits imposed on resources and technology and social constraints on their use. It lies inside the production possibilities curve. One reason why the labor force is less than the total population is because of institutional constraints such as compulsory education and child labor laws.

- The unemployment rate equals the number of unemployed persons divided by the labor force.

- The macroeconomic cost of unemployment is loss of output. According to Okun's Law, each one percentage point increase in the unemployment rate leads to a two percentage point reduction in GDP. Unemployment imposes other costs on society such as alcoholism, suicide, divorce, and crime.

- The unemployment rate varies by a number of socioeconomic variables—race, age, sex, and education. Discouraged workers are not part of the unemployment rate.

- The four kinds of unemployment are frictional (short-term unemployment between jobs), seasonal (unemployment that varies with the seasons), structural (caused by a mismatch of available labor with skill requirements or job locations), and cyclical (caused by deficient aggregate demand). There will always be some unemployment so the natural rate of unemployment is considered to be 4 to 6 percent.

- To keep the unemployment rate from increasing, the output level must increase at least as fast as the labor force increases.

- The U.S. economy has experienced periods of high unemployment (25% during the Great Depression) and periods of low unemployment (1.2% during World War II).

- In order to achieve full employment in the future, we will need to address the structural unemployment that typically occurs with economic growth. Education and training programs can be used to reduce structural unemployment.

Learning Objectives

After reading Chapter 6 and doing the following exercises, you should:

1. Know who is included in the labor force.
2. Understand the relationship between the labor force and economic growth.
3. Know the difference between the physical production possibilities and institutional production possibilities.
4. Be able to calculate the unemployment rate.
5. Understand the various costs associated with unemployment and the loss of output that results.
6. Understand that the unemployment rate varies with age, sex, education, and race.
7. Be able to explain what is meant by discouraged workers and phantom unemployment.
8. Be able to distinguish the nature and causes of cyclical, frictional, structural, and seasonal unemployment.
9. Know the meaning of "full employment."
10. Understand the direct and indirect effects of outsourcing.

Using Key Terms

Fill in the puzzle on the opposite page with the appropriate term from the list of Key Terms at the end of the chapter in the text.

Across

1. Calculated as the number of unemployed people divided by the size of the labor force.
6. Unemployment experienced by people moving between jobs.
7. The percentage of the population working or seeking work is the labor force _____ _____.
11. The relocation of production to foreign countries.
13. Unemployment due to seasonal changes.
14. An individual who is not looking for a job but would accept a job if one were available.
15. Situation in which people work at jobs below their capacity.
16. Can be represented by a rightward shift of the production possibilities curve.

Down

2. The rate of unemployment that prevails in the long run.
3. Alternative combinations of goods and services that can be produced with available resources and technology.
4. The type of unemployment most often experienced by teenagers with few job skills and an inadequate education.
5. Unemployment that occurs when there are not enough jobs.
8. Quantifies the relationship between the shortfall in output and unemployment.
9. The lowest rate of unemployment compatible with price stability.
10. Includes everyone 16 and older who is working for pay or looking for a job.
12. The inability of labor-force participants to find jobs.

Puzzle 6.1

True or False: *Circle your choice and explain why any false statements are incorrect.*

T F 1. Juan says he would like to have a job but hasn't applied for a job in 6 months. Juan is included as unemployed in the calculation of the unemployment rate.

T F 2. When the number of unemployed workers increases, the unemployment rate will always rise.

T F 3. When the economy is growing, the average duration of unemployment declines.

T F 4. A discouraged worker is one who is tired of his job and sees no possibility for advancement.

T F 5. The transition from manufacturing to service industries has accompanied GDP growth, but it has also led to greater frictional unemployment.

T F 6. Teenage unemployment is high because of teenagers' lack of job experience and marketable skills.

T F 7. Cyclical unemployment stems from insufficient aggregate demand.

T F 8. When an economy is producing at full employment, everyone willing and able to work has a job.

T F 9. One of the main reasons for revising the full-employment goal during the 1980s was a change in the age-sex composition of the labor force.

T F 10. Outsourcing results in higher profits and increased productivity for U.S. firms, *ceteris paribus*.

Multiple Choice: *Select the correct answer.*

_____ 1. People become labor force participants when they:
  (a) Take a full-time job.
  (b) Go back to school.
  (c) Return solely to household activities.
  (d) Retire.

_____ 2. The macro consequence of unemployment is:
  (a) Lost income for the individual worker.
  (b) Lost output for the economy.
  (c) A leftward shift in the institutional production-possibilities curve.
  (d) A 4 percent decrease in GDP for every 1 percent increase in unemployment.

_____ 3. Which of the following functions as an institutional constraint and, in doing so, reduces the rate of economic growth?
  (a) Child labor laws.
  (b) Restrictions on the usage of natural resources.
  (c) Restrictions on the usage of technology.
  (d) All of the above.

_____ 4. As economic output increases and an economy moves toward full employment:
  (a) Production moves closer to the institutional production possibilities curve, but not beyond it.
  (b) Production moves beyond the physical production possibilities curve.
  (c) The institutional production possibilities curve shifts outward but not the physical production possibilities curve.
  (d) The physical production possibilities curve shifts outward but not the institutional production possibilities curve.

_____ 5. When the labor force participation rate increases in an economy, *ceteris paribus*:
  (a) Production moves closer to the institutional production possibilities curve, but not beyond it.
  (b) Production moves beyond the physical production possibilities curve.
  (c) The institutional production possibilities curve shifts outward.
  (d) The physical production possibilities curve shifts outward but not the institutional production possibilities curve.

_____ 6. When the growth rate of the labor force is more rapid than the growth rate of the unemployed, then it is certain that:
  (a) The unemployment rate is rising.
  (b) The labor-force participation rate is rising.
  (c) The percentage of the labor force that is employed is rising.
  (d) The labor-force participation rate is falling.

_____ 7. When an economy enters a recession, then:
  (a) The duration of unemployment rises.
  (b) The number of discouraged workers rises.
  (c) The unemployment rate rises.
  (d) All of the above.

_____ 8. According to Okun's Law, a two-percent decrease in unemployment will result in a:
  (a) Two percent increase in real output.
  (b) Four percent increase in real output.
  (c) One percent increase in real output.
  (d) Four percent decrease in real output.

_____ 9. Individuals who are working part-time while seeking full-time employment are classified as:
  (a) Underemployed.
  (b) Unemployed.
  (c) Discouraged workers.
  (d) Phantom unemployed.

_____ 10. The official unemployment statistics may exaggerate the significance of unemployment by including the:
  (a) Underemployed.
  (b) Phantom unemployed.
  (c) Discouraged workers.
  (d) All of the above.

_____ 11. Which of the following are considered possible side effects of increased unemployment?
  (a) Suicides, homicides, and other crimes.
  (b) Heart attacks and strokes.
  (c) Admissions to mental hospitals.
  (d) All of the above.

_____ 12. When a person who mowed lawns all summer seeks employment during the winter, the unemployment rate goes up. This situation is an example of:
  (a) Seasonal unemployment.
  (b) Frictional unemployment.
  (c) Structural unemployment.
  (d) Cyclical unemployment.

13. Frictional unemployment goes up when:
    (a) A student quits work to return to school at the end of the summer.
    (b) A corporation transfers a worker to another city.
    (c) A worker quits one job in order to search for another.
    (d) There is inadequate demand for labor.

14. Which of the following is believed to have contributed to an increase in the level of structural unemployment during the 1970s and 1980s?
    (a) More youth and women in the labor force.
    (b) Increased transfer payments.
    (c) Structural changes in demand.
    (d) All of the above.

15. In terms of the musical chairs analogy in the text, which of the following is a description of cyclical unemployment?
    (a) There are too many chairs.
    (b) There are enough chairs, but it takes time to find one.
    (c) There are enough chairs, but some are not the right size.
    (d) There are too few chairs.

16. Which of the following government programs would be most appropriate to counteract cyclical unemployment?
    (a) Those which stimulate economic growth.
    (b) Those that provide additional health services.
    (c) Those that provide job placement services.
    (d) Those that provide job training.

17. The Employment Act of 1946:
    (a) Committed the government to pursue a goal of "maximum" employment.
    (b) Implied that the economy should avoid cyclical and structural unemployment.
    (c) Implied that frictional unemployment should be kept within a reasonable level.
    (d) All of the above.

18. Which of the following groups would be the most likely to qualify for unemployment benefits?
    (a) People who quit their last jobs.
    (b) People who lose their jobs due to increased foreign competition and are looking for work.
    (c) Mothers who have not worked recently.
    (d) People who are fired from one of the three part-time jobs that they have been working.

19. During which one of the following decades did unemployment levels first rise significantly above the 4 percent level as the result of increasing proportions of both teenagers and women entering the labor force?
    (a) 1960s.
    (b) 1970s.
    (c) 1980s.
    (d) 1990s.

20. Which of the following is true concerning the outsourcing of jobs?
    (a) It occurs because labor is more skilled in other countries than in the United States.
    (b) It is a major reason for current unemployment in the United States.
    (c) It increases specialization.
    (d) It causes firms in the United States to lose money.

Problems and Applications

Exercise 1

The following exercise provides practice in categorizing the population according to labor force participation, employment, and unemployment.

Suppose the population of a country is 1.6 million and the labor force is 1 million, of whom 920,000 are employed. Assume that the full-employment level occurs at a 5 percent unemployment rate and at a real GDP of $100 billion. Answer the indicated questions on the basis of this information:

1. What is the unemployment rate? _____

2. Assume "full employment" is equal to 5 percent unemployment. How many more members of the labor force must find jobs for the economy to achieve full employment? _____

3. On the basis of the information above and the revised version of Okun's Law stated in the text, how much potential GDP has been lost because the economy is not at full employment?
_____

4. On the basis of the information above and the revised version of Okun's Law, what is the GDP for this economy? _____

Exercise 2

This exercise shows how to calculate the unemployment rate and indicates the relationship between the unemployment rate and the growth rate of GDP. Data from 1981-1995 is used to demonstrate both expansionary and contractionary economic situations.

1. Compute the unemployment rate based on the information in Table 6.1, and insert it in column 4.

Table 6.1
Unemployment and real GDP, 1981-1995

Year	(1) Noninstitutional population (thousands)	(2) Civilian labor force (thousands of persons 16 and over)	(3) Unemployment (thousands of persons 16 and over)	(4) Unemployment rate (percent)	(5) Percentage change in real GDP
1981	170,130	108,670	8,273	_____	2.5
1982	172,271	110,204	10,678	_____	−2.1
1983	174,215	111,550	10,717	_____	4.0
1984	176,383	113,544	8,539	_____	6.8
1985	178,206	115,461	8,312	_____	3.7
1986	180,587	117,834	8,237	_____	3.0
1987	182,753	119,865	7,425	_____	2.9
1988	184,613	121,669	6,701	_____	3.8
1989	186,393	123,869	6,528	_____	3.4
1990	188,049	124,787	6,874	_____	1.3
1991	189,765	125,303	8,426	_____	−1.0
1992	191,576	126,982	9,384	_____	2.7
1993	193,550	128,040	8,734	_____	2.2
1994	196,814	131,056	7,996	_____	3.5
1995	198,584	132,304	7,404	_____	2.0

2. In Figure 6.1 graph both the unemployment rate (column 4 of Table 6.1) and the percentage change in real GDP (column 5).

Figure 6.1

3. The relationship between the unemployment rate and the percentage change in the real GDP is best characterized as:
   (a) A direct relationship (the two indicators go up and down together).
   (b) An inverse relationship (the two indicators move in opposite directions).

4. Which indicator seems to change direction first as time passes?
   (a) Percentage change in real GDP.
   (b) The unemployment rate.

5. Which of the following types of unemployment had the largest impact on the unemployment rate from 1981 to 1982 in Figure 6.1?
   (a) Structural unemployment.
   (b) Seasonal unemployment.
   (c) Frictional unemployment.
   (d) Cyclical unemployment.

6. If "full employment" is defined as an unemployment rate of 4-6 percent, in what years was full employment achieved between 1981 and 1995? _____

Exercise 3

This exercise shows the relationship between unemployment and population. It is similar to the problem at the end of the chapter.

Suppose the data in Table 6.2 describe a nation's situation.

Table 6.2
Employment and unemployment

	Year 1	Year 2
Population	500 million	550 million
Labor force	300 million	325 million
Unemployment rate	___ percent	___ percent
Number of unemployed	_____	_____
Number of employed	276 million	276 million

1. Fill in the blanks in Table 6.2 to show the number of unemployed and the unemployment rate.

2. When the population grows and the labor force grows, but the number employed remains constant, the unemployment rate (rises; remains the same; falls).

3. If both the population and the number employed remain constant, but a larger percentage of the population passes through to retirement, the unemployment rate should (rise; remain the same; fall), *ceteris paribus.*

4. The people who immigrate to the United States are generally young and of working age compared to the existing population of the United States. As greater immigration rates are permitted and if the unemployment rate stays constant, the number employed would (rise; remain the same; fall), *ceteris paribus.*

5. Assume each employed person contributes $35,000 worth of goods and services to GDP. If the unemployment rate falls from 8 percent to 6 percent in Year 1, by how much will GDP increase? _____

Exercise 4

The following exercise provides practice in categorizing the various types of unemployment. Identify each of the following cases as an example of seasonal, frictional, structural, or cyclical unemployment.

1. An executive quits her current job and takes several months to find a new job. _____

2. The economy is in a recession and one-fourth of the labor force is without work. _____

3. There is a shortage of workers to fill positions in high-tech industries, while many unskilled workers are unemployed. _____

4. A snowplow driver is unemployed during the summer months. _____

Common Errors

The first statement in each "common error" below is incorrect. Each incorrect statement is followed by a corrected version and an explanation.

1. The government's goal is to eliminate all unemployment. WRONG!

    The government's goal is a low level of unemployment that is compatible with other goals. RIGHT!

    Under the Full Employment and Balanced Growth Act of 1978, Congress set a goal of 4 percent unemployment. While many economists agree that an unemployment rate of 4 to 6 is consistent with "full employment." Regardless of the exact level set for "full employment," the goal is certainly not zero percent unemployment because of both frictional and structural components to unemployment. In addition, the government (and economists) will typically accept a higher level of unemployment when economic goals conflict with one another.

2. A rise in the unemployment rate of 0.1 or 0.2 percent for a month is bad. WRONG!

    Monthly changes in the unemployment rate may not have any significant economic implications. RIGHT!

    Small changes in the unemployment rate tell us nothing about what is happening in the labor force; large changes in seasonal or frictional unemployment are not necessarily bad and could not be easily remedied even if they were.

3. Everyone who is counted as unemployed qualifies for unemployment benefits. WRONG!

    To qualify for unemployment benefits, certain conditions must be met. RIGHT!

    Many of those who are counted as unemployed do not qualify for unemployment benefits. Those who are new entrants to the labor force, those who have not worked at their last job for an extended period, and those who quit their last job are ineligible in many states. In addition some who are among the "seasonally unemployed" may not qualify for benefits.

4. Unemployment only occurs during recessions. WRONG!

    Unemployment can occur anytime, but it increases during a recession. RIGHT!

    There are several types of unemployment. Seasonal, frictional, and structural unemployment occur for reasons other than changes in the business cycle. Only cyclical unemployment occurs because of changes in the business cycle or a recession.

•ANSWERS•

Using Key Terms

Across

1. unemployment rate
6. frictional unemployment
7. participation rate
11. outsourcing
13. seasonal unemployment
14. discouraged worker
15. underemployment
16. economic growth

Down

2. natural rate of unemployment
3. production possibilities
4. structural unemployment
5. cyclical unemployment
8. Okun's Law
9. full employment
10. labor force
12. unemployment

True or False

1. F   Ed is counted as being out of the labor force because he is not actively looking for a job.
2. F   When the number of unemployed workers increases, the unemployment rate will rise only if the labor force increases at a slower rate (or decreases).
3. T
4. F   A discouraged worker is someone who does not have a job and sees no prospect of getting one, thus he has dropped out of the labor force.
5. F   This transition has led to greater structural unemployment.
6. T
7. T
8. F   Full employment does not imply a zero unemployment rate. It is usually defined as between 4 and 6 percent unemployment.
9. T
10. T

Multiple Choice

1. a	5. c	9. a	13. c	17. d
2. b	6. c	10. b	14. d	18. b
3. d	7. d	11. d	15. d	19. b
4. a	8. b	12. a	16. a	20. c

Problems and Applications

Exercise 1

1. The unemployment rate is found as follows:

$$\text{Unemployment rate} = \frac{\text{Unemployed}}{\text{Labor force}} = \frac{(\text{Labor force minus employed})}{\text{Labor force}}$$

$$= \frac{(1,000,000 - 920,000)}{1,000,000} = 8\%$$

2. 30,000. The unemployment rate is 8 percent, which is 3 percent above full employment. Multiplying 3 percent by the labor force of 1 million gives 30,000.

3. Unemployment is 3 percentage points above the full employment level. Okun's Law suggests that each percentage point costs the economy 2 percent of full employment GDP. Multiplying 3 percent unemployment times 2 equals 6 percent. Then multiplying 6 percent times $100 billion equals $6 billion.

4. Full employment GDP = $100 billion; lost output = $6 billion. Thus, GDP = $94 billion

Exercise 2

1. **Table 6.1 Answer**

2. **Figure 6.1 Answer**

Year	(4) Unemployment rate (percent)
1981	7.6
1982	9.7
1983	9.6
1984	7.5
1985	7.2
1986	7.0
1987	6.2
1988	5.5
1989	5.3
1990	5.5
1991	6.7
1992	7.4
1993	6.8
1994	6.1
1995	5.6

3. b
4. a   After a dramatic rise in real GDP, it takes several years for the unemployment rate to reach the lowest level.
5. d
6. 1988, 1989, 1990, 1995

Exercise 3

1. **Table 6.2 Answer**

	Year 1	Year 2
Population	500 million	550 million
Labor force	300 million	325 million
Unemployment rate	8 percent (= 24 ÷ 300)	15 percent
Number of unemployed	24 million (= 300 – 276)	49 million
Number of employed	276 million	276 million

2. Rises
3. Fall
4. Rise
5. $210 billion (With an additional 2 percent (8 percent – 6 percent) of the labor force now employed, there are 6 million more people employed (= 2 percent x 300 million in the labor force). Each worker can produce an average of $35,000 a year in GDP for a total of $210 billion (= 6 million x $35,000) in GDP.

Exercise 4

1. Frictional
2. Cyclical
3. Structural
4. Seasonal

CHAPTER 7

Inflation

Quick Review

- Inflation is defined as an increase in the average level of prices, but not all prices rise during a period of inflation. Some prices may be falling while the *average* increases.

- During an inflationary period, the prices of some goods rise faster than the average. Incomes may not rise as fast as the rate of inflation, and some forms of wealth may lose value. The price, income, and wealth effects spawned by the increase in average prices cause a redistribution of income and wealth.

- At the macro level, inflation leads decision makers to shorten their time horizons, diverts resources to speculative activities, and can cause a phenomenon known as bracket creep because the tax bill is calculated in nominal terms.

- Inflation is typically measured using the Consumer Price Index (CPI), a weighted average of prices paid by consumers at the retail level. The inflation rate is the percentage change in the CPI from one year to the next. Other indexes—the Producer Price Index (PPI) and the GDP deflator—can be used to answer questions about inflation too.

- In the United States, the goal for price stability set by Congress in 1978 called for an inflation rate of less than 3 percent, which reduces the conflict with full employment and allows for quality improvements.

- Inflation can result from excessive pressure on the demand side of the economy, known as demand-pull inflation, and from cost increases on the supply side, known as cost-push inflation.

- Inflationary problems have led to the development of some practical protective measures such as cost-of-living-adjustment (COLA) clauses in various contractual arrangements and adjustable-rate mortgages (ARMs) for lenders.

- It's hard to agree on the ideal inflation rate. But in recent years, many countries have focused on reducing the level of inflation. This makes sense if we consider that inflation interferes with the ability of prices to provide information about relative scarcity in the market.

Learning Objectives

After reading Chapter 7 and doing the following exercises, you should:

1. Understand that inflation is measured as an increase in the *average* level of prices.
2. Understand the difference between average prices and relative prices.
3. Be able to describe how price, income, and wealth effects accomplish redistributions in the economy.
4. Understand that some members of society are subject to money illusion.
5. Be able to explain why the inflationary process causes uncertainty and shortened time horizons, and diverts resources to speculative activity.
6. Understand what a price index is and the difference in the CPI, PPI, and the GDP deflator.
7. Understand that the goal of price stability does not necessarily mean zero inflation.
8. Know that when quality improvements occur, the CPI will overstate the rate of inflation.
9. Know that inflation can originate on both the demand side and the supply side of the economy.
10. Be able to discuss some of the protective mechanisms that reduce the redistributive effects of inflation.

Using Key Terms

Fill in the puzzle on the opposite page with the appropriate term from the list of Key Terms at the end of the chapter in the text.

Across

1. The price of apples compared to the price of other fruit.
5. Computed by the Bureau of Labor Statistics as the average price of consumer goods.
7. The nominal interest rate minus the anticipated rate of inflation.
8. The inflation adjusted value of output.
11. The increase in the average price level over a particular time period.
12. Used to express the purchasing power of income.
13. A decrease in average prices.
14. The price index that refers to all final goods and services.
15. Used in lease and wage agreements to protect real income from inflation.
16. Established at a rate of less than 3 percent inflation in the Full Employment and Balanced Growth Act of 1978.
17. The current dollar value of output.
18. The movement of taxpayers into higher tax brackets as nominal incomes grow.
19. The use of nominal dollars, instead of real dollars, to gauge changes in income or wealth.

Down

2. A home loan used to protect the lender during inflationary periods.
3. The time period used for comparative analysis.
4. An inflation rate in excess of 200 percent, lasting at least one year.
6. The percentage of a typical consumer budget spent on a good; used to compute inflation indexes.
9. Results in a redistribution of income and wealth.
10. Income received in a given time period measured in current dollars.

Puzzle 7.1

True or False: *Circle your choice and explain why any false statements are incorrect.*

T F 1.   It is possible for individual prices to rise or fall during periods of inflation.

T F 2.   Relative price changes are a desirable and essential ingredient of the market mechanism.

T F 3.   Inflation only affects the poor.

T F 4.   When doctors' fees rise faster than aspirin prices, real income falls for people who visit a doctor relative to those who prescribe aspirin for themselves.

T F 5.   If the prices of things you buy do not increase, but the inflation rate is 10 percent, then your real income falls, *ceteris paribus*.

T F 6.   If all individuals were able to anticipate inflation correctly and make appropriate adjustments in their market behavior, there would be no redistribution of real income or real wealth as a result of inflation.

T F 7.   The Consumer Price Index usually increases before the Producer Price Index.

T F 8.   The official goal set by Congress for inflation in the U.S. is three percent.

T F 9.   The CPI overstates the rate of inflation when the quality of the items in the market basket improves.

T F 10. A COLA contributes to the redistribution caused by inflation by adjusting real income based on the rate of inflation.

Multiple Choice: *Select the correct answer.*

_____ 1.   If the price of computers falls 10 percent during a period when the level of average prices falls 5 percent, the relative price of computers compared with other goods:
   (a)   Stays the same.
   (b)   Increases.
   (c)   Decreases.
   (d)   More information is required.

_____ 2.   When an economy experiences a zero rate of inflation, which of the following statements is definitely true?
   (a)   Real incomes improve.
   (b)   There is no redistribution of income and wealth because of inflation.
   (c)   Relative prices do not change.
   (d)   All of the above.

_____ 3.   As a result of inflation:
   (a)   Morale improves.
   (b)   The crime rate decreases.
   (c)   Tension between labor and management increases.
   (d)   Tension between individuals and the government decreases.

_____ 4. Which of the following is a consequence of inflation?
    (a)   A price effect.
    (b)   An income effect.
    (c)   A wealth effect.
    (d)   All of the above.

_____ 5. If actual inflation is greater than anticipated inflation in an economy:
    (a)   Borrowers would experience an increase in real income.
    (b)   Lenders would experience an increase in real income.
    (c)   All workers would experience a decrease in real income.
    (d)   The wealth effect would redistribute purchasing power to people on fixed incomes.

_____ 6. Which of the following groups is likely to lose as a result of unanticipated inflation?
    (a)   Borrowers who have loans at fixed interest rates.
    (b)   Fixed-income groups.
    (c)   Workers under multi-year contracts with COLAs.
    (d)   Mortgage lenders who make adjustable-rate mortgages.

_____ 7. Suppose you get a 10 percent raise during a year in which the price level rises by 10 percent. Then over the year:
    (a)   Your real income falls, but your nominal income remains unchanged.
    (b)   Your real and nominal income both fall.
    (c)   Your real income remains unchanged, but your nominal income rises.
    (d)   Your real income remains unchanged, but your nominal income falls.

_____ 8. Which of the following best describes the impact of uncertainty caused by inflation?
    (a)   Short-run economic decisions become easier to make because people know prices are going to increase.
    (b)   Long-run economic decisions become easier to make because people know prices are going to increase.
    (c)   Investment decisions are more difficult to make because of the uncertain but rising costs.
    (d)   All of the above.

_____ 9. Which of the following characterizes consumers' or businesses' reactions to the uncertainties caused by inflation?
    (a)   Consumers cut back on consumption because they fear that future cost increases will make it difficult to make payments on what they consume.
    (b)   Consumption increases as consumers try to buy products before their prices rise.
    (c)   Businesses decrease investment spending in an attempt to avoid being caught with unprofitable plant and equipment.
    (d)   All of the above.

_____ 10. Which of the following is a macro consequence of inflation?
    (a)   Increased uncertainty.
    (b)   Lengthened time horizons.
    (c)   The wealth effect.
    (d)   The price effect.

_____ 11. Speculation during periods of inflation can result in:
    (a)   People buying resources for resale later rather than using the resources for current production.
    (b)   A movement inside the institutional production-possibilities curve.
    (c)   People buying gold, silver, jewelry, etc. instead of capital for production.
    (d)   All of the above.

_____ 12. At the beginning of 1960 the CPI was 29.6. At the beginning of 2000 it was approximately 170.8. Which of the following most closely approximates the forty-year rate of inflation?
   (a) 141 percent
   (b) 477 percent
   (c) 350 percent
   (d) 550 percent

_____ 13. If you were interested in charting "price changes" for all goods and services produced, which of the following would be the most appropriate to use?
   (a) The CPI.
   (b) The PPI.
   (c) The GDP deflator.
   (d) The COLA.

_____ 14. The reason that policy makers are reluctant to force the economy to a zero percent inflation rate is that:
   (a) Unacceptable levels of unemployment might result.
   (b) Businesses would not be able to raise prices.
   (c) Real incomes would fall.
   (d) Businesses would postpone production decisions.

_____ 15. If the CPI doesn't adjust for product quality improvements, then the CPI tends to:
   (a) Understate the inflation rate.
   (b) Overstate the inflation rate.
   (c) Understate economic growth.
   (d) Be artificially low.

_____ 16. Which one of the following statements about inflation in the U.S. is correct?
   (a) Prior to World War II, the U.S. experienced periods of both deflation and inflation.
   (b) The U.S. experienced inflation virtually every year since 1800.
   (c) Since World War II, the U.S. has consistently met its inflation goal of 3 percent or lower.
   (d) Prior to World War II, the U.S. experienced deflation virtually every year; since World War II, the U.S. has consistently experienced inflation.

_____ 17. COLAs are desired because:
   (a) The real value of wages can be maintained, since COLAs correct for the effects of inflation.
   (b) COLAs help reduce the rate of inflation.
   (c) COLAs help stimulate employment.
   (d) All of the above.

_____ 18. For an economy in which nominal interest rates are equal to real interest rates, which of the following statements is definitely true?
   (a) Anticipated inflation was greater than actual inflation.
   (b) Actual inflation was greater than anticipated inflation.
   (c) Inflation was anticipated.
   (d) No inflation occurred.

_____ 19. The most fundamental function of prices in a market economy is to provide:
   (a) The data necessary to calculate rates of inflation.
   (b) The basis for the calculation of sales tax.
   (c) Information about the relative scarcities of resources and goods and services.
   (d) Maximum profits to producers.

_____ 20. The most desirable inflation rate is the rate:
- (a) At which all prices are constant.
- (b) That least affects the behavior of companies, investors, consumers and workers.
- (c) That maximizes the "wealth effect" of inflation.
- (d) That coincides with an unemployment rate of zero percent.

Problems and Applications

Exercise 1

This exercise emphasizes the redistribution of inflation and deflation.

1. During a period of inflation, a person owns no assets and has no COLA to protect his/her income. This is likely to result in a (negative; positive) (wealth; income) effect.

2. During a period of inflation, a family has a COLA that protects their income, but their rent payment rises more rapidly than the rate of inflation. This family experiences a (negative; positive) (price; wealth) effect.

3. During a period of inflation, a person owns stock which increases in value at a rate less than the rate of inflation. This person experiences a (negative; positive) (wealth; price) effect.

4. During a period of deflation, a person's nominal income remains constant. This results in a (positive; negative) (price; income) effect.

5. During a period of deflation, a person owns a home that decreases in value at a rate less than the rate of deflation. The result of this situation is a (positive; negative) (wealth; income) effect.

Exercise 2

This exercise emphasizes the calculation of real GDP, real income, and the real interest rate.

Use the information in Table 7.1 to answer questions 1-6. Assume 2002 is the base period.

Table 7.1

	Nominal GDP (billions of dollars)	Maria's nominal income	GDP deflator	CPI	Nominal interest rate
2002	$3,200	$28,000	100	100	7%
2003	3,500	31,000	105	108	10%
2004	3,700	35,000	112	114	12%

1. Calculate real GDP for 2003. Use the formula:

$$\text{Real GDP for 2003} = \frac{\text{Nominal GDP}_{2003}}{\text{GDP deflator}_{2003}} \times 100$$

_____

2. Calculate real GDP for 2004. _____

3. Calculate Maria's real income for 2004. Use the formula:

$$\text{Real income for 2004} = \frac{\text{Nominal income}_{2004}}{\text{CPI}_{2004}} \times 100$$

_____

4. By what percentage did consumer prices rise from 2002 to 2003? _____

5. By what percentage did consumer prices rise from 2002 to 2004? _____

6. Use the Consumer Price Index as a measure of the anticipated rate of inflation. Calculate the real interest rate for 2004. (The formula is in the text.) _____

Exercise 3

This exercise focuses on the causes of inflation and the different impacts on the economy.

1. When consumers seek to buy more goods than the economy can produce, the result is _____ inflation.

2. When production costs rise for numerous industries, the result is _____ inflation.

Figure 7.1

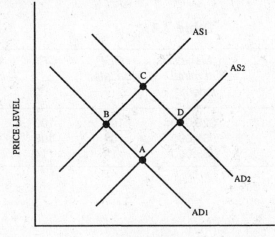

3. Assume the economy is in equilibrium at point A in Figure 7.1. As a result of cost-push inflation, the economy would move to point _____. The price level would (increase, decrease) and the level of output would (increase, decrease).

4. Assume the economy is in equilibrium at point B in Figure 7.1. As a result of demand-pull inflation, the economy would move to point _____. The price level would (increase, decrease) and the level of output would (increase, decrease).

Exercise 4

This exercise will help you see the impact of different inflation rates on the value of money held for different periods of time.

1. Use Table 7.6 in the text to determine the impact of a period of inflation at a particular inflation rate. Calculate the value of $1,000 held for:
   a. Four years' time at an inflation rate of 8%. _____
   b. Five years' time at an inflation rate of 4%. _____
   c. Eight years' time at an inflation rate of 4%. _____
   d. Ten years' time at an inflation rate of 2%. _____
   e. Six years' time at an inflation rate of 10%. _____

2. In which two cases above is the $1,000 worth the greatest amount? _____

3. In which case above is the $1,000 worth the least amount? _____

4. Would you lose more money if you placed $1,000 under your mattress for ten years at an inflation rate of 2% or if you placed $1,000 in a cookie jar for four years at an inflation rate of 8%?

_____

Common Errors

The first statement in each "common error" below is incorrect. Each incorrect statement is followed by a corrected version and an explanation.

1. When the price of a product rises, there is inflation. WRONG!

   When the average level of prices rises, there is inflation. RIGHT!

   The price of a single product may rise while an average of prices of all products falls. Such adjustments in relative prices are essential to the most *efficient* distribution of goods and services through the market. When the average of all prices is rising, however, distribution may not be efficient and capricious redistributions of income may occur.

2. Everyone is worse off during periods of inflation. WRONG!

   Some individuals are worse off as a result of inflation, but other individuals are better off. RIGHT!

   Inflation is an increase in the *average* level of prices of goods and services. People buy and sell different combinations of goods and services and own different assets. The prices for the various goods, services, and assets do not rise at the same rate during a period of inflation (and, in fact, some may even fall) so individuals are affected differently. The result is a redistribution of income and wealth amongst the different individuals and firms. In the end, some people are worse off, but others have gained.

3. Indexation, such as a COLA clause in a contract, protects the *economy* against the effects of inflation. WRONG!

    A COLA clause protects an individual against the effects of inflation. RIGHT!

    Indexation can protect the real incomes of specific groups for which indexation is applied. In other words, it can address some of the micro consequences of inflation. However, if everyone's income is not indexed, then even the micro consequences may not be adequately addressed. In fact, indexation can lead to dramatic changes in relative prices. Furthermore, indexation may lead to anticipation of higher rates of inflation; high current inflation rates may guarantee higher future rates as a result of indexation.

•ANSWERS•

Using Key Terms

Across

1. relative price
5. Consumer Price Index
7. real interest rate
8. real GDP
11. inflation rate
12. real income
13. deflation
14. GDP deflator
15. cost of living adjustment
16. price stability
17. nominal GDP
18. bracket creep
19. money illusion

Down

2. adjustable rate mortgage
3. base period
4. hyperinflation
6. item weight
9. inflation
10. nominal income

True or False

1. T
2. T
3. F   Inflation affects everyone, although the poor and those on fixed incomes tend to be more adversely affected.
4. T

5.	F	If your purchasing power does not change, then your real income hasn't changed.
6.	T	
7.	F	The PPI measures changes in average prices at the producer level, which typically occurs before changes in the CPI.
8.	T	
9.	T	
10.	F	A COLA counteracts the income effect of inflation by adjusting nominal income based on the rate of inflation.

Multiple Choice

1.	c	5.	a	9.	d	13.	c	17.	a
2.	b	6.	b	10.	a	14.	a	18.	d
3.	c	7	c	11.	d	15.	b	19.	c
4.	d	8.	c	12.	b	16.	a	20.	b

Problems and Applications

Exercise 1

1. Negative; income
2. Negative; price
3. Negative; wealth
4. Positive; income
5. Positive; wealth

Exercise 2

1. $3,333.33 billion
2. $3,303.57 billion
3. $30,701.75
4. 8 percent
5. 14 percent
6. 6.44 percent

Exercise 3

1. Demand-pull
2. Cost-push
3. B; increase; decrease
4. C; increase; increase

Exercise 4

1. a. $735
   b. $822
   c. $731
   d. $820
   e. $564
2. b and d
3. e
4. You would lose more money if you placed $1,000 in a cookie jar for four years at 8% inflation.

CHAPTER 8

The Business Cycle

Quick Review

- Business cycles are alternating periods of growth and contraction in the economy. The cycle is measured by changes in the nation's real GDP. The cycles vary in length and intensity. The worst contraction experienced was the Great Depression of the 1930s. Despite the ups and downs, the economy has had an average annual growth rate of approximately 3 percent since 1929.

- Macroeconomic theory attempts to explain the business cycle while macroeconomic policy tries to control the cycle.

- The primary outcomes of the macroeconomy include output (GDP), prices, jobs, growth, and international balances. These outcomes result from the interplay of internal market forces, external shocks, and policy levers.

- The aggregate demand curve slopes downward to the right and the aggregate supply curve slopes upward to the right. The intersection of the aggregate demand and supply curves defines the macro equilibrium.

- The equilibrium may be undesirable because it may not provide the optimal level of employment and output or the optimal price level.

- Even if the equilibrium is desirable, it may be unstable and not last for long because the forces behind the equilibrium can change. Shifts in aggregate demand and/or aggregate supply can lead to unemployment, inflation, or, worse yet, stagflation—a combination of the two.

- The aggregate-demand and aggregate-supply framework provides a convenient way to compare various theories about how the economy works. The theories can be classified as demand-side, supply-side, or eclectic.

- It is also useful to separate the short run from the long run. In the long run, monetarists and classical theorists assert that the aggregate supply curve becomes vertical at the "natural" rate of output.

- Specific policy approaches include fiscal policy (changes in taxes and government spending), monetary policy (the use of money and credit controls), and supply-side policy (favors tax cuts and other policies to increase incentives for producers). The classical approach calls for a laissez-faire policy of nonintervention by the government.

Learning Objectives

After reading Chapter 8 and doing the following exercises, you should:

1. Understand how economic growth is measured and the long-term goal for growth.
2. Have a historical perspective on the business cycle from the Great Depression to the present.
3. Understand why the aggregate supply curve slopes upward to the right, and why the aggregate demand curve slopes downward to the right.
4. Recognize that a given macro equilibrium may not be desirable, and that it may also be unstable.
5. Be able to distinguish the different macro theories about how the economy works.
6. Understand the different macro policies—demand-side, supply-side, and eclectic.

Using Key Terms

Fill in the puzzle on the opposite page with the appropriate term from the list of Key Terms at the end of the chapter in the text.

Across

2. The value of final output produced in a given period, adjusted for changing prices.
3. The idea that whatever is produced by suppliers will always be sold.
9. Potential GDP.
12. The use of tax cuts and government deregulation to shift the aggregate supply curve.
13. The portion of the business cycle when total output decreases.
14. An increase in the average level of prices of goods and services.
15. The concept of nonintervention by government in the market mechanism.

Down

1. A situation in which the economy grows but at a very slow rate.
4. States that an increase in price causes a decrease in quantity demanded of a good.
5. The total quantity of output producers are willing and able to supply at alternative price levels in a given time period, *ceteris paribus*.
6. The combination of price level and real output that is compatible with both aggregate demand and aggregate supply.
7. The area of study that focuses on output, jobs, prices, and growth for the entire economy.
8. The use of money and credit controls to shift the aggregate demand curve.
9. The use of government spending and taxes to shift the aggregate demand curve.
10. Occurs as a result of shifts in aggregate demand and aggregate supply.
11. The total quantity of output demanded at alternative price levels in a given time period, *ceteris paribus*.

True or False: *Circle your choice and explain why any false statements are incorrect.*

T F   1. Business cycles are measured by changes in nominal GDP.

T F   2. During the business cycle, unemployment and production typically move in opposite directions.

T F   3. In the classical view of the economy, the product market is brought into equilibrium by flexible prices, and the labor market is brought into equilibrium by flexible wages.

T F   4. Business cycles result from shifts of the aggregate supply and aggregate demand curves.

T F   5. The U.S. economy has grown at a steady pace since 1930.

T F   6. The economy is in a growth recession if real GDP is decreasing.

T F   7. The full-employment GDP is the same as the equilibrium GDP.

T F   8. Keynes believed that unemployment could exist for long periods of time if aggregate demand was inadequate.

T F   9. Both Keynesian and monetarist theories focus on shifting the aggregate supply curve.

T F 10. Supply-side theorists believe the unwillingness of producers to supply more goods and services at existing prices can prolong an economic downturn.

Multiple Choice: *Select the correct answer.*

_____ 1. Determinants of macro performance include:
    (a)   Internal market forces.
    (b)   External shocks.
    (c)   Policy levers.
    (d)   All of the above.

_____ 2. Business cycles in the United States:
    (a)   Are remarkably similar in length but vary greatly in intensity.
    (b)   Vary greatly in length, frequency, and intensity.
    (c)   Are similar in frequency and intensity.
    (d)   Are similar in length, frequency, and intensity.

_____ 3. Which of the following is inherent in the classical view of a self-adjusting economy?
    (a)   Flexible wages and prices.
    (b)   Inflexible wages and prices.
    (c)   Schiller's Law.
    (d)   Instability.

_____ 4. Keynesian theory became important when classical economic theory did not adequately explain:
    (a)   A prolonged period of both inflation and unemployment.
    (b)   A prolonged growth recession.
    (c)   A depression.
    (d)   A prolonged period of inflation.

_____ 5. In the aggregate demand-aggregate supply diagram:
  (a) More than one equilibrium can occur.
  (b) The horizontal axis measures the average price level.
  (c) The intersection of the two curves marks the macro equilibrium.
  (d) The equilibrium level of output is always at the full employment level.

_____ 6. Which of the following is a reason for a downward-sloping aggregate demand curve?
  (a) The real-balances effect.
  (b) The price effect.
  (c) The inter-state trade effect.
  (d) The savings effect.

_____ 7. The difference between market demand and aggregate demand is:
  (a) Market demand applies to all individuals, and aggregate demand does not.
  (b) Aggregate demand applies to a specific good, and market demand does not.
  (c) Policy levers work only through market demand.
  (d) Market demand applies to a given market while aggregate demand applies to the entire economy.

_____ 8. The foreign-trade effect helps explain the downward slope of the aggregate demand curve because as:
  (a) The U.S. price level falls, people in the United States tend to purchase more imports.
  (b) The U.S. price level falls, people tend to purchase more U.S. produced goods.
  (c) Foreign prices rise, people tend to purchase more U.S. produced goods.
  (d) Foreign prices rise, people in the United States tend to purchase more imports.

_____ 9. When the average price level falls in our economy, consumers tend to buy:
  (a) More imported goods and fewer domestic goods, _ceteris paribus_.
  (b) More imported goods and more domestic goods, _ceteris paribus_.
  (c) Fewer imported goods and more domestic goods, _ceteris paribus_.
  (d) Fewer imported goods and fewer domestic goods, _ceteris paribus_.

_____ 10. Which of the following is a reason why the aggregate supply curve is upward sloping?
  (a) Profit effect.
  (b) Interest rate effect.
  (c) Real-balances effect.
  (d) Foreign trade effect.

_____ 11. The cost effect implies:
  (a) That greater output results in increasingly higher costs.
  (b) A curved, upward-sloping aggregate supply curve.
  (c) That higher costs are reflected in higher average prices.
  (d) All of the above.

_____ 12. In macro equilibrium:
  (a) Aggregate quantity demanded equals aggregate quantity supplied.
  (b) The equilibrium price level and rate of output are both stable.
  (c) Both buyers' and sellers' intentions are satisfied.
  (d) All of the above.

_____ 13. When aggregate supply exceeds aggregate demand, what will happen to the price level?
  (a) Prices will rise.
  (b) Prices will remain the same.
  (c) Prices will fall.
  (d) Prices may either rise or fall depending on the business cycle.

_____ 14. Which of the following combination of shifts of aggregate demand and supply curves would definitely result in higher unemployment?
   (a)   Demand shifts to the left and supply shifts to the right.
   (b)   Demand shifts to the left and supply shifts to the left.
   (c)   Demand shifts to the right and supply shifts to the right.
   (d)   Demand shifts to the right and supply shifts to the left.

_____ 15. Controversies between Keynesian, monetarist, supply-side, and eclectic theories focus on:
   (a)   The shape and sensitivity of aggregate demand and aggregate supply curves.
   (b)   The existence or nonexistence of the aggregate supply curve.
   (c)   The importance of international balances to the economy.
   (d)   All of the above.

_____ 16. According to Keynes, policy makers should respond to a downturn in the business cycle by:
   (a)   Cutting taxes and increasing government spending.
   (b)   Cutting taxes and reducing government spending.
   (c)   Raising taxes and increasing government spending.
   (d)   Raising taxes and reducing government spending.

_____ 17. The eclectic approach to macroeconomic policy relies on:
   (a)   Demand-side policy.
   (b)   A laissez-faire approach.
   (c)   Supply-side policy.
   (d)   Any or all of the above approaches.

_____ 18. Which of the following is _not_ typically used to shift the aggregate demand curve or the aggregate supply curve?
   (a)   Monetary policy.
   (b)   International trade policy.
   (c)   Fiscal policy.
   (d)   A laissez-faire approach.

_____ 19. If equilibrium GDP is less than full employment GDP, an appropriate fiscal policy action would be to:
   (a)   Increase AD by increasing income taxes.
   (b)   Increase AD by increasing government spending.
   (c)   Increase AS by reducing government regulations.
   (d)   Reduce AS by tightening air pollution standards in order to improve air quality.

_____ 20. If an economy is suffering from excessively high rates of inflation, an appropriate monetary policy lever would be to:
   (a)   Decrease AS by decreasing the money supply.
   (b)   Decrease AD by increasing interest rates.
   (c)   Decrease AD by increasing income taxes.
   (d)   Increase AS by increasing the money supply.

Problems and Applications

Exercise 1

This exercise examines the effects of fiscal policy using aggregate supply and demand curves.

Assume the aggregate demand curve (AD_i) and aggregate supply curve (AS_i) are those shown in Figure 8.1. Then suppose the government increases spending, which causes the quantity of output demanded in the economy to rise by $1 trillion per year at every price level. Decide whether the change shifts aggregate demand or aggregate supply from its initial position.

Figure 8.1

AVERAGE PRICE LEVEL

REAL GROSS DOMESTIC PRODUCT
(trillions of dollars per year)

1. Draw the new aggregate demand curve (label it AD_2) or the new aggregate supply curve (label it AS_2) in Figure 8.1.

2. What is the new equilibrium average price? _____

3. What is the new equilibrium output level? _____

4. Which school of thought would be most likely to prescribe the use of fiscal policy in this way?
   _____

5. The shift that occurred in question 1 (above) is consistent with:
   (a) Inflation and a higher unemployment rate.
   (b) Inflation and a lower unemployment rate.
   (c) Deflation and a higher unemployment rate.
   (d) Lower inflation and a lower unemployment rate.

Exercise 2

This exercise will help to explain why the aggregate demand curve slopes downward.

1. Suppose you have $1,000 in savings at the beginning of the year and the price level is 100. If inflation pushes the price level up by 10 percent to 110 during the year, what will be the real value of your savings at year-end? (*Hint:* Refer to the formula in the text for the real value of savings.)
   _____

2. The change in purchasing power in question 1 above, because of a change in the price level, is one explanation for the downward slope of the aggregate demand curve. This explanation is referred to as the _____.

3. The impact of the change in purchasing power in question 1 above would cause a (movement up; leftward shift in) the aggregate demand curve.

Exercise 3

This exercise will demonstrate the impact of shifts in demand and aggregate supply. Answer choices for questions 1-4 are "AD," "AS," or "both AD and AS."

Use Figure 8.2 to answer questions 1-4.

Figure 8.2

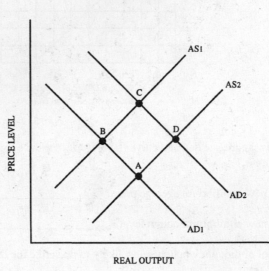

1. Assume the economy is initially in equilibrium at point B in Figure 8.2. Which curve would need to shift in order for a new equilibrium to occur at point C? _____

2. Assume the economy is initially in equilibrium at point D in Figure 8.2. Which curve would need to shift in order for a new equilibrium to occur at point C? _____

3. Assume the economy is initially in equilibrium at point B in Figure 8.2. Which curve would need to shift in order for a new equilibrium to occur at point A? _____

4. Assume the economy is initially in equilibrium at point A in Figure 8.2. Which curve would need to shift in order for a new equilibrium to occur at point C? _____

5. Which policy option might be used to achieve the shift in question 1 above?
    _____

6. Which policy option might be used to achieve the shift in question 3 above?
    _____

108

Exercise 4

This exercise focuses on the long-run aggregate supply curve and the impact of fiscal policy.

Use Figure 8.3 to answer questions 1-7.

Figure 8.3

1. In Figure 8.3, aggregate demand is given as AD_1. Draw the long-run aggregate supply curve according to the classical/monetarist view of long-run stability. The equilibrium level of output should occur at Q_N. Label the curve AS. Label the equilibrium point E_1.

2. T   F Q_N represents the long-run equilibrium output level.

3. What is the equilibrium price level in Figure 8.3, given the long-run aggregate supply curve and AD_1? _____

4. Suppose the government uses fiscal policy to shift the aggregate demand curve in Figure 8.3 to the right. Draw the new aggregate demand curve and label it AD_2. Label the new equilibrium point E_2.

5. The fiscal policy action in question 4 above caused the price level to (rise; fall; stay the same).

6. The fiscal policy action in question 4 above caused the level of real output to (rise; fall; stay the same).

7. T   F   With a vertical long-run aggregate supply curve, fiscal policy is effective in changing the level of real output.

109

Common Errors

The first statement in each "common error" below is incorrect. Each incorrect statement is followed by a corrected version and an explanation.

1. The full-employment GDP is the same as the equilibrium GDP. WRONG!

    The full-employment GDP is not necessarily the same as the equilibrium GDP. RIGHT!

    The full-employment GDP refers to the capacity of the economy to produce goods and services. When resources are fully employed, no additional goods and services can be produced. The equilibrium GDP refers to the equality between the aggregate demand for goods and services and the aggregate supply of those goods and services, not to any particular level of resource employment.

2. Aggregate demand (supply) and market demand (supply) are the same. WRONG!

    Aggregate demand (supply) and market demand (supply) involve very different levels of aggregation. RIGHT!

    Market demand can be found for specific markets only. Products in that market must be homogeneous. The firms in that market are competitors. The market demand is used for microeconomic applications. Aggregate demand applies to all markets within the economy and involves their average prices. Aggregate demand is used for macroeconomic applications, not microeconomic ones. The distinction between aggregate supply and market supply is similar to that between aggregate demand and market demand.

3. A downward-sloping trend of the economic growth rate indicates a recession. WRONG!

    A downward-sloping trend of the real GDP indicates a recession. RIGHT!

    The economic growth rate is measured by the *percentage change* in the real GDP. A recession occurs whenever that percentage change is negative for two quarters. By contrast, in a graph of the real GDP, without any computation of year-to-year changes, it is necessary to look for a downward dip in the real GDP to spot a recession. Three rules for the relationship between the levels and percentage changes of the real GDP should always be remembered when either graph is being examined:
    1. Whenever there is a downward slope to a graph of the real GDP, there will be a negative percentage change in real GDP.
    2. Whenever the graph of the real GDP flattens, the percentage change in the real GDP will approach zero.
    3. Whenever there is an upward slope to a graph of the real GDP, there will be a positive percentage change in real GDP.

•ANSWERS•

Using Key Terms

Across

2. real GDP
3. Say's Law
9. full employment GDP
12. supply-side policy
13. recession
14. inflation
15. laissez faire

Down

1. growth recession
4. law of demand
5. aggregate supply
6. equilibrium
7. macroeconomics
8. monetary policy
9. fiscal policy
10. business cycle
11. aggregate demand

True or False

1. F Business cycles are measured by changes in real GDP.
2. T
3. T
4. T
5. F The U.S. economy has grown at an unsteady pace, with many peaks and troughs in the business cycle.
6. F If real GDP increases but at a rate below the long-term trend, this is known as a growth recession.
7. F Equilibrium GDP does not guarantee full employment. Equilibrium GDP can be greater than, less than, or equal to full employment GDP.
8. T
9. F These are demand-side theories that focus on shifting the aggregate demand curve.
10. T

Multiple Choice

1.	d	5.	c	9.	c	13.	c	17.	d
2.	b	6.	a	10.	a	14.	b	18.	d
3.	a	7.	d	11.	d	15.	a	19.	b
4.	c	8.	b	12.	d	16.	a	20.	b

Problems and Applications

Exercise 1

1. See Figure 8.1 Answer, AD_2.

Figure 8.1 Answer

2. $150
3. $2 trillion
4. Keynesian
5. b

Exercise 2

1. $1,000÷(110÷100) = $1,000÷(1.1) = $909.09
2. Real-balances effect
3. Movement up

Exercise 3

1. AD
2. AS
3. AS
4. Both AD and AS
5. Fiscal or monetary policy
6. Supply-side policy

Exercise 4

Figure 8.3 Answer

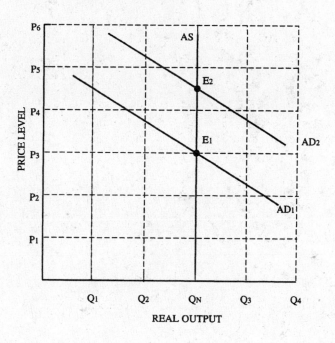

1. See AS and E_1 in Figure 8.3 Answer.
2. T
3. P_3
4. See AD_2 and E_2 in Figure 8.3 Answer.
5. Rise
6. Stay the same
7. F

Aggregate Demand

Quick Review

- John Maynard Keynes challenged the classical approach of laissez faire. He asserted that the economy was inherently unstable and that government intervention was necessary at times.

- The four components of aggregate demand are consumption (C), investment (I), government spending (G), and net exports ($X - M$).

- Disposable income is divided into two parts—that which is spent and that which is saved. Consumption refers to all household spending on goods and services. It can be determined using the consumption function, which is written as $C = a + bY_D$, where a is referred to as "autonomous spending" and bY_D is the income dependent portion of spending.

- The MPC represents the change in consumption because of a change in income and is the slope of the consumption function. In the function above, the MPC is represented by b.

- Any change in the level of autonomous consumption will shift the consumption function up or down, which will in turn shift the aggregate demand curve to the right or left.

- Investment refers to spending by businesses on new plant and equipment and net changes in inventory. It is dependent on interest rates, expectations, and innovation but *not* on current income.

- Government spending includes expenditure on goods and services at the federal, state, and local levels. Decisions on how much to spend are independent of the level of real income.

- Foreign buyers purchase exports from the U.S. economy, and Americans gladly purchase imports from foreign countries. Net exports is the difference between spending on exports and spending on imports.

- Even if the economy is currently in equilibrium at full employment, this may not last if aggregate demand changes. A decrease in spending can push the economy into a recessionary GDP gap, which causes cyclical unemployment. If demand becomes too great the economy may experience an inflationary GDP gap, which results in demand-pull inflation. Either way the economy misses the goals of full employment and price stability.

Learning Objectives

After reading Chapter 9 and doing the following exercises, you should:

1. Know the Keynesian theory of aggregate demand.
2. Understand that equilibrium may not occur at full employment.
3. Know the four components of aggregate demand.
4. Be able to interpret the consumption function.
5. Know how to find the average and marginal propensities to consume.
6. Understand how a shift in the consumption function leads to a shift in aggregate demand.
7. Be able to describe the determinants of C, I, G, and $(X - M)$.
8. Know that the intersection of aggregate supply and aggregate demand determines the equilibrium level of income.
9. Be able to graph a recessionary or an inflationary GDP gap and describe the economic implications.

Using Key Terms

Fill in the puzzle on the opposite page with the appropriate term from the list of Key Terms at the end of the chapter in the text.

Across

1. A change in consumers' spending caused by a change in the value of assets owned by consumers.
5. The total quantity of output producers are willing and able to supply at alternative price levels in a given time period, *ceteris paribus*.
7. Occurs when equilibrium GDP is less than full employment GDP.
9. The fraction of each additional dollar of disposable income spent on consumption.
10. The combination of price level and real output that is compatible with both aggregate demand and aggregate supply.
12. Provides a basis for predicting how changes in income will affect consumer spending.
14. A negative saving flow.
16. The difference between full employment GDP and equilibrium GDP associated with demand-pull inflation.
17. After-tax income of consumers.
18. Unemployment because of an inadequate level of aggregate demand.
19. Alternating periods of expansions and contractions in economic activity.
20. An increase in the price level initiated by excessive aggregate demand.

Down

2. The total quantity of output demanded at alternative price levels in a given time period, *ceteris paribus*.
3. The proportion of total disposable income spent on consumption.
4. The potential GDP for an economy is the same thing as _____ _____ GDP.
6. Equal to 1 - MPC.
8. The value of total output produced at macro equilibrium.
11. The part of disposable income not spent on current consumption.
13. The largest component of aggregate demand.
15. Determined by expectations, interest rates, and technology.

Puzzle 9.1

True or False: *Circle your choice and explain why any false statements are incorrect.*

T F 1. Keynes believed that if market participants were unwilling to buy all of the output produced, the government would have to intervene if the economy were to pull itself out of a recessionary gap.

T F 2. The four components of aggregate demand are consumption, investment, government spending, and net exports.

T F 3. The largest component of aggregate demand is government spending.

T F 4. The question "What fraction of total disposable income is saved?" can be answered by calculating the marginal propensity to save.

T F 5. The slope of the consumption function equals the marginal propensity to consume.

T F 6. The consumption function will shift because of a change in current disposable income.

T F 7. If disposable income is constant, a sudden increase in saving results in a lower level of consumption for society, *ceteris paribus*.

T F 8. Cyclical unemployment can result from a decrease in spending by businesses and government.

T F 9. Investment depends primarily upon the current level of income.

T F 10. If people become overly confident in the economy, an inflationary GDP gap can result.

Multiple Choice: *Select the correct answer.*

_____ 1. Keynes argued that the level of economic activity is predominantly determined by the level of:
(a)   Aggregate supply.
(b)   Aggregate demand.
(c)   Unemployment.
(d)   Interest rates.

_____ 2. If, in the aggregate, consumers spend 90 cents out of every extra dollar received:
(a)   The *APC* is 1.11.
(b)   The *APC* is 0.90.
(c)   The *MPS* is 0.10.
(d)   The *MPC* is 0.10.

_____ 3. Suppose the MPC in an economy is 0.8 and the level of consumption spending independent of current disposable income is $1 billion. If disposable income is $14 billion, what is the level of consumption?
(a) $11.2 billion.
(b) $12.2 billion.
(c) $8.0 billion.
(d) $12.0 billion.

_____ 4. Which of the following is a part of aggregate demand?
(a)   The purchase of athletic shoes for your child.
(b)   The purchase of a new forklift by a hardware store.
(c)   The purchase of a computer by the federal government.
(d)   All of the above.

_____ 5. A change in autonomous consumption would correspond to:
  (a) A shift of both the consumption function and the aggregate demand curve.
  (b) A shift of the consumption function and a movement along the aggregate demand curve.
  (c) A movement along the consumption function and a shift of the aggregate demand curve.
  (d) A movement along both the consumption function and the aggregate demand curve.

_____ 6. In the consumption function $C = a + bY_D$, the value of a is determined in part by:
  (a) Disposable income.
  (b) The level of imports.
  (c) Consumer confidence.
  (d) All of the above.

_____ 7. The line described by the consumption function $C = a + bY_D$ will change its slope when:
  (a) The MPC changes.
  (b) Consumer confidence changes.
  (c) Disposable income changes.
  (d) The MPS is greater than 1.0.

_____ 8. The marginal propensity to consume is the:
  (a) Average consumption per dollar of income.
  (b) Additional consumption because of additional income.
  (c) Additional consumption per dollar paid in taxes.
  (d) Additional dollar amount of consumption because of inflation.

_____ 9. An increase in interest rates would result in:
  (a) A decrease in both aggregate demand and the consumption function.
  (b) A decrease in aggregate demand and an increase in aggregate supply.
  (c) An increase in both aggregate demand and the consumption function.
  (d) An increase in both aggregate demand and aggregate supply.

_____ 10. With respect to the aggregate demand curve, improved consumer confidence would:
  (a) Shift the curve rightward.
  (b) Shift the curve leftward.
  (c) Move the economy down along the curve.
  (d) Move the economy up along the curve.

_____ 11. Determinants of consumption include the:
  (a) Level of wealth.
  (b) Availability of credit.
  (c) Tax rate.
  (d) All of the above.

_____ 12. The terrorist attacks on the World Trade Center and The Pentagon in September 2001 contributed to a recession for the U.S. economy because:
  (a) The decrease in consumer confidence caused the consumption function to shift downward and aggregate demand to decrease.
  (b) The increase in government spending to fight terrorism was primarily in the form of foreign expenditure.
  (c) A decrease in the cost of airline travel caused more people to spend money on flying.
  (d) A decrease in the average price level caused an increase in the aggregate quantity demanded.

_____ 13. Which of the following is included in investment spending?
    (a)   The purchase of a new share of stock issued by IBM.
    (b)   The purchase of a previously owned home.
    (c)   The purchase of a used Sears delivery van by a small business.
    (d)   The purchase of a new computer by a local merchant.

_____ 14. Which of the following causes a movement along the investment demand curve?
    (a)   A change in expenditures.
    (b)   A change in technology.
    (c)   A change in the rate of interest.
    (d)   The current level of income.

_____ 15. The growth in the value of the U.S. stock market in the 1990s caused aggregate demand to increase primarily because of:
    (a)   The price effect.
    (b)   The wealth effect.
    (c)   Increased income.
    (d)   The interest rate effect.

_____ 16. Aggregate demand can shift due to changes in expectations on the part of:
    (a)   U.S. consumers.
    (b)   U.S. businesses.
    (c)   Foreign consumers.
    (d)   All of the above.

_____ 17. Dissaving:
    (a)   Is not possible because that would mean saving is less than zero.
    (b)   Is the result of an inflationary GDP gap.
    (c)   Can be financed with savings from a prior period.
    (d)   Occurs when consumption is greater than real GDP.

_____ 18. If aggregate demand is too great:
    (a)   Equilibrium will still occur at full employment GDP.
    (b)   Cyclical unemployment will occur.
    (c)   There will be an inflationary GDP gap.
    (d)   All of the above.

_____ 19. When consumers, government, businesses, and the foreign sector do not buy all of the output that is produced, then:
    (a)   Inventories accumulate.
    (b)   There is an inflationary GDP gap.
    (c)   The economy will sustain itself at its potential GDP.
    (d)   The aggregate expenditure line should decrease.

_____ 20. When aggregate demand falls below the full-employment level of output, which of the following types of unemployment is most likely to increase?
    (a)   Cyclical.
    (b)   Seasonal.
    (c)   Frictional.
    (d)   Structural.

_____ 21. In graphs with output on the horizontal axis and aggregate expenditures on the vertical axis, a 45-degree line represents:
  (a) The potential growth path for consumption.
  (b) A line marking where aggregate demand and supply intersect for equilibrium (macro).
  (c) The points on which aggregate expenditure equals output.
  (d) Points where consumption equals saving.

_____ 22. Equilibrium (macro) occurs at the output at which:
  (a) The aggregate expenditure curve intersects the 45-degree line.
  (b) The aggregate demand curve intersects the aggregate supply curve.
  (c) Desired expenditure equals the value of output.
  (d) All of the above.

_____ 23. The amount by which the desired rate of total expenditure at full employment is less than full-employment output is the:
  (a) GDP gap.
  (b) Recessionary gap.
  (c) Inflationary gap.
  (d) Budget deficit.

Problems and Applications

Exercise 1

This exercise emphasizes the relationship between consumption and disposable income.

1. Complete columns 4, 5, and 7 in Table 9.1, and then compute the average propensity to consume and the marginal propensity to consume in columns 3 and 6.

Table 9.1
Marginal and average propensity to consume
(billions of dollars per year)

(1) Disposable income	(2) Total consumption	(3) Average propensity to consume	(4) Change in consumption	(5) Change in income	(6) Marginal propensity to consume	(7) Saving
$ 0	$100	----	----	----	----	$_____
1,000	1,000	_____	$900	$1,000	_____	_____
2,000	1,900	_____	_____	_____	_____	_____

2. What is the level of consumption if disposable income increases to $3,000? _____

3. Write the consumption function based on the information in Table 9.1. _____

Exercise 2

This exercise provides practice in using the consumption function and in distinguishing shifts of the consumption function from movements along it.

1. Assume the following consumption function:

$$C = \$200 \text{ billion} + 0.75Y_D$$

In Table 9.2, compute a consumption schedule from the formula.

Table 9.2
Computation of a consumption schedule
(billions of dollars per year)

Disposable income (Y_D)	Autonomous consumption (a)	+	Income-dependent consumption (bY_D)	=	Total consumption (C)
$ 0	_____		_____		$_____
400	_____		_____		_____
1,200	200		0.75 x 1,200		1,100

2. Using the consumption schedule in Table 9.2, draw the consumption function in Figure 9.1 and label it 1. The curve should pass through point *B* if it is correctly drawn.

3. In Table 9.3, fill in the schedule for the consumption function $C = \$300 \text{ billion} + 0.75Y_D$.

4. What is the marginal propensity to consume in Table 9.3? _____

Table 9.3
Consumption function shift
(billions of dollars per year)

Disposable income (Y_D)	Autonomous consumption (a)	+	Income-dependent consumption ($0.75 \times Y_D$)	=	Total consumption (C)
$ 0	$300		_____		$_____
400	300		_____		_____
800	300		_____		_____
1,200	300		_____		_____

5. Using the schedule in Table 9.3, graph the consumption function in Figure 9.1 (label it 2) and draw a 45-degree line from the origin.

6. T   F   In Figure 9.1, the shift in the consumption function from curve 1 to curve 2 shows that at any given level of disposable income, consumption will be greater and savings will be less.

Figure 9.1
Consumption functions

Exercise 3

Choose the diagram (a or b) in Figure 9.2 that best represents the shift in the consumption function that accompanies each of the events described in questions 1-4. Then, try to decide what impact each shift in the consumption function would have on the aggregate demand curve (c or d) for the economy. Place your answers in the blanks provided.

Figure 9.2

1. Consumer confidence falters as a recession becomes more likely. ____ ____

2. Many U.S. households receive a tax refund, which they promptly spend. ____ ____

3. Congress passes new, strict regulations on the distribution and use of credit cards. ____ ____

4. Consumer interest rates are reduced to stimulate the economy. ____ ____

Exercise 4

This examines the relationship between the components of aggregate expenditure (consumption, investment, government spending, and net exports) and the level of income.

1. Complete Table 9.4.

Table 9.4
Disposable income and expenditures
(billions of dollars per year)

At an output of	Desired consumer spending	Desired investment spending	Desired government spending	Net export spending	Aggregate expenditure
$1,000	$ _____	$ 350	$ 400	$ 50	$ 1,750
2,000	1,700	350	400	50	_____
3,000	2,450	_____	400	50	3,250
4,000	3,200	350	400	50	_____
5,000	_____	350	400	50	4,750
6,000	4,700	350	400	_____	5,500

2. What is the equilibrium income level in Table 9.4? _____

3. What is the MPC from Table 9.4? _____

4. If full-employment output occurs at $6,000 billion, there is a _____ gap and aggregate demand is (less than; greater than) the full employment level of output.

5. If full-employment output occurs at $2,000 billion, there is a _____ gap and aggregate demand is (less than; greater than) the full employment level of output.

Exercise 5

The media continually present information about events that shift aggregate demand for the U.S. economy. This exercise uses one of the articles in the text to show the kind of information to look for. Reread the article in the text entitled "Falling Stocks Smash Nest Eggs." Then answer the following questions. Use Figure 9.3 to answer question 1.

Figure 9.3

(a)   (b)

1. Which diagram in Figure 9.3 best represents the shift in consumption spending that the article is describing? _____

2. What should happen to the aggregate demand curve as a result of the change described in the article? _____

3. What happened that encouraged consumers to spend so much? _____
   _____

4. What phrase indicates how consumers have responded to the recent change in the stock market?
   _____

Common Errors

The first statement in each "common error" below is incorrect. Each incorrect statement is followed by a corrected version and an explanation.

1. The economy can spend no more than its income. WRONG!

   The economy *can* spend more than its income. RIGHT!

   The economy can spend more than its income by drawing down inventories of both public and private goods or by consuming capital (allowing it to depreciate) without replacing it. If the economy consumes more than its income, it will actually dissave and experience negative investment.

2. When a person invests in stocks, investment expenditure is increased. WRONG!

   The purchase of stocks has only an indirect relationship to investment expenditure in the economy. RIGHT!

   Investment expenditure refers to purchases of new capital goods (plant, machinery, and the like), inventories, or residential structures. A purchase of stock represents a transfer of ownership from one person to another. Sometimes such purchases are called "financial investments," but they do not represent economic investment.

3. The marginal propensity to consume is consumption divided by income. WRONG!

   The average propensity to consume is consumption divided by income. RIGHT!

   There is a big difference between total consumption and a change in consumption. While the average propensity to consume involves total consumption and total income, the marginal propensity to consume involves changes in consumption and changes in income.

4. Domestic aggregate demand rises when people buy more imports. WRONG!

   Domestic aggregate demand falls when people buy more imports, *ceteris paribus*. RIGHT!

   An increase in imports does not have the same effect on the economy as an increase in consumption. Expenditures on imports do not generate domestic income. If imports increase, they do so at the expense of purchases of U.S. goods, meaning fewer jobs in the United States. Because employment declines, there is less income with which to purchase goods; consumption falls and so does aggregate spending.

5. If the economy is in macroeconomic equilibrium, it must be operating at full employment. WRONG!

    If the economy is in macroeconomic equilibrium, unemployment can still exist. RIGHT!

    There is always a macro equilibrium because equilibrium occurs where aggregate demand and aggregate supply intersect. This equilibrium point may occur at the full-employment level of output, but it can also occur at a level other than full employment.

[CHAPTER 9 APPENDIX COMMON ERRORS]

6. The aggregate expenditure curve is the same as the aggregate demand curve. WRONG!

    The aggregate expenditure curve and aggregate demand curve are related to each other only indirectly. RIGHT!

    The aggregate expenditure curve and aggregate demand curve are two quite different concepts. They have different units on the axes; aggregate expenditure represents the intended expenditures at each *income* level; aggregate demand represents quantity demanded at each average price level for all goods and services.

7. Dissaving is the difference between the 45-degree line and aggregate expenditure curve. WRONG!

    Dissaving is the difference between a curve representing the consumption function and the 45-degree line. RIGHT!

    Both saving and dissaving are defined as the difference between disposable income and consumption. The 45-degree line shows the points at which expenditure equals income. So, when consumption expenditure equals income (the consumption function intersects the 45-degree line), there is zero saving. When the consumption expenditure exceeds income (the consumption function is above the 45-degree line), there will be dissaving.

•ANSWERS•

Using Key Terms

Across
1. wealth effect
5. aggregate supply
7. recessionary GDP gap
9. marginal propensity to consume
10. equilibrium
12. consumption function
14. dissaving
16. inflationary GDP gap
17. disposable income
18. cyclical unemployment
19. business cycle
20. demand-pull inflation

Down

2. aggregate demand
3. average propensity to consume
4. full employment
6. marginal propensity to save
8. equilibrium GDP
11. saving
13. consumption
15. investment

True or False

1. T
2. T
3. F Consumption is the largest component of aggregate spending.
4. F The marginal propensity to save measures the fraction of additional disposable income that is saved.
5. T
6. F There is a movement along a given consumption function when disposable income changes.
7. T
8. T
9. F Investment changes a business's future capacity to produce, so expectations about future sales (i.e., income) are more relevant than current income.
10. T

Multiple Choice

1. b	5. a	9. a	13. d	17. c	21. c
2. c	6. c	10. a	14. c	18. c	22. d
3. b	7. a	11. d	15. b	19. a	23. b
4. d	8. b	12. a	16. d	20. a	

Problems and Applications

Exercise 1

1. **Table 9.1 Answer**

(1)	(2)	(3) Average propensity to consume	(4) Change in consumption	(5) Change in income	(6) Marginal propensity to consume	(7)
Disposable income	Total consumption					Saving
$ 0	$ 100	----	----	----	----	$ -100
1,000	1,000	1.00	$900	$1,000	0.9	0
2,000	1,900	0.95	900	1,000	0.9	100

2. $2800
3. $C = 100 + .9Y_D$

Exercise 2

1. **Table 9.2 Answer**

Disposable income (Y_D)	Autonomous consumption (a)	+	Income-dependent consumption (bY_D)	=	Total consumption (C)
$ 0	200		0		$ 200
400	200		0.75 x 400		500
1,200	200		0.75 x 1,200		1,100

2. **Figure 9.1 Answer**

3. **Table 9.3 Answer**

Disposable income (Y_D)	Autonomous consumption (a)	+	Income-dependent consumption $(0.75 \times Y_D)$	=	Total consumption (C)
$ 0	$300		0		$ 300
400	300		0.75 x 400		600
800	300		0.75 x 800		900
1,200	300		0.75 x 1,200		1,200

4. 0.75; The marginal propensity to consume is the change in consumption (e.g., $600 - $300 billion per year) divided by the corresponding change in income ($400 - $0 billion per year).
5. See Figure 9.1 Answer, line 2.
6. T

Exercise 3

1. a; d
2. b; c
3. a; d
4. b; c

Exercise 4

1. **Table 9.4 Answer**

At an output of	Desired consumer spending	Desired investment spending	Desired government spending	Net export spending	Aggregate expenditure
$1,000	$ 950	$350	$400	$50	$1,750
2,000	1,700	350	400	50	2,500
3,000	2,450	350	400	50	3,250
4,000	3,200	350	400	50	4,000
5,000	3,950	350	400	50	4,750
6,000	4,700	350	400	50	5,500

2. $4,000 billion
3. MPC = 0.75
4. Recessionary GDP; less than
5. Inflationary GDP; greater than

Exercise 5

1. b
2. Aggregate demand should shift to the left.
3. The soaring value of the U.S. stock market and increased home values contributed to the so-called "wealth effect."
4. "Many of the . . . big ticket purchases Americans would have made . . . are on hold."

CHAPTER 10

Self-Adjustment or Instability?

Quick Review

- In the Keynesian view of a market-driven economy, macro equilibrium may not occur at a desirable rate of output.

- Consumer saving is a leakage from the flow of income as are business saving, imports, and taxes. There are several injections, including investment, government purchases, and exports.

- If leakages and injections are not equal at full employment GDP, the economy experiences either a recessionary or an inflationary gap.

- Classical economists believed interest rates and prices would change in response to an imbalance between leakages and injections, and this would bring the economy to a full-employment equilibrium.

- Keynes argued that an initial spending imbalance will be multiplied as it works its way through the economy. If output is greater than desired spending, inventories will accumulate and producers will reduce output. This will cause a decrease in income, which will reduce consumer spending. The spending decrease will lead to further cutbacks in production, more lost income, and still less consumption. This process is known as the multiplier effect.

- The multiplier is calculated as $1 \div (1-MPC)$. It is used to determine the cumulative change in total expenditure because of an initial change in spending.

- A change in spending will shift the aggregate demand curve. Since the aggregate supply curve is upward sloping, any change in aggregate demand will affect both output and the price level. The result is a tradeoff between inflation and unemployment.

- The recessionary GDP gap is the amount by which equilibrium GDP falls short of the full-employment GDP.

- The inflationary gap, measured at full employment, is the amount by which equilibrium GDP exceeds full-employment GDP. In this case inventories are drawn down, prices rise, more people are hired, wages rise, there is an attempt to expand capacity, and interest rates rise.

- Because a change in spending patterns can move the economy away from full-employment equilibrium, the economy is vulnerable to continual booms and busts known as the business cycle.

Learning Objectives

After reading Chapter 10 and doing the following exercises you should:

1. Understand that equilibrium may not occur at a desirable output level.
2. Know the different leakages and injections and how they impact the circular flow.
3. Be able to distinguish between the Keynesian and classical views of the adjustment process in a market-driven economy.
4. Understand the critical distinction between desired investment and actual investment.
5. Be able to describe the multiplier process and calculate the multiplier.
6. Understand the possible divergence between equilibrium GDP and full-employment GDP.
7. Be able to describe how the economy responds to a recessionary GDP gap and an inflationary GDP gap.
8. Be able to describe and demonstrate price and output effects and the inflation-unemployment tradeoff in an AS-AD framework.

Using Key Terms

Fill in the puzzle on the opposite page with the appropriate term from the list of Key Terms at the end of the chapter in the text.

Across

1. The multiple by which an initial change in spending will alter total expenditure after an infinite number of spending cycles.
3. The amount by which equilibrium GDP falls short of full-employment GDP.
4. The rate of real output at which aggregate demand equals aggregate supply.
5. The lowest rate of unemployment compatible with price stability.
7. The amount by which equilibrium GDP exceeds full-employment GDP.
10. Equal to depreciation allowances and retained earnings.
11. Unemployment because of a recessionary gap.

Down

1. The fraction of additional income spent by consumers.
2. An increase in the price level initiated by excessive aggregate demand.
6. The total quantity of output demanded at alternative price levels in a given time period, *ceteris paribus*.
7. An addition of spending to the circular flow of income.
8. Income diverted from the circular flow.
9. The value of total output produced at full employment.

Puzzle 10.1

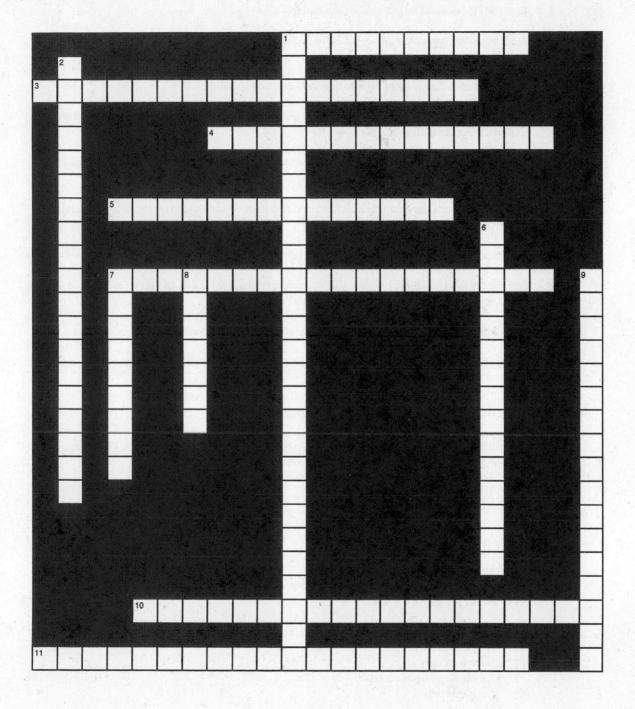

True or False: *Circle your choice and tell why any false statements are incorrect.*

T F 1. As the MPC becomes larger, so does the multiplier.

T F 2. Because saving is a leakage, an increase in saving results in lower equilibrium income for society, *ceteris paribus.*

T F 3. Investment spending is more volatile than consumption spending.

T F 4. If saving and investment are the only leakage and injection, desired investment is greater than desired saving at equilibrium.

T F 5. In a purely private economy, the difference between desired saving and desired investment measures the undesired change in inventory.

T F 6. The multiplier tells the extent to which the rate of output will change in response to an initial change in spending.

T F 7. Equilibrium GDP is always the most desired level of GDP for an economy.

T F 8. When there is an inflationary spiral, there is excess demand for goods and services, and consumers bid up prices by competing for those goods and services.

T F 9. If equilibrium GDP is less than full-employment GDP, then structural unemployment results.

T F 10. The aggregate supply-aggregate demand model can be used to predict how changes in spending behavior will affect output and prices.

Multiple Choice: *Select the correct answer.*

_____ 1. According to the Keynesian view of the macro economy, when the economy is at equilibrium:
  (a) Aggregate supply equals aggregate demand.
  (b) The economy is always at full employment.
  (c) The price level is always stable.
  (d) All of the above are true.

_____ 2. When the economy is at equilibrium:
  (a) Leakages equal injections.
  (b) Inventories are at desired levels.
  (c) Aggregate supply equals aggregate demand.
  (d) All of the above are true.

_____ 3. Equilibrium GDP could be upset by a change in:
  (a) Investment only.
  (b) Injections only.
  (c) Any leakage or injection.
  (d) Leakages only.

_____ 4. A leakage from the circular flow is:
  (a) An export from the economy.
  (b) A decline in the capacity of the economy to produce goods.
  (c) A diversion of income from spending on output.
  (d) A decrease in aggregate supply.

5. When an economy is at full employment and consumption spending decreases, if all other levels of spending remain constant:
   (a) Increased unemployment results.
   (b) Any GDP gap disappears.
   (c) Inventory levels are less than desired until a new equilibrium is reached.
   (d) Changes in consumption spending have no impact on GDP.

6. Given $C = 100 + 0.80Y_D$, the multiplier is:
   (a) 0.20.
   (b) 5.
   (c) 4.
   (d) 8.

7. If actual investment exceeds desired investment then:
   (a) Inventories are increasing.
   (b) Output will increase as a result.
   (c) Demand-pull inflation exists.
   (d) Inventories are being depleted.

8. Keynes emphasized that because there is no automatic adjustment back to full employment:
   (a) Equilibrium GDP might be less than full-employment GDP.
   (b) A long-term recessionary gap could occur.
   (c) Cyclical unemployment could persist.
   (d) All of the above.

9. Suppose that as a result of higher interest rates, desired investment and aggregate demand decrease. Additional decreases in aggregate demand will be the result of:
   (a) Decreases in consumption.
   (b) Decreases in induced expenditures.
   (c) The multiplier effect.
   (d) All of the above.

10. Assuming an upward-sloping aggregate supply curve, when aggregate demand increases:
    (a) Unemployment decreases and the price level decreases.
    (b) Unemployment decreases and the price level increases.
    (c) Unemployment increases and the price level decreases.
    (d) Unemployment increases and the price level increases.

11. Suppose that an economy has an upward-sloping aggregate supply curve and a GDP gap equal to $45 billion. If aggregate demand increases by a total of $45 billion:
    (a) The GDP gap will be eliminated.
    (b) The resulting equilibrium GDP will be lower than full employment GDP because some of the additional spending will drive up prices instead of increasing output.
    (c) The resulting equilibrium GDP will be greater than full employment GDP because of demand-pull inflation.
    (d) Any of the above could occur depending on the size of the multiplier.

_____ 12. Using a consumption function of the form $C = a + bY_D$, which of the following would best measure the total impact on output of a change in autonomous spending?

(a) $\dfrac{1}{MPS}$

(b) $\dfrac{1}{1 - b}$

(c) $\dfrac{1}{1 - MPC}$

(d) All of the above.

_____ 13. When output exceeds desired spending, which of the following is included in the Keynesian adjustment process?

(a) Producers cut output and employment.

(b) Lost income causes a decline in consumer spending.

(c) Lower consumer spending results in additional loss of income.

(d) All of the above.

_____ 14. Because the aggregate supply curve rises more steeply as the economy approaches full employment:

(a) Inflation tends to accelerate.

(b) The GDP gap becomes larger.

(c) Aggregate demand shifts to the left.

(d) The multiplier effect becomes greater.

_____ 15. In which of the following cases would cyclical unemployment tend to increase, *ceteris paribus*?

(a) Undesired inventory depletion.

(b) Total value of goods supplied exceeds the total value of goods demanded.

(c) A period of significant inflation.

(d) Desired investment exceeds desired saving.

_____ 16. If the equilibrium level of output is less than full employment, to achieve a full-employment equilibrium the AD curve must shift to the right by an amount:

(a) Equal to the GDP gap.

(b) Less than the GDP gap because the spending increase causes the multiplier process to occur.

(c) Greater than the GDP gap because the spending increase raises the price level.

(d) Less than the GDP gap because the spending increase raises output and prices.

_____ 17. In an inflationary GDP gap situation:

(a) Savings dollars are readily available and interest rates fall.

(b) There are sufficient resources available and wages tend to decrease.

(c) There is excess demand for goods and consumers bid up prices.

(d) All of the above.

_____ 18. A rightward shift in the aggregate demand curve will cause:

(a) Both higher prices and higher output if the aggregate supply curve is upward sloping.

(b) Higher prices and lower output if the aggregate supply curve is upward sloping.

(c) No change in prices, but higher output, if the aggregate supply curve is upward sloping.

(d) Lower prices and higher output if the aggregate supply curve is upward sloping.

_____ 19. With an MPC of 0.50, an increase of $2 billion in autonomous consumption would cause:

(a) An initial increase of $1 billion in income.

(b) $500 million in multiplier effects.

(c) Income to change by a total of $4 billion.

(d) Income to change by a total of $2 billion.

_____ 20. A basic conclusion of Keynesian analysis is that:
   (a)   The economy is vulnerable to abrupt changes in spending behavior.
   (b)   The economy does not self adjust to reach full employment or stable price levels.
   (c)   Equilibrium GDP may not be consistent with full employment or price stability.
   (d)   All of the above.

Problems and Applications

Exercise 1

This exercise focuses on a recessionary GDP gap caused by a change in investment spending.

Assume the economy is initially in equilibrium on AD$_3$ in Figure 10.1 and full-employment GDP occurs at Q$_3$. Use Figure 10.1 to answer questions 1-7.

Figure 10.1

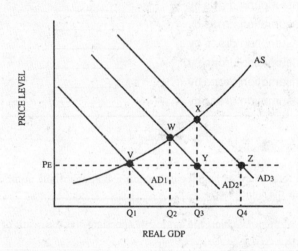

1.   Suppose the rate of investment decreases and aggregate demand shifts initially to AD$_2$. The new equilibrium real GDP occurs at _____.

2.   The decline in investment spending causes a (decrease; increase) in household income and consumption. Aggregate demand shifts to the (right; left) to (AD$_1$; AD$_3$). The final equilibrium is at a real GDP level of _____.

3.   T   F   The real GDP gap is equal to the distance Q$_3$ - Q$_1$.

4.   If equilibrium output is less than full-employment, there is a (recessionary; inflationary) GDP gap.

5.   When equilibrium output is less than full-employment output, at the full-employment level actual investment is (less than; greater than; equal to) desired investment because undesired inventories are (less than; greater than; equal to) zero.

6.   When aggregate expenditure is (less than; greater than; equal to) the full-employment level of output, a recessionary GDP gap exists.

7.   A recessionary GDP gap causes (seasonal; structural; cyclical; frictional) unemployment.

137

Exercise 2

The following exercise shows how the multiplier works and how to calculate it.

1. Suppose the economy was at full employment but suddenly experienced a $100 billion decrease in business expenditures because of a decrease in the value of corporate stocks. Follow the impact of this sudden change through the economy by completing Table 10.1. (Refer to Table 10.1 in the text.) Assume the marginal propensity to consume is 0.80. (Hint: Consumption will decrease in each round by the "change in spending in the previous cycle" times the MPC.) Then use Table 10.1 to answer questions 2-7.

Table 10.1

Spending cycles	Decrease in expenditure	Change in spending (billions of dollars per year)	Cumulative decrease in aggregate spending (billions of dollars per year)
First cycle:	GDP gap emerges	$100	$100
Second cycle:	consumption drops by	_____	_____
Third cycle:	consumption drops by	_____	_____
Fourth cycle:	consumption drops by	_____	_____
Fifth cycle:	consumption drops by	_____	_____
Sixth cycle:	consumption drops by	_____	_____
Seventh cycle:	consumption drops by	_____	_____

2. Compute the multiplier. _____

3. What is the total change in aggregate spending after an infinite number of cycles? (Multiply $100 billion times the multiplier.) _____

4. How much of the total change in aggregate spending was the result of a change in investment?
   _____

5. How much of the total change in aggregate spending was the result of a change in consumption?
   _____

6. T   F   A large portion of the change in aggregate spending in question 3 was due to the multiplier effect.

Exercise 3

This exercise emphasizes the short-run trade-off between unemployment and inflation.

Assume the economy is initially on AD_1. The full-employment level of output is Q_1 and the desired price level is P_2. Use Figure 10.2 to answer questions 1-3.

Figure 10.2

1. Assume price level P₁ is considered inflationary. If the AD curve is shifted to AD₂ to reduce the price level, the result is a _____ in the level of output and an _____ in the level of unemployment.

2. If AD is shifted back to the right to AD₁, output returns to the full-employment level, but the price level _____.

3. Because the AS curve is _____ sloping, any shift in AD will cause a trade-off between _____.

Exercise 4

This exercise focuses on an inflationary GDP gap situation.

1. Figure 10.9 in the text illustrates an inflationary gap situation. An increase in investment caused AD to shift to _____ and the resulting multiplier effects caused AD to shift again to _____.

2. When AD shifts to the right, the price level _____.

3. In the situation in question 2, actual investment is (less than; greater than; equal to) desired investment and _____ are being depleted.

4. Producers will respond to the increased demand by (increasing; decreasing) production.

5. The resulting economic situation is referred to as _____ inflation.

Exercise 5

Reread the article in the text titled "U.S. Slowdown Helps Derail Asia." Then answer questions 1-4.

Figure 10.3

1. Which of the diagrams in Figure 10.3 represents the shift in the Asian economies because of the U.S. slowdown? _____

2. The downturn in the U.S. economy has resulted in a _____ in demand for Asian exports.

3. How have Asian manufacturers responded to the downturn? _____
   _____

4. The slowdown in the U.S. economy causes a decrease in demand for Asian exports, which causes a decrease in demand for U.S. exports in Asia. This is called the _____ _____ effect.

Common Errors

The first statement in each "common error" below is incorrect. Each incorrect statement is followed by a corrected version and an explanation.

1. Since saving and investment must be the same by definition, a closed economy must be at expenditure equilibrium because investment equals saving. WRONG!

   Intended investment equals intended saving at expenditure equilibrium in a closed economy. RIGHT!

   If there are excess inventories or if people are forced to save because they cannot spend on desired goods and services, then the income level may be different from equilibrium income. Do not confuse actual investment and actual saving with intended investment and intended saving.

2. If consumers save more, interest rates will fall and investment will rise. WRONG!

   When consumption falls as a result of increased saving, investment may be discouraged. RIGHT!

   Interest rates *may* fall because of increased saving. However, Keynes showed that businesses may invest less when they expect to sell less. The lower consumption that results from increased saving may actually cause businesses to reduce investment.

3. Expenditure equilibrium and full-employment GDP are always the same. WRONG!

   Expenditure equilibrium and full-employment GDP are determined in different ways. RIGHT!

Expenditure equilibrium occurs where the aggregate expenditure curve and the 45-degree line intersect. The full-employment GDP occurs at the GDP level where the market supply and market demand curves for labor are in equilibrium. For most purposes, we can consider the two levels to be independent of each other.

Be careful! While it is possible to determine the expenditure equilibrium or income level by glancing at the aggregate spending curve and the 45-degree line, it is not possible to determine full-employment GDP this way. Full-employment GDP is shown simply as a vertical line.

•ANSWERS•

Using Key Terms

Across

1. multiplier
3. recessionary GDP gap
4. equilibrium GDP
5. full employment
7. inflationary GDP gap
10. gross business saving
11. cyclical unemployment

Down

1. marginal propensity to consume
2. demand-pull inflation
6. aggregate demand
7. injection
8. leakage
9. full-employment GDP

True or False

1. T
2. T
3. T
4. F At equilibrium, leakages must equal injections. In a closed private economy, the only leakages and injections are saving and investment.
5. T
6. F The multiplier tells how much total spending will change in response to an initial change in spending. Whenever the AS curve is upward sloping, the total change in output will be less than the total change in spending.
7. F Equilibrium GDP does not necessarily mean that the economy is experiencing full employment or stable price levels.
8. T
9. F Cyclical unemployment results.
10. T

Multiple Choice

1. a	5. a	9. d	13. d	17. c
2. d	6. b	10. b	14. a	18. a
3. c	7. a	11. b	15. b	19. c
4. c	8. d	12. d	16. c	20. d

Problems and Applications

Exercise 1

1. Q_2
2. Decrease; left; AD_1; Q_1
3. T
4. Recessionary
5. Greater than; greater than
6. Less than
7. Cyclical

Exercise 2

1. **Table 10.1 Answer**

Spending cycles	Amount	Cumulative decrease in aggregate spending
First cycle:	$100.00	$100.00
Second cycle:	80.00	180.00
Third cycle:	64.00	244.00
Fourth cycle:	51.20	295.20
Fifth cycle:	40.96	336.16
Sixth cycle:	32.77	368.93
Seventh cycle:	26.22	395.15

2. Multiplier = 1÷(1-MPC) = 1÷(1-0.8) = 5
3. $500 billion
4. $100 billion
5. $400 billion
6. T

Exercise 3

1. Decrease; increase
2. Increases
3. Upward sloping; inflation and unemployment

Exercise 4

1. AD_5; AD_6
2. Increases
3. Less than; inventories
4. Increasing
5. Demand-pull

Exercise 5

1. c
2. Decrease
3. Layoffs; decreased production
4. International multiplier

CHAPTER 11

Fiscal Policy

Quick Review

- Keynes concluded that the macroeconomy would not automatically correct spending imbalances. He said government intervention was necessary to shift the economy's aggregate demand in the appropriate direction.

- The primary tools of fiscal policy are changes in taxes, government spending on goods and services and income transfers.

- Fiscal expansion can be accomplished with an increase in government spending. The required increase in AD does not come completely from government purchases. Successive rounds of spending, kicked off by the initial government purchases, ripple through the economy through the multiplier process.

- The aggregate demand curve must shift by more than the GDP gap because some of the shift is felt in a price level change. The fiscal stimulus required to get the economy to full employment can be calculated by the following:

  Desired fiscal stimulus = AD shortfall ÷ the multiplier

  The same thing can be accomplished with a tax cut, which is calculated in two steps. First determine the desired fiscal stimulus and then determine the desired tax cut using:

  Desired tax cut = desired fiscal stimulus ÷ *MPC*

- A tax cut of a given size will be less expansionary than a spending increase of the same size because part of the tax cut leaks into saving before the first private-sector spending takes place.

- Fiscal restraint can be accomplished with cuts in government spending, increased taxes, or reduced income transfers. The desired fiscal restraint is the same as the fiscal stimulus except it causes a decrease in AD.

- Greater borrowing by government might crowd out an equal amount of private spending. Tax cuts can go to businesses or households and favor investors or consumers. Either way, the mix of output is affected. Changes in transfers lead to a different mix of output also.

Learning Objectives

After reading Chapter 11 and doing the following exercises, you should:

1. Understand that government intervention may be necessary to achieve full employment.
2. Know the tools of fiscal policy.
3. Understand how fiscal stimulus and fiscal restraint can be used to stabilize the economy.
4. Be able to explain why tax cuts are less expansionary than increases in government purchases of an equal size.
5. Understand that any fiscal policy initiative will be multiplied through the economy.
6. Understand that the AD curve must shift by more than the GDP gap to close the gap.
7. Be able to calculate the AD shortfall or excess, the multiplier, and the desired fiscal stimulus or restraint.
8. Be able to explain how fiscal stimulus can be offset by the "crowding out" of private expenditure.
9. Understand how fiscal policy can change the mix of output for an economy.

Using Key Terms

Fill in the puzzle on the opposite page with the appropriate term from the list of Key Terms at the end of the chapter in the text.

Across

2. The use of fiscal policy to reduce aggregate demand.
5. The use of the federal government budget to change macroeconomic outcomes.
8. An inflationary _____ _____ occurs when equilibrium GDP is greater than full-employment GDP.
10. Personal income minus personal taxes.
11. The total quantity of output demanded at alternative price levels in a given time period, *ceteris paribus*.
12. Government spending in the form of Social Security, welfare, and unemployment benefits.
13. The combination of price level and real output that is compatible with both aggregate demand and aggregate supply.
14. If equilibrium GDP is less than full-employment GDP, there is a _____ GDP gap.

Down

1. The change in consumption divided by the change in disposable income.
2. Tax cuts or spending increases intended to shift aggregate demand to the right.
3. The total quantity of output producers are willing and able to supply at alternative price levels in a given time period, *ceteris paribus*.
4. A decrease in private-sector borrowing caused by increased government borrowing.
6. The amount by which aggregate demand must increase to achieve full-employment equilibrium after allowing for price-level changes.
7. Equal to $1 \div (1 - MPC)$.
9. The amount by which aggregate demand must be reduced to achieve full-employment equilibrium after allowing for price-level changes.

Puzzle 11.1

True or False: *Circle your choice and indicate why any false statements are incorrect.*

T   F   1.   Fiscal policy works principally through shifts of the aggregate supply curve.

T   F   2.   From a Keynesian perspective, the way out of a recession includes an increase in government spending, a tax cut, or an increase in transfer payments.

T   F   3.   If the AS curve is horizontal (i.e., flat), the GDP gap is equal to the desired fiscal stimulus (or restraint).

T   F   4.   Increasing government expenditures by the amount of the AD shortfall will achieve full employment.

T   F   5.   Fiscal policy involves changes in government spending and taxes.

T   F   6.   When there is excess aggregate demand, desired fiscal restraint equals the desired AD reduction divided by the multiplier.

T   F   7.   A tax cut contains less stimulus to the economy than an increase in government spending of the same size because some of the tax cut is saved.

T   F   8.   Both government purchases of goods and services and government transfer payments are part of AD.

T   F   9.   Every dollar of new government spending has a multiplied impact on aggregate demand.

T   F   10.   Crowding out is the idea that an increase in government spending may cause a reduction in private-sector spending.

Multiple Choice: *Select the correct answer.*

_____ 1.   Fiscal policy works principally through shifts of:
   (a)   The aggregate supply curve.
   (b)   The aggregate demand curve.
   (c)   The full-employment output line.
   (d)   The 45-degree line.

_____ 2.   Which of the following is a tool of fiscal policy?
   (a)   Increasing government purchases of goods and services.
   (b)   Increasing taxes.
   (c)   Increasing income transfers.
   (d)   All of the above.

_____ 3.   In a diagram of aggregate demand and aggregate supply curves, the GDP gap is measured:
   (a)   As the vertical distance between the equilibrium price and the price at which the aggregate demand would intersect aggregate supply at full employment.
   (b)   As the horizontal distance between the equilibrium output and the full employment output.
   (c)   As the horizontal distance between the aggregate demand and the aggregate supply curves at the equilibrium price.
   (d)   As the amount of the AD shortfall or excess.

_____ 4. If the economy is operating below full employment, which of the following policies will increase aggregate spending but will not increase the size of the government?
   (a) Increase government spending and leave taxes unchanged.
   (b) Increase government spending and taxes by the same amount.
   (c) Leave government spending unchanged and decrease taxes.
   (d) Decrease government spending and leave taxes unchanged.

_____ 5. The GDP gap will differ from the AD shortfall when:
   (a) The aggregate supply curve slopes upward.
   (b) The multiplier effect raises spending.
   (c) The budget is balanced.
   (d) All of the above.

_____ 6. To eliminate the AD shortfall of $100 billion when the economy has an *MPC* of 0.80, the government should increase its purchases by:
   (a) $20 billion.
   (b) $100 billion.
   (c) $500 billion.
   (d) $800 billion.

_____ 7. Assuming an *MPC* of 0.75, the change in total spending for the economy as a result of a $100 billion new government spending injection would be:
   (a) $40 billion.
   (b) $75 billion.
   (c) $750 billion.
   (d) $400 billion.

_____ 8. $1 \div (1 - MPC)$ multiplied by a new spending injection gives the:
   (a) *MPC*.
   (b) Multiplier.
   (c) Total change in income generated from the new spending.
   (d) First-round income that is gained from the new spending.

_____ 9. An *MPS* of 0.10 means a $100 tax increase ultimately causes:
   (a) Spending to fall by $1,000.
   (b) Spending to fall by $900.
   (c) Spending to rise by $90.
   (d) Spending to rise by $100.

_____ 10. Suppose the consumption function is $C = 100 + .5Y_D$. If the government stimulates the economy with $100 billion in increased government spending, aggregate expenditure would ultimately rise by:
   (a) $50 billion.
   (b) $80 billion.
   (c) $200 billion.
   (d) $400 billion.

_____ 11. When the government tries to correct for an aggregate demand shortfall in the economy, it must take into account that:
   (a) The total change in spending equals the government's spending and the multiplier effects of that spending.
   (b) The desired stimulus should be set at the AD shortfall divided by the multiplier.
   (c) Prices will rise unless the AS curve is horizontal.
   (d) All of the above.

12. The desired fiscal stimulus that will eliminate an AD shortfall should equal the:
    (a) Desired AD increase ÷ the multiplier.
    (b) Desired tax cut x *MPC*.
    (c) Desired income transfer x *MPC*.
    (d) All of the above.

13. The desired tax cut necessary to close an AD shortfall is given by:
    (a) Desired fiscal stimulus ÷ multiplier.
    (b) Desired fiscal stimulus ÷ *MPC*.
    (c) (Desired fiscal stimulus ÷ multiplier) ÷ *MPC*.
    (d) Desired fiscal stimulus x *MPC*.

14. For the balanced-budget multiplier to equal 1, the budget:
    (a) Need not be balanced, but the changes in taxes and spending must be equal.
    (b) Must be balanced before the changes in taxes and spending take place.
    (c) Must be balanced and the change in spending must equal the change in taxes.
    (d) Must be balanced, but the changes in taxes and spending may be unequal amounts.

15. Which of the following is most powerful in shifting the aggregate demand curve?
    (a) A increase in Social Security payments of $10 billion.
    (b) A reduction in personal income taxes of $10 billion.
    (c) An increase in defense spending of $10 billion.
    (d) All of the changes above affect aggregate demand equally.

16. The initial, or first round, increase in consumption because of a tax cut is equal to:
    (a) *MPC* x the amount of the tax cut.
    (b) *MPC* x (multiplier x the amount of the tax cut).
    (c) Amount of the tax cut ÷ *MPS*.
    (d) Multiplier x the amount of the tax cut.

17. If the desired fiscal restraint is $10 billion and the desired AD decrease is $100 billion, we can conclude that the desired tax:
    (a) Increase is $11.11 billion.
    (b) Increase is $10 billion.
    (c) Cut is $11.11 billion.
    (d) Cut is $10 billion.

18. Crowding out occurs when the government:
    (a) Increases taxes, thus causing a decrease in consumption.
    (b) Issues debt, thus making it more difficult for the private sector to issue debt.
    (c) Prints money, which displaces currency.
    (d) Does all of the above.

19. Which of the following are factors which may limit the effectiveness of fiscal policy in the real world?
    (a) The crowding out effect.
    (b) Time lags between the recognition of a macro problem and the implementation of corrective measures.
    (c) Political considerations that could alter the content and timing of fiscal policy.

(d)   All of the above are factors.

_____ 20.   The federal government approves a new highway that injects $100 million of new spending into the economy during the first year of the project. *Ceteris paribus*, if the consumption function for this economy is given by the equation $C = 500 + 0.75Y_D$, how much is the increase in spending for the second round of the multiplier process?

(a) $400 million.
(b) $100 million.
(c) $75 million.
(d) $56.25 million.

Problems and Applications

Exercise 1

This exercise shows how to use the aggregate demand and supply curves to analyze macro equilibrium, the AD shortfall, excess AD, and the GDP gap.

Table 11.1
Aggregate demand and supply*

Price Index (1)	Aggregate Supply (Qs) (2)	Aggregate Demand (Qd) Full Employment (3)	Aggregate Demand (Qd) AD1 (4)	Aggregate Demand (Qd) AD2 (5)
2.6	24	-	-	-
2.2	23	0	-	14
1.8	22	6	0	22
1.0	18	18	8	-
0.8	16	21	10	-
0.6	12	24	12	-
0.4	4	27	14	-

(* Quantity is measured in billions of units in columns 2 through 5.)

1.   Use the first two columns in Table 11.1 to draw the aggregate supply curve for an economy in Figure 11.1. Then use columns 1 and 3 to draw the aggregate demand curve at full employment. Label the aggregate supply curve AS and the aggregate demand curve at full employment AD_F.

Figure 11.1
Aggregate demand and supply

2. When macro equilibrium is achieved at full employment, the full-employment real output is
    _____. The corresponding full-employment price index is _____.

3. Now draw the aggregate demand curve corresponding to columns 1 and 4 labeling it AD_1. For this
    aggregate demand curve, the equilibrium real output is _____. The corresponding equilibrium
    price index is _____.

4. Assume the economy is on AD_1. In Figure 11.1 indicate the GDP gap, which is _____ billion
    units of output, and the AD (excess; shortfall), which is _____ billion units of output.

5. Which of the following government policies could be used to shift AD to full employment?
    (a) The government increases taxes.
    (b) The government provides tax incentives to encourage more saving.
    (c) The government eliminates investment tax credits, which results effectively in higher taxes
         on investment goods.
    (d) A trade agreement is approved, which suddenly results in U.S. exports rising faster than
         imports.
    (e) Foreign governments place limits on imports from the U.S.
    (f) Government cuts back on its expenditures.

6. Now draw the aggregate demand curve corresponding to columns 1 and 5 labeling it AD_2. For
    this aggregate demand curve, the equilibrium real output is _____. The corresponding
    equilibrium average price index is _____.

7. Assume the economy is on AD_2. In Figure 11.1 indicate the GDP gap, which is _____ units of
    output, and the AD (excess; shortfall), which is _____ units of output.

150

8. Which of the following government policies could be used to shift AD to full employment?
   (a)   The government lowers interest rates.
   (b)   The government cuts taxes.
   (c)   The government cuts its expenditures.
   (d)   The government raises tariffs, which increases the cost of imports.
   (e)   The government subsidizes exports to help domestic firms sell abroad.
   (f)   The government eliminates IRAs and other instruments that encourage saving, which results in greater autonomous consumption.

Exercise 2

This exercise emphasizes the impact of various fiscal policies on total spending.

Assume the economy can be described by the consumption function: $C = \$400$ billion $+ 0.8Y_D$.

1. Calculate the cumulative change in total spending if the government increases purchases of goods and services by \$100 million. _____

2. Calculate the cumulative change in total spending if the government reduces taxes by \$100 million. _____

3. Calculate the cumulative change in total spending if the government increases transfer payments by \$100 million. _____

4. The \$100 million increase in government spending on goods and services had a (smaller, larger) impact on total spending than the \$100 million decrease in taxes because there is a savings (leakage; injection) out of the tax change.

5. Calculate the cumulative change in total spending if the government increases purchases of goods and services by \$100 million and at the same time increases taxes by \$100 million to finance the spending. _____

6. The situation described in question 5 represents a _____ _____ expenditure.

Exercise 3

The media often provide information on multiplier effects in the economy. This exercise will use one of the articles in the text to show the kind of information to look for.

Reread the article "Economy Is Already Feeling the Impact of Federal Government's Spending Cuts" in the text. Then answer the following questions:

1. Which passages indicate the cause of the change in the economy? _____
_____

2. The change in the economy is (more; less) of a/an (injection; leakage).

3. What statement indicates the estimated impact of the "belt tightening" on GDP? _____
_____

4. What evidence of secondary changes in income are reported? _____
_____

Exercise 4

This exercise shows how the multiplier works to eliminate a GDP gap.

Refer to Figure 11.2 to answer questions 1-4. Assume the *MPC* equals 0.90 and the current level of aggregate demand is equal to AD$_1$.

Figure 11.2

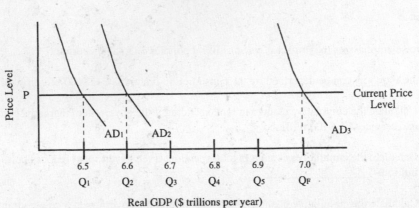

1. What is the equilibrium level of real GDP if aggregate demand is equal to AD$_1$? _____

2. What is the full employment level of real GDP? _____

3. What is the size of the GDP gap? _____

4. What is the value of the multiplier? _____

5. An increase in government spending of $50 billion would cause consumption to increase by $ _____ billion in the second spending cycle.

6. An increase in government spending of $50 billion would cause a cumulative increase in aggregate demand equal to $ _____ billion and would result in an equilibrium real GDP equal to $ _____ trillion.

Common Errors

The first statement in each "common error" below is incorrect. Each incorrect statement is followed by a corrected version and an explanation.

1. In order for the federal government to increase spending, taxes must be increased. WRONG!

    Increased spending by the federal government has the strongest impact on the economy if it is *not* accompanied by a tax increase. RIGHT!

    The federal government can finance spending in excess of taxes by borrowing. This topic is discussed further in Chapter 12.

2. If the government increases spending and taxes by the same amount, there will be no effect on income. WRONG!

Income increases by the amount of government spending, even if taxes are increased by the same amount. RIGHT!

The full impact of the increased government spending turns into income for the people who provide goods and services to the government. Part of the increased taxes, however, comes from people's savings, which had been leakages from the economy. So consumption decreases by less than the loss of taxes. This in turn means that income generated by consumption spending is not cut back by the amount of taxes. Therefore, the economy experiences a smaller cutback in incomes as a result of increased taxes than from stimulus from increased government spending.

•ANSWERS•

Using Key Terms

Across

2. fiscal restraint
5. fiscal policy
8. GDP gap
10. disposable income
11. aggregate demand
12. income transfers
13. equilibrium
14. recessionary

Down

1. marginal propensity to consume
2. fiscal stimulus
3. aggregate supply
4. crowding out
6. AD shortfall
7. multiplier
9. AD excess

True or False

1. F Fiscal policy works through shifts in the AD curve.
2. T
3. F If the AS curve is horizontal (i.e., flat), the GDP gap is equal to the AD shortfall (or excess).
4. F The effect of the multiplier must be taken into account even when AS is flat. In this case, government expenditures should be increased by an amount equal to the AD shortfall divided by the multiplier.
5. T
6. T
7. T
8. F Only government purchases of goods and services are part of AD. Government transfer payments are not part of AD because they do not represent a direct purchase of goods and services.
9. T
10. T

Multiple Choice

1.	b	5.	a	9.	b	13.	b	17.	a
2.	d	6.	a	10.	c	14.	a	18.	b
3.	b	7.	d	11.	d	15.	c	19.	d
4.	c	8.	c	12.	d	16.	a	20.	c

Problems and Applications

Exercise 1

1. See Figure 11.1 Answer, AS and AD_F.

Figure 11.1 Answer

2. At full employment, the price index is 1.0 at an output of 18 units.
3. See Figure 11.1 Answer, AD_1. At AD_1, the price index is 0.6 at an output of 12 units.
4. See Figure 11.1 Answer. GDP gap = 6.0 units; AD shortfall = 12 units.
5. d   We are looking for more of an injection or less of a leakage, and we find higher United States exports, which is more of an injection.
6. See Figure 11.1 Answer, AD_2. At AD_2, the price index is 1.8 at an output of 22 units.
7. See Figure 11.1 Answer. GDP gap = -4.0 units; excess AD = 16 units.
8. c   We are looking for more of a leakage or less of an injection, and we find lower government expenditures, which is less of an injection.

Exercise 2

1. $500 million increase
2. $400 million increase [($100 million x 0.8) x multiplier = $80 million x 5]
3. $400 million increase
4. Larger; leakage
5. $100 million increase
6. Balanced budget

Exercise 3

1. "Skeptical about the federal government's pledge to tighten its belt?" and "Federal purchases of goods and services dropped 3.3% in 1992 . . . " tell us that G has been reduced.
2. Less; injection
3. ". . . cuts in purchases by the federal government knocked as much as 0.5 percentage point off the gross domestic product last year . . . "
4. 400,000 jobs were lost in 1992 and the same was expected for the next year.

Exercise 4

1. 6.5 trillion
2. 7.0 trillion
3. $7 trillion - $6.5 trillion = $500 billion
4. Multiplier = $1 \div (1 - MPC) = 1 \div (1 - 0.9) = 10$
5. $45 billion
6. 10 x $50 billion = $500 billion; $7.0 trillion

CHAPTER 12

Deficits, Surpluses, and Debt

Quick Review

- When the federal government's revenues fall short of its expenditures in any fiscal year, there is a budget deficit. The U.S. Treasury issues IOUs (e.g., Treasury bonds) and sells them to cover the difference. If revenues are greater than expenditures, there is a budget surplus.

- Policy makers distinguish between "cyclical deficits," which are caused by short-run changes in economic conditions, and the "structural deficit," which measures the deficit that would result *if* the economy were at full employment. When GDP slows or inflation subsides, the cyclical deficit increases. The impact of fiscal policy as a stimulus or restraint is measured by the structural deficit.

- "Automatic stabilizers," such as unemployment compensation, *increase* as the economy weakens and decrease when the economy improves.

- When government purchases goods and services, the resources used to produce them are denied to the rest of society. Rates of investment and economic growth may both be reduced when government borrowing pushes interest rates up. This is called "crowding out."

- If you add up all of the Treasury's IOUs that are outstanding, the sum is the national debt. The national debt is a liability of the government, but it represents an asset to those who own it.

- Historically, the United States has accrued debt during wars, recessions, and tax cuts. In recent years, the debt increased during the recessions of 1980-82 and 1990-91 and the tax cuts of 1981-1984 and 2001-2003.

- Most of the debt is owned "internally" by banks and other financial institutions, the Federal Reserve, and individuals. The interest payments redistribute income from taxpayers to bondholders and the opportunity costs are incurred when the debt financed activity occurs.

- Debt that is purchased and held by foreigners is called the external debt. It allows us to avoid opportunity costs presently. When foreign holdings of U.S. debt come due, payment on the debt means that dollars must flow out of the country. As a result, future generations will have less output to consume. Currently, 22 percent of the national debt is owned by foreigners.

- The Gramm-Rudman-Hollings Act (1985) and the Budget Enforcement Act of 1990 were efforts to stop the continuation of budget deficits and the resulting debt.

Learning Objectives

After reading Chapter 12 and doing the following exercises, you should:

1. Understand the cause of budget deficits and the relationship between deficits and the national debt.
2. Be able to distinguish between discretionary spending and uncontrollables.
3. Be able to describe the operation and importance of automatic stabilizers.
4. Be able to distinguish cyclical deficits from structural deficits.
5. Understand the economic effects of deficits and be able to explain "crowding out."
6. Understand the history of the national debt and how it reached its present size.
7. Know who owns the debt, and understand the implications of internal and external ownership.
8. Understand the real burden of the debt.
9. Understand that the only way to stop the debt from growing is to eliminate budget deficits.
10. Be aware of attempts to address the deficit problem.

Using Key Terms

Fill in the puzzle on the opposite page with the appropriate term from the list of Key Terms at the end of the chapter in the text.

Across

1. A reduction in private-sector borrowing and spending caused by increased government borrowing.
6. Tax increases or spending cuts designed to reduce aggregate demand.
10. A spending or revenue item that responds automatically and countercyclically to national income.
11. The twelve-month accounting period used by the federal government.
12. When the government borrows funds to pay for spending that exceeds tax revenues.
13. Promissory notes issued by the U.S. Treasury.
15. The amount by which government spending exceeds revenues.
17. The idea that in order to get more public-sector goods, some private-sector goods must be given up.
18. Equal to the total stock of all outstanding Treasury bonds.
20. Tax cuts or spending increases designed to shift aggregate demand to the right.
22. An excess of government revenues over government expenditures in a given time period.
23. U.S. government debt held by foreign households and institutions.
24. The issuance of new bonds to replace the bonds that mature.
25. An explicit limit on the size of the annual budget deficit.
26. An explicit limit on the size of the national debt.

Down

2. Spending decisions not determined by past legislative commitments.
3. U.S. Treasury bonds are an _____ for the people who own them.
4. The most desirable combination of output given the available resources and technology.
5. Payments to individuals for which no current goods or services are exchanged.
7. The U.S. Treasury bonds are a _____ for the federal government.
8. The portion of the budget deficit that widens when unemployment or inflation increases.
9. Use of the government budget to stabilize the economy.
14. The structural _____ reflects fiscal-policy decisions.
16. The U.S. government debt owned by U.S. households, institutions, and government agencies.
19. The interest required to be paid each year on outstanding debt.
21. An increase in private-sector borrowing and spending caused by decreased government borrowing.

Puzzle 12.1

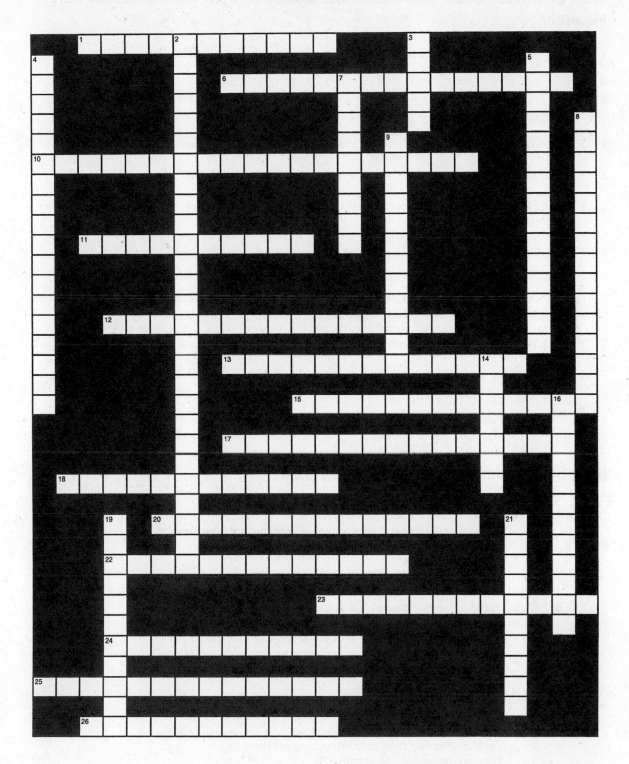

True or False: *Circle your choice and explain why any false statements are incorrect.*

T F 1. According to Keynes, a balanced budget would be appropriate only if all other injections and leakages were in balance and the economy was in full employment.

T F 2. Automatic stabilizers reduce government expenditures and decrease budget deficits when the economy is in a recession.

T F 3. Approximately 20 percent of the expenditures in the federal budget are "uncontrollable."

T F 4. The cyclical deficit narrows when unemployment or inflation increase.

T F 5. Part of the deficit arises from cyclical changes in the economy; the rest is the result of discretionary fiscal policy.

T F 6. Discretionary fiscal policy is stimulative if the structural deficit is shrinking (or the surplus is growing).

T F 7. In general, a budget surplus tends to change the mix of output in the direction of more public-sector goods and fewer private-sector goods.

T F 8. When foreigners help finance U.S. deficits, U.S. residents can consume more than they produce.

T F 9. The true burden of the debt is the reduction in national wealth when the federal government borrows money by selling bonds.

T F 10. The national debt is both an asset and a liability to future generations.

Multiple Choice: *Select the correct answer.*

_____ 1. Deficit spending results whenever the government:
    (a) Faces interest expense from government debt amassed from previous deficits.
    (b) Finances expenditures that exceed tax revenues.
    (c) Refinances the debt.
    (d) All of the above.

_____ 2. Deficit spending can be financed in the same year by:
    (a) Borrowing from foreign sources.
    (b) Borrowing from the banking system and the private sector.
    (c) U.S. Treasury bonds.
    (d) All of the above.

_____ 3. A budget deficit is incurred whenever:
    (a) Tax revenues fall short of expenditures over the fiscal year.
    (b) Discretionary fiscal spending is used to achieve macro equilibrium.
    (c) The U.S. Treasury engages in refinancing activities.
    (d) The government uses fiscal policy.

_____ 4. According to Keynes, it was acceptable for the budget to be unbalanced if:
    (a) The economy was below full employment.
    (b) Leakages and injections were out of balance.
    (c) The economy was above full employment.
    (d) All of the above.

_____ 5. Discretionary fiscal spending includes:
    (a) Income taxes.
    (b) Unemployment benefits.
    (c) A one-time expenditure for a highway.
    (d) Social Security payments.

_____ 6. Uncontrollable government spending includes:
    (a) Interest payments on the national debt.
    (b) Medicare benefits.
    (c) Pensions for retired government workers.
    (d) All of the above.

_____ 7. Automatic stabilizers tend to stabilize the level of economic activity because:
    (a) They are changed quickly by Congress.
    (b) They increase the size of the multiplier.
    (c) They increase spending during recessions and decrease spending during inflationary periods.
    (d) They control the rate of change in prices.

_____ 8. The major reason budget deficits were reduced during the 1990s and surpluses were experienced in 1998-2001 was:
    (a) President Clinton's deficit reduction policies.
    (b) The significant reductions in federal spending implemented by Congress.
    (c) Structural surpluses during the period.
    (d) The growing U.S. economy.

_____ 9. In contrast to the structural deficit, the cyclical deficit reflects:
    (a) Fluctuations in economic activity.
    (b) Fiscal-policy decisions.
    (c) Changes in discretionary fiscal policy.
    (d) Changes in the "full-employment" deficit.

_____ 10. The structural deficit represents:
    (a) Federal revenues minus federal expenditures at full employment under current fiscal policy.
    (b) Federal revenues minus federal expenditures under current fiscal policy at current output.
    (c) A measure of the size of recessionary or inflationary gaps.
    (d) The difference between expenditures at full employment and expenditures at cyclical unemployment.

_____ 11. The magnitude of a fiscal stimulus is measured by the:
    (a) Decrease in the structural deficit (or increase in the structural surplus).
    (b) Increase in the structural deficit (or decrease in the structural surplus).
    (c) Increase in the total budget deficit.
    (d) Increase in the cyclical deficit (or decrease in the cyclical surplus).

_____ 12. Crowding out occurs when the government:
    (a) Increases taxes, causing a decrease in consumption.
    (b) Prints money, which displaces currency.
    (c) Borrows, making it more difficult for the private sector to borrow.
    (d) Expenditures displace saving.

_____ 13. When the federal government runs a budget surplus, it is:
   (a)   Providing a fiscal stimulus to the economy.
   (b)   Adding a leakage to the circular flow.
   (c)   Adding an injection to the circular flow.
   (d)   Reducing leakages to the circular flow.

_____ 14. Which of the following uses of a budget surplus has the potential of increasing the private sector's proportion of output?
   (a)   Cutting taxes.
   (b)   Paying off a portion of the national debt.
   (c)   Increasing transfer payments.
   (d)   All of the above have the potential.

_____ 15. When the U.S. Treasury issues new bonds to replace bonds that have matured, it is engaging in:
   (a)   Debt refinancing.
   (b)   Debt servicing.
   (c)   Income transfers.
   (d)   Discretionary fiscal spending.

_____ 16. If all of the national debt were owned internally, then:
   (a)   We would not have to worry about raising taxes to pay the interest on the debt.
   (b)   We would still have to worry about the effect of interest payments on the distribution of income.
   (c)   The federal government would have to stop refinancing the debt.
   (d)   The Federal Reserve System would have no use for government debt.

_____ 17. Externally held U.S. debt results in:
   (a)   A burden to the United States when newly issued bonds are sold to foreigners.
   (b)   A burden to the United States when foreign-owned bonds are cashed in and proceeds are used to buy goods and services produced in the United States.
   (c)   A burden incurred by foreigners when bonds are sold in the United States.
   (d)   No burden to the United States.

_____ 18. A deficit ceiling limits:
   (a)   The amount by which government spending can exceed government revenue.
   (b)   The amount of the national debt.
   (c)   The trade deficit.
   (d)   Inflation.

_____ 19. Which of the following statements about the U.S. national debt is _not_ correct?
   (a)   The national debt represents both a liability and asset.
   (b)   The primary burden of the debt is incurred when the deficit-financed activity takes place.
   (c)   The primary economic costs of the debt are being passed on to future generations.
   (d)   Future generations will bear some of the debt burden when it is externally financed.

_____ 20. Which of the following policies can the government use to pay for Social Security in the future?
   (a)   An increase in income taxes.
   (b)   A decrease in Social Security benefits.
   (c)   A decrease in spending for other government programs.
   (d)   All of the above.

Problems and Applications

Exercise 1

After doing this exercise you should understand the relationship between deficits, bonds, debt, and interest payments. You should see how continual deficits lead to larger and larger interest payments and larger and larger debt. Keep in mind that it is difficult to eliminate deficits when interest payments are an important factor contributing to the deficits.

1. Suppose government expenditures for country XYZ in the year 2000 are $1 trillion and taxes are $800 billion. Compute the deficit and place the answer in column 1 of Table 12.1 for the year 2000.

Table 12.1
Deficits, bonds, debts, and interest payments for XYZ
(billions of dollars per year)

Year	(1) Deficit	(2) Newly issued bonds	(3) Total debt	(4) Interest payment
1999	$0	$0	$0	$0
2000	_____	_____	_____	_____
2001	_____	_____	_____	_____
2002	_____	_____	_____	_____
2003	_____	_____	_____	_____
2004	_____	_____	_____	_____
2005	_____	_____	_____	_____
2006	_____	_____	_____	_____
2007	_____	_____	_____	_____

2. To finance the deficit, the government must sell bonds of an equivalent amount to cover the revenue shortfall. What is the dollar amount necessary to finance the debt? Place the answer in column 2 of Table 12.1 for the year 2000.

3. Assume that up to 1999 the government had zero debt (as shown in the 1999 row of Table 12.1). What is the total debt after the government has borrowed to cover the deficit in the year 2000? Place the answer in column 3 of Table 12.1 for the year 2000.

4. What will be the interest payment on the total debt in the year 2000 if the interest rate is 10 percent per year? Place the answer in column 4 of Table 12.1 for the year 2000. Assume all bonds are sold January 1 with interest due December 31.

5. For the years 2001 through 2007, the government spends $1 trillion each year plus any interest payment on the previous years' debt and receives tax revenues of only $800 billion each year. The interest rate is still 10 percent per year. Fill in the rest of Table 12.1.

6. Graph and label the deficit (column 1 of Table 12.1) and interest payment (column 4) in Figure 12.1 for 2000-2007.

Figure 12.1

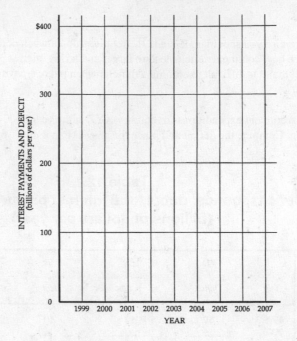

7. T F With continual deficits, interest payments on past deficits will become a bigger part of current deficits, *ceteris paribus*.

8. T F In this example, if both taxes and government expenditures increased at 5 percent per year as a result of bigger government, both the deficit and the debt would become smaller.

Exercise 2

This exercise focuses on the ratio of the national debt to GDP, which is an important measure of the burden of the debt.

Table 12.2 National debt and GDP
(billions of dollars per year)

Year	Country A			Country B		
	Debt	GDP	Debt/GDP	Debt	GDP	Debt/GDP
1999	$200	$1,000	_____	$200	$1,000	_____
2000	250	1,250	_____	250	1,150	_____
2001	280	1,400	_____	280	1,000	_____
2002	320	1,600	_____	320	1,000	_____
2003	400	2,000	_____	400	1,200	_____

1. Calculate the debt/GDP ratio for Country A and Country B in Table 12.2.

164

2. During the period from 1999 to 2003 both countries in Table 12.2 are experiencing (budget deficits; budget surpluses; a balanced budget) each year.

3. Even though the size of the debt is the same for the two countries in Table 12.2 for each year, the debt is likely to be a greater burden for Country _____ because the debt/GDP ratio is _____.

4. Given the information in Table 12.2, what is the most likely cause for the increase in the debt/GDP ratio from 2000 to 2001 for Country B? _____

5. The actual amount of debt increases each year for Country A in Table 12.2. The size of the debt/GDP ratio (increases; decreases; stays the same) because GDP (increases; decreases; stays the same) each year.

Exercise 3

This exercise explores the impact of government spending on private-sector spending.

Use Figure 12.2 to answer questions 1-6.

Figure 12.2

1. If all debt is held internally and the government finances additional spending by borrowing, then an increase in government purchases would move the economy from point K to point _____.

2. If the economy moves from point E to point A because of increased government spending, the amount of private sector spending crowded out is equal to the distance _____.

3. Assume the government has a budget surplus and uses it to reduce the accumulated debt. As a result interest rates (rise; fall) and the economy moves from point E to point _____.

4. The situation described in question 3 is referred to in the text as the _____ effect.

5. External financing of the debt allows the economy to move from point E to point _____.

6. In question 5, external financing allows public-sector goods to (increase; decrease; stay the same) while private-sector goods (increase; decrease; stay the same).

Exercise 4

Reports on fiscal policy typically involve changes in the deficit and the debt.

Reread the article titled "Fiscal Policy in the Great Depression" in the text.

1. President Hoover believed that the federal budget should always be (balanced; in deficit; in surplus).

2. What did President Hoover propose to resolve the problem with the federal budget?
    _____

3. From 1931 to 1933 the structural deficit _____. This fiscal restraint caused the _____ curve to shift to the (left; right).

4. What finally occurred that caused a huge increase in government spending, which ended the Great Depression? _____

Common Errors

The first statement in each "common error" below is incorrect. Each incorrect statement is followed by a corrected version and an explanation.

1. Our grandchildren will feel the burden of the deficit. WRONG!

    Our grandchildren may feel the burden of the debt. RIGHT!

    Deficit and debt are concepts that are often confused. While deficits occur because of the excess of expenditures over taxes during a given year, the debt can be calculated at any given point in time and represents the cumulative effect of running deficits over our entire history. It is the debt on which transfers such as interest payments are made, not the deficit. Such transfers may result in opportunity costs. However, a deficit may reflect expenditures on capital, which will benefit future generations and thus may not be a burden.

2. The national debt must be paid off eventually. WRONG!

    The national debt is paid off continually through refinancing. RIGHT!

    No Treasury bond has a maturity date more than thirty years in the future. Some bonds have maturity dates that come much sooner—in ten or twenty years. Treasury bills are sold at auction and have maturity dates of 360 days or less with 30-day intervals (i.e., 30, 60, 90, and so on). Suppose the federal government has balanced budgets for the next thirty years. The entire debt will have come due at some point. What will happen? It would be refinanced as it comes due and replaced with new debt.

3. There is nothing "behind" the national debt. WRONG!

    The federal government owns many physical assets and has the ability to tax. RIGHT!

    The proceeds of bond sales by the federal government are used to do many things, including the purchase of assets. Every item owned by the federal government—from the White House to

Old Faithful—is an asset that could be sold to help pay off the national debt. Stealth bombers, office buildings, computers, and the like, are all assets that were needed over the years and are as much an asset as the debt is a liability. By raising taxes, the government can at least theoretically run a surplus and pay off the debt.

•ANSWERS•

Using Key Terms

Across
1. crowding out
6. fiscal restraint
10. automatic stabilizer
11. fiscal year
12. deficit spending
13. treasury bonds
15. budget deficit
17. opportunity cost
18. national debt
20. fiscal stimulus
22. budget surplus
23. external debt
24. refinancing
25. deficit ceiling
26. debt ceiling

Down
2. discretionary fiscal spending
3. asset
4. optimal mix of output
5. income transfers
7. liability
8. cyclical deficit
9. fiscal policy
14. structural deficit
16. internal debt
19. debt service
21. crowding in

True or False
1. T
2. F As an economy falls into a recession, automatic stabilizers tend to increase government spending (and reduce tax receipts) thus making budget deficits larger.
3. F Approximately 80 percent of the expenditures in the federal budget are uncontrollable.
4. F The cyclical deficit widens when unemployment increases or inflation decreases.
5. T
6. F Such policies are restrictive.
7. F Unless the government spends the surplus, the proportion of private goods and services produced will tend to increase.
8. T
9. F The true burden of the national debt is the private goods and services that are forgone (i.e., crowded out) as a result of government borrowing.
10. T

Multiple Choice

1. b		5. c		9. a		13. b		17. b
2. d		6. d		10. a		14. d		18. a
3. a		7. c		11. b		15. a		19. c
4. d		8. d		12. c		16. b		20. d

Problems and Applications

Exercise 1

1-5. **Table 12.1 Answer**

Year	(1) Deficit	(2) Newly issued bonds	(3) Total debt	(4) Interest payment
2000	$200	$200	$ 200	$ 20 = (0.10 x 200)
2001	220	220	420 = (200 + 220)	42 = (0.10 x 420)
2002	242	242	662 = (420 + 242)	66 = (0.10 x 662)
2003	266	266	928 = (662 + 266)	93 = (0.10 x 928)
2004	293	293	1,221 = (928 + 293)	122 = (0.10 x 1,221)
2005	322	322	1,543 = (1,221 + 322)	154 = (0.10 x 1,543)
2006	354	354	1,897 = (1,543 + 354)	190 = (0.10 x 1,897)
2007	390	390	2,287 = (1,897 + 390)	229 = (0.10 x 2,287)

6. **Figure 12.1 Answer**

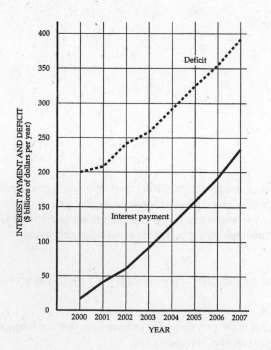

7. T Compare relative sizes of columns 1 and 4 in Table 12.1 Answer.
8. F

Exercise 2

1. **Table 12.2 Answer**

Year	Country A			Country B		
	Debt	GDP	Debt/GDP	Debt	GDP	Debt/GDP
1999	$200	$1000	0.20	$200	$1000	0.20
2000	250	1250	0.20	250	1150	0.22
2001	280	1400	0.20	280	1000	0.28
2002	320	1600	0.20	320	1000	0.32
2003	400	2000	0.20	400	1200	0.33

2. Budget deficits
3. B; greater
4. Recession
5. Stays the same; increases

Exercise 3

1. E
2. H_2-H_1
3. Fall; K
4. Crowding-in
5. B
6. Increase; stay the same

Exercise 4

1. Balanced
2. A decrease in government spending and an increase in taxes
3. Decreased; AD; left
4. World War II

CHAPTER 13

Money and Banks

Quick Review

- Money facilitates market exchanges and allows for specialization. It makes an economy more efficient than one that relies on barter. Anything that serves simultaneously as a medium of exchange, a store of value, and a standard of value can be thought of as money.

- The money supply (M1) is composed of transactions accounts, currency in circulation, and traveler's checks.

- The banking system can create money by making loans. When a bank decides to make a loan, it simply credits the transactions account of the borrower. Because transactions accounts are included in M1, this causes an increase in the money supply.

- In the United States, the Federal Reserve System requires banks to maintain some minimum ratio of bank reserves to total deposits. Any reserves above the required level are considered to be excess reserves. A bank may use its excess reserves to make new loans.

- As the new loans are spent, the dollars flow back into the banking system and additional loans are made. This process continues to occur over and over again and is known as *deposit creation*.

- The banking system as a whole can increase the volume of deposits by the amount of the excess reserves times the money multiplier. The money multiplier is equal to 1/required reserve ratio.

- Banks perform a strategic role in the economy by transferring money from savers to spenders and by creating additional money through lending. An increase in the money supply, because of deposit creation, leads to an increase in aggregate demand. A reduction in the money supply leads to a decrease in aggregate demand.

- Deposit creation is constrained by the willingness of market participants to use and accept checks. It is also constrained by the willingness of businesses and individuals to borrow, and the willingness of banks to make loans. Regulations of the Federal Reserve System also limit deposit creation.

Learning Objectives

After reading Chapter 13 and doing the following exercises, you should:

1. Know the basic history of money and the functions of money.
2. Be familiar with the composition and measures of the money supply ($M1$, $M2$).
3. Know how banks create money by making loans.
4. Know the function of the reserve requirement.
5. Be able to calculate required and excess reserves.
6. Be able to work through the steps of deposit creation using balance sheets (T-accounts).
7. Be able to calculate and explain the money multiplier.
8. Know the banking system's role in the circular flow of economic activity.
9. Know the constraints on deposit creation.

Using Key Terms

Fill in the puzzle on the opposite page with the appropriate term from the list of Key Terms at the end of the chapter in the text.

Across

1. Assets held by a bank to fulfill its deposit obligations.
5. Total reserves minus required reserves.
7. An account that allows direct payment to a third party.
9. Represent a leakage from the flow of money because they cannot be used to make loans.
10. The reciprocal of the required reserve ratio.

Down

2. Tends to increase with an increase in the money supply because new loans are used to purchase additional goods and services.
3. The process by which bank lending causes the money supply to increase.
4. The direct exchange of one good for another without the use of money.
6. Currency held by the public, plus balances in transactions accounts.
8. The ratio of bank reserves to total transactions deposits.
10. Throughout history gold coins, tobacco, and bullets have functioned in this role.

Puzzle 13.1

True or False: *Circle your choice and explain why any false statements are incorrect.*

T F 1. The terms "transactions-account balances" and "checking accounts" mean the same thing.

T F 2. Credit cards are a form of money because they are used to facilitate exchanges.

T F 3. When you get a loan at a bank, the bank creates money.

T F 4. The withdrawal of money from a checking account causes the money supply to get smaller.

T F 5. The minimum-reserve ratio is established by the Federal Reserve System.

T F 6. The higher the legal minimum-reserve ratio, the greater the lending power of the banks.

T F 7. If the minimum-reserve ratio is 20 percent, then $1 of reserves can support $5 in transactions-account balances.

T F 8. The amount any one bank can lend is equal to its total reserves.

T F 9. A bank transfers money from savers to spenders by lending a fraction of the deposits it holds.

T F 10. If people stop using checks and instead switch to cash, banks will not be able to acquire or maintain reserves and the lending activity will cease.

Multiple Choice: *Select the correct answer.*

_____ 1. Money is anything:
   (a) That can be used to barter.
   (b) That a government declares to have value.
   (c) That has value.
   (d) Generally accepted as a medium of exchange.

_____ 2. Which of the following is a necessary characteristic of money?
   (a) It serves as a medium of exchange.
   (b) Its value must be supported by government reserves of gold and silver.
   (c) The government declares it to have value.
   (d) All of the above are necessary characteristics.

_____ 3. Barter:
   (a) Facilitates specialization in production.
   (b) Is most efficient for an economy.
   (c) Is the direct exchange of one good or service for another.
   (d) All of the above are correct.

_____ 4. The different components of the money supply reflect:
   (a) Variations in liquidity and accessibility of assets.
   (b) Whether deposits are domestic or international.
   (c) How often depositors use their accounts.
   (d) All of the above.

5. $M1$ refers to:
   (a) One component of the money supply.
   (b) Currency held by the public plus transactions-account balances.
   (c) The smallest of the money-supply aggregates watched by the Fed.
   (d) All of the above.

6. Which of the following appears in $M2$ but not in $M1$?
   (a) Credit-union share drafts.
   (b) Treasury bills.
   (c) Saving account balances.
   (d) U.S. savings bonds.

7. Immediately after cash is deposited into a bank, the composition of the money supply:
   (a) And the size of the money supply both change.
   (b) Changes, but the size of the money supply remains the same.
   (c) Remains the same, but the size of the money changes.
   (d) And the size of the money supply both remain the same.

8. Suppose the total amount of transactions accounts on the books of all of the banks in the system is $1 million and the minimum-reserve ratio is 0.20. The amount of required reserves for the banking system is, then:
   (a) $20,000,000.
   (b) $500,000.
   (c) $200,000.
   (d) $800,000.

9. When the reserve requirement changes, which of the following will change for an individual bank?
   (a) Transactions-account balances, lending capacity.
   (b) Transactions-account balances, total reserves, excess reserves.
   (c) Total reserves, required reserves, excess reserves.
   (d) Required reserves, excess reserves, lending capacity.

10. Banks are required to keep a minimum amount of funds in reserve because:
    (a) Depositors may decide to withdraw funds.
    (b) It provides a constraint on the bank's ability to create money.
    (c) It provides a constraint on the bank's ability to affect aggregate demand.
    (d) All of the above are correct.

11. Suppose a bank has $4 million in deposits, a required reserve ratio of 25 percent, and reserves of $1 million. Then it has excess reserves of:
    (a) $10,000.
    (b) $0.
    (c) $400,000.
    (d) $1,600,000.

12. Suppose a bank has $100,000 in deposits, a required reserve ratio of 5 percent, and bank reserves of $25,000. Then it can make new loans in the amount of:
    (a) $20,000.
    (b) $5,000.
    (c) $2,500.
    (d) $25,000.

_____ 13. A higher reserve requirement:
  (a) Further limits deposit creation.
  (b) Increases the ability of banks to make loans.
  (c) Lowers the interest rate.
  (d) Increases the borrowing capability of borrowers.

_____ 14. If people never withdrew cash from banks and there was no reserve requirement, how much money could the banking system potentially create for a given amount of new deposits?
  (a) Zero.
  (b) The same amount as the new deposits.
  (c) The amount of new deposits multiplied by the reserve ratio.
  (d) An infinite amount of money.

_____ 15. If the minimum-reserve ratio is 10 percent, the money multiplier is:
  (a) 9.
  (b) 10.
  (c) 0.10.
  (d) 1.10.

_____ 16. Suppose a banking system has $100,000 in deposits, a required reserve ratio of 15 percent, and total bank reserves for the whole system of $25,000. Then the whole system can potentially make new loans in the amount of:
  (a) $10,000.
  (b) $15,000.
  (c) $66,667.
  (d) $166,667.

_____ 17. The main goal of banks is to:
  (a) Earn a profit.
  (b) Create money.
  (c) Lend all of its deposits.
  (d) Minimize its reserve ratio.

_____ 18. Which of the following are constraints on the deposit-creation process of the banking system?
  (a) The willingness of consumers and businesses to continue using and accepting checks rather than cash.
  (b) The willingness of consumers, businesses, and government to borrow money.
  (c) The reserve requirement.
  (d) All of the above.

_____ 19. Deposit insurance:
  (a) Lowers the bankruptcy rate for banks.
  (b) Lowers the number and magnitude of bank runs.
  (c) Must be subsidized and run by the government in order to have credibility.
  (d) All of the above.

_____ 20. Which of the following could cause the money supply to decrease?
  (a) An increase in depositor confidence in the banking system.
  (b) An increase in the amount of borrowing by businesses and individuals.
  (c) A decrease in lending activity by banks.
  (d) Rapid growth on the part of the economy.

Problems and Applications

Exercise 1

Use the information from the Balance Sheet in Table 13.1 to answer questions 1–5.

Table 13.1 Bank of Arlington

Assets		Liabilities	
Required reserves	$200,000	Transactions accounts	$1,000,000
Other assets	800,000		
Total	$1,000,000	Total	$1,000,000

1. Suppose that the Bank of Arlington is just meeting its reserve requirement. The reserve ratio must be _____, and the money multiplier must be _____.

2. To be in a position to make loans, the Bank of Arlington must acquire some (required reserves; excess reserves).

3. If we assume that the reserve ratio is changed to 15 percent, the Bank of Arlington would have required reserves of _____ and excess reserves of _____.

4. With a 15 percent reserve ratio the Bank of Arlington is in a position to make new loans totaling _____.

5. With a 15 percent reserve ratio, the entire banking system can increase the volume of loans by _____.

Exercise 2

This exercise shows how the multiplier process works.

Assume that all banks in the system lend all of their excess reserves, that the reserve ratio for all banks is 0.25, and that all loans are returned to the banking system in the form of transactions deposits. Use the information from the Balance Sheets in Table 13.2, Table 13.3, Table 13.4, and Table 13.5 to answer questions 1–6.

Table 13.2 Bank A - Initial Balance Sheet

Assets		Liabilities	
Required reserves	$25,000	Transactions accounts	$100,000
Excess reserves	0		
Other assets	75,000		
Total	$100,000	Total	$100,000

1. Bob takes $10,000 out of his cookie jar and deposits it in a transactions account in Bank A. Fill in the blanks in Bank A's balance sheet in Table 13.3 after the deposit. (Remember that some of the deposit will show up in required reserves and the remainder will become part of excess reserves.)

Table 13.3 Bank A - Balance Sheet After Bill's Deposit

Assets		Liabilities	
Required reserves	$_____	Transactions accounts	$_____
Excess reserves	_____		
Other assets	75,000		
Total	$_____	Total	$_____

Now assume that Bank A lends all of its excess reserves to Maria, who spends the money on a car. The car dealership deposits the money in its transactions account in Bank B. Bank B's initial balance sheet is the same as Bank A's initial balance sheet.

2. Fill in the blanks in Bank B's balance sheet after the car dealership makes its deposit.

Table 13.4 Bank B - Balance Sheet After Car Dealership's Deposit

Assets		Liabilities	
Required reserves	$_____	Transactions accounts	$_____
Excess reserves	_____		
Other assets	75,000		
Total	$_____	Total	$_____

Now assume Bank B lends all of its excess reserves to Mike, who spends the money on college tuition. The university deposits the money in Bank C. Bank C's initial balance sheet is the same as Bank A's initial balance sheet.

3. Fill in the blanks in Bank C's balance sheet after the university makes its deposit.

Table 13.5 Bank C - Balance Sheet After University's Deposit

Assets		Liabilities	
Required reserves	$_____	Transactions accounts	$_____
Excess reserves	_____		
Other assets	75,000		
Total	$_____	Total	$_____

4. Add together the loans made by each bank because of the initial $10,000 deposit made by Bob.

Bank A lent $_____
Bank B lent $_____
Bank C lent $_____

Total loans made so far $_____

5. The money multiplier for this exercise equals _____.

6. The potential deposit creation for the banking system in this exercise is _____.

Exercise 3

Reread the article "The Cashless Society" in the text. Use the article to answer the following questions.

1. Which form of money ($M1$, $M2$,... etc.) is most affected according to the article? _____

2. According to the article, the ruble is no longer accepted as payment for goods and services. In this situation, which of the functions of money is the ruble not performing? _____
    _____

3. Because the ruble has lost its value, people are using _____ to acquire goods and services.

4. Which passage indicates the impact on the Russian economy as a result of barter? _____
    _____

Exercise 4

This exercise focuses on the reserve requirement and its impact on the money supply.

1. Given the following reserve ratios, calculate the money multiplier for each.

    a. Reserve ratio = 10 percent   Money multiplier = _____
    b. Reserve ratio = 15 percent   Money multiplier = _____
    c. Reserve ratio = 20 percent   Money multiplier = _____

2. As the reserve ratio increases, the money multiplier (increases; decreases).

3. As the money multiplier decreases, potential deposit creation (increases; decreases).

4. T   F   An increase in the reserve ratio functions as a constraint on the deposit creation of the banking system.

Common Errors

The first statement in each "common error" below is incorrect. Each incorrect statement is followed by a corrected version and an explanation.

1. Banks can't create money. WRONG!

    Banks can and do create money. RIGHT!

    It should be obvious by now that banks and other depository institutions are very important participants in the money-supply process. They create money by granting loans to borrowers and accomplish their role by adding to their customers' transactions accounts. The accounts are money just as much as the coins and currency in your wallet are money. The banks create (supply) money, but only in response to borrowers' demands for it. Without customers demanding loans, banks wouldn't be able to create money at all.

2. Banks hold your deposits in their vaults. WRONG!

Banks don't hold your deposits in their vaults. (And neither do other depository institutions.) RIGHT!

You can look at this two ways. First, when you deposit your paycheck, there's nothing for the bank to "hold" in its vault, except the check, and that is returned to the person who wrote it. Second, if you deposited coin or cash, it's all put together and you can't distinguish any one person's deposit from any other person's deposit. Even then, when "cash in vault" becomes too large, much of it is shipped away by armored truck to the Federal Reserve Bank. (This is described in Chapter 14.) Thus, banks don't hold your deposits in their vaults.

3. Gold and silver are intrinsically valuable and are necessary to secure the value of a currency. WRONG!

Money can serve as a store of value, a standard of value, and a medium of exchange without being backed by gold and silver. RIGHT!

While precious metals such as gold and silver have frequently been used to back currencies, they do not back the dollar today. Like other commodities, their value in terms of dollars continually fluctuates in response to supply and demand conditions. International monetary authorities have attempted to "demonetize" the precious metals and have been successful in holding the price of these metals down in terms of the major currencies. Nevertheless, during periods of calamity and fear, these precious metals are hoarded because people believe these items have intrinsic value; they then do take the role of a store of value.

4. Banks are irresponsible if they fail to store all of the money that is deposited with them so that it is available on demand. WRONG!

Banks must lend most of the money that is deposited with them so that they can earn interest and pay interest on those deposits. RIGHT!

If banks allowed money just to sit in the vault, no productive use could be made of the money. Banks are useful as the intermediary between savers, who have the money, and spenders, who wish to borrow the money. Through their lending activity, banks promote efficiency. That means the money is not sitting idle in the bank's vault.

•ANSWERS•

Using Key Terms

Across

1. bank reserves
5. excess reserves
7. transactions account
9. required reserves
10. money multiplier

Down

2. aggregate demand
3. deposit creation
4. barter
6. money supply
8. reserve ratio
10. money

True or False

1. F Transactions accounts permit direct payment to a third party by check or debit card. In addition to traditional checking accounts, NOW accounts, ATS accounts, credit union share drafts, and demand deposits at mutual savings banks also serve this purpose.
2. F Credit cards are a payment service, not a final form of payment, i.e., credit card balances must be paid by cash or check.
3. T
4. F The single action of withdrawal simply changes the composition of the money supply from, for example, a transactions account balance to cash. However, the banking system now has less money to lend out and the potential exists for a reduction in the money supply.
5. T
6. F The higher the reserve ratio, the lower the lending power of the banks.
7. T
8. F The amount any one bank can lend is equal to its excess reserves.
9. T
10. T

Multiple Choice

1. d	5. d	9. d	13. a	17. a
2. a	6. c	10. d	14. d	18. d
3. c	7. b	11. b	15. b	19. b
4. a	8. c	12. a	16. c	20. c

Problems and Applications

Exercise 1

1. 0.20; 5
2. Excess reserves
3. $150,000; $50,000
4. $50,000
5. $333,333.33

Exercise 2

1. **Table 13.3 Answer**

Assets		Liabilities	
Required reserves	$27,500	Transactions accounts	$110,000
Excess reserves	7,500		
Other assets	75,000		
Total	$110,000	Total	$110,000

2. **Table 13.4 Answer**

Assets		Liabilities	
Required reserves	$26,875	Transactions accounts	$107,500
Excess reserves	5,625		
Other assets	75,000		
Total	$107,500	Total	$107,500

3. **Table 13.5 Answer**

Assets		Liabilities	
Required reserves	$26,406.25	Transactions accounts	$105,625.00
Excess reserves	4,218.75		
Other assets	75,000.00		
Total	$105,625.00	Total	$105,625.00

4. Bank A lent $7,500.00
   Bank B lent $5,625.00
   Bank C lent $4,218.75
   Total loans made so far $17,343.75
5. $1 \div \text{reserve ratio} = 1 \div 0.25 = 4$
6. Potential deposit creation = initial excess reserves x money multiplier = $7,500 x 4 = $30,000

Exercise 3

1. *M*1
2. Medium of exchange
3. Barter
4. "Barter is poisoning the development of capitalism . . . because it consumes huge amounts of time that would be better spent producing goods."

Exercise 4

1. a. 10
   b. 6.67
   c. 5
2. Decreases
3. Decreases
4. T

CHAPTER 14

The Federal Reserve System

Quick Review

- The Federal Reserve System (Fed) controls the money supply by limiting the amount of loans that the banking system can provide from any given level of reserves, and it also controls the amount of reserves in the system.

- The Federal Reserve System is composed of twelve regional banks located across the country. The regional banks provide the following services for the private banks in their region: check clearing, holding bank reserves, providing currency, and providing loans to the private banks.

- The Board of Governors of the Federal Reserve System is the key decision-maker in setting monetary policy. Board members are appointed by the president of the United States for fourteen-year terms. The Federal Open Market Committee (FOMC) directs Fed transactions in the bond market.

- There are three primary levers of monetary policy: reserve requirements, discount rates, and open-market operations. Changing the reserve requirement changes both the money multiplier and the level of excess reserves in the banking system. It is the least frequently used tool.

- The process in which the Fed lends money to private banks is known as "discounting." Changing the discount rate makes it more or less attractive for private banks to borrow from the Fed.

- The principal monetary policy tool is open-market operations, which involves the buying or selling of U.S. government bonds in the open market by the Fed. When the Fed buys or sells bonds, this changes the price of bonds and their yields.

- If the Fed buys bonds, there is an increase in bank reserves and the lending capacity for the banking system increases. If the Fed sells bonds, there is a decrease in bank reserves and the lending capacity decreases.

- In order to increase the money supply the Fed can decrease the reserve requirement, decrease the discount rate, or buy bonds. To decrease the money supply the Fed can do just the opposite.

- Congress passed legislation in 1980 to give the Fed greater control of the money supply, but the rise in foreign institutions and nonbank financial entities has made it more difficult for the Fed to control the money supply.

Learning Objectives

After reading Chapter 14 and doing the following exercises, you should:

1. Be familiar with the organization, structure, and functions of the Federal Reserve System.
2. Know that the Fed can use the reserve requirement as one of its tools to change the money supply.
3. Know what the money multiplier is and how it is used.
4. Know that the discount rate can be used by the Fed to change the money supply.
5. Know the significance of the federal funds rate and the Federal Funds Market.
6. Understand how the Open Market Committee can achieve a given policy objective by buying or selling securities.
7. Understand how the Fed can change the price of a bond and its yield.
8. Be able to demonstrate the inverse relationship between interest rates and bond prices.
9. Know the background and provisions of the Monetary Control Act of 1980 and recent changes in the structure of the financial system.

Using Key Terms

Fill in the puzzle on the opposite page with the appropriate term from the list of Key Terms at the end of the chapter in the text.

Across

5. The interest rate one bank charges another bank when lending reserves.
6. Equal to total reserves minus required reserves.
8. The interest rate the Fed charges a bank when lending reserves.
10. Represent a leakage from the flow of money because they cannot be used to make loans.
12. The choice of where to place idle funds.

Down
1. The reciprocal of the required reserve ratio.
2. The use of money and credit controls to influence the macroeconomy.
3. The purchase and sale of government securities by the Fed in order to change bank reserves.
4. The annual interest payment divided by the bond's purchase price.
7. Controlled by the Fed through the use of the reserve requirement, the discount rate, and open market operations.
9. Refers to the Fed lending reserves to private banks.
11. A certificate acknowledging a debt and terms for repayment.

Puzzle 14.1

True or False: *Circle your choice and explain why any false statements are incorrect.*

T   F   1.   The Federal Reserve banks hold deposits of banks and other business firms.

T   F   2.   The Board of Governors is responsible for setting monetary policy.

T   F   3.   The Fed is not one bank but is actually twelve regional banks with central control located in Washington D.C.

T   F   4.   The fourteen-year terms for the Board of Governors give the Fed a measure of political independence.

T   F   5.   Monetary policy is the use of money and government spending to influence macroeconomic activity.

T   F   6.   If the Fed wishes to create the conditions under which the money supply can be increased, it can increase the reserve requirement.

T   F   7.   When the Fed buys bonds from the public, it increases the flow of reserves into the banking system.

T   F   8.   The FOMC implements monetary policy by adjusting reserve requirements and discount rates.

T   F   9.   Open-market operations are the principal mechanism for altering the reserves of the banking system.

T   F   10.   To increase the lending capacity of banks, the Fed sells securities.

Multiple Choice: *Select the correct answer.*

_____   1.   Suppose that Brian receives a check for $100 from a bank in Atlanta. He deposits the check in his account at his Baltimore bank. Brian's Baltimore bank will collect the $100 from the:
(a)   Atlanta bank.
(b)   Baltimore bank's regional Federal Reserve Bank.
(c)   The central Federal Reserve Bank in Washington.
(d)   Board of Governors.

_____   2.   Which of the following is a service performed by the Federal Reserve banks?
(a)   Clearing checks between commercial banks.
(b)   Holding reserves of commercial banks.
(c)   Providing currency to commercial banks.
(d)   All of the above.

_____   3.   The formulation of general Federal Reserve policy is the responsibility of the:
(a)   Federal Open Market Committee.
(b)   Federal Advisory Council.
(c)   Board of Governors.
(d)   Regional Federal Reserve banks.

_____ 4. Members of the Federal Reserve Board of Governors:
   (a)   Are appointed to fourteen-year terms by the president of the United States.
   (b)   Are relatively immune to short-term political pressures.
   (c)   May not be reappointed after serving a full term.
   (d)   All of the above are true.

_____ 5. Which of the following is responsible for buying and selling government securities to influence reserves in the banking system?
   (a)   The Board of Governors.
   (b)   The twelve regional Federal Reserve Banks.
   (c)   The Federal Open Market Committee.
   (d)   The Executive Branch of the government.

_____ 6. Which of the following is _not_ one of the tools of monetary policy used by the Fed?
   (a)   Expulsion from Fed membership.
   (b)   Changing the reserve requirement.
   (c)   Changing the discount rate.
   (d)   Performing open-market operations.

_____ 7. When the Fed wishes to increase the excess reserves of the member banks, it:
   (a)   Raises the discount rate.
   (b)   Buys securities.
   (c)   Raises the reserve requirement.
   (d)   Sells securities.

_____ 8. The reserve requirement is:
   (a)   A powerful tool that can cause abrupt changes in the money supply.
   (b)   The most often used tool on the part of the Fed.
   (c)   A tool that has little impact on the money supply.
   (d)   Effective in changing excess reserves but not the money multiplier.

_____ 9. Which of the following can be used by a bank to increase reserves?
   (a)   Selling securities.
   (b)   Borrowing from the discount window.
   (c)   Borrowing in the Fed funds market.
   (d)   All of the above.

_____ 10. The federal funds market is a market in which:
   (a)   Banks lend excess reserves to other banks.
   (b)   Government securities are bought and sold.
   (c)   Reserves are discounted outside the Fed's control.
   (d)   The Fed lends to member banks.

_____ 11. Discounting refers to the Fed's practice of:
   (a)   Selling securities at the federal funds rate.
   (b)   Lending reserves to private banks.
   (c)   Lending at the prime rate.
   (d)   Purchasing securities at the lowest available federal funds rate.

_____ 12. The most frequently used tool on the part of the Fed is:
   (a)   The reserve requirement.
   (b)   The discount rate.
   (c)   Open-market operations.
   (d)   The Fed funds rate.

_____ 13. Suppose that the Fed desires to sell more bonds than people are willing to purchase. The most likely result of this situation would be a:
    (a)   Decrease in the price of bonds.
    (b)   Switch to another type of monetary policy lever by the Fed.
    (c)   Switch to fiscal policy.
    (d)   Purchase of the unsold bonds by the Fed.

_____ 14. When the Fed buys bonds from the public:
    (a)   It decreases the flow of reserves to the banking system.
    (b)   It increases the flow of reserves to the banking system.
    (c)   It decreases the money supply.
    (d)   It decreases the discount rate.

_____ 15. If the Fed buys bonds from the public, which of the following changes are likely to occur?
    (a)   The public's holdings of bonds would decrease.
    (b)   *M1* would increase.
    (c)   Excess reserves would increase.
    (d)   All of the above would occur.

_____ 16. The Fed can increase the Federal Funds rate by:
    (a)   Selling bonds.
    (b)   Buying bonds.
    (c)   Simply announcing a lower rate since the Fed has direct control of this interest rate.
    (d)   Changing the money multiplier.

_____ 17. In recent years the Fed has shifted away from:
    (a)   Money-supply targets to interest rate targets.
    (b)   Interest rate targets to money-supply targets.
    (c)   Using fiscal policy.
    (d)   Using monetary policy.

_____ 18. An increase in the discount rate:
    (a)   Reduces the cost of reserves borrowed from the Fed.
    (b)   Signals the Fed's desire to restrain money growth.
    (c)   Signals the Fed's desire to support credit creation.
    (d)   Signals the Fed's eagerness to lend additional reserves.

_____ 19. Assuming a reserve requirement of 25 percent, if the Fed sells $10 billion of bonds in the open market, the lending capacity of the banking system will eventually:
    (a)   Increase by $2.5 billion.
    (b)   Decrease by $2.5 billion.
    (c)   Increase by $40 billion.
    (d)   Decrease by $40 billion.

_____ 20. Which of the following has contributed to the reduction in Fed control of the money supply?
    (a)   An increase in the amount of consumer deposits held in nonbank financial institutions.
    (b)   Banks are no longer the exclusive source of credit cards.
    (c)   A significant portion of U.S. dollars are held as deposits abroad.
    (d)   All of the above.

Problems and Applications

The first three exercises demonstrate how monetary policy might work in a hypothetical situation.

Exercise 1

This exercise is similar to a problem in the text, which shows how to understand the accounts for the entire banking system. The focus of this exercise is the reserve requirement.

Suppose the Fed wishes to expand $M1$. Carefully read the assumptions below and then work through the exercise step-by-step to achieve the policy objective. Assume:

- The banks in the system have initially $300 million of transactions account liabilities.
- The banking system initially has no excess reserves.
- The initial reserve requirement is 0.20.
- The banks make loans in the full amount of any excess reserves that they acquire.
- All loans flow back into the banking system as transactions accounts.

The combined balance sheet of the banks in the system is as shown in Table 14.1.

Table 14.1
Balance sheet of banking system when reserve requirement is 0.20 (millions of dollars)

Assets		Liabilities	
Total reserves	$ 60	Transactions accounts	$300
Required $60			
Excess $0			
Securities	100		
Loans	140		
Total	$300	Total	$300

1. Suppose the Fed lowers the reserve requirement to 0.10. How many dollars of excess reserves does this create? $ _____.

2. How large are required reserves now? $ _____.

3. How large are total reserves now? $ _____.

4. What is the additional lending capacity of the banking system due to the change in the reserve requirement from 0.20 to 0.10? $ _____.

5. Reconstruct the balance sheet in Table 14.2 to show the new totals for the accounts affected in the banking system because of the loans generated in question 4 above.

Table 14.2
Balance sheet of banking system when reserve requirement is 0.10
(millions of dollars)

Assets		Liabilities	
Total reserves	$ _____	Transactions accounts	$ _____
Required _____			
Excess _____			
Securities	_____		
Loans	_____		
Total	$ _____	Total	$ _____

6. The money supply (*M1*) has expanded by $ _____.

7. Total reserves have increased by $ _____.

8. Loans have increased by $ _____.

Exercise 2

This exercise shows how the money supply can be changed. The focus of this exercise is open-market policy.

Suppose the banking system faces the balance sheet given in Table 14.3 and suppose further that:

- The banking system initially has no excess reserves.
- The reserve requirement is 0.25.
- The banks make loans in the full amount of any excess reserves that they acquire.
- All loans flow back into the banking system as transactions accounts.

Table 14.3
Balance sheet of banking system (millions of dollars)

Assets		Liabilities	
Total reserves	$ 75	Transactions accounts	$300
Required $75			
Excess $0			
Securities	100		
Loans	125		
Total	$300	Total	$300

1. Suppose the Fed Open Market Committee buys $10 million of securities from the commercial banking system. This action causes excess reserves to increase by $ _____.

2. Complete the balance sheet in Table 14.4 after loans have been made. Assume the banking system expands its loans and transactions accounts by the maximum amount. (Remember: The reserve ratio is 0.25.)

Table 14.4
Balance sheet of banking system after expansion of loans and deposits (millions of dollars)

Assets		Liabilities	
Total reserves	$_____	Transactions accounts	$_____
Required _____			
Excess _____			
Securities	_____		
Loans	_____		
Total	$_____	Total	$_____

3. As a result of the open-market operations, the money supply has expanded by a total of $ _____.

4. Total reserves have increased by $ _____.

5. Loans have increased by $ _____.

Exercise 3

This exercise demonstrates what might happen when the Fed lowers the discount rate.

Suppose the Fed wants to expand the money supply by changing the discount rate. It is faced with the balance sheet of the banking system as shown in Table 14.5. Carefully read the assumptions below and then work through the exercise step-by-step to achieve the policy objective. Assume that:

- The banking system initially has no excess reserves.
- The initial reserve requirement is 0.20.
- The banks in the system respond to each percentage point drop in the discount rate by borrowing $2 million from the Fed.
- The banks make loans in the full amount of any excess reserves that they acquire.
- All loans flow back into the banking system as transactions deposits.

Table 14.5
Balance sheet of banking system (millions of dollars)

Assets		Liabilities	
Total reserves	$ 70	Transactions accounts	$350
Required $70			
Excess $0			
Securities	70		
Loans	210		
Total	$350	Total	$350

1. Suppose the Fed lowers the discount rate by 1 percentage point and that the banking system responds as indicated in the assumption above. As a result of this policy initiative, the banks in the system will now borrow _____ from the Fed, all of which is (excess; required) reserves. On the basis of this lending potential, the banks together can expand their loans by _____ .

2. In Table 14.6, assume the banks have made the additional loans. Complete the balance sheet to show the final effect of the change in the discount rate.

Table 14.6
Final balance sheet of banking system (millions of dollars)

Assets		Liabilities	
Total reserves	$_____	Transactions accounts	$_____
Required _____			
Excess _____			
Securities	_____		
Loans	_____	Borrowed from the Fed	$_____
Total	$_____	Total	$_____

3. The effect of lowering the discount rate is an increase in the money supply of _____ .

Exercise 4

In order to understand how open-market operations work, it is important to understand how the bond market works. The following exercise will demonstrate how the Fed can make bonds more or less attractive for people to buy.

1. Assume you purchase a bond for $1,000. The face value of the bond is $1,000 and the bond pays 10 percent interest annually. What is the dollar amount of the annual interest payment? _____

2. What is the yield on the bond? (*Hint*: Refer to the bond yield formula in the text.) _____

3. Now assume that instead of paying $1,000 for the bond, you buy the same bond for $850. (The annual interest payment stays the same because it is based on the face value of the bond.) Calculate the yield on the bond now. _____

4. When the price of a bond decreases, the yield (increases; decreases) and the bond becomes (more; less) attractive to people. There is a (direct; inverse) relationship between the bond price and the bond yield.

Exercise 5

This exercise provides information from the media about changes in policy by the Federal Reserve.

Reread the article in the text titled "Fed Cuts Deposit-Reserve Requirements" and answer questions 1-5.

1. What central monetary authority is mentioned in the article?_____

2. What phrase in the article indicates the monetary instrument that is being used by the central monetary authority?_____

3. Which instrument is being used?
   (a) Reserve requirement.
   (b) Open-market operations.
   (c) Discount rate.
   (d) Other (Specify: _____)

4. What passage indicates in which direction the monetary instrument(s) is being changed by the central monetary authority to influence the money supply?_____

5. The policy initiative (lowers; raises) the quantity of money relative to what it would have been without the change.

Common Errors

The first statement in each "common error" below is incorrect. Each incorrect statement is followed by a corrected version and an explanation.

1. Bank reserves are required for the safety of depositors' money. WRONG!

   Bank reserves are for control of the money supply. RIGHT!

   Many people have the idea that bank reserves provide for the safety of depositors' money. They don't. The statistics in this chapter indicate that the amount of demand deposits is several times larger than that of reserves. Reserves are for control of the money supply. The FDIC provides for safety of deposits by insuring them. Reserves are not principally for depositors' safety.

2. Deposits of cash are necessary to start the process of lending and deposit creation. WRONG!

   To start the lending process, the banks must acquire reserves from outside the banking system. RIGHT!

   Many find it difficult to understand that for deposit creation to occur, the banking system needs only to acquire reserves from outside the system or be able to stretch existing reserves further. It may acquire reserves by selling a security to the Fed or by borrowing from the Fed. An individual bank, however, may acquire reserves from another bank. So to the extent that it has increased its reserves, another bank's reserves have shrunk. Thus, the system has no more reserves after the transaction than it had before, and so the system's lending capacity is unchanged.

3. When the Fed sells government bonds in open-market operations, it is increasing the money supply. WRONG!

   When the Fed sells government bonds, the buyers pay with reserves, which means there are fewer reserves and less money. RIGHT!

   The key here is to realize that payment of reserves to the Fed means that there are fewer reserves available to the entire banking system. By selling bonds the Fed is tightening monetary policy.

•ANSWERS•

Using Key Terms

Across

5. federal funds rate
6. excess reserves
8. discount rate
10. required reserves
12. portfolio decision

Down

1. money multiplier
2. monetary policy
3. open market operations
4. yield
7. money supply
9. discounting
11. bond

True or False

1. F   Federal Reserve banks hold *reserves* for banks and other types of financial institutions.
2. T
3. T
4. T
5. F   Monetary policy is the use of changes in the money supply and credit conditions to influence the macroeconomy.
6. F   The Fed has to *reduce* the reserve requirement to increase the money supply.
7. T
8. F   The FOMC implements monetary policy by buying and selling bonds.
9. T
10. F   The Fed *buys* securities to increase the lending capacity.

Multiple Choice

1. b	5. c	9. d	13. a	17. a
2. d	6. a	10. a	14. b	18. b
3. c	7. b	11. b	15. d	19. d
4. d	8. a	12. c	16. a	20. d

Problems and Applications

Exercise 1

1. $30 million
2. $30 million
3. $60 million
4. $300 million

5. **Table 14.2 Answer**

Assets		Liabilities	
Total reserves	$ 60	Transactions accounts	$600
Required $60			
Excess $0			
Securities	100		
Loans	440		
Total	$600	Total	$600

6. $300 million
7. Zero
8. $300 million

Exercise 2

1. $10 million

2. **Table 14.4 Answer**

Assets		Liabilities	
Total reserves	$ 85	Transactions accounts	$340
Required $85			
Excess $0			
Securities	90		
Loans	165		
Total	$340	Total	$340

3. $40 million
4. $10 million
5. $40 million

Exercise 3

1. $2 million; excess; $10 million

2. **Table 14.6 Answer**

Assets		Liabilities	
Total reserves	$ 72	Transactions accounts	$360
Required $72			
Excess $0			
Securities	70		
Loans	220	Borrowed from the Fed	$ 2
Total	$362	Total	$362

3. $10 million

Exercise 4

1. $100
2. 10 percent
3. 11.76 percent
4. Increase; more; inverse

Exercise 5

1. The Federal Reserve Board
2. The title: "Deposit-Reserve Requirements" or "The Fed cut ... the percentage of deposits that banks are required to hold as reserves."
3. a
4. "The Fed *cut* to 10% from 12% the percentage of checking-account deposits that banks are required to hold as reserves."
5. Raises

CHAPTER 15

Monetary Policy

Quick Review

- By controlling the banks' ability to make loans ("create money"), the Federal Reserve System controls the money supply. The goal of monetary policy is to provide the appropriate level of aggregate demand in the economy to achieve the output, employment, and price level goals.

- The demand for money includes the transactions demand, the precautionary demand, and the speculative demand. The supply of money and demand for money together determine the equilibrium interest rate, or the price of money.

- From a Keynesian perspective, an increase in the money supply will drive the interest rate down and stimulate greater investment spending, thus shifting the aggregate demand curve to the right. Monetary restraint works in the opposite direction. A decrease in the money supply causes the interest rate to increase, which causes investment to decrease and aggregate demand to decrease.

- Monetary policy may not be as effective as expected. Will the banks be willing to lend? Will the increase in the money supply force the interest rate down, or will the Keynesian liquidity trap prevent the interest rate from falling? Will low expectations leave the business sector without incentives to increase investment?

- Attempts to apply monetary restraint also may not be as effective as expected. If the money supply is reduced, will optimistic firms and households borrow more in spite of higher interest rates? Finally, since the money market is a global one, if domestic interest rates get too high, will borrowers look abroad?

- Monetarists believe that the link between the money supply and aggregate demand is more direct. They use the equation of exchange ($MV = PQ$) to demonstrate the relationship. Assuming V is constant, any increase in M must be translated into greater spending.

- Some monetarists also believe that Q is constant, creating a vertical aggregate supply curve at the natural rate of unemployment. Thus, an increase in M translates into an increase in P. Monetarists, as a result, advocate steady, predictable changes in the money supply.

- Monetarists note that real interest rates are fairly stable. The real interest rate is equal to the nominal interest rate minus the anticipated inflation rate.

- Monetarists and Keynesians argue that monetary policy can affect nominal interest rates, thus changing the composition of GDP and the distribution of income.

- Monetarists and Keynesians are led to radically different views about the effectiveness of monetary *and* fiscal policy. The Fed has adopted an eclectic approach to policy making and uses several measures of the money supply and interest rates to gauge the state of the economy.

Learning Objectives

After reading Chapter 15 and doing the following exercises, you should:

1. Know the determinants of the transactions, precautionary, and speculative demands for money.
2. Know how the equilibrium interest rate is determined and how changes in the money supply affect it.
3. Understand how changes in the money supply are transmitted to aggregate demand.
4. Understand expansionary and restrictive monetary-policy initiatives and know the constraints on both.
5. Know how the equation of exchange is expressed and the assumptions on which it is based.
6. Understand the relationship between the natural rate of unemployment and the aggregate supply curve.
7. Know the mechanism by which changes in *M* affect GDP in the monetarist model.
8. Understand and be able to calculate the real rate of interest.
9. Be able to contrast Keynesian and monetarist views of how fiscal and monetary policies work.
10. Be able to articulate the effects of monetary policy on the mix of output and the distribution of income.

Using Key Terms

Fill in the puzzle on the opposite page with the appropriate term from the list of Key Terms at the end of the chapter in the text.

Across

2. The Federal Reserve System can use its powers to alter the _____ _____.
4. Money held for future financial opportunities.
8. Equal to the nominal rate of interest minus the inflation rate.
9. The quantities of money people are willing and able to hold at alternative interest rates, *ceteris paribus.*
11. The choice of how and where to hold idle funds.
12. The interest rate that banks charge other banks for borrowed reserves is the _____ _____ rate.
13. A decrease in private-sector borrowing and spending because of an increase in government spending.
15. The number of times per year a dollar is used to purchase final goods and services.
16. Determined by the intersection of the money demand curve and the money supply curve.
17. The total quantity of output demanded at alternative price levels in a given time period, *ceteris paribus.*

Down

1. Money held for everyday purchases.
3. Money held for emergencies.
5. The mathematical formula used by monetarists to explain how monetary policy works.
6. The long-run rate of unemployment determined by structural forces.
7. The use of money and credit controls to influence the macroeconomy.
10. The portion of the money demand curve that is horizontal.
14. The price paid for the use of money.

Puzzle 15.1

True or False: *Circle your choice and explain why any false statements are incorrect.*

T F 1. People who hold idle money balances incur no costs.

T F 2. The downward slope of the money-demand curve indicates that the quantity of money people are willing and able to hold increases as interest rates fall.

T F 3. When the Fed buys securities and causes interest rates to fall, investment spending increases, thereby increasing AD.

T F 4. Monetary policy affects the macro economy by shifting aggregate supply.

T F 5. If the interest rate is in the liquidity-trap range, monetary policy is ineffective.

T F 6. The liquidity trap occurs because the opportunity cost of holding money is low at low interest rates.

T F 7. Monetarists believe that changes in the money supply increase aggregate demand by lowering interest rates.

T F 8. According to the equation of exchange, total spending will rise if the money supply grows and velocity is stable.

T F 9. The assumption of a natural rate of unemployment implies that M is stable in the equation of exchange.

T F 10. Monetarists believe an increase in government spending will lead to the "crowding out" of an equal amount of private spending.

Multiple Choice: *Select the correct answer.*

_____ 1. The opportunity cost of holding money will increase if:
(a) Interest rates rise.
(b) Bond yields fall.
(c) Bond prices rise.
(d) All of the above.

_____ 2. By adding together the speculative, transactions, and precautionary demands for money, one can obtain:
(a) The market demand curve for money.
(b) The Keynesian liquidity trap.
(c) The monetarist demand-for-money curve.
(d) The market supply curve for money.

_____ 3. The intersection of the market demand for money and the market supply of money establishes the:
(a) Equilibrium of supply and demand of investment goods.
(b) Real rate of interest.
(c) Equilibrium rate of interest.
(d) Equilibrium average price level for the economy.

_____ 4. If the supply curve of money is vertical, what should happen to the equilibrium interest rate and equilibrium quantity of money as a result of a recession, *ceteris paribus*?
   (a) Equilibrium interest rate should go up.
   (b) Equilibrium interest rate should go down, but equilibrium quantity would remain unchanged.
   (c) Both equilibrium interest rate and equilibrium quantity should go up.
   (d) Equilibrium interest rate should go down, and equilibrium quantity should go up.

_____ 5. Given an upward-sloping aggregate supply curve, which of the following is most likely if the Fed pursues restrictive monetary policy?
   (a) The equilibrium price level and output will both increase.
   (b) The equilibrium output will decrease and the price level will stay the same.
   (c) The equilibrium price level will decrease and the output will stay the same.
   (d) The equilibrium price level and output will both decrease.

_____ 6. In the Keynesian model, the effectiveness of monetary policy depends on which of the following?
   (a) The Fed's ability to influence the money supply.
   (b) The sensitivity of interest rates to changes in the money supply.
   (c) The sensitivity of investment spending to changes in interest rates.
   (d) All of the above.

_____ 7. Which of the following is a series of events used by Keynesians to describe the steps by which expansionary monetary policy works in the short run?
   (a) Increase in *M*, decrease in interest rate, increase in *I*.
   (b) Decrease in interest rate, increase in *M*, increase in *I*.
   (c) Increase in *M*, decrease in *I*, decrease in interest rate.
   (d) Increase in *M*, increase in interest rate, increase in *I*.

_____ 8. Monetary policy will be most effective if:
   (a) The demand curve for money is horizontal and the investment demand curve is downward sloping.
   (b) The demand curve for money is downward sloping but the investment demand curve is vertical.
   (c) The demand curve for money and the investment demand curve are downward sloping, but neither is vertical nor horizontal.
   (d) The demand curve for money and the investment demand curve are vertical or both curves are horizontal.

_____ 9. Which of the following is likely to occur if the Fed lowers the minimum reserve ratio?
   (a) Equilibrium interest rate and the rate of investment should both go up.
   (b) Equilibrium interest rate should go up, and the rate of investment should go down.
   (c) Equilibrium interest rate should go down, and the rate of investment should go up.
   (d) Equilibrium interest rate and the rate of investment should both go down.

_____ 10. Which of the following Fed actions is most likely to increase the aggregate demand curve?
   (a) Buying bonds in the open market.
   (b) Raising the discount rate.
   (c) Raising the reserve requirement.
   (d) Raising the federal funds rate.

_____ 11. Monetary stimulus will fail if:
   (a) The investment demand curve is perfectly inelastic.
   (b) Expectations of a boom cause the investment demand curve to shift to the right, offsetting interest-rate effects that would stimulate the economy.
   (c) The investment demand curve is elastic.
   (d) All of the above.

_____ 12. When the money market is in equilibrium in the liquidity trap:
   (a) The demand for money is perfectly insensitive to interest rates.
   (b) An increase in the money supply does not affect interest rates.
   (c) There is no speculative demand for money.
   (d) Investment spending falls to zero.

_____ 13. Which of the following acts as a constraint on expansionary monetary policy?
   (a) The responsiveness of interest rates to a change in the money supply.
   (b) Low business expectations.
   (c) The reluctance of banks to lend money.
   (d) All of the above.

_____ 14. Which of the following positions can be attributed to the monetarists?
   (a) "Only money matters."
   (b) "Velocity is constant."
   (c) "Government expenditures crowd out private expenditures."
   (d) All of the above are monetarist positions.

_____ 15. Which of the following is a monetarist assumption, which plays a key role in explaining the monetarist view that fiscal policy is ineffective?
   (a) The liquidity trap.
   (b) Crowding out.
   (c) Unstable velocity of money.
   (d) A vertical aggregate demand curve.

_____ 16. Given monetarist assumptions about the shape of the aggregate supply curve, which of the following would most likely result if the Fed pursues expansionary monetary policy?
   (a) The equilibrium price level and output would both increase.
   (b) The equilibrium price level and output would both decrease.
   (c) The equilibrium price level would increase but output would stay the same.
   (d) The equilibrium output would increase but the price level would stay the same.

_____ 17. Monetarists argue that the velocity of money:
   (a) Is constant.
   (b) Is reduced when fiscal policy puts idle money balances to work.
   (c) Increases when there is a recession because people accumulate money balances.
   (d) Increases as much as total spending falls so that MV remains constant.

_____ 18. The existence of a natural rate of unemployment implies that in the long run:
   (a) V in the equation of exchange is actually very unstable.
   (b) Monetary policy affects only the rate of inflation.
   (c) Q in the equation of exchange varies in proportion to M.
   (d) The rate of unemployment can be permanently reduced by more expansionary monetary and fiscal policies.

_____ 19. An increase in the money supply will:
   (a) Always cause inflation.
   (b) Never causes inflation.
   (c) Cause inflation only if aggregate supply is horizontal.
   (d) Cause inflation if aggregate supply is upward sloping or vertical.

_____ 20. Which of the following provides the correct policy targets of the three groups mentioned?
   (a)   Keynesians target the money supply, monetarists target interest rates, and the Fed targets a mix of the two.
   (b)   Keynesians target interest rates, monetarists target steady money growth, and the Fed targets a mix of the two.
   (c)   The Fed targets the money supply, monetarists target interest rates, and Keynesians target a mix of the two.
   (d)   The Fed targets interest rates, monetarists target steady money growth, and Keynesians target a mix of the two.

Problems and Applications
Exercise 1

This exercise focuses on the relationship between the money supply, interest rates, and aggregate demand.

Use Figure 15.1 to answer questions 1-7.

Figure 15.1

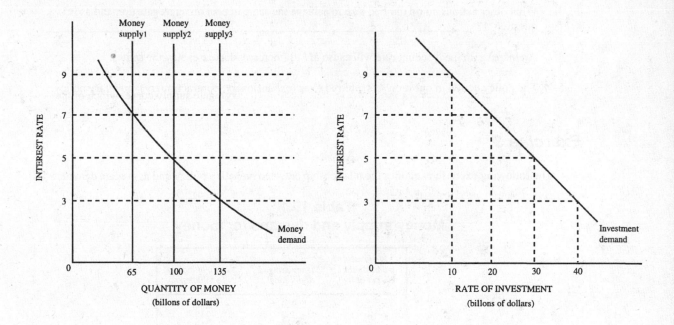

1. Assume the Federal Reserve sets the quantity of money at Money supply 2. The equilibrium interest rate is _____ percent and the equilibrium quantity of money is _____.

2. At the equilibrium interest rate in question 1 the rate of investment is equal to _____.

3. Now, suppose the Federal Reserve increases the money supply by $35 billion. The new equilibrium interest rate is _____ percent.

4. As a result of the (increase; decrease) in the interest rate, the rate of investment will (increase; decrease) to _____.

5. This (increase; decrease) in the rate of investment will cause aggregate _____ to (increase; decrease) or shift to the _____.

6. Now assume the Federal Reserve decides to change the money supply to Money supply 1. As a result of this change the equilibrium interest rate will (rise; fall), which will cause the rate of investment to (rise; fall).

7. Based on question 6, the change in the rate of investment will cause the level of aggregate demand to (rise; fall).

Exercise 2

This exercise examines what might happen if the Federal Reserve decided to change the discount rate.

1. A decrease in the discount rate will cause *M1* to (increase; decrease; stay the same).

2. This change in the money supply will cause aggregate (demand; supply) to shift to the (left; right).

3. What other actions could the Fed take to achieve the same impact on aggregate demand as in question 1? _____

4. An increase in the discount rate will cause *M1* to (increase; decrease; stay the same).

5. The policy action in question 4 is referred to as (expansionary; contractionary) monetary policy.

Exercise 3

The following exercise examines the relationship between monetary policy and aggregate demand.

Table 15.1
Money supply and demand for money

Nominal interest rate (% per year)	Money demand ($ billions)	Supply of money ($ billions)
2	320	240
4	280	240
6	240	240
8	200	240

On the basis of Table 15.1, answer the indicated questions. Assume for every 1 percentage point decline in the interest rate, aggregate spending shifts upward by $20 billion.

1. In Table 15.1, the equilibrium interest rate is _____ percent per year.

2. If the interest rate in Table 15.1 is 8 percent, then there is a (surplus; shortage) of money, and the interest rate will (rise; fall; remain constant).

3. Assume the anticipated inflation rate is 4 percent. At the equilibrium nominal interest rate in Table 15.1, the real interest rate will be _____ percent per year.

4. If the real rate of interest is negative then, *ceteris paribus*:
   (a) The nominal interest rate is negative.
   (b) Monetary policy is tight.
   (c) The inflation rate is negative.
   (d) It pays to borrow.

5. Suppose the Fed buys $8 billion worth of securities on the open market and that the reserve requirement is 0.2. If the money supply expands to its maximum potential, the new equilibrium rate of interest in Table 15.1 would be, *ceteris paribus*, _____ percent per year.

6. The change in the equilibrium interest rate in Table 15.1 as a result of the Fed's purchase of $8 billion worth of securities would be _____ percentage points.

7. If every 1 percentage point decline in the interest rate causes investment to increase by $20 billion the change in the interest rate in question 6 would cause investment to (increase; decrease) by _____ .

Exercise 4

This exercise will help you check your understanding of how monetary and fiscal policy affect the economy.

1. Consider each of the statements in Table 15.2. Decide whether you think each was made by a monetarist or a Keynesian, and place a check in the appropriate column. If you have difficulty, reread Tables 15.2 and 15.3 in the text.

Table 15.2
Comparing Keynesian and Monetarist views on monetary policy

	Monetarist	Keynesian
1. An increase in government spending will raise total spending.	_____	_____
2. A reduction in taxes will leave real output unaffected.	_____	_____
3. Real interest rates are determined by real growth.	_____	_____
4. Prices may be affected by increases in G or reductions in T.	_____	_____
5. Changes in the money supply definitely affect both the price level and aggregate spending.	_____	_____
6. Changes in M definitely affect changes in the normal interest rate.	_____	_____
7. Changes in M may cause changes in V and Q.	_____	_____
8. Changes in M definitely cannot lower the unemployment rate.	_____	_____
9. The liquidity trap may prevent the nominal interest rate from falling.	_____	_____
10. Monetary and fiscal policy must be used together to stabilize aggregate demand.	_____	_____

Exercise 5

The media often feature articles about changes in government policies that affect the money supply or about events that change the demand for money. This exercise will use one of the articles in the text to show the kind of information to look for.

Reread the article titled "Deflation Still Haunts the Bank of Japan." Then answer the following questions.

1. Which passage specifically indicates why the Bank of Japan decided to raise the money supply?
   _____

2. An increase in the money supply should cause the aggregate demand curve to _____
   _____

3. How should the price level respond to this change? _____

4. Prior to targeting the money supply, the Bank of Japan had targeted _____.

Common Errors

The first statement in each "common error" below is incorrect. Each incorrect statement is followed by a corrected version and an explanation.

1. When the interest rate goes down, the demand for money increases. WRONG!

   When the interest rate goes down, the quantity of money demanded increases. RIGHT!

   Don't fail to distinguish between a change in demand and a change in quantity demanded. Remember that each demand schedule (speculative, transactions, precautionary) is drawn on the assumption of *ceteris paribus*. Unless there is a change in one of the things held constant (e.g., expectations), there will be no change in demand when the interest rate falls, only a change in quantity demanded.

2. High nominal rates of interest mean high real rates of interest. WRONG!

   High nominal interest rates and high real interest rates do not necessarily coincide. RIGHT!

   High nominal interest rates and high real interest rates will coincide only if the average level of prices is not changing rapidly enough to offset the differential. For example, if the nominal rate is 10 percent and prices are rising at 10 percent, the real rate of interest is zero.

3. Monetary policy is easy to determine and to administer. WRONG!

   Monetary policy is difficult to determine and to administer. RIGHT!

   One could easily get the idea that monetary policy is easy to administer and that the Fed always knows the rate at which the money supply should grow. This is not true. Many variables intervene to make monetary policy difficult to prescribe and implement. Such variables include timing and the duration of a given policy, unanticipated events on the fiscal side, and problems abroad. The Fed's policy makers analyze the data available and do the best they can to achieve a given objective, which often involves compromises. The process is much more difficult than turning a printing press on and off.

•ANSWERS•

Using Key Terms

Across
2. money supply
4. speculative demand for money
8. real rate of interest
9. demand for money
11. portfolio decision
12. federal funds
13. crowding out
15. income velocity of money
16. equilibrium rate of interest
17. aggregate demand

Down
1. transactions demand for money
3. precautionary demand for money
5. equation of exchange
6. natural rate of unemployment
7. monetary policy
10. liquidity trap
14. interest rate

True or False

1. F   Holding money balances incurs an opportunity cost, e.g., giving up interest that could be earned on those balances.
2. T
3. T
4. F   Monetary policy affects the macro economy by shifting aggregate demand.
5. T
6. T
7. F   Monetarists believe that, according to the equation of exchange (MV = PQ), a change in the money supply must alter total spending, regardless of how interest rates change, given the assumption of a constant V.
8. T
9. F   A natural rate of unemployment implies that Q is constant in the equation of exchange.
10. T

Multiple Choice

1. a	5. d	9. c	13. d	17. a
2. a	6. d	10. a	14. d	18. b
3. c	7. a	11. a	15. b	19. d
4. b	8. c	12. b	16. c	20. b

Problems and Applications

Exercise 1

1. 5; $100 billion
2. $30 billion
3. 3
4. Decrease; increase; $40 billion
5. Increase; demand; increase; right
6. Rise; fall
7. Fall

Exercise 2

1. Increase
2. Demand; right
3. An open-market purchase of government securities or a decrease in the reserve requirement
4. Decrease
5. Expansionary

Exercise 3

1. 6
2. Surplus; fall
3. 2
4. d
5. 4
6. -2
7. Increase; $40 billion

Exercise 4

Table 15.1 Answer

	Monetarist	Keynesian
1.		x
2.	x	
3.	x	
4.		x
5.	x	
6.	x	
7.		x
8.	x	
9.		x
10.		x

Exercise 5

1. ". . . to ease the price declines hammering Japanese companies."
2. Increase or shift to the right
3. Increase
4. Interest rates

CHAPTER 16

Supply-Side Policy: Short-Run Options

Quick Review

- The responses of the economy to demand side policies depend on the slope of the aggregate supply (AS) curve. The Monetarist model views the aggregate supply curve as vertical at the natural rate of unemployment, while the simple Keynesian model views aggregate supply as flat until full employment is reached. The consensus view is that aggregate supply is an upward-sloping curve that becomes vertical at full employment.

- If aggregate supply is upward sloping, a shift in aggregate demand (AD) results in a tradeoff between output and price level. This relationship between unemployment and inflation is drawn in the Phillips curve.

- If AS shifts to the left, unemployment and inflation both increase and the Phillips curve shifts to the right. This is known as stagflation.

- Supply-side policy attempts to shift the AS curve to the right. This causes a decrease in unemployment and inflation, both positive outcomes for the economy.

- Supply-side tax cuts are incentive-based and work on the assumption that people and firms will produce more if they get to keep a larger fraction of what they earn. Supply-siders favor tax cuts to provide incentives to encourage saving *and* investment

- Just how much supply will respond to a tax cut is measured by the tax elasticity of supply.

- Human capital incentives are important because they emphasize the quality of the labor force and reduce structural employment barriers, thus helping shift the aggregate supply curve to the right. Worker training, spending on education, and affirmative-action programs have a positive impact on the stock of human capital.

- Deregulation of both product and factor markets has provided a powerful stimulus to aggregate supply because it eliminates barriers to the efficient employment of resources, thus reducing costs at every level of output.

- Agreements like the North American Free Trade Agreement (NAFTA), which eliminated trade barriers between Canada, the United States and Mexico, have the potential to shift aggregate supply to the right by reducing the cost of imported inputs and finished goods.

- Infrastructure development enhances aggregate supply by reducing costs in transportation, communication, and so on. This improves market transactions and increases production possibilities.

Learning Objectives

After reading Chapter 16 and doing the following exercises, you should:

1. Understand why the success of demand-side policies depends on the aggregate-supply response.
2. Understand the nature of the inflation–unemployment tradeoff and the Phillips curve.
3. Understand the supply-side options for improving the inflation–unemployment tradeoff.
4. Understand why marginal tax rates affect work incentives, investment, and saving.
5. Know the significance of the tax elasticity of supply.
6. Be able to describe human capital and its relationship to structural unemployment.
7. Understand why deregulation of factor and product markets influences aggregate supply.
8. Understand that a reduction in trade barriers increases aggregate supply.
9. Know why the development and maintenance of infrastructure is important to aggregate supply.

Using Key Terms

Fill in the puzzle on the opposite page with the appropriate term from the list of Key Terms at the end of the chapter in the text.

Across

4. The amount of output produced by a worker in a given time period.
5. The percentage change in quantity supplied divided by the percentage change in tax rates.
8. The simultaneous occurrence of unemployment and inflation.
10. The total quantity of output producers are willing and able to supply at alternative price levels in a given time period, *ceteris paribus*.
11. Payments such as Social Security, welfare, and unemployment benefits.
12. The transportation, communications, judicial, and other systems that facilitate market exchanges.
13. Business expenditure on new plant and equipment and inventory changes.

Down

1. The skills and knowledge of the workforce.
2. Unemployment because of a mismatch between the skills of the workforce and the requirements of jobs.
3. A lump-sum refund of taxes paid.
6. Disposable income minus consumption.
7. The tax rate imposed on the last dollar of income received.
9. The _____ _____ was developed by a New Zealand economist to summarize the relationship between inflation and unemployment.

Puzzle 16.1

True or False: *Circle your choice and explain why any false statements are incorrect.*

T   F   1.   Below full employment, the simple Keynesian model contends that increased aggregate demand raises output only, not prices (*P*).

T   F   2.   Rightward shifts of the aggregate supply curve decrease both the price level and output.

T   F   3.   Investment in human capital reduces saving and shifts the aggregate supply curve leftward.

T   F   4.   The Phillips curve shows a direct relationship between unemployment and the rate of inflation.

T   F   5.   A basic contention of supply-side economists is that we should decrease regulation of the production process.

T   F   6.   In the consensus view, the aggregate supply curve has a gentle, accelerating upward slope.

T   F   7.   As the marginal tax rate increases, there is more incentive to work because workers want to maintain their "after tax" income level.

T   F   8.   A reduction in tax rates will yield larger tax revenues only if the absolute value of the tax elasticity of supply is greater than 1.0.

T   F   9.   A leftward shift of the aggregate supply curve increases inflationary pressures and reduces employment.

T   F   10.   Discrimination against any group can shift the aggregate supply curve to the left when the best person for a given job is not hired.

Multiple Choice: *Select the correct answer.*

_____   1.   According to the simple Keynesian model, the aggregate supply curve is:
(a)   First horizontal, then upward sloping, and finally vertical.
(b)   Vertical.
(c)   Horizontal until full employment is reached, and then it becomes vertical.
(d)   Upward sloping.

_____   2.   Stagflation is caused by:
(a)   An increase in aggregate demand.
(b)   A decrease in aggregate demand.
(c)   An increase in aggregate supply.
(d)   A decrease in aggregate supply.

_____   3.   Lower unemployment and a lower inflation rate can best be achieved with a:
(a)   Rightward shift of the Phillips curve.
(b)   Rightward shift of the aggregate supply curve.
(c)   Rightward shift of the aggregate demand curve.
(d)   Leftward shift of the aggregate supply curve.

_____ 4. The Phillips curve shows:
  (a) An inverse relationship between the unemployment rate and inflation.
  (b) A direct relationship between the unemployment rate and inflation.
  (c) An inverse relationship between output and the unemployment rate.
  (d) A direct relationship between inflation and output.

_____ 5. What is the slope of the aggregate supply curve according to monetarists?
  (a) Horizontal until full employment is reached, and then vertical.
  (b) Vertical.
  (c) Horizontal at all production levels.
  (d) Upward sloping.

_____ 6. Supply-side policies are designed to achieve:
  (a) A leftward shift in the Phillips curve.
  (b) A rightward shift of the aggregate supply curve.
  (c) Both a lower inflation rate and a lower unemployment rate.
  (d) All of the above.

_____ 7. In contrast to monetarists and Keynesians, the supply-side policies are designed to:
  (a) Shift the Phillips curve leftward.
  (b) Raise inflation and lower unemployment.
  (c) Move the economy down the Phillips curve to a lower inflation rate.
  (d) Move the economy down the supply curve.

_____ 8. Which of the following shifts, _ceteris paribus_, will cause lower rates of both unemployment and inflation?
  (a) An increase in aggregate demand.
  (b) A decrease in aggregate demand.
  (c) An increase in aggregate supply.
  (d) A decrease in aggregate supply.

_____ 9. The impact on the economy of a given shift in aggregate demand depends on the:
  (a) Shape of the aggregate supply curve.
  (b) Response of consumers to a change in spending.
  (c) Position of the aggregate supply curve.
  (d) All of the above.

_____ 10. Declining investment in infrastructure:
  (a) Will lead to greater delays and higher opportunity costs.
  (b) Has characterized the United States since 1960.
  (c) Shifts both aggregate demand and aggregate supply.
  (d) All of the above.

_____ 11. According to supply-side theory, which of the following would cause a rightward shift in the aggregate supply curve?
  (a) Lifting trade restrictions.
  (b) Increasing transfer payments to the unemployed.
  (c) Eliminating government-funded training programs for the structurally unemployed.
  (d) Eliminating job-search assistance.

_____ 12. Which of the following will definitely lead to a larger value on the misery index?
  (a)   A movement along the Phillips curve.
  (b)   An outward shift of the aggregate demand curve.
  (c)   Stagflation.
  (d)   A rightward shift of the money supply curve.

_____ 13. If the marginal tax rates increase, then:
  (a)   The labor supply will increase.
  (b)   Entrepreneurship is discouraged.
  (c)   Investment increases.
  (d)   Savings increases.

_____ 14. The tradeoff between unemployment and inflation is the result of an aggregate supply curve that is:
  (a)   Horizontal.
  (b)   Vertical.
  (c)   Upward sloping.
  (d)   Downward sloping.

_____ 15. Which of the following groups would use a decrease in government regulation to increase the incentive to work and produce?
  (a)   Supply-siders.
  (b)   Monetarists.
  (c)   Keynesians.
  (d)   All of the above.

_____ 16. If the absolute value of the tax elasticity of supply is 0.5, a tax _cut_ of 5 percent would:
  (a)   Increase output by 2.5 percent and decrease tax revenues.
  (b)   Increase output by 10 percent and decrease tax revenues.
  (c)   Increase output by 2.5 percent and increase tax revenues.
  (d)   Decrease output by 2.5 percent and decrease tax revenues.

_____ 17. Which of the following changes in trade policy will increase aggregate supply?
  (a)   Increased tariffs on imported factors of production.
  (b)   The implementation of a quota on finished goods.
  (c)   The relaxation of immigration laws to allow more immigration.
  (d)   All of the above.

_____ 18. The marginal tax rate indicates the:
  (a)   Change in taxes resulting from a change in fiscal policy.
  (b)   Tax rate imposed on total income.
  (c)   Tax rate imposed on taxable income.
  (d)   Tax rate imposed on the last dollar of income.

_____ 19. If a new tax policy raises the tax rate 2% but causes the quantity supplied to fall by 10%, the absolute value of the tax elasticity of supply is:
  (a)   0.5.
  (b)   2.
  (c)   5.
  (d)   10.

_____ 20.   If the government reduces the regulations that impact businesses, supply-side economists believe
            unemployment will:
            (a)   Increase and the price level will decrease.
            (b)   Decrease and the price level will decrease.
            (c)   Increase and the price level will increase.
            (d)   Decrease and the price level will increase.

Problems and Applications

Exercise 1

This exercise will focus on how aggregate supply and demand changes affect the equilibrium output and price index.

The aggregate demand curve and aggregate supply curve for all of the goods in an economy are presented in Figure 16.1. The economy is assumed to be on aggregate demand curve *B* in the current fiscal year.

Figure 16.1
Aggregate supply and demand curves

QUANTITY
(billions of units per year)

1.   Four aggregate demand curves (*A*, *B*, *C*, and *D*) are shown in Figure 16.1, corresponding to four
     alternative government policies for the upcoming fiscal year.

     For the following government policy initiatives, choose the aggregate demand curve in Figure 16.1
     that best portrays the expected impact of each policy. Place the letter of your choice in the blank
     provided. Each letter can be used more than once, and some blanks can have more than one letter.

     a. _____   Money supply is expanded, taxes are cut, government increases its expenditures.
     b. _____   Government does nothing.
     c. _____   Government decides to balance the budget by reducing government spending and raising
                taxes.
     d. _____   Government increases expenditures and cuts taxes.

2.   Indicate the equilibrium price index and output for each policy in Table 16.1.

Table 16.1
Equilibrium prices for four government policies

Aggregate demand curve	A	B	C	D
Equilibrium price index	_____	_____	_____	_____
Equilibrium output	_____	_____	_____	_____

3. Place an "X" in the appropriate column in Table 16.2 to indicate the aggregate demand curve that is most likely to result in each of the outcomes listed. More than one answer per outcome is possible.

Table 16.2
Macroeconomic outcomes

(Place an "X")	Aggregate demand curve			
	A	B	C	D
Depression	___	___	___	___
Deflation	___	___	___	___
Highest unemployment	___	___	___	___
Recession	___	___	___	___
Zero inflation	___	___	___	___
Full employment	___	___	___	___
Price stability	___	___	___	___
Maximum output	___	___	___	___
Highest inflation	___	___	___	___

4. Suppose aggregate demand shifts to the left. Determine the change to the equilibrium price level and output level (increase or decrease) for each of the aggregate supply curves in Table 16.3.

Table 16.3

Aggregate supply curve	Change in price level	Change in output level
upward sloping	_____	_____
horizontal	_____	_____
vertical	_____	_____

Exercise 2

1. Suppose the price index is currently 1.2 as shown by demand curve B in Figure 16.1. Compute the inflation rate under each of the four policies, assuming the supply curve remains the same. The formula is:

$$\frac{\text{equilibrium price index} - 1.2}{1.2} \times 100\%$$

Enter your answers for each policy in the appropriate blank of column 1 in Table 16.4.

Table 16.4 Inflation rates, equilibrium output, and unemployment rates under four government policies

Aggregate demand curve	(1) Equilibrium price change	(2) Equilibrium output (billions of units per year)	(3) Unemployment rate
A	_____%	_____	_____%
B	_____	_____	_____
C	_____	_____	_____
D	_____	_____	_____

2. In column 2 of Table 16.4, indicate the equilibrium output associated with each of the policies. Use Figure 16.1 to find this information.

3. Which of the following best represents the U.S. unemployment rate?
   (a) The number of people divided by the U.S. labor force.
   (b) The number of people employed divided by the U.S. population.
   (c) The number of people counted as unemployed divided by the U.S. labor force.
   (d) The number of people unemployed divided by the U.S. population.

4. Table 16.5 shows hypothetical data for the U.S. population, the labor force, the number of people who are employed, and the number of people who are unemployed at each production rate for the economy. Compute the unemployment rate at each production rate in the table.

Table 16.5 Computation of the unemployment rate

Production rate (billions of units per year)	2	3	4
U.S. population (millions)	200	200	200
Labor force (millions)	100	100	100
Number of people unemployed (millions)	15	8	5
Number of people employed (millions)	85	92	95
Unemployment rate (percent)	_____	_____	_____

5. Using the information in Table 16.5, complete column 3 in Table 16.4, which shows the unemployment rate corresponding to each government policy.

6. The government's dilemma is:
   (a) That it cannot reach an unemployment level of 5 percent without experiencing inflation of at least 8 percent.
   (b) That it cannot reach stable prices (0 percent increase) without experiencing an unemployment rate of 8 percent or more.
   (c) That when it makes gains in holding inflation below 8 percent, unemployment increases.
   (d) Expressed by all of the above statements.

219

7. Which of the four aggregate demand curves from Figure 16.1 places the economy closest to full-employment output and moderate inflation?
   (a) Aggregate demand curve A.
   (b) Aggregate demand curve B.
   (c) Aggregate demand curve C.
   (d) Aggregate demand curve D.

Exercise 3

Suppose corporate taxes are reduced to encourage productivity, and as a result, firms in the economy supply $1 trillion more in output at every price level. As a result, the average price level decreases by $50 at every level of real GDP.

Figure 16.2

REAL GROSS DOMESTIC PRODUCT
(trillions of dollars per year)

1. Draw the new aggregate demand curve (label it D_2) or aggregate supply curve (label it S_2) in Figure 16.2.

2. What is the new equilibrium price level? _____

3. What is the new equilibrium output level? _____

4. Which type of economic policy is this tax change most consistent with? _____

5. The shift that occurred in Figure 16.2 (above) should result in:
   (a) Stagflation (inflation and a higher unemployment rate).
   (b) Inflation and a lower unemployment rate.
   (c) Deflation and a higher unemployment rate.
   (d) A lower price level and lower unemployment rate.

220

Exercise 4

Suppose taxpayers are required to pay a base tax of $400 plus 20 percent on any income over $1,000.

1. Compute the amount of taxes to be paid at the income levels in Table 16.6 by filling in columns 2, 3, and 4.

Table 16.6
Tax calculations

(1)	(2)	(3)	(4)	(5)	(6)
		Tax on income	Total	Total tax after change	
Income	Base tax +	over $1,000 =	tax		In marginal
($ per year)	($ per year)	($ per year)	($/year)	In base tax	tax rate
$ 5,000	_____	_____	_____	_____	_____
$10,000	_____	_____	_____	_____	_____
$15,000	_____	_____	_____	_____	_____

2. Suppose further that the taxing authority wishes to raise taxes by $500 for people with incomes of $10,000. If the marginal tax rates remain unchanged, what will the new base tax have to be? _____

3. In column 5 of Table 16.6, compute the resulting taxes at each income level with the new base tax.

4. If the base tax of $400 is to remain unchanged, what will the *marginal tax rate* have to be if $500 is to be added to the tax paid by people with incomes of $10,000? _____

5. Use the new marginal tax rate to complete column 6.

6. If taxes are to be increased (columns 5 and 6), a change in the base is:
   (a) More progressive and helpful to work incentives than raising taxes by changing the marginal tax rate.
   (b) More progressive and harmful to work incentives than raising taxes by changing the marginal tax rate.
   (c) More regressive and helpful to work incentives than raising taxes by changing the marginal tax rate.
   (d) More regressive and harmful to work incentives than raising taxes by changing the marginal tax rate.

Common Errors

The first statement in each "common error" below is incorrect. Each incorrect statement is followed by a corrected version and an explanation.

1. Labor productivity increases when more is produced per dollar of wages. WRONG!

   Labor productivity increases when more units of product are produced per unit of labor. RIGHT!

   Productivity changes are not directly related to wage levels. Wage levels reflect a large number of influences embodied in the demand and supply curves for labor. Productivity, however, is a physical measure of the relation between units of product and the amount of labor needed to produce them.

2. The Phillips curve is simply a demand curve. WRONG!

Although the Phillips curve is related to supply and demand curves, it is not the same as either a demand or a supply curve. RIGHT!

Table 16.7 shows some of the major differences separating Phillips curves, market demand curves, and aggregate demand curves. The axes of the three curves are very different.

Table 16.7
Characteristics of three types of demand curve

| Type of curve | Sources of differences | | |
	x-axis	y-axis	Market
Phillips curve	Unemployment	Inflation	Aggregate labor market
Market demand curve	Quantity per time period	Price	Single market
Aggregate demand curve	Quantity per time period	Price index	Aggregate product market

3. We can't have full employment with price stability. WRONG!

Full employment with price stability is possible, although it may be difficult to achieve. RIGHT!

Look at the definition of full employment again. It is the lowest rate of unemployment with price stability. Although we may be able to increase production above full employment, it will cause inflation.

•ANSWERS•

Using Key Terms

Across
4. labor productivity
5. tax elasticity of supply
8. stagflation
10. aggregate supply
11. transfer payments
12. infrastructure
13. investment

Down

1. human capital
2. structural unemployment
3. tax rebate
6. saving
7. marginal tax rate
9. Phillips curve

True or False

1. T
2. F   Increases in AS decrease the price level but increase output.
3. F   Investment in human capital can shift AS rightward.
4. F   The Phillips curve indicates an inverse relationship between unemployment and inflation.
5. T
6. T
7. F   There is less incentive to work when the additional income earned is taxed at a higher rate.
8. T
9. T
10. T

Multiple Choice

1.	c	5.	b	9.	d	13.	b	17.	c
2.	d	6.	d	10.	d	14.	c	18.	d
3.	b	7.	a	11.	a	15.	a	19.	c
4.	a	8.	c	12.	c	16.	a	20.	b

Problems and Applications

Exercise 1

1.   a. C or D   b. B   c. A   d. C or D

2. **Table 16.1 Answer**

Aggregate demand curve	A	B	C	D
Equilibrium price index	1.1	1.2	1.3	1.8
Equilibrium output	2.0	3.0	4.0	4.0

223

3. **Table 16.2 Answer**

	Aggregate demand curve			
(Place an "x")	A	B	C	D
Depression	_X_	___	___	___
Deflation	_X_	___	___	___
Highest unemployment	_X_	___	___	___
Recession	___	_X_	___	___
Zero inflation	___	_X_	___	___
Full employment	___	___	_X_	___
Price stability	___	_X_	___	___
Maximum output	___	___	_X_	_X_
Highest inflation	___	___	___	_X_

4. **Table 16.3 Answer (millions of dollars)**

Aggregate supply curve	Change in price level	Change in output level
upward sloping	decrease	decrease
horizontal	no change	decrease
vertical	decrease	no change

Exercise 2

1. See Table 16.4 answer, column 1.

Table 16.4 Answer

Aggregate demand curve	(1) Equilibrium price change	(2) Equilibrium output (billions of units per year)	(3) Unemployment rate
A	– 8.3%	2.0	15%
B	0.0	3.0	8
C	8.3	4.0	5
D	50.0	4.0	5

2. See Table 16.4 answer, column 2.
3. c

4. **Table 16.5 Answer**

Production rate (billions of units per year)	2	3	4
Unemployment rate (percent)	15	8	5

5. See Table 16.4 answer, column 3.

6. d
7. c

Exercise 3

1. See Figure 16.2 Answer, S_2.

Figure 16.2 Answer

2. $100
3. $2 trillion
4. Supply-side policy
5. d

Exercise 4

1. See Table 16.6 Answer, columns 2-4.

Table 16.6 Answer

(1)	(2)	(3)		(4)	(5)	(6)
		Tax on income		Total	Total tax after change	
Income	Base tax +	over $1,000	=	tax		In marginal
($ per year)	($ per year)	($ per year)		($/year)	In base tax	tax rate
$ 5,000	$400	$ 800 (= $ 4,000x0.2)		$1,200	$1,700	$1,424
$10,000	$400	1,800 (= 9,000x0.2)		2,200	2,700	2,704
$15,000	$400	2,800 (= 14,000x0.2)		3,200	3,700	3,984

2. $900 (= $400 + $500)
3. See Table 16.6 Answer column 5.
4. 25.6 percent; This is found by solving the following equation, which indicates people with $10,000 in income have a tax of $2,700 (= $2,200 + $500):

$$\$2,700 = \$400 + (\$10,000 - \$1,000)X$$
$$\$2,300 = \$9,000X$$
$$X = 25.6 \text{ percent}$$

5. See Table 16.6 Answer column 6.
6. c

CHAPTER 17

Growth and Productivity: Long-Run Possibilities

Quick Review

- Economic growth refers to increases in real GDP. Growth is desired by virtually every society because it provides for possible improvements in the standard of living.

- In the short run, economic growth can be achieved by increased capacity utilization, represented by a movement toward the production-possibilities curve.

- In the long run, growth requires an increase in capacity itself, represented by a rightward shift of the production-possibilities curve. This results in a rightward shift in the long-run aggregate supply curve as well.

- GDP per capita is a basic measure of living standards. GDP per worker is a measure of productivity. Increases in productivity, rather than increases in the quantity of resources available, have been the primary source of past U.S. economic growth.

- The sources of productivity gains include improved labor skills, increased investment and the resulting increase in the nation's capital stock, technological advances, and improved management skills and techniques.

- Government policies play a role in fostering economic growth. Policies that encourage growth include education and training, immigration, and programs that promote investment and saving. All of these can lead to increases in both the quality and quantity of resources available.

- Macroeconomic policies impact the long-run aggregate supply curve. Budget deficits may reduce the level of economic growth through "crowding out." This occurs when increased government spending, financed by borrowing, causes a reduction in the level of private investment. Budget surpluses can increase economic growth and cause "crowding in."

- Political and economic stability and economic freedom also contribute to economic growth.

- Continued economic growth is desirable as long as it brings a higher standard of living for a country and an increased ability to produce and consume goods and services that society desires.

Learning Objectives

After reading Chapter 17 and doing the following exercises, you should:

1. Know the difference between economic growth in the short run versus the long run.
2. Know the difference between GDP per capita and GDP per worker.
3. Understand the sources of productivity growth.
4. Understand how government policy can promote economic growth.
5. Know that economic freedom and stability can foster growth.
6. Understand the nature of environmental constraints that can limit growth.
7. Recognize what society can do to reduce the external costs imposed by economic growth.
8. Understand how the market mechanism may automatically generate solutions to resource exhaustion and constraints on growth.

Using Key Terms

Fill in the puzzle on the opposite page with the appropriate term from the list of Key Terms at the end of the chapter in the text.

Across

2. The proportion of the adult population that is employed.
5. According to the text, Malthus believed food supplies would increase in this manner.
9. Output per unit of input.
12. An increase in private-sector borrowing and spending because of a decrease in government borrowing.
13. All persons over the age of sixteen who are working for pay or are looking for work.
14. An increase in quantity by a constant proportion each year.
15. Gross investment minus depreciation.

Down

1. The percentage change in real output from one period to another.
3. The alternative combinations of final goods and services that can be produced in a given time period with all available resources and technology.
4. The time period used for comparative analysis.
6. A decrease in private-sector borrowing and investment because of increased government borrowing.
7. The knowledge and skills possessed by the labor force.
8. Total GDP divided by total population.
10. An increase in output or real GDP.
11. The actual quantity of goods and services produced, valued in constant prices.

True or False: *Circle your choice and explain why any false statements are incorrect.*

T F 1. World economic growth has virtually eliminated poverty in most of the world.

T F 2. Once an economy is on its production-possibilities curve, further increases in output require an expansion of productive capacity.

T F 3. An increase in nominal GDP always means there has been an outward shift in the production-possibilities curve.

T F 4. Growth in real GDP per capita is achieved when population grows more rapidly than output.

T F 5. A primary determinant of labor productivity is the rate of capital investment.

T F 6. Malthus believed that population grew arithmetically and that the means of subsistence grew geometrically.

T F 7. Economic growth is an exponential process because gains made in one year accumulate in future years.

T F 8. Increases in the size of the labor force and capital stock have been less important than productivity advances in causing U.S. real GDP to grow.

T F 9. Over time, research and development are credited with the greatest contributions to economic growth in the U.S.

T F 10. Overall, immigration has had a negative impact on the U.S. economy over time.

Multiple Choice: *Select the correct answer.*

_____ 1. A major difference between short-run and long-run economic growth is that short-run growth:
(a) Moves the economy to the production-possibilities curve, while long-run growth shifts the curve outward.
(b) Increases capacity utilization, while long-run economic growth increases capacity.
(c) Moves the economy up the aggregate supply curve, while long-run economic growth shifts the aggregate supply curve outward.
(d) All of the above.

_____ 2. Which of the following would likely contribute to an improvement in the productivity of labor?
(a) Greater expenditures on training and education.
(b) Policies to stimulate the saving and investment process.
(c) Greater expenditures on research and development.
(d) All of the above.

_____ 3. In order to produce a combination of goods and services outside the production possibilities curve, an economy:
(a) Would have to use more of its existing resources.
(b) Would have to raise the prices of goods and services so that firms would produce more.
(c) Would have to find more resources or develop new technology.
(d) Will never be able to produce a combination of goods and services outside its current production possibilities curve.

4. A sustained net growth in real output of 4 percent per year will cause real output to double in about:
   (a) 4 years.
   (b) 18 years.
   (c) 10 years.
   (d) 25 years.

5. The best measure of productivity could be calculated with data on:
   (a) Real GDP and hours worked by the labor force.
   (b) Real GDP and the population of the United States.
   (c) Nominal GDP and the number of people in the U.S. labor force.
   (d) Nominal GDP and the population of the United States.

6. A major goal of short-run macroeconomic policy is to:
   (a) Shift the production-possibilities curve outward.
   (b) Move toward the production-possibilities curve.
   (c) Shift the aggregate supply curve leftward.
   (d) Shift the aggregate supply curve rightward.

7. Which of the following is the best measure of the standard of living?
   (a) The ratio of current GDP to GDP in the base period.
   (b) Investment as a percentage of GDP.
   (c) GDP per capita.
   (d) GDP per worker.

8. Assume U.S. real GDP in 1929 was $942 billion with a population of 122 million people and U.S. real GDP in 1930 was $858 billion with 123 million people. The real GDP per capita for this time period:
   (a) Increased.
   (b) Increased and then decreased.
   (c) Remained unchanged.
   (d) Decreased.

9. Which of the following measures the growth rate of an economy?
   (a) The ratio of current real GDP to real GDP in the base period.
   (b) Investment as a percentage of GDP.
   (c) Real GDP divided by nominal GDP.
   (d) GDP per worker.

10. Which of the following measures productivity?
    (a) The ratio of current GDP to GDP in the base period.
    (b) Percentage increase in GDP.
    (c) GDP per capita.
    (d) GDP per worker.

11. When the production-possibilities curve shifts outward, we can also be sure that:
    (a) Aggregate supply has increased.
    (b) Output has increased.
    (c) GDP per capita has increased.
    (d) All of the above occur when the production possibilities curve shifts outward.

12. The exponential process:
    (a) Explains why increases in GDP in one year accumulate in future years.
    (b) Is a measure of productivity.
    (c) Is included in an arithmetic progression.
    (d) All of the above.

_____ 13. Which of the following policy levers definitely enhances productivity?
    (a) Higher taxes.
    (b) More government regulation.
    (c) Development of human capital.
    (d) A higher labor to capital ratio.

_____ 14. In recent decades, a primary source of growth in U.S. output has been:
    (a) Rapid growth of the money supply.
    (b) Increased capacity utilization.
    (c) Increased number of workers.
    (d) Increased productivity per worker.

_____ 15. Sources of productivity growth include:
    (a) Higher skills.
    (b) More capital.
    (c) Improved management.
    (d) All of the above.

_____ 16. Which of the following could impede productivity improvements?
    (a) Crowding out.
    (b) Technological advances.
    (c) Higher ratios of capital to labor.
    (d) All of the above.

_____ 17. Which of the following situations will cause the greatest increase in labor productivity?
    (a) An increase in the labor force and capital remains constant.
    (b) An increase in both the labor force and capital, but the labor force increases more rapidly.
    (c) An increase in both the labor force and capital, but the capital increases more rapidly.
    (d) A decrease in capital and the labor force remains constant.

_____ 18. Current U.S. problems with congested highways, air quality and global warming are primarily the result of:
    (a) Too many goods and services.
    (b) The mix of output produced.
    (c) Too much government regulation.
    (d) Excessively high levels of GDP per capita.

_____ 19. Growth in GDP per capita is attained only when:
    (a) There is growth in population.
    (b) There is growth in output.
    (c) The growth of output exceeds population growth.
    (d) Population is held constant.

_____ 20. From the long-run perspective of economic growth, household saving:
    (a) Threatens growth because of the paradox of thrift.
    (b) Is the basic source of investment financing in the U.S.
    (c) Is a leakage that constrains economic growth.
    (d) Shifts the institutional production possibilities curve inward.

Problems and Applications

Exercise 1

This exercise focuses on the difference in short-run growth versus long-run growth.

Refer to Figure 17.1 to answer questions 1-4.

Figure 17.1

1. Assume the economy is producing at point E. A movement to point B represents an increase in (short-run; long-run) growth.

2. The movement from point E to point B results in increased output because of (increased use of existing capacity; increased capacity).

3. Assume the economy is now producing at point B. A movement to point D represents an increase in (short-run; long-run) growth.

4. The movement from point B to point D results in increased output because of (increased use of existing capacity; increased capacity). This type of growth implies a (leftward; rightward) shift in the _____ _____ curve.

Exercise 2

The following exercise shows how gross domestic product can be used to indicate the standard of living and the rate of economic growth in an economy.

1. Using the data provided complete Table 17.1.

Table 17.1

	1990	1998	Percentage change
(1) U.S. real GDP (billions of dollars)	$6707.9	$8515.7	_____
(2) U.S. population (thousands)	249,973	270,509	_____
(3) U.S. per capita GDP (dollars per person)	$26,834	$31,480	_____
(4) World population (thousands)	5,329,000	5,927,000	_____

2. Using the information in Table 17.1, the U.S. standard of living (increased; decreased) from 1990 to 1998.

3. Why must the world economic growth be greater than the U.S. economic growth to maintain the same standard of living? _____

   _____

4. From 1990 to 1998, what was the average annual growth rate for real GDP in the U.S? _____

5. If the growth rate calculated in question 4 was the actual growth rate each year (not the average), how long should it take for real GDP to double according to Table 17.1 in the text? _____

Exercise 3

The focus of this exercise is on the value of investment in spurring economic growth. This exercise will help you with a problem at the end of the chapter.

Reread the *World View* article titled "Comparative Investment and Growth." Suppose two hypothetical economies are currently characterized by the following data:

	Country A	Country B
GDP	$10 trillion	$5 trillion
Consumption	4 trillion	3 trillion
Investment	4 trillion	1 trillion
Government spending	2 trillion	1 trillion

1. What is the investment rate ($I \div$ GDP) for Country A? _____

2. What is the investment rate ($I \div$ GDP) for Country B? _____

3. Based on the information above, which country is likely to have the higher growth rate of GDP? _____ Why? _____

234

4. According to the article in the text, which two countries had the highest investment rate?
   _____

5. Which two countries had the highest growth rate for GDP? _____

Common Errors

The first statement in each "common error" below is incorrect. Each incorrect statement is followed by a corrected version and an explanation.

1. Zero economic growth treats everyone equally. WRONG!

   Zero economic growth treats groups unequally. RIGHT!

   Zero economic growth in its simplest dimensions means that GDP would not grow from year to year. Income per capita therefore could not grow unless population declined. Yet we know that U.S. population is growing, although slowly, as a result of new births and increased longevity, and more recently as a result of immigration. If GDP were not to grow, the only way for those at the bottom of the income distribution to have more would be for someone at the top to take less.

2. As long as output increases as rapidly as the population, the standard of living will improve. WRONG!

   As long as output increases more rapidly than the population, the standard of living will improve. RIGHT!

   Standard of living is typically measured using real GDP per capita. In order for the standard of living to increase, real GDP must grow faster than the population. If they both grow at the same rate, the standard of living will remain constant.

3. There is no way to hold off the doomsday prophecy. WRONG!

   Much has been done in the last decade to avoid the cataclysmic predictions of the doomsday prophets. RIGHT!

   Much has been done by federal, state, and local governments to overcome some of the problems that seemed most acute. The air is cleaner in many areas and so is the water. Higher oil prices spur research into new sources of power and new ways to conserve energy. All of this activity helps us meet the doomsday challenge each time it arises.

Using Key Terms

Across

2. employment rate
5. arithmetic growth
9. productivity
12. crowding in
13. labor force
14. geometric growth
15. net investment

Down

1. growth rate
3. production possibilities
4. base period
6. crowding out
7. human capital
8. GDP per capita
10. economic growth
11. real GDP

True or False

1. F   Over half of the world's population lives in poverty.
2. T
3. F   An increase in *nominal* GDP does not necessarily mean that production has increased.
4. F   Growth in real GDP per capita is achieved when output grows more rapidly than population.
5. T
6. F   Malthus believed that population grew geometrically but the means of subsistence grew only arithmetically.
7. T
8. T
9. T
10. F   Immigration has significantly increased the labor force and contributed to the outward shift of the U.S. production possibilities curve over time.

Multiple Choice

1.	d	5.	a	9.	a	13.	c	17.	c
2.	d	6.	b	10.	d	14.	d	18.	b
3.	c	7.	c	11.	a	15.	d	19.	c
4.	b	8.	d	12.	a	16.	a	20.	b

Problems and Applications

Exercise 1

1. Short-run
2. Increased use of existing capacity
3. Long-run
4. Increased capacity; rightward; long-run AS

Exercise 2

1. **Table 17.1 Answer**

	1990	1998	Percentage change
(1) U.S. real GDP (billions of dollars)	$6707.9	$8515.7	27.0%
(2) U.S. population (thousands)	249,973	270,509	8.2%
(3) U.S. per capita GDP (dollars per person)	$26,834	$31,480	17.3%
(4) World population (thousands)	5,329,000	5,927,000	11.2%

2. Increased
3. Since the world population growth rate is faster than that of the U.S., it takes higher economic growth to maintain the same standard of living.
4. 3.375%
5. 21.33 years

Exercise 3

1. I ÷ GDP = $4 trillion ÷ $10 trillion = 0.40 or 40 percent
2. I ÷ GDP = $1 trillion ÷ $5 trillion = 0.20 or 20 percent
3. Country A; because it has a higher investment rate
4. China and Thailand
5. China and Singapore

PART 7 Policy Constraints

CHAPTER 18

Global Macro

Quick Review

- Trade impacts domestic economic performance. Exports (X) are an injection into the circular flow and imports (M) are a leakage from it.

- The multiplier in an open economy reflects consumers' desire to spend some of every extra dollar on imports, which is called the marginal propensity to import (MPM). The multiplier for the open economy becomes $1/(MPS + MPM)$.

- The marginal propensity to import may interfere with fiscal policy in achieving domestic goals. Because the multiplier is smaller in an open economy than in a closed economy, any tax or spending change will have to be larger to achieve a given income or employment goal.

- Our exports (determined abroad) are seldom equal to our imports (determined at home). We expect either a trade surplus, $(X - M) > 0$, or a trade deficit, $(X - M) < 0$. Although the trade deficit permits us to consume more goods than we produce, it may complicate fiscal policy. A fiscal expansion will worsen any trade deficit, *ceteris paribus*.

- If the U.S. has a trade deficit, our trading partners must have an overall trade surplus.

- Capital flows involve the movement of money across international borders. Capital inflows occur when foreigners lend to us (e.g., by purchasing Treasury bonds or other U.S. assets) and outflows occur when we purchase assets from other countries.

- Capital flows are seldom in balance. When the outflow of dollars exceeds the inflow of dollars, the U.S. experiences a capital deficit; when the inflow exceeds the outflow, there is a capital surplus.

- Capital imbalances can alter macro outcomes. If the Fed decreases the growth of the money supply, domestic interest rates increase. This action attracts foreigners to U.S. bonds and other assets, which causes a capital inflow and an increase in the money supply.

- The critical link between economies in both trade and finance is the exchange rate.

- Specialization and trade increase world efficiency and output, and stimulate improvements in productivity, as producers anywhere must compete with producers everywhere. As a result, consumption possibilities increase.

- The gains from trade and cooperation among nations are enormous and have been pursued with great resolve by blocks of countries. The International Monetary Fund, the Group of Seven, and the European Union are all attempts at global coordination.

Learning Objectives

After reading Chapter 18 and doing the following exercises, you should:

1. Understand how international transactions affect U.S. economic performance and the ability to use macroeconomic policy.
2. Be able to explain why the open-economy multiplier is smaller than the closed-economy multiplier.
3. Understand why fiscal policy initiatives have less impact in an open economy than in a closed economy.
4. Be able to show how trade and capital flows can counteract normal macro policy initiatives.
5. Be aware of the foreign repercussions of U.S. policy initiatives.
6. Know the principal vocabulary of the trade and capital accounts.
7. Be able to relate exchange rate changes to the question of competitiveness in international trade.
8. Understand the various attempts at global coordination.

Using Key Terms

Fill in the puzzle on the opposite page with the appropriate term from the list of Key Terms at the end of the chapter in the text.

Across

2. The ability of a country to produce a specific good at a lower opportunity cost than its trading partners.
3. Income diverted from the circular flow, such as imports.
9. Equal to 1 - *MPC*.
12. Equal to exports minus imports.
13. The amount by which exports exceed imports.
14. Equal to 1 ÷ (1 - *MPC*).
15. The amount by which the capital outflow exceeds the capital inflow.

Down

1. The fraction of each additional dollar of income that is spent on imports.
4. Goods and services purchased from foreign sources.
5. A situation in which capital inflows are greater than capital outflows.
6. A decrease in private-sector borrowing and spending because of an increase in government borrowing.
7. A situation in which imports exceed exports.
8. Output per unit of input.
10. Goods and services sold to foreign sources.
11. The price of one country's currency in terms of another country's currency.

True or False: *Circle your choice and explain why any false statements are incorrect.*

T F 1. The main reason countries specialize and trade with each other is to acquire goods and services they cannot produce themselves.

T F 2. The open economy multiplier is smaller than the closed economy multiplier, *ceteris paribus*.

T F 3. Imports act like an automatic stabilizer for the economy.

T F 4. An increase in net exports will lower the equilibrium level of income, *ceteris paribus*.

T F 5. When the United States has a trade deficit, the value of what the United States consumes is more than the value of what it produces.

T F 6. When the dollar gets weaker, U.S. products become less competitive in the world market.

T F 7. Stimulative fiscal policy will increase both aggregate demand and a trade deficit, *ceteris paribus*.

T F 8. Trade stimulates improvements in productivity because of increased competition.

T F 9. A trade surplus is accompanied by a capital inflow; a trade deficit, by a capital outflow.

T F 10. The "Group of Eight" is an informal attempt to coordinate the global macro policy of the eight largest industrial countries.

Multiple Choice: *Select the correct answer.*

_____ 1. The open-economy multiplier is smaller than the closed-economy multiplier:
  (a) Because imports are a leakage from the circular flow.
  (b) Because the marginal propensity to import is greater than zero.
  (c) Because the denominator is greater for the open-economy multiplier than for the closed-economy multiplier.
  (d) For all of the above reasons.

_____ 2. The marginal propensity to import relates:
  (a) Domestic consumption to the foreign level of income.
  (b) Changes in the domestic level of income to changes in the foreign level of income.
  (c) Changes in the domestic imports with changes in domestic income.
  (d) Changes in domestic consumption with changes in imports.

_____ 3. An increase in U.S. exports:
  (a) Must increase unemployment in the rest of the world.
  (b) Means the rest of the world must be importing more.
  (c) Means the rest of the world must have a trade deficit.
  (d) Means the rest of the world must have a trade surplus.

_____ 4. If the marginal propensity to import is 0.2 and the marginal propensity to consume is 0.8, the open-economy multiplier is:
 (a) 0.4.
 (b) 2.5.
 (c) 4.0.
 (d) 2.0.

_____ 5. A decrease in the marginal propensity to import will:
 (a) Reduce the size of the open-economy multiplier.
 (b) Shift the aggregate supply curve rightward.
 (c) Increase the size of the open-economy multiplier.
 (d) Shift the aggregate demand curve leftward.

_____ 6. With respect to the circular flow of economic activity:
 (a) Exports are a leakage.
 (b) Imports are a leakage.
 (c) Imports and exports are both leakages.
 (d) Exports and imports are both injections.

_____ 7. World output of goods and services increases with specialization because:
 (a) The world's resources are being used more efficiently.
 (b) Each country's production possibilities curve is shifted outward.
 (c) Each country's workers are able to produce more than they could before specialization.
 (d) All of the above are correct.

_____ 8. When a trade deficit rises:
 (a) Exports rise, imports fall, or both.
 (b) Net exports fall.
 (c) The aggregate demand curve increases.
 (d) The level of income will rise, _ceteris paribus_.

_____ 9. An increase in U.S. imports:
 (a) Means the rest of the world must be exporting more.
 (b) Must increase unemployment in the rest of the world.
 (c) Means the rest of the world must have a trade deficit.
 (d) Means the rest of the world must have a trade surplus.

_____ 10. There is a tradeoff between the objective of reducing a trade deficit and the objective of reaching full employment because:
 (a) Net exports rise as income increases.
 (b) As income increases, the trade deficit rises.
 (c) Imports fall as income increases.
 (d) Fiscal policy and monetary policy must be used to achieve the objective.

_____ 11. Comparative advantage refers to the ability of a country to:
 (a) Produce a specific good with fewer resources than other countries.
 (b) Sell a good at a higher price than other countries.
 (c) Produce a specific good at a lower opportunity cost than other countries.
 (d) Maximize its economic welfare by producing all the goods and services it needs domestically.

_____ 12. French wine producers would gain an advantage over U.S. wine producers in world markets if:
 (a) The euro weakened relative to the U.S. dollar.
 (b) The American dollar weakened against other currencies.
 (c) The French inflation rate rose relative to the American inflation rate.
 (d) French interest rates rose relative to American interest rates.

_____ 13. A net capital inflow into the U. S. means that the U. S. is:
  (a) Consuming more than it produces, and net exports are positive.
  (b) Consuming more than it produces, and net exports are negative.
  (c) Consuming less than it produces, and net exports are positive.
  (d) Consuming less than it produces, and net exports are negative.

_____ 14. The International Monetary Fund (IMF):
  (a) Receives its funds from contributions from all the countries of the world.
  (b) Lends funds to nations whose currency is in trouble.
  (c) Often insists on changes in a nation's monetary, fiscal and/or trade policies as a condition for an IMF loan.
  (d) All of the above are correct.

_____ 15. A capital outflow occurs for the U.S. when, _ceteris paribus_:
  (a) Citizens of the United States buy foreign stock.
  (b) U.S. corporations abroad repatriate their profits.
  (c) Foreigners purchase real estate in the United States.
  (d) All of the above occur.

_____ 16. If the Fed cuts interest rates to stimulate aggregate demand, this could cause:
  (a) A capital outflow.
  (b) A capital inflow.
  (c) The value of the dollar to increase.
  (d) The value of the euro to decrease.

_____ 17. When the U.S. dollar is strong, _ceteris paribus_:
  (a) Imports become more expensive.
  (b) U.S. producers become more competitive in foreign markets.
  (c) U.S. goods become more expensive for foreigners to buy.
  (d) U.S. exports should increase.

_____ 18. A common currency, like the euro, facilitates trade by:
  (a) Eliminating the uncertainties associated with fluctuating exchange rates.
  (b) Eliminating currency conversion costs.
  (c) Easing the flow of financial capital across national boundaries.
  (d) All of the above facilitate trade.

_____ 19. For a given amount of fiscal stimulus, an open economy will experience, _ceteris paribus_, a shift in aggregate demand that is:
  (a) Greater than in a closed economy resulting in a larger increase in GDP.
  (b) Less than in a closed economy resulting in a larger increase in GDP.
  (c) Less than in a closed economy resulting in a smaller increase in GDP.
  (d) Greater than in a closed economy resulting in a smaller increase in GDP.

_____ 20. Which of the following is true about the Group of Seven?
  (a) It is composed of the seven largest industrialized nations.
  (b) It assesses the global economic outlook.
  (c) It coordinates global macroeconomic policy.
  (d) All of the above.

Problems and Applications

Exercise 1

Using the consumption function and the marginal propensity to import, it is possible to compare the multiplier effect for an open economy versus the multiplier effect for a closed economy.

Assume that an economy is characterized by the consumption function

$$C = 100 + 0.75Y_D$$

where all figures are in billions of dollars.

1. What is the marginal propensity to consume for this closed economy? _____

2. Compute the marginal propensity to save for the closed economy. _____

3. Compute the multiplier for this closed economy. _____

4. If government expenditures were to increase by $100 billion, how much would income increase in this closed economy? _____

5. Now suppose the economy has been opened up to imports and has a marginal propensity to import equal to 0.25.

   Assuming that the consumption function is the same as in the beginning of this exercise, compute the multiplier for this open economy. _____

6. Now, if government expenditures increase by $100 billion, how much does income increase in this open economy? _____

7. T   F   Imports reduce the effectiveness of fiscal policy. (Compare your answers in questions 4 and 6 above.)

Figure 18.1

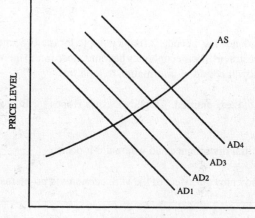

245

8. Refer to Figure 18.1. Assume the economy is originally on AD_1. For a closed economy, a fiscal policy stimulus shifts aggregate demand to AD_3. In an open economy, the same fiscal policy stimulus would shift aggregate demand to _____, *ceteris paribus*.

Exercise 2

This exercise shows the impact of fiscal policy on the trade balance.

Assume the following information for a hypothetical economy.

Table 18.1 Data in billions of dollars

	Year 1	Year 2
GDP	$800	$_____
Exports	50	50
Imports	60	_____
Net exports	_____	_____
Import/GDP ratio	_____	_____

1. Calculate the level of net exports in Year 1 in Table 18.1.

2. Assume the government increases spending form Year 1 to Year 2, which causes GDP to increase by $200 billion. Calculate GDP for Year 2 in Table 18.1.

3. As a result of the increase in government spending, the demand for imports increases. Assume imports increase by $10 for every $100 increase in GDP. Calculate the level of imports for Year 2 in Table 18.1.

4. Assume exports do not change. Calculate the level of net exports for Year 2 in Table 18.1.

5. Calculate the import/GDP ratio for Year 1 and for Year 2 in Table 18.1.

6. In an open economy, fiscal stimulus tends to (increase; decrease) a trade deficit by (increasing; decreasing) imports.

Exercise 3

Economic interdependence has become a frequent topic for the U.S. media. As countries forge greater links through trade and investment, their economies become more interdependent. This exercise will use one of the articles in the text to show the kind of information to look for.

Reread the article in the text entitled "Tragedy Dashes Hopes for Europe's Economy." Then answer the following questions.

1. What was the initial disturbance and where did it occur? _____

2. Which phrase indicates the effect of the U.S. economy's problems on the level of European exports?
   _____

3. Which phrase suggests the interdependence between the U.S. economy and Europe? _____
   _____

Common Errors

The first statement in each "common error" below is incorrect. Each incorrect statement is followed by a corrected version and an explanation.

1. A stronger dollar means American firms are stronger and more competitive. WRONG!

    A stronger dollar puts U.S. firms at a competitive disadvantage, *ceteris paribus*. RIGHT!

    When the dollar becomes stronger, this means the dollar can now purchase more of a foreign currency. It also means it takes more of a foreign currency to purchase one U.S. dollar. U.S. manufactured items now cost more. The stronger dollar effectively causes the price of U.S. manufactured items to increase for foreign countries, and this puts U. S. firms at a competitive disadvantage.

2. Foreign trade does not impact the effectiveness of domestic fiscal and monetary policy. WRONG!

    Foreign trade can significantly impact the effectiveness of domestic fiscal and monetary policy. RIGHT!

    Imports and exports result in financial flows into and out of the economy. The movement of goods across borders not only affects the exchange rates, but also the spending multipliers. In a closed economy the spending multiplier is equal to $1 \div MPS$, while in an open economy the spending multiplier is equal to $1 \div (MPS + MPM)$. Thus, in an open economy, the spending multiplier is smaller and fiscal and monetary policies have less impact than in a closed economy.

3. Trade surpluses are good for the economy, and trade deficits are bad for the economy. WRONG!

    Trade surpluses and deficits are neither *inherently* bad nor *inherently* good. RIGHT!

    When we run a trade deficit, we get the benefits of foreign resources *net*. That's good. But persistent deficits can be bad for the economy if they lead to restrictive policies designed to cut down on imports and to a continual depreciation of the exchange rate. Our persistent trade deficits (foreigners' trade surpluses) mean foreigners will eventually accumulate more of our currency than they want to hold. Capital inflows will not be able to stem the glut of the currency. As a result, our currency will depreciate and foreign goods will become more expensive.

4. The U.S. trade deficit means U.S. producers are inefficient. WRONG!

    The U.S. trade deficit means U.S. producers are having difficulty competing. RIGHT!

    The trade deficit reflects more than our (in)efficiency. As an example, U.S. agricultural producers are extremely efficient, but they have had difficulty exporting because the dollar was so strong for so long. A weaker dollar helps our producers compete. Before we believe the rhetoric concerning competitiveness, we need to know what is happening to exchange rates.

•ANSWERS•

Using Key Terms

Across
2. comparative advantage
3. leakage
9. marginal propensity to save
12. net exports
13. trade surplus
14. multiplier
15. capital deficit

Down
1. marginal propensity to import
4. imports
5. capital surplus
6. crowding out
7. trade deficit
8. productivity
10. exports
11. exchange rate

True or False

1. F   Getting goods and services they can't produce themselves is one reason to trade, but the main reason countries specialize and trade is to increase total output, incomes, and living standards.
2. T
3. T
4. F   Net exports are a part of GDP, so an increase will cause equilibrium income to increase.
5. T
6. F   U.S. products become more competitive (i.e., relatively lower priced) when the U.S. dollar becomes weaker.
7. T
8. T
9. F   A trade deficit is associated with a capital inflow and a trade surplus is associated with a capital outflow.
10. T

Multiple Choice

1.	d	5.	c	9.	a	13.	b	17.	c
2.	c	6.	b	10.	b	14.	d	18.	d
3.	b	7.	a	11.	c	15.	a	19.	c
4.	b	8.	b	12.	a	16.	a	20.	d

Problems and Applications

Exercise 1

1. 0.75; Refer to the consumption function
2. 0.25 (= 1 - 0.75)
3. 4 (= 1 ÷ MPS)
4. $400 billion (= $100 billion x 4)
5. 2 [= 1 ÷ (MPS + MPM) = 1 ÷ (0.25 + 0.25)]
6. $200 billion (= $100 billion x 2)
7. T
8. AD_2

Exercise 2

1. **Table 18.1 Answer**

	Year 1	Year 2
GDP	$800	$1,000
Exports	50	50
Imports	60	80
Net exports	-10	-30
Import/GDP ratio	0.075	0.080

2. See Table 18.1 Answer.
3. See Table 18.1 Answer.
4. See Table 18.1 Answer.
5. See Table 18.1 Answer.
6. Increase; increasing

Exercise 3

1. Terrorist attacks on the United States
2. "The U.S. buys 22 percent of Europe's exports."
3. "Economists estimate a percentage-point drop in U.S. economic growth translates into a half-percentage point decline in European growth. "

CHAPTER 19
Theory and Reality

Quick Review

- Government policy-makers have many tools with which to design and implement the ideal "package" of macro policies.

- The basic tools of fiscal policy are taxes and government spending. Automatic stabilizers, such as income taxes and unemployment benefits, help to stabilize any disruptions in the economy by responding automatically to changes in national income.

- Monetary policy, controlled by the Federal Reserve, uses open market operations, changes in the discount rate, and occasional changes in the reserve requirement to impact the macroeconomy. Both monetary and fiscal policy shift the aggregate demand curve.

- Supply-side policy focuses on shifting the aggregate supply curve, which allows for economic growth. Tax cuts, government deregulation, education, training, and research are supply-side tools.

- To end a recession, we can cut taxes, increase government spending, or expand the money supply. To curb inflation, we can reverse each of these policy levers. To overcome stagflation, fiscal and monetary policies can be combined with supply-side incentives.

- Recurring economic slowdowns with accompanying increases in unemployment and nagging inflation suggest that obstacles may stand in the way of successful policy-making. In addition, there are opportunity costs for all policy decisions, and economic goals may even conflict with one another.

- Policymaking is an inexact science for many reasons. Measurement problems exist because the data are incomplete and take months or years to report. Furthermore, we must rely on inherently uncertain forecasts about the economy, and we are unsure just how the economy will respond to specific policy choices. Implementation problems occur because of the time it takes Congress and the President to agree on an appropriate plan of action. Finally, there is always the possibility that policies are more politically desirable than economically appropriate.

- Those who favor discretionary policies believe that active intervention is necessary. Others (monetarists and new classical economists) believe fine-tuning is not possible and favor fixed policy rules.

Learning Objectives

After reading Chapter 19 and doing the following exercises, you should:

1. Know the three basic types of policies and each of the policy levers.
2. Know how the concept of "opportunity cost" defines the basic policy tradeoffs faced in the economy.
3. Be able to prescribe policies to eliminate an AD shortfall.
4. Be able to design policies to deal with excess AD.
5. Be able to suggest policies to control stagflation.
6. Know the general theories of several groups of economists.
7. Evaluate how effective policy makers have been in battling inflation and unemployment.
8. Be able to explain how measurement problems impede the development of effective policies.
9. Understand the concept of a leading indicator.
10. Understand the design problems encountered in administering policy and the problems that are inherent in economic forecasting.
11. Know the "rational-expectations" argument about the effectiveness of policy.
12. Recognize the lags involved in policy implementation.
13. Know the advantages and problems of both rules and discretion in making policy.

Using Key Terms

Fill in the puzzle on the opposite page with the appropriate term from the list of Key Terms at the end of the chapter in the text.

Across

4. Spending or revenue item that responds automatically and countercyclically to changes in national income.
5. Alternating periods of economic expansion and contraction.
8. The idea that people make decisions on the basis of all available information, including the anticipated effects of government intervention.
9. A period during which real GDP grows, but at a rate below the long-term trend.
10. A situation of inflation and substantial unemployment.
11. Equal to $1 \div (1 - MPC)$.
12. Spending increases or tax cuts intended to increase aggregate demand.
13. Focuses on providing incentives to work, invest, and produce.
14. The use of money and credit controls to change macroeconomic outcomes.
16. The difference between equilibrium GDP and full-employment GDP when there is demand-pull inflation.
17. The use of spending and revenue items to change macroeconomic outcomes.

Down

1. The lowest rate of unemployment compatible with price stability.
2. Continuous responses to changing economic conditions.
3. The number of times money turns over in a given time period.
6. Federal revenues at full employment minus federal expenditures at full employment.
7. Spending decreases or tax hikes intended to decrease aggregate demand.
15. If equilibrium GDP is less than full-employment GDP there is a recessionary _____ _____.

Puzzle 19.1

True or False: *Circle your choice and explain why any false statements are incorrect.*

T   F   1.   The failure of macroeconomic policy is reflected in the fact that since World War II, the ups and downs of the business cycle have become more severe.

T   F   2.   It is often the case that good economic policy and political objectives are in conflict.

T   F   3.   Automatic stabilizers tend to smooth out the business cycle.

T   F   4.   Macroeconomic forecasts from different computer models are usually surprisingly similar because the models are based on the same macroeconomic theories.

T   F   5.   Monetary policy is controlled by Congress.

T   F   6.   Monetarists and new classical economists favor rules rather than discretionary macro policies.

T   F   7.   Modern Keynesians and monetarists believe the government should use changes in the money supply as a method to eliminate a GDP gap.

T   F   8.   The new classical economists favor steady, predictable policies, such as a constant growth rate in the money supply.

T   F   9.   External shocks can make economic forecasts invalid.

T   F   10. Supply-side economists focus on the expansion of capacity through lower marginal tax rates and policies to increase work and investment incentives.

Multiple Choice: *Select the correct answer.*

_____ 1.   A supply-side policy cure to stagflation would include:
   (a)   Reduced government spending.
   (b)   Tax incentives to encourage investment.
   (c)   Open-market operations when the Fed buys securities.
   (d)   A higher reserve requirement.

_____ 2.   Fine-tuning is most consistent with:
   (a)   Keynesian or Neo-Keynesian economics.
   (b)   Monetarist or new classical economics.
   (c)   Supply-side economics or new classical economics.
   (d)   A laissez-faire policy.

_____ 3.   Which of the following is an accurate statement concerning the performance of macroeconomic policy in the United States?
   (a)   We have frequently failed to reach our goals of full employment, price stability and vigorous economic growth.
   (b)   The business cycle continues to exist.
   (c)   The ups and downs of the business cycle have been less severe since World War II.
   (d)   All of the above are accurate.

_____ 4. Monetary policy to eliminate a recession might include:
   (a) Infrastructure development.
   (b) The sale of securities in the open market by the Fed.
   (c) A decrease in the marginal tax rate.
   (d) A decrease in the discount rate.

_____ 5. When Federal Reserve Board chairman Alan Greenspan announced a goal of "zero inflation," which of the following was most consistent with his new goal?
   (a) A lower discount rate.
   (b) A lower minimum reserve ratio.
   (c) Sales of securities in the open market.
   (d) Increased government spending.

_____ 6. Which of the following groups feels that output and employment gravitate to a long-term rate determined by structural forces in the labor and product markets?
   (a) Monetarists.
   (b) Keynesians.
   (c) New classical economists.
   (d) Supply-side economists.

_____ 7. An increase in the discount rate during an inflationary period would be a policy consistent with the views of:
   (a) Monetarists.
   (b) Modern Keynesians.
   (c) Monetarists and supply-siders.
   (d) New classicals and "Old" Keynesians.

_____ 8. A supply-side policy to reduce AD excess would include:
   (a) Tax incentives to encourage saving.
   (b) Reduced government spending.
   (c) The purchase of securities by the Fed.
   (d) A higher reserve requirement.

_____ 9. Which of the following is the Monetarist policy for fighting a recession?
   (a) Increase government spending.
   (b) Expand the money supply at a faster rate.
   (c) Provide tax incentives to increase investment.
   (d) Patience (i.e., laissez faire).

_____ 10. Which of the following supply-side efforts has the George W. Bush administration embraced?
   (a) Deficit reduction.
   (b) Reduced marginal tax rates.
   (c) A zero-inflation target.
   (d) All of the above.

_____ 11. Expansionary fiscal and monetary policy are _not_ effective when the aggregate:
   (a) Supply curve is horizontal.
   (b) Supply curve is vertical.
   (c) Supply curve is upward sloping but not vertical.
   (d) Demand curve is vertical.

_____ 12. The opportunity costs of different policies must be weighted to solve which of the following obstacles?
- (a) Design problems.
- (b) Measurement problems.
- (c) Goal conflicts.
- (d) Implementation problems.

_____ 13. Which of the following is a reason that many economic policies fail, even if they are properly designed to achieve economic goals?
- (a) Measurement difficulties prevent policy makers from correctly identifying what is actually happening in the economy.
- (b) People often react in ways that may undercut new government policies.
- (c) There are significant lags in response to policy.
- (d) All of the above are reasons for the failure of economic policy.

_____ 14. Advocates of "fixed policy rules" believe:
- (a) That "fixed policy rules" can improve macro outcomes.
- (b) Appropriate macro policy would include constant increases in the money supply and balanced federal budgets.
- (c) That in view of the many practical problems associated with implementing fiscal and monetary policy, the economy would be better off if discretionary policy were abandoned.
- (d) All of the above.

_____ 15. During a severe recession, appropriate economic policy might include:
- (a) An open market sale by the Fed, a decrease in the discount rate, or an increase in the budget deficit.
- (b) A decrease in government spending, a decrease in the discount rate, or a decrease in government regulations.
- (c) An open market purchase by the Fed, a decrease in the discount rate, or a decrease in government regulations.
- (d) An open market purchase by the Fed, a decrease in tax rates, or a decrease in the budget deficit.

_____ 16. Which of the following groups feels that output and employment gravitate to their natural levels?
- (a) Keynesians.
- (b) Monetarists.
- (c) New Classical economists.
- (d) Marxists.

_____ 17. Leading economic indicators are used to address:
- (a) Goal conflicts.
- (b) Design problems.
- (c) Measurement problems.
- (d) Implementation problems.

_____ 18. Congress is responsible for:
- (a) Monetary policy.
- (b) Fiscal policy and supply-side policy.
- (c) Monetary and fiscal policy.
- (d) Monetary, fiscal, and supply-side policy.

_____ 19. The order of policy lags can best be stated as follows:
- (a) Formulation, recognition, and implementation lags.
- (b) Implementation, formulation, and recognition lags.
- (c) Recognition, formulation, and implementation lags.
- (d) Formulation, implementation, and recognition lags.

_____ 20. Which of the following groups believes that people will realize what the government is attempting to do and will take action to offset government policy?
(a) New Classical economists.
(b) Keynesians.
(c) Monetarists.
(d) Marxists.

Problems and Applications

Exercise 1

This exercise will help you recognize the inherent tradeoffs in the economy.

Table 19.1 presents data on interest rates, government expenditures, taxes, exports, imports, investment, consumption, a price index, and unemployment for four levels of equilibrium income (GDP). These items appear frequently in newspaper articles about the economy.

Table 19.1 Level of key economic indicators, by GDP level (billions of dollars per year)

Interest rate	30%	20%	10%	0%
Government expenditures	$ 100	$ 100	$ 100	100
Taxes	25	75	125	175
Budget balance	____	____	____	____
Exports	300	300	300	300
Imports	260	280	300	320
Investment	10	90	170	250
Consumption	750	790	830	870
Nominal GDP	____	____	____	____
Price index	1.00	1.00	1.02	1.10
Real GDP (constant dollars)	____	____	____	____
Unemployment rate	15%	7%	4%	3.5%

1. Compute the federal budget balance, nominal GDP, and real GDP in Table 19.1, for each level of interest rate. (*Hint:* Remember the formula $C + I + G + [X - M] = GDP$.)

2. Which policy is the government most likely using to reach each of the situations in Table 19.1?
(a) Fiscal policy.
(b) Monetary policy.
(c) Wage and price controls.
(d) Labor policy.

3. Which of the following statements best explains why the amount paid in taxes might change as the level of GDP changes, as shown in Table 19.1?
(a) Taxpayers experience stagflation as income increases.
(b) As taxpayers' incomes rise, their marginal tax rates rise.
(c) The income tax is regressive.
(d) Automatic stabilizers link taxes with income.

4. The most likely explanation for why the price index changes as the level of GDP changes, as shown in Table 19.1, is that as:
   (a) People receive greater income, they can be more discriminating buyers and find the lowest prices.
   (b) Firms receive more orders, productivity rises, allowing inflation to ease.
   (c) People receive greater income, they spend it, and if the economy is near full employment, prices begin to rise.
   (d) Businesses receive greater income, they have an incentive to expand capacity and must pass the cost of the increased capacity on to consumers in the form of higher prices.

5. The most logical reason for why unemployment changes as the level of GDP changes, as shown in Table 19.1, is that as GDP rises:
   (a) People do not need jobs and leave the labor force.
   (b) Automatic stabilizers provide increased benefits to the unemployed, keeping them out of the labor force.
   (c) Inflation causes real income to fall and employment to decrease.
   (d) Aggregate demand rises, stimulating the derived demand for labor.

Exercise 2

This exercise shows the difficulties faced by policy makers because of the inevitable tradeoffs in the economy.

Table 19.2 presents data on government expenditure, taxes, the price index, unemployment, and pollution for four levels of equilibrium income (GDP). These items appear frequently in newspaper articles about the economy.

Table 19.2 Level of key economic indicators, by GDP level
(billions of dollars per year)

| Indicator | Nominal GDP | | | |
	$120	$160	$200	$240
Government expenditure	$ 0	$ 20	$ 35	$ 50
Taxes	$ 18	$ 24	$ 30	$ 36
Budget balance	$_____	$_____	$_____	$_____
Price index	1.00	1.00	1.02	1.20
Real GDP (constant dollars)	$_____	$_____	$_____	$_____
Unemployment rate	15%	7%	4%	3.5%
Pollution index	1.00	1.10	1.80	1.90

1. Compute the federal budget balance and real GDP in Table 19.2 for each level of nominal GDP.

2. Choose the government expenditure level that is best at accomplishing all of the following goals, according to Table 19.2. $_____
   • Lowest level of taxes.
   • Lowest pollution index.
   • Lowest inflation rate.

3. Which of the following might induce a policy maker to choose a higher government expenditure level than the one that answers question 2?
   (a) High unemployment.
   (b) An inability by government to provide public goods and services.
   (c) Low real income.
   (d) All of the above.

4. Choose the government expenditure level that is best at accomplishing all of the following goals, according to Table 19.2. $_____
   • Lowest unemployment rate.
   • Largest amount of government spending.
   • Highest level of real income.

5. The policy that best satisfies the goals in question 4, is most likely to result in:
   (a) A recession.
   (b) Rapid economic growth accompanied by inflation.
   (c) Stagflation.
   (d) Deflation.

6. Choose the government expenditure level that is best at accomplishing all of the following goals, according to Table 19.2. $_____
   • Balancing the federal budget.
   • Maintaining pollution at reasonably low levels.
   • Maintaining price stability.

7. At which government expenditure level does full employment occur? (Use 4 percent unemployment as full employment.) $_____

8. If you are a policy maker faced with the alternatives in Table 19.2, can you say that one of the alternative government expenditure levels is clearly better than all the others? _____

Exercise 3

This exercise tests your ability to choose the appropriate policy initiative to overcome various undesirable economic conditions.

Choose a policy from the list below that would be appropriate to correct the economic conditions at the top of Table 19.3. Place the letter of each item in Table 19.3 only once.

a. Deregulation.
b. Discount rate lowered.
c. Discount rate raised.
d. Government spending decreases.
e. Government spending increases.
f. Open-market operations (Fed buys government securities).
g. Open-market operations (Fed sells government securities).

h. Reserve requirement higher.
i. Reserve requirement lower.
j. Job and skill training.
k. Tax cuts.
l. Tax incentives to alter the structure of supply and demand.
m. Tax incentives to encourage saving.
n. Tax increases.

Table 19.3 Economic policies

	Recession	Inflation	Stagflation
Fiscal policy	1._____	6._____	
	2._____	7._____	
Monetary policy	3._____	8._____	
	4._____	9._____	
	5._____	10._____	
Supply-side policy		11._____	12._____
			13._____
			14._____

Exercise 4

The media often provide information about the government's slow response to the economy's needs. This exercise will use one of the articles in the text to show the kind of information to look for.

Reread the article in the text titled "Deficit-Cutting Wilts in Heat from Voters." Then answer the following questions.

1. Which *one* of the following obstacles to success is best illustrated by the article?
   (a)   Goal conflicts.
   (b)   Measurement problems.
   (c)   Design problems.
   (d)   Implementation problems.

2. Which passage specifically mentions the obstacle you have chosen? _____
   _____

3. Which passage indicates the decision-maker who is responsible for determining the policy?
   _____

4. Which passage indicates the situation that requires a policy response? _____
   _____

Common Errors

The first statement in each "common error" below is incorrect. Each incorrect statement is followed by a corrected version and an explanation.

1. Fiscal and monetary policy should be consistently applied to stimulate the economy. WRONG!

   Fiscal and monetary policies must be tailored to the specific economic problems faced by the government. RIGHT!

The government sometimes needs to apply apparently contradictory monetary and fiscal policies in order to attain quite different goals. For example, an expansionary fiscal policy may be needed to stimulate the economy, but a contractionary monetary policy may be needed to raise interest rates so that foreign capital will be enticed into the United States. A policy maker must weigh the various goals and decide on the appropriate mix of tools to achieve them.

2. Fiscal, monetary, and stagflation policies are effective regardless of the income level of the economy. WRONG!

The state of the economy in relation to full employment is important in determining the effectiveness of the various policies. RIGHT!

If the economy is experiencing an excess aggregate demand, wage-price controls will prove ineffective in curbing inflation. At relatively low levels of GDP, however, wage-price controls can be effective in holding down inflation. Work-force policies are often more effective in matching people with jobs when many people are looking for work than when unemployment is low. It is easier for the government to increase expenditures to stimulate the economy when there is a recession than to cut them back when there is excess aggregate demand.

3. The government has the power to prevent unemployment and inflation, but it just doesn't want to use it. WRONG!

While the government has the power to move the economy closer to any one goal, it faces a tradeoff between different goals that prevents it from achieving all of them. RIGHT!

Remember that the Phillips curve shows that a tradeoff exists between unemployment and inflation. Government policies to lower unemployment may lead to a worsening of inflation. The government must choose between the different goals.

•ANSWERS•

Using Key Terms

Across
4. automatic stabilizer
5. business cycle
8. rational expectations
9. growth recession
10. stagflation
11. multiplier
12. fiscal stimulus
13. supply-side policy
14. monetary policy
16. inflationary GDP gap
17. fiscal policy

Down
1. natural rate of unemployment
2. fine tuning
3. velocity of money
6. structural deficit
7. fiscal restraint
15. GDP gap

True or False

1. F   The ups and downs of the business cycle have become less severe since World War II, possibly indicating partial success.
2. T
3. T
4. F   Macroeconomic forecasts often differ because the models are based on different macroeconomic theories (e.g., Keynesian, supply-side).
5. F   Monetary policy is controlled by the Federal Reserve.
6. T
7. F   Modern Keynesians would agree to the use of changes in the money supply, but monetarists would take a "hands off" approach, believing that as sales and output decline, interest rates will decline (because of lower demand) and the lower rates will stimulate investment without government intervention.
8. F   New classicals believe that the only policies that work are those that are unexpected because rational people will anticipate the impact of announced policies and take protective actions that will render the announced policies ineffective.
9. T
10. T

Multiple Choice

1.	b	5.	c	9.	d	13.	d	17.	c
2.	a	6.	a	10.	b	14.	d	18.	b
3.	d	7.	b	11.	b	15.	c	19.	c
4.	d	8.	a	12.	c	16.	b	20.	a

Problems and Applications

Exercise 1

1. **Table 19.1 Answer (billions of dollars per year)**

Interest rate	30%	20%	10%	0%
Budget balance	$ −75	$ −25	$ 25	$ 75
Nominal GDP	900	1,000	1,100	1,200
Real GDP (constant dollars)	900	1,000	1,078	1,091

At the 30 percent interest rate, the following calculations should have been made, in billions of dollars per year:

Budget balance = $25 - $100 = - $75

Nominal GDP = $750 + $10 + $100 + $40 = $900

2. a   3. b   4. c   5. d

Exercise 2

1. **Table 19.2 Answer (billions of dollars per year)**

Indicator	Nominal GDP			
	$120	$160	$200	$240
Budget balance	$ 18	$ 4	$ -5	$ -14
Real GDP (constant dollars)	120	160	196	200

2. $0   4. $50 billion   6. $20 billion   8. No
3. d   5. b   7. $35 billion

Exercise 3

1. **Table 19.3 Answer**

	Recession	Inflation	Stagflation
Fiscal	1. k Tax cuts 2. e Government spending increases	6. n Tax increases 7. d Government spending decreases	
Monetary policy	3. b Discount rate lowered 4. f Open-market operations (Fed buys government securities) 5. i Reserve requirement lower	8. c Discount rate raised 9. g Open-market operations (Fed sells government securities) 10. h Reserve requirement higher	
Supply-side policy		11. m Tax incentives to encourage saving	12. a Deregulation 13. l Tax incentives to alter the structure of supply and demand 14. j Job and skill training

Exercise 4

1. a; However, there is implicit evidence of design problems concerning the best way to cut the deficit.
2. "Even before his proposal [to cut the deficit] took shape, more than 3,000 New Mexico constituents sent him identical postcards opposing any effort to cap entitlement programs." The passage shows the conflict between deficit cutting and the need for inflation-indexed entitlement programs to protect different groups.
3. "Senate, which voted 69 to 28 to reject the proposal"
4. "digging out of the massive federal deficit"

PART 8 Product Markets: The Basics

CHAPTER 20

The Demand for Goods

Quick Review

- Economic theory about consumer behavior focuses on demand (the willingness and ability to buy specific quantities of a good at various prices) and does not try to explain why people want the things they do.

- Utility is the satisfaction obtained from a particular good or service. Total utility is the total amount of satisfaction from consuming a particular quantity of a good or service; marginal utility is the satisfaction from consuming an additional unit of a good or service.

- The law of diminishing marginal utility says that the satisfaction from additional units of a good or service decreases as more of the good or service is consumed. This provides the basis for the law of demand. Marginal utility is combined with price in order to derive the law of demand.

- According to the law of demand, consumers will buy more of a good at a lower price, *ceteris paribus*. The nonprice determinants of demand—tastes, income, expectations, and the price and availability of other goods—are held constant when the demand curve is drawn. If any of these determinants change, the demand curve will shift.

- Price elasticity of demand measures the response of demand to a change in price. It is calculated as the percentage change in quantity demanded divided by the percentage change in price.

- The coefficient (E) that results from the elasticity calculation is always negative because of the law of demand, so its absolute value is used. If $|E| > 1$, demand is elastic; $|E| < 1$, demand is inelastic; and $|E| = 1$, demand is unitary elastic.

- Price elasticity determines the impact of a price change on total revenue ($P \times Q$). If price falls and demand is elastic, total revenue will increase; if price falls and demand is inelastic, total revenue will decrease. The opposite is true for a price increase.

- The determinants of price elasticity include the price of the good relative to income, the availability of substitutes, and the designation of the good as a necessity or a luxury.

- Income elasticity measures the response of demand to a change in income. Cross-price elasticity measures the response of demand for one good to a change in price of a related good.

- Optimal consumption occurs when utility is maximized. This is determined by comparing the marginal utility per dollar spent for each good or service.

- Advertising is intended to increase the willingness of consumers to purchase a good. If advertising is successful, the demand curve will shift to the right.

Learning Objectives

After reading Chapter 20 and doing the following exercises, you should:

1. Be able to distinguish the demand for a good from the desire for it.
2. Be able to show how any change in the price of a good, in the price of a substitute, in the price of a complement, in incomes, in tastes, or in expectations will affect the demand curve.
3. Know how the law of diminishing marginal utility and the law of demand relate to each other.
4. Be able to draw a demand curve from a demand schedule and create a demand schedule by looking at a demand curve.
5. Be able to distinguish between a change in demand (a shift of the curve) and a change in quantity demanded (a movement along the demand curve).
6. Know the determinants of elasticity.
7. Be able to compute the price elasticity of demand between two points on the demand curve.
8. Be able to determine on the basis of the elasticity of demand what will happen to total revenue when price changes.
9. Understand income elasticity, cross-price elasticity and their role in demand theory.
10. Know how a consumer makes the optimal consumption decision.
11. Understand the role of advertising in the theory of demand.

Using Key Terms

Fill in the puzzle on the opposite page with the appropriate term from the list of Key Terms at the end of the chapter in the text.

Across

1. Items for which an increase in the price of good X causes a decrease in the demand for good Y.
6. In the cartoon in the text, the fourth hamburger does not provide as much satisfaction as the first hamburger because of the law of _____ _____ _____.
12. The quantity of a good demanded in a given time period increases as its price falls, *ceteris paribus*.
13. The satisfaction obtained from the entire consumption of a good.
14. The quantity of a product sold times the price at which it is sold.
15. If two goods can be used in place of each other, they are _____ _____.
17. Equal to the percentage change in quantity demanded divided by the percentage change in income.
18. The percentage change in quantity demanded of good X divided by the percentage change in the price of good Y is the _____ _____ of demand.
19. The best forgone alternative.

Down

2. Influenced by tastes, income, expectations, and other goods.
3. Measures the response of consumers to a change in price.
4. The combination of goods that maximizes the total utility attainable from available income.
5. The additional satisfaction from consuming one more unit of a good or service.
7. When one of the underlying determinants of demand changes, there is a _____ _____ _____.
8. An item for which quantity demanded falls when income rises.
9. A curve describing the quantities of a good a consumer is willing and able to buy at alternative prices.
10. Consumers buy more of such an item when their incomes rise.
11. The assumption that everything else is constant.
16. Satisfaction obtained from goods and services.

Puzzle 20.1

True or False: *Circle your choice and explain why any false statements are incorrect.*

T F 1. Sellers use advertising to change the consumer's utilities, thus causing a shift in the consumer's demand curve.

T F 2. The law of demand differs from the law of diminishing marginal utility in that it considers what a person is able to pay for a good or service, not just the person's desire for a good or service.

T F 3. When the price of a good is expected to fall next month, then the current demand curve should shift to the right.

T F 4. According to the law of diminishing marginal utility, the total utility we obtain from a product declines as we consume more of it.

T F 5. If there is no budget constraint, utility maximization is achieved when marginal utility is zero.

T F 6. If demand is elastic, a rise in price raises total revenue.

T F 7. Elasticity of demand is constant along straight-line demand curves.

T F 8. The price elasticity of demand is influenced by all the determinants of demand.

T F 9. A demand curve is perfectly elastic if consumers reduce their quantity demanded to zero if price rises by even the slightest amount.

T F 10. A negative cross-price elasticity indicates goods are substitutes because a positive percentage increase in one good results in a negative percentage increase in the other.

Multiple Choice: *Select the correct answer.*

_____ 1. As more of a good is consumed, then total utility typically:
   (a) Increases at a decreasing rate.
   (b) Decreases as long as marginal utility is negative.
   (c) Decreases as long as marginal utility is positive.
   (d) Is negative as long as marginal utility is decreasing.

_____ 2. Which of the following statements exemplifies the law of diminishing marginal utility?
   (a) Spinach gives me no satisfaction, so I won't spend my income for any of it.
   (b) The more soda I drink, the more I want to drink.
   (c) The more I go to school, the more I want to do something else.
   (d) Since we need water more than we need diamonds, water is more valuable.

_____ 3. Both the law of demand and the law of diminishing marginal utility:
   (a) State that quantity and price are inversely related.
   (b) Reflect declining increments of satisfaction from consuming additional units of product.
   (c) Reflect both the willingness and the ability of buyers to buy goods and services.
   (d) Can be illustrated by means of demand curves.

_____ 4. Which of the following is a reason why a demand curve is typically downward sloping?
    (a) The law of diminishing marginal utility.
    (b) Consumers are not willing to pay as much for a good with low marginal utility than for a good with a high marginal utility.
    (c) Consumers have limited budgets.
    (d) All of the above are reasons.

_____ 5. _Ceteris paribus_, as the number of substitutes for a good increase, the:
    (a) Price elasticity of demand will become smaller.
    (b) Price elasticity of demand will become larger.
    (c) Cross-price elasticity of demand will become negative.
    (d) Income elasticity of demand will become negative.

_____ 6. Which of the following causes demand to be more elastic with respect to price?
    (a) Shorter periods of time to adjust to a change in price.
    (b) A steeper demand curve for a given price and quantity.
    (c) More substitutes.
    (d) If the good takes up a smaller portion of the consumer's budget.

_____ 7. Which of the following is likely to have a price elasticity coefficient greater than 1.0?
    (a) Cigarettes.
    (b) Coffee.
    (c) An addictive drug.
    (d) Meals at a restaurant.

_____ 8. Suppose your college or university raises tuition by 4 percent and as a result 2 percent fewer students enroll next semester. What is the value of the price elasticity of demand?
    (a) 0.50.
    (b) 2.0.
    (c) 8.0.
    (d) 6.0.

_____ 9. A demand curve is described as perfectly elastic if:
    (a) The same quantity is purchased regardless of price.
    (b) The same price is charged regardless of quantity sold.
    (c) Only price can change.
    (d) It is vertical.

_____ 10. Total revenue declines when demand is:
    (a) Elastic and price rises, causing a demand shift.
    (b) Elastic and price rises, causing a movement along the demand curve.
    (c) Inelastic and price rises, causing a demand shift.
    (d) Inelastic and price rises, causing a movement along the demand curve.

_____ 11. One of the airline industry's arguments against deregulation of airfares was that the resulting fall in prices would lower airline total revenue. Instead, total revenue rose. Assuming the increase in total revenue was due solely to the lower fares, it can be concluded that:
    (a) Airline representatives thought demand for plane trips was elastic.
    (b) Quantity demanded of airline service increased by a greater percentage than the percentage fall in price.
    (c) Demand for airline service increased with the fall in prices.
    (d) Airlines were more profitable after deregulation.

_____ 12. If a state legislature wishes to raise revenue by increasing certain sales taxes, it would increase sales taxes on goods that:
   (a)   Have inelastic demand.
   (b)   Are bought by those with high incomes.
   (c)   Are illegal.
   (d)   Have elastic demand.

_____ 13. Assume that a good has a downward sloping, linear demand curve. Beginning at a very low price, as the price of this good increases, total revenue:
   (a)   Increases indefinitely.
   (b)   Decreases initially and then increases.
   (c)   Remains constant.
   (d)   Increases initially and then decreases.

_____ 14. Assume that the price elasticity of demand for Great Fit Shoe Co. shoes is 1.5. If the company decreases the price of each pair of shoes, total revenues will:
   (a)   Increase because more shoes will be sold.
   (b)   Decrease because the company will be receiving less revenue per pair of shoes.
   (c)   Increase because the percentage increase in the number sold is greater than the percentage decrease in the price.
   (d)   Impossible to predict because we do not know the percentage change in price.

_____ 15. When the price of postage stamps increases, the demand for long-distance telephone service increases, _ceteris paribus_. Postage stamps and long-distance service are therefore:
   (a)   Elastic.
   (b)   Inelastic.
   (c)   Complements.
   (d)   Substitutes.

_____ 16. Which of the following elasticities would be most useful in determining the impact of a recession on the demand for airline travel?
   (a)   The income elasticity of air travel.
   (b)   The price elasticity of demand for air travel.
   (c)   The cross-price elasticity of demand for air travel with respect to income.
   (d)   The cross-price elasticity of income with respect to air travel.

_____ 17. Suppose the cross-price elasticity of demand for automobiles with respect to the gasoline price is -0.20. If gasoline prices rise 20 percent, then automobile sales should, _ceteris paribus_:
   (a)   Fall 4 percent.
   (b)   Fall 100 percent.
   (c)   Rise 4 percent.
   (d)   Rise 100 percent.

_____ 18. If the price elasticity of demand is 2.0 and a firm raises its price by 8 percent, the quantity sold by the firm will:
   (a)   Increase by 16 percent.
   (b)   Decrease by 16 percent.
   (c)   Increase by 4 percent.
   (d)   Decrease by 4 percent.

_____ 19. To maximize utility when purchasing two or more goods, the consumer should choose that good which:
   (a) Is priced the lowest.
   (b) Has the highest price elasticity.
   (c) Delivers the most marginal utility per dollar.
   (d) Provides the most satisfaction.

_____ 20. The objective of advertising is to:
   (a) Increase demand and increase the price elasticity of demand.
   (b) Increase demand and decrease the price elasticity of demand.
   (c) Increase demand only.
   (d) Decrease demand and make the price elasticity of demand unitary.

[CHAPTER 20 APPENDIX QUESTIONS]

_____ 21. An indifference curve shows:
   (a) The maximum utility that can be achieved for a given consumer budget.
   (b) The maximum utility that can be achieved for different amounts of a good.
   (c) The combinations of goods giving equal utility to a consumer.
   (d) The optimal consumption combinations between two goods.

_____ 22. A budget line represents:
   (a) Consumption possibilities.
   (b) The combinations of goods giving equal utility to a consumer.
   (c) The combinations of goods a consumer can afford.
   (d) The amount of income that is required to purchase a given amount of a good.

_____ 23. Where the budget line and an indifference curve are tangent, there is:
   (a) An optimal consumption point.
   (b) A point indicating the quantity and price that would appear on a demand curve.
   (c) A point where the ratio of marginal utility to price is equal for two goods.
   (d) All of the above.

Problems and Applications

Exercise 1

This exercise will help you draw demand curves using demand schedules. It should also give you practice in constructing market demand curves.

   1. Market demand is:
   (a) The total quantity of a good or service that people are willing and able to buy at alternative prices in a given period of time, _ceteris paribus_.
   (b) The sum of individual demands.
   (c) Represented as the horizontal sum of individual demand curves.
   (d) All of the above.

2. Table 20.1 presents a hypothetical demand schedule for cars manufactured in the United States.

Table 20.1 Demand for U.S. cars

Price	Number of new U.S. cars (millions per year)
$10,000	9.0
9,000	10.0

Graph this demand curve in Figure 20.1.

Figure 20.1

3. Table 20.2 presents a similar demand schedule for imported cars.

Table 20.2
Demand for foreign cars

Price	Number of new foreign cars (millions per year)
$10,000	1.0
9,000	2.0

Graph this demand curve in Figure 20.2.

Figure 20.2

4. In Table 20.3 calculate the demand schedule for cars (both foreign and domestically produced) at the two prices shown.

Table 20.3
Market demand for new cars

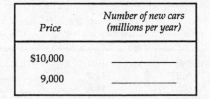

Price	Number of new cars (millions per year)
$10,000	_____
9,000	_____

5. In Figure 20.3 draw the domestic market demand curve for both foreign and domestic cars.

Figure 20.3

Exercise 2

This exercise should give you practice in computing and interpreting the price elasticity of demand. This exercise is similar to a problem in the text.

1. T F The midpoint formula for the price elasticity of demand is

$$\frac{(p_2 - p_1) \div [1 \div 2 (p_1 + p_2)]}{(q_2 - q_1) \div [1 \div 2 (q_1 + q_2)]}$$

2. If you answered "true" to problem 1, you goofed. The percentage change in quantity, $(q_2 - q_1) \div [1/2(q_1 + q_2)]$, should be on the top, not the bottom. The correct formula is

$$\frac{(q_2 - q_1) \div [1 \div 2 (q_1 + q_2)]}{(p_2 - p_1) \div [1 \div 2 (p_1 + p_2)]}$$

Apply this formula to the information in Table 20.4, which represents a hypothetical demand schedule for cars. Remember to use the absolute value of this expression, which makes the coefficient always positive. (When calculating elasticities, answers will vary depending on the number of decimal places used. To achieve the book answer you will need to round each calculation to 2 decimal places.)

Table 20.4
Market demand schedule for cars

Price	Number of new U.S. cars (millions per year)	Elasticity of demand
$10,000	10.0	——
9,000	12.0	_____
8,000	14.0	_____
7,000	16.0	_____

3. According to Table 20.4, the price elasticity of demand for U.S. cars is (elastic; inelastic) between $9,000 and $8,000.

4. According to Table 20.4, what is the total revenue for new U.S. cars at a price of $8,000?

5. If the price of new U.S. cars increases from $8,000 to $9,000, total revenue will (increase; decrease; stay the same).

6. Graph the first two columns of Table 20.4 in Figure 20.4.

Figure 20.4
Market demand curve

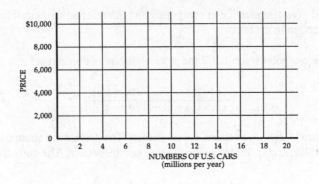

7. T F The curve is a linear demand curve.

8. What is the slope of the demand curve? _____

9. Moving down a linear demand curve results in:
   (a) More inelastic demand and a changing slope.
   (b) More inelastic demand but a constant slope.
   (c) More elastic demand and a changing slope.
   (d) More elastic demand and a constant slope.

10. T F While elasticity reflects a ratio of percentage changes in two variables, the slope reflects only changes in the variables, not percentage changes.

Exercise 3

This exercise focuses on calculating income elasticity and cross-price elasticity. It is similar to a problem in the text.

1. Use Table 20.5 to calculate the income elasticity of demand for peanut butter. Refer to the formula in the text. (Remember to round to 2 decimal places.)

Table 20.5

	Income (per year)	Demand for peanut butter (jars per year)		Income elasticity of demand
a	$10,000	12		
b	$20,000	7	a to b	_____
c	$40,000	3	b to c	_____
d	$80,000	1	c to d	_____

2. Based on Table 20.5, peanut butter is a (normal; inferior) good because as income rises, the quantity demanded of peanut butter (rises; falls), and the income elasticity of demand is (negative; positive).

3. Use Table 20.6 to calculate the cross-price elasticity of demand for jelly when the price of peanut butter changes. Refer to the formula in the text. (Remember to round to 2 decimal places.)

Table 20.6

	Price of peanut butter (per jar)	Demand for jelly (jars per year)		Cross-price elasticity of demand
a	$2.00	12		
b	$3.00	10	a to b	_____
c	$4.00	7	b to c	_____
d	$5.00	2	c to d	_____

4. Based upon Table 20.6, peanut butter and jelly are (substitute; complementary) goods because as the price of peanut butter rises, the demand for jelly (falls; rises) and the cross-price elasticity of demand is (negative; positive).

Exercise 4

This exercise shows the relationship between total and marginal utility. It also gives practice in identifying the law of diminishing marginal utility.

Suppose there are two types of entertainment you enjoy: an evening at home with friends, and an "event" entertainment, such as a sports event or a rock concert. The number of times that you experience each type of entertainment during a month determines the total utility of each type of entertainment for that month. Suppose Table 20.7 represents the total utility you achieve from consuming various quantities of the two types of entertainment.

Table 20.7
Total and marginal utility of two types of entertainment per month

Days of entertainment per month	Evening at home		Event	
	Total utility	Marginal utility	Total utility	Marginal utility
0	0	_____	0	_____
1	170	_____	600	_____
2	360	_____	1,250	_____
3	540	_____	1,680	_____
4	690	_____	2,040	_____
5	820	_____	2,350	_____
6	930	_____	2,550	_____
7	1,030	_____	2,720	_____
8	1,110	_____	2,820	_____
9	1,170	_____	2,820	_____
10	1,170	_____	2,760	_____
11	1,120	_____	2,660	_____
12	1,020	_____	2,460	_____

1. Complete Table 20.7 by computing the marginal utility of each type of entertainment.

2. The law of diminishing marginal utility means:
    (a)   The total utility of a good declines as more of it is consumed in a given time period.
    (b)   The marginal utility of a good declines as more of it is consumed in a given time period.
    (c)   The price of a good declines as more of it is consumed in a given period of time.
    (d)   All of the above.

3. The law of diminishing marginal utility is in evidence in Table 20.7 for:
    (a)   Both types of entertainment.
    (b)   Home entertainment only.
    (c)   Event entertainment only.
    (d)   Neither type of entertainment.

    (Hint: You should be able to tell by looking at the marginal utility columns in Table 20.7. Does the marginal utility become smaller as you go down the column?)

4. In Figure 20.5 graph the total utility curve for evenings at home.

Figure 20.5

5. In Figure 20.6 graph the marginal utility curve for evenings at home.

Figure 20.6

6. On the basis of the two graphs above, marginal utility becomes zero only when:
   (a) Total utility is zero.
   (b) Total utility reaches a maximum.
   (c) Total utility is rising.
   (d) Total utility is falling.

7. When total utility is rising, it is certain that:
   (a) Marginal utility is rising.
   (b) Marginal utility is negative.
   (c) Marginal utility is positive.
   (d) Marginal utility is zero.

Exercise 5

The principle of utility maximization is used to determine optimal consumption. This exercise builds on the previous exercise.

Suppose you hold a part-time job that gives you $120 a month extra spending money. On any day of the month you can spend that money on either of two types of entertainment—an evening at home with friends, for which you usually spend $10 for snacks and drinks, or an "event" entertainment, which costs $30. Table 20.8 shows the hypothetical marginal utility that each type of entertainment provides for you during the month.

Table 20.8
Total and marginal utility of two types of entertainment per month

Days of entertainment per month	Evening at home (price = $10)		Event entertainment (price = $30)	
	Marginal utility	MU / price	Marginal utility	MU / price
0	0	0	0	—
1	180	18	600	____
2	180	18	600	____
3	170	17	480	____
4	140	14	360	____
5	140	14	360	____
6	140	14	360	____
7	100	10	360	____
8	100	10	0	____
9	100	10	0	____
10	0	0	0	____

1. Finding the optimal level of consumption with a given income involves choosing successive *increments* of a good (service), *each of which* yields:
    (a) The largest total utility.
    (b) The largest marginal utility per unit of product or activity purchased.
    (c) The largest marginal utility for each dollar spent.
    (d) All of the above.

2. Divide marginal utility by the price of the event entertainment to complete Table 20.8.

Before you spend any money on any activity:

3. Which activity has the highest MU/*p* ratio? _____

4. Judging by the MU/*p* ratio, how many days of event entertainment should you buy before spending anything on at-home entertainment? _____

5. If you had $120 to spend on entertainment, how much money would you have left after buying two days of event entertainment? _____

6. Should you spend the entire balance from question 5 on at-home entertainment? _____

7. After you have bought three at-home nights and two events, how much income is left from the original $120? _____

278

8. Based on MU/*p*, which activity should you purchase with the income remaining in question 7?
    _____

9. T   F   When your income is $120, optimal consumption occurs with three evenings of each type of entertainment.

Appendix
Exercise 6

This exercise provides practice in interpreting an indifference map and total utility.

For questions 1-7 refer to Figure 20A.2 in the appendix for Chapter 20.

1. At point E, the consumption combination includes _____ cokes and _____ video games.

2. At point D, the consumption combination includes _____ cokes and _____ video games.

3. Based on the indifference map, the consumer receives:
    (a)   Greater satisfaction at point E than at point D.
    (b)   Greater satisfaction at point D than at point E.
    (c)   Equal satisfaction at point D and at point E.
    (d)   Satisfaction cannot be determined from an indifference map.

4. At point B, the consumption combination includes _____ cokes and _____ video games.

5. At point C, the consumption combination includes _____ cokes and _____ video games.

6. Compare combinations B and C to point E. In each case, point E provides (greater, lesser) satisfaction than point B or point C.

7. For the given indifference map, the level of total utility is greatest at any point along curve
    _____.

Common Errors

The first statement in each "common error" below is incorrect. Each incorrect statement is followed by a corrected version and an explanation.

1. The law of demand and the law of diminishing marginal utility are the same. WRONG!

    The law of demand and the law of diminishing marginal utility are not the same. RIGHT!

    Do not confuse utility and demand. Utility refers only to expected satisfaction. Demand refers to both preferences and ability to pay. This distinction should help you to keep the law of diminishing marginal utility separate from the law of demand.

2. Figures 20.8a and 20.8b represent simple graphs drawn from a demand schedule.

Figure 20.8a

Price (dollars per unit)	Output quantity per unit of time
10	1
2	3

WRONG!

Figure 20.8b

Price (dollars per unit)	Output quantity per unit of time
10	1
2	3

RIGHT!

The first graph has been drawn without any units indicated. It is something of an accidental tradition in economics to show price on the *y*-axis and quantity on the *x*-axis. This convention is sometimes confusing to mathematicians, who want to treat quantity as a function of price, according to the definition in the text. In Figure 20.8a the axes have been reversed and incorrect points have been chosen.

Be careful! When you are drawing a new graph, make a special effort to understand the units that are placed on the axes. Also, make sure you know the kinds of units in which each axis is measured. If you are drawing a graph from a table (or schedule), you can usually determine what should be on the axes by looking at the heading above the column from which you are reading the numbers.

Make sure price is shown on the *y*-axis (vertical) and quantity on the *x*-axis (horizontal). If you mix up the two, you may confuse a graph showing perfectly elastic demand with one showing perfectly inelastic demand.

3. The formula for the price elasticity of demand is

$$\frac{\text{Change in price}}{\text{Change in quantity}} \qquad \text{WRONG!}$$

The formula for the price elasticity of demand is

$$\frac{\text{Percentage change in quantity demanded}}{\text{Percentage change in price}} \qquad \text{RIGHT!}$$

The concept of elasticity allows us to compare relative changes in quantity and price without having to worry about the units in which they are measured. In order to do this, we compute percentage changes of both price and quantity. A change in price *causes* people to change the quantity they demand in a given time period. By putting the quantity changes in the numerator, we can see that if the quantity response is very large in relation to a price change, the elasticity will also be very large. If the quantity response is small in relation to a price change, then demand is price inelastic (elasticity is small).

Be careful! Do not confuse slope and elasticity. The formula for the slope of the demand curve is the *wrong* formula shown above. The formula for the price elasticity of demand is the *right* formula. Remember to take the absolute value of the elasticity too.

4. A flat demand curve has an elasticity of zero. WRONG!

A flat demand curve has an infinite elasticity. RIGHT!

When price remains constant even when quantity changes, the elasticity formula requires us to divide by a zero price change. In fact, as demand curves approach flatness, the elasticity becomes larger and larger. By agreement we say it is infinite.

5. The person for whom a good or service has the greatest utility has the greatest desire for more of it. WRONG!

The good that has the greatest *marginal* utility for a person, with respect to price, is the good that he or she desires more. RIGHT!

Utilities of one good for many people cannot be compared. Utilities of various goods for one person can be compared. Marginal utility with respect to price, not total utility, is the best indicator of how to make a choice.

6. An expected price change has the same effect as a change in the current price. WRONG!

An unexpected price change shifts the demand curve, whereas a current price change is a movement along the demand curve. RIGHT!

If prices are expected to rise in the near future, people will demand more of the commodity today in order to beat the rise in price. Demand increases and the quantity demanded will rise. However, if the price rises today, by the law of demand people reduce the quantity demanded! Furthermore, demand itself does not change. A current price change and an expected price change have very different effects.

7. When a buyer purchases a good, the demand for the good decreases. WRONG!

When a buyer purchases a good, demand is not affected. RIGHT!

Demand refers only to the *willingness* and *ability* of a buyer to buy. The potential for purchase, not the actual purchase, is the focus of demand. Demand is defined over a given period of time. If a buyer buys a good during that period of time, he or she is still counted as demanding the good—even after it is purchased.

8. Both income and cross-price elasticities must be interpreted using absolute values. WRONG!

The absolute value is used only for the price elasticity of demand. RIGHT!

The law of demand guarantees that the price elasticity of demand would always have a negative sign. However, the income and cross-price elasticities may be either positive or negative, and the sign provides important information about the demand for a good. The sign of the income elasticity indicates if a good is a normal good or an inferior good. The sign on the cross-price elasticity indicates whether a good is a substitute or a complement.

•ANSWERS•

Using Key Terms

Across
1. complementary goods
6. diminishing marginal utility
12. law of demand
13. total utility
14. total revenue
15. substitute goods
17. income elasticity of demand
18. cross-price elasticity
19. opportunity cost

Down
2. demand
3. price elasticity of demand
4. optimal consumption
5. marginal utility
7. shift in demand
8. inferior good
9. demand curve
10. normal good
11. *ceteris paribus*
16. utility

True or False

1. T
2. T
3. F   Consumers will plan to wait until next month's lower prices to purchase this good. The current demand curve will shift to the left.
4. F   The marginal utility will decline. The total utility will increase as long as the marginal utility is positive.
5. T
6. F   A rise in the price will result in lower total revenues. A *decrease* in the price will raise total revenues if demand is elastic.
7. F   Price elasticity of demand will be more elastic (i.e., consumers more responsive) at higher prices. Elasticity cannot be compared to slope.
8. T
9. T
10. F   A *positive* cross-price elasticity indicates substitutes. An *increase* in the price of one good, for example, would result in an *increase* in the demand for the substitute.

Multiple Choice

1. a	5. b	9. b	13. d	17. a	21. c
2. c	6. c	10. b	14. c	18. b	22. c
3. b	7. d	11. b	15. d	19. c	23. d
4. d	8. a	12. a	16. a	20. b	

Problems and Applications

Exercise 1

1. d

2. **Figure 20.1 Answer**

3. **Figure 20.2 Answer**

283

4. **Table 20.3 Answer**

Price	Number of new cars (millions per year)
$10,000	10.0
9,000	12.0

5. ## Figure 20.3 Answer

Exercise 2

1. F
2. ## Table 20.4 Answer

Price	Number of new U.S. cars (millions per year)	Elasticity of demand
$10,000	10.0	---
9,000	12.0	1.73
8,000	14.0	1.64
7,000	16.0	1.23

3. Elastic
4. $112,000 million
5. Decrease
6. ## Figure 20.4 answer

7. T

284

8. The slope can be estimated by using the coordinates of any two points on the demand curve. The slope is computed by dividing the change in the variable on the y-axis by the change in the variable on the x-axis. For example, using the first and last points in Table 20.4, we would have

$$\frac{\text{Change in } y\text{-axis}}{\text{Change in } x\text{-axis}} = \frac{p_1 - p_2}{q_1 - q_2} = \frac{10{,}000 - 7{,}000}{10{,}000{,}000 - 16{,}000{,}0000} = \frac{3{,}000}{-6{,}000{,}000} = -.0005 \text{ per car}$$

Regardless of what pair of points is chosen, the slope should be the same (except for differences that result from rounding).

9. b; As noted in the previous problem, the slope is the same regardless of which pair of points is tried.

10. T

Exercise 3

1. **Table 20.5 Answer**

	Income (per year)	Demand for peanut butter (jars per year)		Income elasticity of demand
a	$10,000	12		
b	$20,000	7	a to b	-0.79
c	$40,000	3	b to c	-1.19
d	$80,000	1	c to d	-1.49

2. Inferior; falls; negative

3. **Table 20.6 Answer**

	Price of peanut butter (per jar)	Demand for jelly (jars per year)		Cross-price elasticity of demand
a	$2.00	12		
b	$3.00	10	a to b	-0.45
c	$4.00	7	b to c	-1.21
d	$5.00	2	c to d	-5.05

4. Complementary; falls; negative

Exercise 4

1. **Table 20.7 Answer**

Days of entertainment per month	Evening at home Marginal utility	Event Marginal utility
0	—	—
1	170	600
2	190	650
3	180	430
4	150	360
5	130	310
6	110	200
7	100	170
8	80	100
9	60	0
10	0	−60
11	−50	−100
12	−100	−200

2. b
3. a

4. **Figure 20.5 Answer**

5.   **Figure 20.6 Answer**

DAYS OF ENTERTAINMENT AT HOME
(per month)

6.   b
7.   c

Exercise 5

1.   c
2.   **Table 20.8 Answer**

	Event entertainment (price = $30)	
Days of entertainment per month	Marginal utility	$\frac{MU}{price}$
0	0	0
1	600	20
2	600	20
3	480	16
4	360	12
5	360	12
6	360	12
7	360	12
8	0	0
9	0	0
10	0	0

3.   Event entertainment
4.   2
5. $60 [= $120 - ($30 x 2)]
6.   No
7. $30 [= $120 - $60 - (3 x $10)]
8.   Event entertainment
9.   T

Exercise 6

1. 3 cokes; 5 video games
2. 2 cokes; 8 video games
3. c
4. 2 cokes; 5 video games
5. 3 cokes; 4 video games
6. Greater
7. I_2

CHAPTER 21

The Costs of Production

Quick Review

- The production function determines how much output can be obtained from varying amounts of factor inputs. Every point on the production function is efficient, meaning that, given current technology, the maximum output is being produced.

- The output of any factor depends on the amount of other resources available to it. Fixed factors constrain the firm's ability to produce output. As more of a variable input is applied to a fixed input, at some point, the marginal physical product of the variable input begins to get smaller in size. This short-run situation is referred to as the *law of diminishing returns*. In the long run, all factor inputs are variable.

- The dollar costs incurred because of fixed inputs are called fixed costs; those for variable factors are called variable costs. In the short-run, even if output is zero, there are fixed costs. The total cost of producing any level of output is the sum of fixed and variable costs. Because fixed costs do not change as output changes, the rate of increase in total cost is determined by variable costs only.

- Marginal cost (*MC*) is the increase in total cost associated with a one-unit increase in production. Average total cost (*ATC*) is the total cost of production divided by the rate of output. The *ATC* curve starts at a high level and declines as production increases because of fixed costs. At a point, the *ATC* curve begins to rise because of rising marginal costs that result from the law of diminishing returns. This results in a U-shaped *ATC* curve.

- Economic costs include both explicit and implicit costs associated with the use of *all* resources in the production process, whether they receive a monetary payment or not. Accounting costs include only those costs for which an explicit payment is made.

- In the short run some costs are fixed. The producer decides how much output to produce with existing facilities. In the long run there are no fixed costs. The producer must decide whether to build, buy, or lease plant and equipment.

- If minimum average costs decrease as the size of the firm increases, then there are economies of scale. If minimum *ATC* increases as the firm gets larger, then there are diseconomies of scale.

- Advances in technology shift the production function upward and the cost curves downward. Along with improved quality of inputs, technology improvements have historically been the major source of productivity growth in the U.S. economy.

Learning Objectives

After reading Chapter 21 and doing the following exercises, you should:

1. Know the relationship between the production function and the firm's ability to produce goods and services.
2. Understand the nature and determinants of marginal productivity.
3. Be able to draw a graph relating the marginal physical product and total product curves.
4. Be able to define and explain the law of diminishing returns.
5. Understand the relationship between the production function and the short-run cost curves.
6. Understand the difference between variable costs and fixed costs.
7. Know how to define and calculate the total, average, and marginal costs of production and be able to show their relationship to marginal productivity.
8. Understand the relationship between average and marginal cost curves.
9. Understand the distinction between economic costs and accounting costs.
10. Know the distinction between long-run costs and short-run costs.
11. Be able to explain economies of scale, diseconomies of scale, and constant returns to scale.
12. Understand the impact of technological improvements on the production function.

Using Key Terms

Fill in the puzzle on the opposite page with the appropriate term from the list of Key Terms at the end of the chapter in the text.

Across

1. The resources used to produce a good or service.
5. Costs of production that don't change when the rate of output is altered.
7. The market value of all resources used to produce a good or service.
9. Equal to the wage rate divided by marginal physical product.
11. The marginal physical product of a variable input declines as more of it is employed with a given quantity of other (fixed) inputs.
13. Maximum output of a good attainable from the resources used.
14. Any time a dollar payment is made for the use of a resource there is a(an) _____ cost.
15. Average total cost minus average fixed cost.
17. Includes both explicit and implicit costs.
18. The change in total output associated with one additional unit of input.
21. A technological relationship expressing the maximum quantity of a good attainable from different combinations of factor inputs.
22. Output per unit of input.
23. A period in which some inputs are fixed.

Down

2. Total cost divided by the quantity produced in a given time period.
3. The most desired forgone alternative.
4. Reductions in minimum average costs that come about through increases in the size of plant and equipment.
6. A situation in which an increase in plant size does not reduce minimum average costs.
8. Total fixed cost divided by the quantity produced in a given time period.
10. The portion of economic cost that does not receive an explicit payment.
12. Determine how fast total costs rise.
16. This curve is typically rising because of the law of diminishing returns.
19. The difference between total revenue and total cost.
20. A period in which all inputs are variable.

Puzzle 21.1

True or False: *Circle your choice and explain why any false statements are incorrect.*

T F 1. If the workers are very efficient, a firm can produce beyond the given production function.

T F 2. The productivity of labor is affected by changes in the mix of other factors being used in the production process.

T F 3. If *MPP* is increasing with output, the marginal cost of production is falling, *ceteris paribus*.

T F 4. The total cost at a zero level of output is always the amount of fixed costs.

T F 5. The marginal cost curve can intersect the average total cost curve and the average variable cost curve at any point.

T F 6. The difference between the accountant's and the economist's measurement of costs equals the opportunity costs of resources that do not have a value.

T F 7. As output increases, marginal costs eventually increase because *MPP* begins to decline.

T F 8. With greater output, falling average fixed costs eventually outweigh falling average variable costs, and then average total cost starts to rise.

T F 9. Economies of scale result from the law of diminishing returns.

T F 10. Improved technology shifts the production function upward and the cost curves downward.

Multiple Choice: *Select the correct answer.*

_____ 1. Which of the following would cause a firm's production function to shift upward?
    (a) An increase in production by the firm.
    (b) Hiring more workers.
    (c) Increased training for the firm's workers.
    (d) An increase in factor costs.

_____ 2. When a firm produces at the least-cost output level, it is:
    (a) Producing the output at the minimum *MC* curve.
    (b) Using the fewest resources to produce a good or service.
    (c) Producing the output where the *AVC* curve is at a minimum.
    (d) Producing the best combination of goods and services.

_____ 3. Technical efficiency is achieved for a given set of resources when a firm produces:
    (a) The quantity of output indicated by the production function.
    (b) Below the opportunity cost for the resources.
    (c) The minimum necessary output to cover the opportunity cost of resources.
    (d) All of the above.

_____ 4. The law of diminishing returns indicates that the greater use of a variable input, holding other factors fixed, results in:
    (a) A declining rate of increase in total output for each additional unit of input.
    (b) A rising *MC* curve.
    (c) A declining *MPP* curve.
    (d) All of the above.

5. Rising marginal costs are the result of:
    (a) The law of diminishing returns.
    (b) Decreasing *MPP*.
    (c) Adding more variable factors of production to a fixed quantity of other factors of production.
    (d) All of the above are correct.

6. Given the cost of the variable input, marginal cost will increase with greater output if:
    (a) Marginal physical product is declining.
    (b) Marginal physical product is increasing.
    (c) Total variable cost is decreasing.
    (d) Total fixed cost is increasing.

7. For which of the following costs would the cost curve appear as a flat line and the associated average cost curve decline continuously?
    (a) Total costs.
    (b) Variable costs.
    (c) Fixed costs.
    (d) Marginal costs.

8. If an additional unit of labor costs $20, and has an *MPP* of 40 units of output, the marginal cost is:
    (a) $0.20.
    (b) $0.50.
    (c) $20.00.
    (d) $800.00.

9. Which of the following can you compute if you know only the total cost at an output level of zero?
    (a) Fixed cost.
    (b) Variable cost.
    (c) Marginal cost.
    (d) Average total cost.

10. When output increases and the marginal cost curve is:
    (a) Below the *ATC*, the *ATC* is downward sloping.
    (b) Equal to the *ATC*, the *ATC* is at its lowest point.
    (c) Above the *ATC*, the *ATC* is upward sloping.
    (d) All of the above.

11. As output increases, changes in short-run total costs result from changes in:
    (a) Variable costs.
    (b) Fixed costs.
    (c) Profit.
    (d) The price elasticity of demand.

12. Which of the following is equivalent to *ATC*?
    (a) *FC + VC*.
    (b) *AFC + AVC*.
    (c) Change in output divided by change in total cost.
    (d) Total cost times the quantity produced.

_____ 13. The _ATC_ at a given output level multiplied by the number of units produced at that output level equals:
  (a)   Marginal cost.
  (b)   Total fixed cost.
  (c)   Total variable cost.
  (d)   Total cost.

_____ 14. Which one of the following curves is falling when marginal cost is below it?
  (a)   Average variable cost curve.
  (b)   Average total cost curve.
  (c)   Average fixed cost curve.
  (d)   All of the above.

_____ 15. Which of the following costs will always increase as output increases?
  (a)   Total costs.
  (b)   Average total costs.
  (c)   Marginal costs.
  (d)   Fixed costs.

_____ 16. Economies of scale are reductions:
  (a)   In average total cost that result from declining average fixed costs.
  (b)   In average fixed cost that result from reducing the firm's scale of operations.
  (c)   In average total cost that result from increasing the firm's scale of operations.
  (d)   In average fixed cost resulting from improved technology and production efficiency.

_____ 17. Which of the following contributes to the typical U shape of the _ATC_ curve?
  (a)   The initial dominance of diminishing returns.
  (b)   The eventual dominance of the rising _AVC_ curve.
  (c)   The steady impact of a rising _AFC_ curve.
  (d)   All of the above.

_____ 18. In economics, the long run is the time period in which:
  (a)   All inputs are fixed.
  (b)   All inputs are variable.
  (c)   Some inputs are fixed.
  (d)   Producers decide how much to produce with existing plant and equipment.

_____ 19. In defining economic costs, economists recognize:
  (a)   Only explicit costs while accountants recognize only implicit costs.
  (b)   Only explicit costs while accountants recognize explicit and implicit costs.
  (c)   Explicit and implicit costs while accountants recognize only implicit costs.
  (d)   Explicit and implicit costs while accountants recognize only explicit costs.

_____ 20. The long-run average cost curve is constructed from:
  (a)   The minimum points of the short-run marginal cost curves.
  (b)   The minimum points of the short-run average cost curves.
  (c)   The lowest average cost for producing each level of output.
  (d)   The minimum points of the long-run marginal cost curves.

Problems and Applications

Exercise 1

This exercise shows how to compute and graph the marginal physical product of a factor of production. It also demonstrates the law of diminishing returns.

In the text, an example of jeans production was used to show how many sewing machines and workers were needed per day to produce various quantities of jeans per day. A similar table is given here.

Table 21.1
The production of jeans
(pairs per day)

Capital input (sewing machines per day)	Labor input (workers per day)							
	0	1	2	3	4	5	6	7
0	0	0	0	0	0	0	0	0
1	0	15	34	44	48	50	51	46
2	0	20	46	64	72	78	81	80
3	0	21	50	73	82	92	99	102

1. Suppose a firm has two sewing machines and can vary only the amount of labor input. On the basis of Table 21.1, fill in column 2 of Table 21.2 to show how much can be produced at different levels of labor input when there are only two sewing machines.

Table 21.2
The production of jeans with two sewing machines

(1) Labor input (workers per day)	(2) Production of jeans (pairs per day)	(3) Marginal physical product (pairs per worker)
0	_____	—
1	_____	_____
2	_____	_____
3	_____	_____
4	_____	_____
5	_____	_____
6	_____	_____
7	_____	_____

2. Graph the total output curve in Figure 21.1.

Figure 21.1

3. Compute the marginal physical product of each extra worker per day. Place the answers in column 3 of Table 21.2.

4. Graph the marginal physical product curve in Figure 21.2.

Figure 21.2

5. The law of diminishing returns states that the marginal physical product of a factor will:
   (a) Become negative as output increases.
   (b) Always decline as output increases.
   (c) Increase and then decline as output increases.
   (d) Begin to decline as more of the factor is used.

6. At what amount of labor input does the law of diminishing returns first become apparent in Figure 21.2?
   (a) 0-1.
   (b) 1-2.
   (c) 2-3.
   (d) 3-4.

7. In Figure 21.1 at 4 units of labor, total output:
   (a) Is rising with increased labor usage.
   (b) Is falling with increased labor usage.
   (c) Remains constant with increased labor.

8. T F When marginal physical product declines, total output declines.

Exercise 2

This exercise shows the relationship between the various costs of production.

1. Complete Table 21.3 using the information given about output and the costs of production. (Hint: Refer to the table in Figure 21.5 in the text if you need help getting started.)

Table 21.3 Costs of Production

Rate of Output	Fixed Cost	Variable Cost	Total Cost	Average Total Cost	Marginal Cost
0	$ _____	$ _____	$ 10	--------	-------
1	_____	6	_____	$ _____	$ _____
2	_____	10	_____	_____	_____
3	_____	16	_____	_____	_____
4	_____		36	_____	_____
5	_____	40	_____	_____	_____
6	_____	_____	68	_____	_____

2. When the average total cost is rising, marginal cost is (above; below; equal to) average total cost.

3. When the average total cost is falling, marginal cost is (above; below; equal to) average total cost.

Exercise 3

This exercise shows the relationship between fixed costs, variable costs, accounting cost, and economic cost.

1. Fixed costs are defined as:
   (a) Costs that do not change with inflation.
   (b) Costs that are set firmly (without escalator clauses) in a contract.
   (c) Costs of production that do not change when the rate of production is altered.
   (d) Average costs that do not change when the rate of production is altered.

2. Variable costs include:
   (a) Costs of production that change when the rate of production is altered.
   (b) All costs in the long run.
   (c) The difference between total and fixed costs.
   (d) All of the above.

Table 21.4 Expense statements for parachute business (dollars per week)

Weekly expense	Parachutes produced per week		
	0	100	200
Lease on building	$1,500	$1,500	$1,500
Sewing machines	600	600	600
Nylon	0	400	700
Utilities (electricity, etc.)	0	150	200
Labor	0	650	750
Testing and certification	800	800	800

Use the information in Table 21.4 to answer the following questions.

3. Which items are considered to be fixed costs? _____

4. Calculate variable costs at an output level of 100 parachutes per week. _____

5. Calculate total costs at an output level of 100 parachutes per week. _____

6. Now assume the owner of the parachute business buys the building he is currently leasing so he no longer has a lease expenditure. Calculate the accounting cost at an output level of 200 parachutes per week. _____

7. Assume the owner still owns the building. Calculate the economic cost at an output level of 200 parachutes per week. Explain why there is a difference in the accounting cost at an output level of 200 parachutes and the economic cost. _____

Exercise 4

This exercise focuses on average total costs.

Table 21.5 represents the cost data for producing cement in three different plants, where Plant 1 is the smallest and Plant 3 is the largest.

Table 21.5
Costs associated with three plants

Output (tons per day)	1	2	3	4	5	6	7	8	9	10
Average total cost:										
Plant 1	$10	9	8	7	8	9	10	11	12	13
Plant 2	12	10	8	6	5	4	5	6	8	10
Plant 3	13	12	11	9	7	5	3	2	3	4

1. Given the three plant sizes in Table 21.5, the cement industry experiences (economies of scale; diseconomies of scale; constant returns to scale) because as plant size increases the minimum average total cost (increases; decreases; stays the same).

2. Which plant should be used to produce 2 tons of cement per day? _____

3. Which plant should be used to produce 8 tons of cement per day? _____

4. For which levels of output is Plant 2 the best choice? _____

Exercise 5

Suppose the marginal physical product of worker A is 10 units per hour and her wage is $15 per hour. Suppose the marginal physical product of worker B is 5 units per hour and her wage is $10 per hour. Given this information, answer questions 1-4.

1. Calculate the unit labor cost for worker A. _____

2. Calculate the unit labor cost for worker B. _____

3. T   F   Worker B is less costly per unit because her wage rate is lower.

4. T   F   Unit labor costs can be used to measure productivity.

Exercise 6

The news media often provide information on events that affect productivity and costs. This exercise will use one of the articles in the text to show the kind of information to look for.

Reread the article in the text titled "Funeral Giant Moves In on Small Rivals," and then answer the following questions.

1. What is the strategy employed by SCI to achieve economies of scale? _____
   _____

2. Which phrase(s) indicates how SCI grew to more than 230,000 units? _____
   _____

3. Which phrase indicates one way that SCI achieves lower costs than its rivals? _____
   _____

4. Which phrase demonstrates that economies of scale have allowed SCI to reap greater profits than its smaller rivals? _____

Common Errors

The first statement in each "common error" below is incorrect. Each incorrect statement is followed by a corrected version and an explanation.

1. A rising marginal cost means average cost is rising. WRONG!

   A rising average cost curve means the marginal cost curve is above the average cost curve. RIGHT!

It is important to remember the basic relationships between the average cost curves and the marginal cost curve:

a. When the average cost curve rises, the marginal cost curve is above the average cost curve.

b. When the average cost curve falls, the marginal cost curve is below the average cost curve.

c. When the average cost curve is flat, the marginal cost curve equals the average cost curve.

2. Total output starts falling when diminishing returns occur. WRONG!

Diminishing returns set in when marginal physical product begins to decline. RIGHT!

The law of diminishing returns describes what happens to *marginal physical product,* not total output. Marginal physical product will typically begin to decline long before total output begins to decline. For total output to decline, the marginal physical product must be negative.

3. A firm's productivity increases when labor is willing to accept lower wages. WRONG!

A firm's productivity increases when more output can be produced per unit of labor used. RIGHT!

Productivity is not defined on the basis of the prices of factors of production. Productivity depends simply on the amount of output that is produced by the factors of production.

4. The term "economies of scale" refers to the shape of the short-run average cost curve. WRONG!

The term "economies of scale" refers to the shape of the long-run average cost curve. RIGHT!

The short-run average cost curve and the long-run average cost curve may have similar shapes. But the shape of the short-run curve results from the law of diminishing returns. In the long run, all factors, and therefore all costs, are variable. Thus the shape of the long-run average cost curve is the result of other forces, such as the specialization and division of labor, the use of different sources of power, and so on. Remember, even though the long-run average cost curve is a summary of many short-run average cost curves, and even though the shapes of the two curves may be similar, the reasons for the shapes of the curves are quite different. The term "economies of scale" applies only to the long-run average cost curve.

5. The marginal cost curve rises because factor prices rise when more of a good is produced. WRONG!

The marginal cost curve rises because the marginal productivity of the variable factor declines. RIGHT!

The marginal cost curve moves in the direction opposite to that of the marginal product curve. Changes in factor prices would shift the whole marginal cost curve but would not explain its shape and would not affect the marginal product curve.

6. Marginal physical product begins to decline because inferior factors must be hired to increase output. WRONG!

Declining marginal physical product occurs even if all of the factors are of equal quality. RIGHT!

Many people incorrectly attribute diminishing returns to the use of inferior factors of production. Diminishing returns result from an increasing ratio of the variable input to the fixed input. There is always a point where the variable input begins to have too little of the fixed input to work with. Result? Diminishing marginal product!

7. Diminishing returns means there are diseconomies of scale. WRONG!

Diminishing returns refers to the short-run shape of a marginal physical product curve and diseconomies of scale refers to the shape of the long-run average cost curve. RIGHT!

As suggested in the previous Common Error, diminishing returns is a short-run phenomenon; at least one input in the production process is fixed. Diminishing returns is reflected in diminishing marginal productivity and a rising short-run marginal cost curve. However, when all factors are variable—as they are in the long run—then it is possible to talk about economies or diseconomies of scale. Diseconomies of scale results in a rising long-run average cost curve. It is quite common to have short-run diminishing returns and long-run economies of scale, particularly in the public utilities.

•ANSWERS•

Using Key Terms

Across

1.	factors of production
5.	fixed costs
7.	total cost
9.	unit labor cost
11.	law of diminishing returns
13.	efficiency
14.	explicit
15.	average variable cost
17.	economic cost
18.	marginal physical product
21.	production function
22.	productivity
23.	short run

Down

2.	average total cost
3.	opportunity cost
4.	economies of scale
6.	constant returns to scale
8.	average fixed cost
10.	implicit cost
12.	variable costs
16.	marginal cost
19.	profit
20.	long run

True or False

1. F   The production function represents the maximum output that can be obtained from a given mix of inputs, i.e., technical efficiency.
2. T
3. T

4. T
5. F   The marginal cost curve always intersects the minimum point of the average total cost
       curve and the minimum point of the average variable cost curve.
6. F   The difference is the opportunity cost of resources that are not given an explicit payment.
7. T
8. F   Rising AVC (MC) will eventually overcome falling AFC and cause the ATC to increase.
9. F   Economies of scale is a long-run phenomenon. The law of diminishing returns does not
       apply in the long run because there are no fixed inputs in the long run.
10. T

Multiple Choice

1.	c	5.	d	9.	a	13.	d	17.	b
2.	b	6.	a	10.	d	14.	d	18.	b
3.	a	7.	c	11.	a	15.	a	19.	d
4.	d	8.	b	12.	b	16.	c	20.	c

Problems and Applications

Exercise 1

1.   See Table 21.2 Answer, column 2.

Table 21.2 Answer

(1)	(2)	(3)
0	0	---
1	20	20
2	46	26
3	64	18
4	72	8
5	78	6
6	81	3
7	80	-1

2. **Figure 21.1 Answer**

3. See Table 21.2 Answer, column 3.

4. **Figure 21.2 Answer**

5. d   6. c   7. a   8. F

Exercise 2

1. **Table 21.3 Answer**

Rate of Output	Fixed Cost	Variable Cost	Total Cost	Average Total Cost	Marginal Cost
0	$ 10	$ 0	$ 10	--------	-------
1	10	6	16	$16.00	$ 6
2	10	10	20	10.00	4
3	10	16	26	8.67	6
4	10	26	36	9.00	10
5	10	40	50	10.00	14
6	10	58	68	11.33	18

2. Above
3. Below

Exercise 3

1. c
2. d
3. Lease on the building, sewing machines, and testing and certification
4. $1,200
5. $4,100
6. $3,050
7. $4,550; The economic cost is greater because it includes the implicit cost of the building; the accounting cost does not.

Exercise 4

1. Economies of scale; decreases
2. Plant 1
3. Plant 3
4. 4 to 6 tons per day

Exercise 5

1. $15 ÷ 10 = $1.50 per unit of output
2. $10 ÷ 5 = $2.00 per unit of output
3. F   Unit labor cost, not wage rate, is used to determine cost.
4. T

Exercise 6

1. SCI uses a large number of small plants.
2. "But we're in the era of acquisitions and consolidations..."
3. "SCI is able to get cheaper prices on caskets and other products from suppliers," and "if funeral homes clustered in the same markets cut costs by sharing vehicles, personnel, services, and supplies."
4. "...give SCI a profit of 31 cents on every dollar it takes in...vs. 12 cents for the industry as a whole."

CHAPTER 22
The Competitive Firm

Quick Review

- Profit is the difference between revenues and costs. Because economists include implicit costs in assessing the costs of production, economic profits are smaller than accounting profits.

- Market power is determined by the number and relative size of firms in an industry. Market power affects the behavior of producers and influences market outcomes. Market structure ranges from monopoly to perfect competition.

- A perfectly competitive firm cannot influence the price of its output and is referred to as a price taker. It is important to distinguish the firm's demand curve from the market-demand curve. The firm's demand curve is perfectly flat because the firm produces such a small part of total market output, while the market demand curve is downward-sloping, reflecting the law of demand.

- In an effort to maximize profits, in the short run, a competitive firm will choose the rate of output where price equals marginal cost.

- In the short run, a firm continues to operate as long as it can cover its variable costs. A firm *shuts down* if variable costs of production cannot be covered. The point where price equals minimum *AVC* is the shutdown point.

- In the long run a firm must cover all costs, both explicit and implicit, or exit from the market. This is the firm's investment decision.

- A competitive firm's marginal cost curve above the average total cost curve is its short-run supply curve.

- The determinants of supply include the price of inputs, technology, and expectations. If any of these determinants change, the firm's supply curve will shift.

- Changes in tax laws can affect both the production decision (short run) and the investment decision (long run).

Learning Objectives

After reading Chapter 22 and doing the following exercises, you should:

1. Know the difference between economic profits and accounting profits, and how profits are maximized.
2. Know the different market structures and the basic characteristics of each.
3. Understand why competitive firms are "price takers" and recognize the differences between the firm's demand and the market demand.
4. Know the relationships among total, average, and marginal costs (or revenue).
5. Recognize the difference between long-run and short-run decisions.
6. Know the profit maximization rule and the importance of marginal revenue and marginal cost.
7. Understand graphically how a firm determines profit, price, and production rate in the short run.
8. Understand how the firm makes the "shutdown" decision and the long-run investment decision.
9. Understand how various taxes affect the firm's output decision.

Using Key Terms

Fill in the puzzle on the opposite page with the appropriate term from the list of Key Terms at the end of the chapter in the text.

Across

2. The value of all resources used in production.
4. Costs of production that don't change when the rate of output is altered.
6. The competitive _____ _____ _____ says firms should produce the rate of output where $MR = MC$.
7. The change in total revenue that results from a one-unit increase in quantity sold.
9. The opportunity cost of capital.
11. The period in which the quantity of some inputs cannot be changed.
12. The increase in total costs associated with a one-unit increase in production.
13. The ability to alter the market price of a good or service.
14. The long-run decision to enter or exit an industry.
17. The number and relative size of firms in an industry.
18. The price of a product multiplied by the quantity sold in a given time period.
19. The value of resources used, even when no direct payment is made, is the _____ cost.
20. Costs of production that change when the rate of output changes.
21. A period of time long enough for all inputs to be varied.
22. Represented by a direct payment made for the use of a resource.

Down

1. A market in which no buyer or seller has market power.
3. The sole supplier of a good or service.
5. A firm that must take whatever price the market offers for the goods it produces.
6. The choice of a short-run rate of output by a firm.
8. Total revenue minus total economic cost.
10. The rate of output where price equals minimum AVC.
15. The marginal cost curve is the short-run _____ _____ for a competitive firm.
16. Eventually becomes zero in a competitive industry because of market entry.

Puzzle 22.1

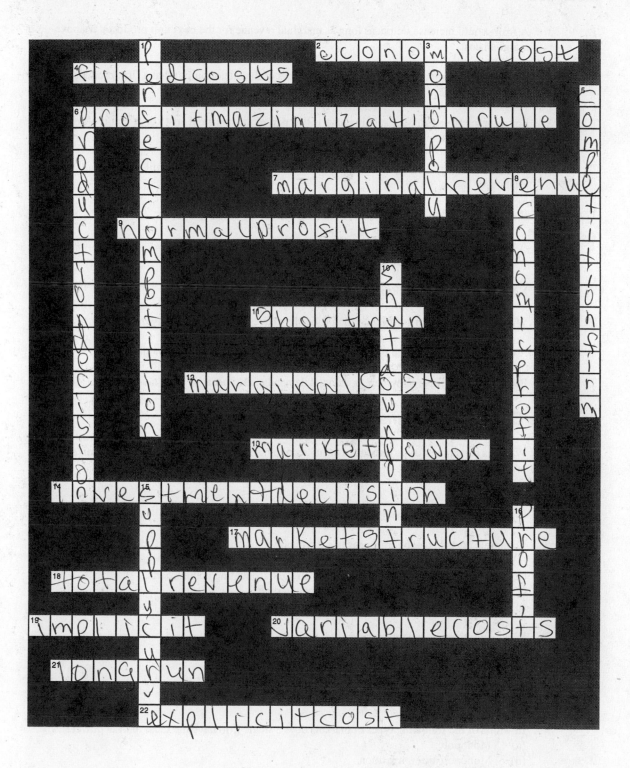

True or False: *Circle your choice and explain why any false statements are incorrect.*

T F **1.** A firm should increase output as long as marginal revenue for the next unit produced is above marginal cost.

T F **2.** If the price of a good remains the same regardless of the rate of output that a firm produces, the demand curve faced by the firm is perfectly elastic.

T **F** **3.** For a competitive firm, the supply curve is that part of the marginal cost curve that is above the short-run average total cost curve.

T **F** **4.** Since a firm's goal is to maximize profits, it should expand production until total revenue equals total cost.

T **F** **5.** If a firm maximizes revenue, it is maximizing profit.

T F **6.** A firm can minimize its losses by continuing to produce in the short run when price is less than *ATC* but greater than *AVC*.

T F **7.** Normal profit is when a firm's revenues just cover its economic costs.

T **F** **8.** When businesses earn zero economic profit, they have no incentive to stay in business.

T F **9.** A change in the tax rate on corporate profits will affect the firm's investment decision.

T F **10.** Perfectly competitive firms face horizontal demand curves because they have no market power.

Multiple Choice: *Select the correct answer.*

a **1.** Whereas consumers try to maximize utility, economists assume that firms try to maximize:
  (a) Profits.
  (b) Revenues.
  (c) Sales.
  (d) Production in a given period of time, *ceteris paribus*.

a **2.** Economic costs and economic profits are typically:
  (a) Greater and smaller, respectively, than their accounting counterparts.
  (b) Smaller and greater, respectively, than their accounting counterparts.
  (c) Both smaller than their accounting counterparts.
  (d) Both larger than their accounting counterparts.

c **3.** When a producer can control the market price for the good it sells:
  (a) The producer is an entrepreneur.
  (b) The producer is certain to make a profit.
  (c) The producer has market power.
  (d) The producer is a perfectly competitive firm.

a **4.** In which of the following types of markets does a single firm have the most market power?
  (a) Monopoly.
  (b) Monopolistic competition.
  (c) Oligopoly.
  (d) Perfect competition.

_d_ 5. Normal profit implies that:
   (a)   Economic profit is zero.
   (b)   All factors employed are earning an amount equal to their opportunity costs.
   (c)   The factors employed are earning as much as they could in the best alternative employment.
   (d)   All of the above.

_b_ 6. The market equilibrium price occurs where:
   (a)   Price equals the minimum of average variable cost.
   (b)   Market supply crosses market demand.
   (c)   A firm's marginal revenue equals marginal cost.
   (d)   A firm's marginal cost equals average cost.

_b_ 7. A competitive firm:
   (a)   Has a large advertising budget.
   (b)   Has output so small relative to the market supply that is has no effect on market price.
   (c)   Can alter the market price of the good(s) it produces.
   (d)   Can raise price to increase profit.

_c_ 8. If a perfectly competitive firm can sell 100 computers at $500 each, in order to sell one more computer, the firm:
   (a)   Must lower its price.
   (b)   Can raise its price.
   (c)   Can sell the 101st computer at $500.
   (d)   Cannot sell an additional computer at any price because the market is at equilibrium.

_c_ 9. A competitive firm's profits are maximized where:
   (a)   Market supply crosses the firm's marginal cost.
   (b)   Price equals the minimum of total cost.
   (c)   Price equals marginal cost.
   (d)   Marginal cost equals total revenue.

_b_ _a_ 10. If price is greater than marginal cost, a perfectly competitive firm should increase output because:
   (a)   Marginal costs are increasing.
   (b)   Additional units of output will add to the firm's profits (or reduce losses).
   (c)   The price they receive for their product is increasing.
   (d)   Total revenues would increase.

_b_ _a_ 11. If a perfectly competitive firm wanted to maximize its total _revenues_, it would produce:
   (a)   The output where _MC_ equals price.
   (b)   As much output as it is capable of producing.
   (c)   The output where the _ATC_ curve is at a minimum.
   (d)   The output where the marginal cost curve is at a minimum.

_d_ _b_ 12. Total profit is:
   (a)   _TR - TC_.
   (b)   _Q_ x (_P - ATC_).
   (c)   (_P_ x _Q_) - _TC_.
   (d)   All of the above.

_b_ 13. When price exceeds average variable cost but not average total cost, the firm should, in the short run:
   (a)   Shut down.
   (b)   Produce at the rate of output where price = _MC_.
   (c)   Minimize per-unit losses by producing at the rate of output where _ATC_ is minimized.
   (d)   Raise the price it charges.

a 14. A firm should shut down (stop producing) whenever:
   (a) Minimum average variable cost exceeds price.
   (b) Minimum average total cost exceeds price.
   (c) It is taking a loss.
   (d) Marginal cost exceeds marginal revenue.

a 15. A firm that makes an investment decision views all factors of production as:
   (a) Variable over the long run.
   (b) Variable over the short run.
   (c) Fixed over the long run.
   (d) Fixed over the short run.

d 16. The marginal cost curve:
   (a) Will be affected by changes in the cost of inputs.
   (b) Will eventually slope upward to the right as output increases.
   (c) Above the *AVC* is the short run supply curve for a competitive firm.
   (d) All of the above.

a 17. The market supply curve is calculated by:
   (a) Summing the quantities supplied of individual supply curves at each price.
   (b) Averaging the quantities supplied of individual supply curves at each price.
   (c) Summing the prices of individual supply curves at each price.
   (d) Averaging the prices of individual supply curves.

c 18. The short-run supply curve, for a perfectly competitive firm, is equivalent to the *MC* curve:
   (a) Above *ATC*.
   (b) Above *AFC*.
   (c) Above *AVC*.
   (d) Beyond its minimum point.

a 19. Taxes affect average total cost and marginal cost curves as follows:
   (a) Profit taxes affect neither, property taxes affect only average total cost, and payroll taxes affect both average and marginal costs.
   (b) Payroll taxes affect neither, property taxes affect only average total cost, and profit taxes affect both average and marginal costs.
   (c) Payroll taxes affect neither, property taxes affect only marginal cost, and profit taxes affect both average and marginal costs.
   (d) Property taxes affect neither, payroll taxes affect only marginal cost, and profit taxes affect both average and marginal costs.

d 20. If a perfectly competitive firm finds that economic profits are negative in the short run, it should shut down:
   (a) And go out of business.
   (b) If price is less than *ATC* but greater than *AVC*.
   (c) If price is less than *MC* but greater than *AVC*.
   (d) If price is less than *AVC*.

Problems and Applications

Exercise 1

This exercise uses total cost and total revenue to determine how much output a competitive firm should produce.

Refer to Figure 22.1 to answer questions 1-5.

Figure 22.1

1. Profit is the difference between _____ _____ and _____ _____.

2. This firm earns a profit at all output levels between _____ and _____ units.

3. What is the profit maximizing rate of output for this firm? _____

4. This firm experiences losses at all rates of output below _____ units.

5. Total costs increase more rapidly after 90 units of output because of the law of _____ _____.

Exercise 2

This exercise shows how the equilibrium price is determined in a competitive market and how the profit maximizing rate of output is determined in a perfectly competitive market.

1. Using the information in Table 22.1 draw the market demand curve for chicken eggs in Figure 22.2. Label the curve *D*. (Assume the demand curve is linear or a straight line.)

311

Table 22.1
Market demand for eggs

Quantity (millions of eggs per day)	Price (per dozen)
2	$ 1.00
4	$ 0.50

Figure 22.2
Market demand and market supply curves

2. Using the information in Table 22.2 draw the market supply curve for chicken eggs in Figure 22.2. Label the curve *S*. (Assume the supply curve is linear or a straight line.)

Table 22.2
Market supply of eggs

Quantity (millions of eggs per day)	Price (per dozen)
4	$ 1.00
2	$ 0.50

3. Use the information in Table 22.3 to determine the marginal cost at each output level for an individual egg farmer.

Table 22.3
Production costs for an individual egg farmer

Quantity (eggs per minute)	Total cost	Marginal cost
0	$ 4.00	---------
1	$ 4.20	_____
2	$ 4.65	_____
3	$ 5.40	_____
4	$ 6.50	_____
5	$ 7.90	_____

4. Use the information in Table 22.3 to draw the marginal cost curve for the individual egg farmer in Figure 22.3.

Figure 22.3
Costs of egg production

5. Use the market equilibrium price from Figure 22.2 to draw a line at the price that the individual farmer faces in Figure 22.3.

6. For a competitive firm, *MR* always equals _____.

7. According to the profit-maximization rule, this egg farmer should produce _____ eggs per minute.

8. At an output level of 2 eggs per minute, for the individual farmer, *MC* is (greater; less) than price and the farmer should (increase; decrease) output in order to maximize profit.

Exercise 3

This exercise provides practice in using graphs in a perfectly competitive market situation.

Figure 22.4
Production costs

1. Label the three curves given in Figure 22.4 for a firm in a perfectly competitive market situation.

2. What is the profit maximizing rate of output for this firm? _____

3. Shade the area that represents total profit at the profit maximizing rate of output.

4. Given a perfectly competitive market, does this graph depict a short-run or long-run situation? Explain how you know. _____

Exercise 4

This exercise gives you a chance to calculate total revenue, total profit, and marginal cost and to find the output that will yield maximum profit.

1. Complete the following formulas: (a) Price X quantity = _____
   (b) Change in total cost ÷ change in output = _____
   (c) Total revenue - total cost = _____

2. After checking your answers for question 1, complete Table 22.4.

Table 22.4
Cost and revenue data

Qty.	Price	Total revenue	Total cost	Profit	Marginal cost
0	$7	$_____	$ 5.00	$_____	--------
1	7	_____	7.00	_____	_____
2	7	_____	11.00	_____	_____
3	7	_____	18.00	_____	_____
4	7	_____	27.00	_____	_____
5	7	_____	39.00	_____	_____

3. In Figure 22.5, graph price and marginal cost.

Figure 22.5

Quantity (items per hour)

4. What is the profit maximizing level of output for this firm? _____

5. At an output level of 4 items this firm would (increase; decrease) profit by producing more.

Exercise 5

This exercise focuses on the shutdown decision.

Refer to Figure 22.6 to answer questions 1-6.

Figure 22.6

1. What is the profit-maximizing production rate for the firm if the price is $23? _____

2. What is the profit-maximizing production rate for the firm if the price is $15? _____

3. At a price of $12 this firm is earning a (profit; loss) and should (continue to produce; shut-down) because the price is greater than (ATC; AVC).

4. The shutdown price for a firm is any price below the minimum of the _____ curve.

5. At a price of $8 this firm will minimize losses by (continuing to produce; shutting down). In this case total revenues are (less; greater) than total variable costs.

6. The shutdown point for this firm occurs at a price of _____.

Common Errors

The first statement in each "common error" below is incorrect. Each incorrect statement is followed by a corrected version and an explanation.

1. Zero economic profits mean that a firm should go out of business. WRONG!

   Zero economic profits mean that a firm is still earning accounting profits. RIGHT!

   Since economic profits take into account economic costs, economic profits will be less than accounting profits if there are implicit costs. If a firm is covering its opportunity costs, it can still remain in business even if its economic profits are zero.

2. If a firm cannot cover all of its costs, it should shut down production. WRONG!

   If a firm cannot cover its variable costs, it should shut down production. RIGHT!

   The decision to shut down production depends only on variable costs. Even if the firm cannot cover its total costs, the firm will minimize losses in the short run by continuing to produce as long as variable costs are covered. If variable costs cannot be covered, then the firm should shut down. When a firm shuts down, it loses all its fixed costs.

3. If a firm is taking a loss, it is not maximizing profits. WRONG!

   A firm may be maximizing profits even if it is making zero profits or taking a loss. RIGHT!

   Minimizing losses is essentially the same as maximizing profits. A firm is maximizing profits as long as there is nothing it can do to make larger profits. Remember, even if the firm is taking a loss, it will not shut down if it can cover variable costs.

4. A price taker chooses the price that maximizes profit. WRONG!

   A price taker chooses the rate of output in order to maximize profit at the market price. RIGHT!

   In a perfectly competitive market, price is determined by the interaction of market supply and market demand. The individual firm can sell all the output it can produce at the market price, but it will not sell any output at a higher price. Since all the output can be sold at the market price, there is no incentive to sell the output for a lower price. Perfectly competitive firms adjust output so that marginal cost equals price. At this level of output, profit is maximized. This explains why perfectly competitive firms are called price takers.

5. A firm should always increase the rate of production as long as it is making a profit. WRONG!

    A profitable firm should increase production rates only as long as additional revenues from the increase in production exceed the additional associated costs. RIGHT!

    If the increase in production rates generates more costs than revenue, the firm will be less profitable. In this case, continued expansion will ultimately result in zero profits.

•ANSWERS•

Using Key Terms

Across

2. economic cost
4. fixed costs
6. profit maximization rule
7. marginal revenue
9. normal profit
11. short run
12. marginal cost
13. market power
14. investment decision
17. market structure
18. total revenue
19. implicit
20. variable costs
21. long run
22. explicit cost

Down

1. perfect competition
3. monopoly
5. competitive firm
6. production decision
8. economic profit
10. shutdown point
15. supply curve
16. profit

True or False

1. T
2. T
3. F   The supply curve is that part of the marginal cost curve above the *AVC* curve.
4. F   A firm should expand production until *MR* equals *MC*. To produce where total revenue equals total cost yields a profit of zero.

5. F To maximize revenue, a firm would produce as much output as it possibly can. To maximize profit, the firm should produce the output where the difference between *TR* and *TC* is the greatest.
6. T
7. T
8. F A firm that earns zero economic profits is covering all its economic costs, including a normal profit to the entrepreneur. There is no better use for the firm's resources (i.e., it is earning exactly what it could earn in the next best option).
9. T
10. T

Multiple Choice

1.	a	5.	d	9.	c	13.	b	17.	a
2.	a	6.	b	10.	b	14.	a	18.	c
3.	c	7.	b	11.	b	15.	a	19.	a
4.	a	8.	c	12.	d	16.	d	20.	d

Problems and Applications

Exercise 1

1. Total revenue; total cost
2. 90; 220
3. 160 units
4. 90
5. Diminishing returns

Exercise 2

1. See Figure 22.2 answer.
2. See Figure 22.2 answer.

Figure 22.2 Answer

318

3. **Table 22.3 Answer**

Quantity	Marginal cost
0	$ ------
1	0.20
2	0.45
3	0.75
4	1.10
5	1.40

4. See Figure 22.3 answer.
5. See Figure 22.3 answer.

Figure 22.3 Answer

6. Price
7. 3
8. Less; increase

Exercise 3

1. **Figure 22.4 Answer**

2. 4 items per hour
3. See Figure 22.4 answer.
4. Short run; there is an economic profit (price is greater than minimum *ATC*)

319

Exercise 4

1. a. Total revenue
    b. Marginal cost
    c. Profit

2. **Table 22.4 Answer**

Quantity	Total revenue	Profit	Marginal cost
0	$ 0.00	$ -5.00	-------
1	7.00	+ 0.00	$ 2.00
2	14.00	+ 3.00	4.00
3	21.00	+ 3.00	7.00
4	28.00	+ 1.00	9.00
5	35.00	- 4.00	12.00

3. **Figure 22.5 Answer**

4. 3 items per day
5. Decrease

Exercise 5

1. 39 units
2. 31 units
3. Loss; continue to produce; *AVC*
4. *AVC*
5. Shutting down; less
6. $10

CHAPTER 23

Competitive Markets

Quick Review

- In a competitive industry, the market supply curve is the sum of the marginal cost curves of individual firms. Economic profits encourage new firms to enter a competitive market. As entry occurs, the market supply curve shifts to the right and the equilibrium price decreases.

- The characteristics of a perfectly competitive market are 1) many firms, 2) perfect information, 3) low barriers to entry, 4) identical products, 5) marginal cost pricing, and 6) zero economic profit in the long run.

- The short-run production decision leads perfectly competitive firms to produce where price equals MC.

- The limit to the competitive price and profit squeeze is reached when price is driven down to the level of minimum average total cost (ATC). If the market price falls below the minimum ATC, firms will exit from the industry. Price stabilizes when entry and exit cease. This long-run equilibrium occurs when economic profits reach zero.

- In the short run, if a firm is not able to cover variable costs, it will reduce its losses by shutting down production.

- In an effort to earn economic profits, competitive firms are always searching for better and more efficient production methods. Technological advances cause MC and ATC to decrease.

- The process of competition benefits consumers because it results in the optimal mix of output and the most efficient use of resources.

- In competitive markets there is a persistent pressure on prices and profits. Firms must keep costs as low as possible by adopting the most efficient technologies. Competitive firms must also respond quickly to changes in demand by producing the goods and services demanded by buyers in order to earn a profit. The penalties for not responding are losses and the potential failure of the firm.

Learning Objectives

After reading Chapter 23 and doing the following exercises, you should:

1. Know how the absence of market power relates to the shape of demand and supply curves from the point of view of buyers and sellers.
2. Be able to tell why the demand curve facing a competitive firm is flat.
3. Be able to list the characteristics of the competitive market structure and describe the role of competition in the U.S. economy.
4. Know how barriers to entry influence the competitive process.
5. Know the difference between the firm's demand curve and the market demand curve.
6. Know why above-normal profits disappear in competitive industries.
7. Understand how a competitive market structure affects prices, cost, output, and profits in the short and long run.
8. Be able to identify the signals for the entry and exit of firms.
9. Be able to show the effects of shifts of market demand or supply on individual demand or supply.
10. Describe how marginal cost pricing leads to efficiency in the allocation of resources.

Using Key Terms

Fill in the puzzle on the opposite page with the appropriate term from the list of Key Terms at the end of the chapter in the text.

Across

3. The choice of a short-run rate of output by catfish farmers.
4. The offer of goods at a price equal to their marginal cost.
6. Competitive markets promote _____ because price is driven down to the level of minimum average costs.
7. In a perfectly competitive industry, firms will enter a market if _____ _____ exists.
8. A market in which no buyer or seller has market power.
10. Equal to price minus average total cost.
11. This curve is the sum of the marginal cost curves of all the individual firms.
12. The rate of output at which price equals minimum *AVC*.
13. The price signal the consumer receives in a competitive market is an accurate reflection of

    _____ _____.
14. The increase in total cost associated with a one-unit increase in production.
15. Total cost divided by the quantity produced.
16. Determined by the intersection of market demand and market supply.
17. Allows for indirect communication between producers and consumers by way of market sales and purchases.

Down

1. Occurs where price equals minimum *ATC*.
2. Occurs where price equals marginal cost.
5. Obstacles that make it difficult or impossible for new firms to enter an industry.
9. The decision to build, buy, or lease plant and equipment.

Puzzle 23.1

True or False: *Circle your choice and explain why any false statements are incorrect.*

T   F   1.   The market supply curve is a horizontal summation of the MC curves above minimum AVC of the individual firms.

T   F   2.   A competitive firm's production decision aims to maximize profits at the production rate where the ATC is at a minimum.

T   F   3.   If a perfectly competitive firm raises its price above the market price, it will lose all of its sales.

T   F   4.   As long as an economic profit is available, a market will continue to attract new entrants.

T   F   5.   In competitive markets, economic losses are a signal to firms that better options are available for its resources.

T   F   6.   In a competitive market, firms sell their products at a price greater than MC.

T   F   7.   Since perfectly competitive firms earn zero economic profits in the long run, all firms will leave the industry.

T   F   8.   Perfectly competitive firms are forced to be technically efficient by government regulations.

T   F   9.   In the long-run equilibrium for a perfectly competitive market, the price of the product will equal the minimum marginal cost.

T   F   10.   In a competitive market, competition forces firms to continually search for more efficient methods of production.

Multiple Choice: *Select the correct answer.*

_____ 1. A competitive firm:
   (a)   Is able to keep other potential producers out of the market.
   (b)   Would like to keep other potential producers out of the market but cannot do so.
   (c)   Is powerless to alter its own rate of production.
   (d)   Will not care if more producers enter the market.

_____ 2. Which of the following is consistent with a competitive market?
   (a)   A small number of firms.
   (b)   Exit of small firms when profits are high for large firms.
   (c)   Zero economic profit in the long run.
   (d)   Marginal revenue lower than price for each firm.

_____ 3. In a perfectly competitive market in the long run:
   (a)   Economic profits induce firms to enter until profits are normal.
   (b)   Economic losses induce firms to exit until profits are normal.
   (c)   Economic profit is zero at equilibrium.
   (d)   All of the above.

_____ 4. The exit of firms from a market:
  (a) Shifts the market supply curve to the right.
  (b) Reduces profits of existing firms in a market.
  (c) Reduces the equilibrium output in the market.
  (d) All of the above.

_____ 5. Which of the following conditions is *not* characteristic of a perfectly competitive market?
  (a) The market price is determined by an organization of sellers.
  (b) Products are homogeneous.
  (c) Barriers to enter the industry are low.
  (d) There are many firms.

_____ 6. In a competitive market, if the market demand curve is tangent to the minimum point of the *ATC* curve, a firm may seek to earn economic profits by:
  (a) Producing at the rate of output where price equals demand.
  (b) Decreasing production costs through technological improvements.
  (c) Decreasing price.
  (d) Increasing price.

_____ 7. The entry of firms into a market:
  (a) Pushes the equilibrium price downward.
  (b) Reduces profits of existing firms in the market.
  (c) Shifts the market supply curve rightward.
  (d) All of the above.

_____ 8. *Ceteris paribus*, when firms leave a competitive market:
  (a) The equilibrium price increases.
  (b) Profits for the existing firms in the market decrease.
  (c) The equilibrium level of output increases.
  (d) The market supply curve shifts to the right.

_____ 9. A competitive market promotes technical efficiency in the long run by pushing prices to the minimum of:
  (a) Short-run *AVC*.
  (b) Short-run *MC*.
  (c) Long-run *ATC*.
  (d) Long-run *TC*.

_____ 10. Which of the following conditions always characterizes a firm that is in short-run competitive equilibrium where profits are maximized?
  (a) Price equals minimum average total cost.
  (b) Price equals marginal cost.
  (c) There are no economic profits.
  (d) All of the above characterize such a firm.

_____ 11. *Ceteris paribus*, the market supply curve will *not* shift as a result of a change in:
  (a) Technology.
  (b) The number of firms in the industry.
  (c) The current income of buyers.
  (d) Expectations about potential profits in an industry.

_____ 12. In a competitive market where firms are incurring losses, which of the following should be expected as the industry moves to long-run equilibrium, *ceteris paribus?*
  (a)   A higher price and fewer firms.
  (b)   A lower price and fewer firms.
  (c)   A higher price and more firms.
  (d)   A lower price and more firms.

_____ 13. In long-run competitive equilibrium:
  (a)   Price equals the minimum of the long-run average total cost curve.
  (b)   Economic profit is maximized.
  (c)   Price equals the minimum of the long-run marginal cost curve.
  (d)   All of the above.

_____ 14. In which of the following cases would a firm enter a market?
  (a) P = short-run ATC.
  (b) P > long-run ATC.
  (c) P < short-run ATC.
  (d) P < long-run ATC.

_____ 15. The constant quest for profits in competitive markets results in:
  (a)   Zero economic profits in the long run.
  (b)   The production of goods and services that consumers demand.
  (c)   Product and technological innovation.
  (d)   All of the above are correct.

_____ 16. When economic profits exist in the market for a particular product, this is a signal to producers that:
  (a)   Consumers would like more scarce resources devoted to the production of this product.
  (b)   The market is oversupplied with this product.
  (c)   The best mix of goods and services are being produced with society's scarce resources.
  (d)   Price is at the minimum of the ATC curve.

_____ 17. In a competitive market where firms are experiencing economic losses, which of the following would *not* be expected?
  (a)   A decrease in MR for the remaining firms.
  (b)   A decrease in market supply.
  (c)   An increase in total revenue for the remaining firms.
  (d)   An increase in output for the remaining firms.

_____ 18. In a perfectly competitive market, efficiency in production occurs because of:
  (a)   The profit motive.
  (b)   The competition from many other firms selling an identical product.
  (c)   Low barriers to entry.
  (d)   All of the above.

_____ 19. When a computer firm is producing an output where the price is greater than the MC, then from society's standpoint:
  (a)   The firm is producing too much because society is giving up more to produce additional computers than the computers are worth.
  (b)   The firm is producing too much because society would be willing to give up more alternative goods in order to get additional computers.
  (c)   The firm is producing too little because society is giving up more to produce additional computers than the computers are worth.
  (d)   The firm is producing too little because society would be willing to give up more alternative goods in order to get additional computers.

_____ 20. Marginal cost pricing results in the most desirable mix of output from the consumer's standpoint because:
- (a) Firms are forced by law to produce at the most technically efficient output level.
- (b) The price consumers are willing to pay reflects the value of the output, which is given up.
- (c) Prices are forced down to the lowest possible level.
- (d) Economic profits are zero.

Problems and Applications

Exercise 1

This exercise focuses on the market supply curve and how a competitive industry adjusts to long-run equilibrium.

Assume the HDTV industry is a competitive market and initially there are economic profits in the industry.

1. The lure of economic profits will cause (more; less) firms to enter the industry over time, which will cause the market supply curve to _____.

2. Market price is determined by the intersection of _____
_____.

3. If the market supply shifts to the right, *ceteris paribus*, market price will (increase; decrease).

4. As long as new producers enter the market, market output will (expand; contract) and economic profits will (increase; decrease).

5. Economic profits will approach _____ for this industry in the long run.

6. In long-run competitive equilibrium, price will be equal to minimum _____.

Exercise 2

This exercise uses information from a table to determine revenues, costs, and profits.

Use Table 23.1 to answer questions 1-9.

Table 23.1

Output	Price	Total revenue	Total cost	Total profit	Marginal revenue	Marginal cost	Average total cost
0	----	----	$10	____	----	----	----
1	$13	____	15	____	____	____	____
2	13	____	22	____	____	____	____
3	13	____	31	____	____	____	____
4	13	____	44	____	____	____	____
5	13	____	61	____	____	____	____

1. It is obvious that Table 23.1 refers to a perfectly competitive firm because _____ is constant regardless of the level of output.

2. The fixed cost for this firm is equal to _____.

3. Calculate total revenue, total profit, marginal revenue, marginal cost, and average total cost for this firm.

4. What is the profit maximizing rate of output for this firm? _____

5. The short-run competitive equilibrium occurs where _____.

6. The long-run competitive equilibrium occurs where _____.

7. The minimum for average total cost for this firm is _____. This amount is (greater; less) than the current price so this firm is operating in the (short; long) run.

8. In this case, firms will _____ the industry because economic _____ exist.

9. What happens to price as new firms enter the market? _____

Exercise 3

When the hand-held calculator was invented in the 1970s, the market responded in competitive fashion. This exercise focuses on the adjustments made in a competitive market in both the short run and the long run.

Figure 23.1 presents the cost curves that are relevant to a firm's production decision, and Figure 23.2 shows the market demand and supply curves for the calculator market. Use Figures 23.1 and 23.2 and the knowledge of cost curves that you have gained from the text to answer questions 1-10.

**Figure 23.1
Firm**

**Figure 23.2
Market (all firms)**

1. If the market demand and supply curves are S_1 and D_1, the market equilibrium price will be:
   (a) P_1.
   (b) P_2.
   (c) P_3.
   (d) P_4.

2. Suppose the demand for calculators shifts to D_4. This shift might be caused by:
   (a) An increase in the number of consumers.
   (b) An increase in consumers' incomes.
   (c) A rise in the price of a substitute good.
   (d) All of the above.

3. If the demand curve is at D_4, the quantity supplied by the *firm* will be:
   (a) q_1.
   (b) q_2.
   (c) q_3.
   (d) q_4.

4. Suppose a recession results in a shift in the demand curve for calculators to D_1. Then the *firm* will produce:
   (a) q_1.
   (b) q_2.
   (c) q_3.
   (d) q_4.

5. In the short run, the firm will continue to produce some output until demand changes enough to drive price below:
   (a) P_1.
   (b) P_2.
   (c) P_3.
   (d) P_4.

6. At prices below P_1, the firm will shut down (produce no output) because:
   (a) Its loss will be less than if it produces at any level of output.
   (b) Its loss will be limited to its fixed costs.
   (c) Total revenue is less than total variable cost.
   (d) All of the above are the case.

7. The fact that the quantity supplied by the firm changes whenever the market price changes indicates that:
   (a) The firm is a price setter.
   (b) The firm is a price taker.
   (c) The firm has monopoly power.
   (d) The firm has no control over the quantity it produces.

8. Since the firm will not produce any output if the market price falls below P_1:
   (a) The firm's supply curve is that part of the *MC* curve above the minimum point on the *ATC* curve.
   (b) The average variable cost curve is the firm's supply curve.
   (c) The average total cost curve is the firm's supply curve.
   (d) The firm's supply curve is that part of its marginal cost curve that lies above its average variable cost curve.

9. If the price is P_3, and the demand curve is D_3 in the long run:
    (a) Returns to the firm are below average, and firms will leave the industry.
    (b) Returns are above average, and new firms will have an incentive to enter the market.
    (c) Returns are about average, and there is no incentive for firms to move into or out of the industry.
    (d) We really can't say without more information.

10. Long-run competitive equilibrium occurs at a price of:
    (a) P_1.
    (b) P_2.
    (c) P_3.
    (d) P_4.

Exercise 4

Newspapers provide information about competitive markets in the form of want ads, market prices, and advertising.

Reread the article in the text entitled "Whiskered Catfish Stir a New Trade Controversy." Then answer the following questions.

1. Which phrase indicates the change in the U.S. catfish market? _____
    _____.

2. Which passage indicates entry into the catfish market? _____
    _____

3. What causes entry into a competitive market? _____

4. As more producers enter the catfish industry, what will happen to profits? _____

5. On the basis of information in the article, the catfish market appears to be:
    (a) A local market.
    (b) A regional market.
    (c) A national market.
    (d) An international market.

Common Errors

The first statement in each "common error" below is incorrect. Each incorrect statement is followed by a corrected version and an explanation.

1. The demand curve for a competitive market is flat. WRONG!

    The demand curve for a competitive firm is flat. RIGHT!

    The error above results from failure to distinguish between the market and the firm. Review Exercise 3 if this distinction is not clear.

2. Competitive firms do not make profits. WRONG!

   Competitive firms can make economic profits in the short run. RIGHT!

   In the long run, firms enter an industry and compete away economic profits. In the short run, a change in demand or supply may cause price to change and may bestow temporary economic profits on a firm. In the personal computer example in the text, technological changes shifted the supply curve and provided temporary profits.

   Be careful! Always distinguish between short-run profit-maximizing production rates and price levels and long-run equilibrium production rates and price levels. While industries have a tendency to move toward long-run equilibrium, they may never reach it because of shocks that buffet a market.

3. Since competitive firms make zero profits in the long run, they cannot pay their stockholders and so they should shut down. WRONG!

   Since competitive firms make zero economic profits in the long run, they are able to pay all factors of production, including the entrepreneurs, to keep the firms in existence. RIGHT!

   Be careful! Keep the accounting and economic definitions of such words as "profit" separate and distinct. Keep movements along the supply curve (firms increase production rates) separate from shifts of the supply curve (firms enter or exit). Avoid confusing short-run responses (increasing production rates in existing plants) with long-run responses (entry or exit).

•ANSWERS•

Using Key Terms

Across

3. production decision
4. marginal cost pricing
6. efficiency
7. economic profit
8. competitive market
10. profit per unit
11. market supply
12. shutdown point
13. opportunity cost
14. marginal cost
15. average total cost
16. equilibrium price
17. market mechanism

Down

1. long-run competitive equilibrium
2. short-run competitive equilibrium
5. barriers to entry
9. investment decision

True or False

1. T
2. F   The firm maximizes profits at the output rate where price $(MR) = MC$.
3. T
4. T
5. T
6. F   In a competitive market, firms sell their products at a price equal to MC.
7. F   Zero economic profits are an indication that there is no better use for a firm's resources. As a result, once economic profits reach zero, there is no further exit (or entry).
8. F   Competition forces perfectly competitive firms to be technically efficient.
9. F   The price of the product will equal the minimum ATC.
10. T

Multiple Choice

1.	b	5.	a	9.	c	13.	a	17.	a
2.	c	6.	b	10.	b	14.	b	18.	d
3.	d	7.	d	11.	c	15.	d	19.	d
4.	c	8.	a	12.	a	16.	a	20.	b

Problems and Applications

Exercise 1

1. More; shift to the right
2. Market supply and market demand
3. Decrease
4. Expand; decrease
5. Zero
6. ATC

Exercise 2

1. Price
2. $10
3. **Table 23.1 Answer**

Output	Price	Total revenue	Total cost	Total profit	Marginal revenue	Marginal cost	Average total cost
0	----	----	$10	$-10	----	----	----
1	$13	$13	15	-2	$13	$5	$15.00
2	13	26	22	4	13	7	11.00
3	13	39	31	8	13	9	10.33
4	13	52	44	8	13	13	11.00
5	13	65	61	4	13	17	12.20

4. 4 units of output
5. $P = MC$
6. $P = MC$ = minimum ATC
7. $10.33; less; short
8. Enter; profits
9. Decreases

Exercise 3

1.	a	3.	d	5.	a	7.	b	9.	b
2.	d	4.	a	6.	d	8.	d	10.	b

Exercise 4

1. ". . . the U.S. catfish production has plunged in the past year."
2. ". . . imports from Vietnam have soared from 575,000 pounds in 1998 to as much as 20 million pounds this year."
3. Economic profit
4. Decrease
5. d

333

CHAPTER 24
Monopoly

Quick Review

- Market power is the ability to alter the price of a good or service. A monopolist is the sole supplier in a given market and has market power, which it can use to influence price and output.

- The demand curve faced by a monopolist is the downward-sloping market demand curve. As a result, in order to sell more output a monopolist must lower its price for all output, so the marginal revenue curve is always less than price.

- In making the production decision, monopolists attempt to maximize profits. They produce the level of output at which marginal cost equals marginal revenue. When compared to the competitive producer, the monopolist will charge a higher price and will produce a smaller output.

- If market demand is sufficient, monopolists will reap economic profits that are a signal for other firms to enter the market. In order to maintain its monopoly status, barriers to entry such as patents, legal harassment, exclusive licensing, bundled products, and government franchises are necessary.

- The existence of market power in the economy influences the answers we get to the WHAT, HOW, and FOR WHOM questions. By restricting output, the monopolist forces some resources to move where they will earn less and keeps economic profits for itself. Monopolists tend to be less efficient than competitive firms are since they are not compelled by competitive forces to adopt the newest and most efficient technologies.

- Arguments in favor of a monopoly include: 1) economic profits give the firm the financial resources to pursue research and development, 2) monopoly profits may encourage entrepreneurial activity, 3) if economies of scale exist over the entire market, society will be best served by having a single firm (a natural monopolist) produce all the output, 4) potential competition, perhaps from foreign producers attracted by economic profits, is sufficient to constrain the monopolist from exploiting its market power. If a market is contestable, the economic outcomes may be more like that of the perfectly competitive market.

- The government is empowered to prevent or regulate the abuse of market power. The Sherman Act, the Clayton Act, and the Federal Trade Commission Act form the legal foundation for antitrust activities.

Learning Objectives

After reading Chapter 24 and doing the following exercises, you should:

1. Know the meaning of market power.
2. Know why a monopolist has market power and a downward-sloping demand curve, and why price and marginal revenue diverge.
3. Be able to show the relationship between the market demand and individual demand curve for a monopolist.
4. Know the difference between marginal cost pricing for a competitive firm and profit maximization for a monopoly.
5. Be able to determine a monopolist's most profitable rate of production.
6. Be able to show why a monopoly typically results in higher profits, less output, and higher prices than would occur in a competitive market.
7. Be able to contrast the long-run results in a competitive market with that of a monopoly.
8. Be able to describe the advantages and disadvantages of monopoly versus competition.
9. Be able to distinguish price discrimination from other types of pricing.
10. Be able to distinguish economies of scale from constant returns to scale and diseconomies of scale.
11. Understand why a natural monopoly occurs.
12. Know how and why antitrust policy is used to control monopoly.
13. Understand the idea of "contestable" markets.

Using Key Terms

Fill in the puzzle on the opposite page with the appropriate term from the list of Key Terms at the end of the chapter in the text.

Across

2. The change in total revenue that results from a one-unit increase in the quantity sold.
7. Based on the _____ _____ _____, firms should produce at the rate of output where marginal revenue equals marginal cost.
9. The ability to alter the market price of a good or service.
10. An industry in which one firm can achieve economies of scale over the entire range of market supply.
11. Total cost divided by the quantity produced in a given time period.
12. Government intervention to alter market structure or prevent abuse of market power.
13. For a monopolist, this short-run choice is made by locating the intersection of marginal cost and marginal revenue.

Down

1. The sale of an identical good at different prices to different consumers by a single seller.
2. A market structure in which there is only one firm.
3. The percentage change in quantity demanded divided by the percentage change in price.
4. Obstacles that make it difficult or impossible for would-be producers to enter a particular market.
5. Gives one producer an advantage over several smaller producers and acts as a barrier to entry.
6. An imperfectly competitive industry which is restrained by potential competition.
8. The pricing method characteristic of competitive markets but not a monopoly.

Puzzle 24.1

True or False: *Circle your choice and explain why any false statements are incorrect.*

T F 1. Since a competitive firm can sell unlimited quantities of output at the prevailing price, it can affect the market price of a good or service.

T F 2. The monopolist has a flat (i.e., horizontal) demand curve because of high barriers to entry.

T F 3. The demand curve for the monopolist is exactly the same as the market demand curve.

T F 4. Monopolists maximize profits at the output level at which price equals marginal cost.

T F 5. Since both monopolists and competitive firms maximize profits at the output level at which marginal revenue equals marginal cost, monopolists and competitive markets with the same marginal cost curves and market demand curves will produce the same output.

T F 6. In the long run, a monopolist can continue to earn economic profits.

T F 7. When compared to a competitive market, monopolists tend to charge a higher price and produce a larger output.

T F 8. Price discrimination can occur because of the differences in the demand curves among buyers.

T F 9. The theory of contestable markets focuses on market structure rather than market behavior.

T F 10. U.S. policy regarding antitrust is based on three laws, the Sherman Act, the Clayton Act, and the Federal Trade Commission Act.

Multiple Choice: *Select the correct answer.*

_____ 1. Which of the following is the result of a monopolist's market power?
(a) It faces a downward-sloping demand curve.
(b) When it produces an extra unit of output, it must lower its price on all of its units.
(c) Its marginal revenue curve is below its demand curve.
(d) All of the above are results.

_____ 2. For a monopolist, the demand curve facing the firm is:
(a) The same as for the perfectly competitive firm.
(b) The same as the market-demand curve.
(c) Always below marginal revenue.
(d) Perfectly elastic.

_____ 3. When a monopolist sells an additional unit of output, the marginal revenue will be lower than the price because:
(a) The price of all the units sold will have to be lowered in order to sell the additional unit.
(b) The monopolist faces a flat (horizontal) demand curve for its product.
(c) Costs increase as more output is produced.
(d) Economies of scale exist for monopolists.

_____ 4. Which of the following is most likely *not* a monopolist?
(a) The only doctor in a small community.
(b) A large soft-drink firm such as Coca-Cola.
(c) The only grocery store in a small, country town.
(d) The water company in your area.

_____ 5. Which of the following rules will always be satisfied when a firm has maximized profit?
   (a) P = lowest level of long-run average costs.
   (b) $P = MC$.
   (c) $MR = MC$.
   (d) $P = ATC$.

_____ 6. In a monopoly and perfect competition, a firm should expand production when:
   (a)   Price is below marginal cost.
   (b)   Price is above marginal cost.
   (c)   Marginal revenue is below marginal cost.
   (d)   Marginal revenue is above marginal cost.

_____ 7. Suppose a monopoly produces a drug and sells 100 prescriptions at $100 each. In order to sell 101 prescriptions, the firm must lower the price to $99. What is the marginal revenue of the 101st unit sold?
   (a) $-1.
   (b) $1.
   (c) $99.
   (d) $9,999.

_____ 8. Monopoly might be considered to be more desirable than perfect competition because:
   (a)   The monopolist has more incentive to keep costs down.
   (b)   Economies of scale can only be fully realized by a single firm in a natural monopoly.
   (c)   Marginal revenue is less than price for a monopoly.
   (d)   It is the best way to increase output above the competitive level of production.

_____ 9. Which of the following can help a firm maintain a monopoly situation?
   (a)   A license.
   (b)   Exclusive control over important resources.
   (c)   A patent.
   (d)   All of the above.

_____ 10. A monopolist with many plants produces less than would be produced if all of the plants were competing with one another in a competitive market:
   (a)   Because the market demand curve is perfectly inelastic for the monopolistic firm but not for the competitive firms.
   (b)   Because the market demand curve slopes downward for the monopolistic market and for the competitive market.
   (c)   Because the marginal revenue curve is below the demand curve for the monopolistic firm but not for the competitive firms.
   (d)   Because profit is maximized where $MR = MC$ for the monopolistic firm but not for the competitive firms.

_____ 11. The price charged by a profit-maximizing monopolist in the long run occurs:
   (a)   At the minimum of the long-run average total cost curve.
   (b)   Where $P = MR = MC$.
   (c)   At a price on the demand curve above the intersection where $MR = MC$.
   (d)   At a price on the long-run average total cost curve below the point where $MR = MC$.

_____ 12. When a monopoly continues to make above-normal profits in the long run, you can be sure that:
   (a)   It produces more efficiently than a competitive market can.
   (b)   Barriers to entry prevent other firms from competing away the above-normal profits.
   (c)   There is a conspiracy between the government and the monopolist to maintain high prices.
   (d)   It has an inelastic demand curve, which gives it greater revenues at every price.

_____ 13. If a monopoly used marginal cost pricing to determine its output and price, which of the following statements would be true?
  (a) The monopolist would not be maximizing its profits.
  (b) The monopolist would produce a higher level of output than it would if it was maximizing its profits.
  (c) The monopolist would produce the optimal level of output from the consumer's standpoint.
  (d) All of the above would be true.

_____ 14. Monopolists are:
  (a) Price setters, but competitive firms are price takers.
  (b) Price takers, as are competitive firms.
  (c) Price takers, but competitive firms are price setters.
  (d) Price setters, as are competitive firms.

_____ 15. Price discrimination allows a producer to:
  (a) Reap the highest possible average price for the quantity sold.
  (b) Increase the elasticity of consumer demand.
  (c) Minimize marginal costs.
  (d) Decrease total costs.

_____ 16. Which of the following is an example of price discrimination by a "10-Minute Oil Change" firm?
  (a) Charging a lower price if the customer does not want their car vacuumed.
  (b) Charging a lower price for cars that use 4 quarts of oil instead of the typical 5 quarts.
  (c) Charging women a lower price because it is Tuesday.
  (d) All of the above.

_____ 17. The argument that concentration of market power enhances research and development efforts may be weak because:
  (a) Monopolies cannot afford basic research.
  (b) A monopoly may have no clear incentive to pursue new research and development.
  (c) No one has attempted to gather any empirical evidence.
  (d) No existing monopoly has a research and development program.

_____ 18. According to the theory of contestable markets, monopoly may _not_ be a problem if:
  (a) The structure of a market is competitive.
  (b) Firms can exit from the market.
  (c) Antitrust regulations are enforced.
  (d) Potential competition exists.

_____ 19. The primary purpose of anti-trust policy in the United States is to:
  (a) Issue patents.
  (b) Encourage competition.
  (c) Limit foreign competition.
  (d) Regulate monopolies.

_____ 20. Which of the following was the first to prohibit conspiracies in restraint of trade?
  (a) The Sherman Act.
  (b) The Clayton Act.
  (c) The Federal Trade Commission Act.
  (d) The Gramm-Rudman Act.

Problems and Applications

Exercise 1

This exercise provides practice in calculating total revenue and marginal revenue, and shows the relationship between marginal revenue and demand.

1. Use the information given in Table 24.1 to calculate total revenue and marginal revenue.

Table 24.1 Revenue data

	Quantity	Price	Total Revenue	Marginal Revenue
A	0	$12.00	$_____	-------
B	1	11.00	_____	$_____
C	2	10.00	_____	_____
D	3	9.00	_____	_____
E	4	8.00	_____	_____
F	5	7.00	_____	_____
G	6	6.00	_____	_____

2. Use the information from Table 24.1 to graph the demand curve and the marginal revenue curve in Figure 24.1. Label each curve and label the points (B through G) on the demand curve.

Figure 24.1 Demand and marginal revenue curves

3. For a monopoly, price is determined from the _____ curve, directly above the point where _____ .

341

4. For a monopoly, marginal revenue is always (greater; less) than price, after the first unit, because the firm must (raise; lower) its price to sell additional output.

Exercise 2

This exercise reviews costs and revenues and provides further experience with profit maximization.

Figure 24.2 represents cost curves for a monopolist. Use Figure 24.2 to answer questions 1-4.

Figure 24.2 Cost curves and profit maximization

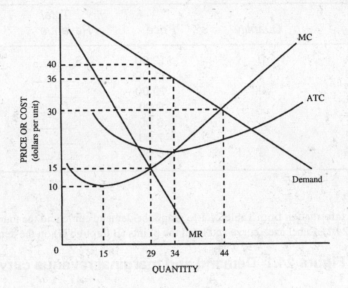

1. What is the profit-maximizing rate of output for the monopolist in Figure 24.2? _____

2. What price will the monopolist charge in Figure 24.2? _____

3. This monopolist (is; is not) earning an economic profit because, at the profit-maximizing rate of output in Figure 24.2, ATC is (above; below) the demand curve.

4. Now assume the curves in Figure 24.2 represent a perfectly competitive market. What is the profit-maximizing rate of output? _____ What price will the firms charge at this output? _____ How do price and output compare to the profit-maximizing rate of output and price for a monopolist?
_____

Exercise 3

This exercise emphasizes the relationship between costs and revenues for a monopolist and determination of profit maximization.

1. Use the data in Table 24.2 to calculate total revenue, marginal revenue, and marginal cost for a monopolist.

Table 24.2 Revenue and cost data

Quantity	Price	Total revenue	Marginal revenue	Total cost	Marginal cost
0	$14	$_____	----	$13	----
1	13	_____	$_____	15	$_____
2	12	_____	_____	18	_____
3	11	_____	_____	23	_____
4	10	_____	_____	30	_____
5	9	_____	_____	39	_____
6	8	_____	_____	51	_____

2. For a monopolist, the profit-maximizing rate of output occurs where marginal revenue equals _____.

3. In this case, the profit-maximizing rate of output is _____ units.

4. At the profit-maximizing rate of output, the monopolist will charge _____ for the product.

5. At the profit-maximizing rate of output, this monopolist earns a profit of _____.

6. In order to sell one additional unit, the monopolist would have to (decrease; increase; make no change in) price.

7. Since this monopolist is earning a profit, the *ATC* curve must be (above; below; equal to) the demand curve at the profit-maximizing rate of output.

8. Now suppose the data in Table 24.2 represent a perfectly competitive market. The profit-maximizing rate of output occurs where marginal cost equals _____.

9. In this case, the profit-maximizing rate of output would be _____ units at a price of _____.

10. At the competitive profit-maximizing rate of output, profits equal _____.

11. Compared to a perfectly competitive market, a monopoly charges a (higher; lower) price, produces a (higher; lower) output, and earns a (greater; smaller) profit.

Exercise 4

Reread the article titled "New Competition May Mean Bad News for CNN" and then answer the following questions.

1. What phrase indicates that CNN has monopoly power in the 24-hour news market? _____
_____

2. What barriers to entry have kept other networks from competing with CNN? _____
_____

3. Why are competitors trying to overcome the barriers to entry? _____
_____

Common Errors

The first statement in each "common error" below is incorrect. Each incorrect statement is followed by a corrected version and an explanation.

1. Monopolists have supply curves. WRONG!

   Monopolists have marginal cost curves, but not supply curves. RIGHT!

   The marginal cost indicates the quantity that a competitive firm will supply at a given price. (*Remember*: Price equals marginal cost for the profit maximizing competitive firm.) But we cannot tell what a monopolist will supply at a given price by looking at the marginal cost curve. We need to know marginal revenue, and therefore the demand curve, before we can tell what quantity the firm will supply. (*Remember*: Marginal cost equals marginal revenue when profits are maximized.)

   Be careful! Do not label the marginal cost curve of a monopolist (or any noncompetitive firm) as a "supply" curve in your diagrams.

2. When there are economies of scale, a firm can simply increase production rates in the short run and unit costs will decline. WRONG!

   When there are economies of scale, a firm can choose a plant size designed for increased production rates at lower unit costs. RIGHT!

   Economies of scale are not realized through production decisions in the short run. They are realized through investment decisions, by the choice of an optimal-sized plant for higher production rates. Scale refers to plant size or capacity, not to production rates within a plant of a given size. Think of economies of scale in terms of investment decisions concerning choices of optimal capacity for the long run, not production decisions concerning the lowest cost production in the short run.

3. The profit maximizing and shutdown rules are different for a monopoly than for a competitive firm. WRONG!

   The profit maximizing and shutdown rules are the same for a monopoly as they are for all other profit maximizing firms. RIGHT!

   All firms that want to maximize profits should produce at the output level where $MC = MR$, regardless of the market structure. In addition, all firms should continue to produce in the short run only if they can cover variable costs. The shutdown point occurs where price equals AVC.

•ANSWERS•

Using Key Terms

Across
2. marginal revenue
7. profit maximization rule
9. market power
10. natural monopoly
11. average total cost
12. antitrust
13. production decision

Down

1. price discrimination
2. monopoly
3. price elasticity of demand
4. barriers to entry
5. economies of scale
6. contestable market
8. marginal cost pricing

True or False

1. F   A competitive firm has no control over the market price because it is such a tiny part of the relatively huge market. Because it is relatively insignificant, it can sell as much as it wants at the market price.
2. F   The monopolist typically has a relatively inelastic demand curve because of barriers to entry, i.e., few substitutes.
3. T
4. F   Monopolists maximize profits where $MR = MC$.
5. F   Monopolists will tend to produce less than the output that would be produced in a competitive market because the MR curve is below the demand curve for the monopolist.
6. T
7. F   When compared to a competitive market, monopolists tend to charge a higher price and produce a lower output.
8. T
9. F   The theory focuses on behavior rather than structure, i.e., not how many producers exist in a market but how many could potentially exist.
10. T

Multiple Choice

1. d	5. c	9. d	13. d	17. b
2. b	6. d	10. c	14. a	18. d
3. a	7. a	11. c	15. a	19. b
4. b	8. b	12. b	16. c	20. a

Exercise 1

1. **Table 24.1 Answer**

Quantity	Total revenue	Marginal revenue
0	$ 0.00	-----
1	11.00	$ 11.00
2	20.00	9.00
3	27.00	7.00
4	32.00	5.00
5	35.00	3.00
6	36.00	1.00

2. **Figure 24.1 Answer**

3. Demand; $MC = MR$
4. Less; lower

Exercise 2

1. 29 units
2. $40
3. Is, below
4. 44 units; $30; price is less and output is greater for the perfectly competitive firm

Exercise 3

1. **Table 24.2 Answer**

Quantity	Price	Total revenue	Marginal revenue	Total cost	Marginal cost
0	$14	$ 0	----	$13	----
1	13	13	$ 13	15	$ 2
2	12	24	11	18	3
3	11	33	9	23	5
4	10	40	7	30	7
5	9	45	5	39	9
6	8	48	3	51	12

2. Marginal cost
3. 4
4. $10
5. $10
6. Decrease
7. Below
8. Price
9. 5; $9
10. $6
11. Higher; lower; greater

Exercise 4

1. ". . . with the market to itself . . . "
2. ". . . huge distribution hurdles caused by lack of space on crowded cable systems . . . "
3. "Last year . . . CNN . . . generated about $227 million in operating profit for Turner Broadcasting System Inc."

CHAPTER 25
Oligopoly

Quick Review

- Market structure is based on the number and relative size of firms in an industry. Three structures are referred to as imperfectly competitive—duopoly, oligopoly, and monopolistic competition.

- The determinants of market power, that is, the extent to which the firm can influence market outcomes, are determined by the number of producers, the size of each firm, barriers to entry, and the availability of substitute products.

- Market power is commonly measured by calculating the concentration ratio: the proportion of total market output produced by the largest producers, typically the top four.

- An oligopoly is a market structure consisting of a few interdependent firms. Because of the small number of firms involved in an oligopoly, it can potentially behave as a shared monopoly.

- An oligopolist's pricing decision is often depicted with a kinked demand curve. This reflects the idea that rival firms will follow price decreases but will not follow price increases. This leads to a demand curve that is flatter above the equilibrium price and steeper below.

- If oligopolists are successful in coordinating their efforts, they can restrict industry output and reap monopoly-like profits. Strategies such as collusion, price leadership, and price-fixing can be used to accomplish this goal.

- Barriers to entry are the key to maintaining economic profits in the long run. Patents, control of a distribution system, government regulation, and nonprice competition are used to eliminate competition. Mergers and acquisitions can also be used to limit entry.

- Market power contributes to market failure when it results in significant misallocation of resources. Antitrust laws explicitly forbid many of the practices described in this chapter.

- The Herfindahl-Hirshman Index (HHI) is used to measure industry concentration. The Justice Department also examines market structure, barriers to entry, and consumer welfare to determine if government intervention is necessary.

Learning Objectives

After reading Chapter 25 and doing the following exercises, you should:

1. Be able to describe the different market structures.
2. Know the determinants of market power.
3. Be able to calculate and interpret concentration ratios and the Herfindahl-Hirshman Index.
4. Be aware of some of the economy's most concentrated industries.
5. Know how market structure affects market behavior and market outcomes.
6. Understand and be able to describe the kinked demand curve model of oligopoly.
7. Know the difference between the long-run market outcomes resulting from perfectly competitive markets and oligopoly.
8. Understand the setting in which game theory is useful in studying business decision making.
9. Be able to describe the coordination problem inherent in the shared-monopoly idea of oligopoly.
10. Know some techniques which oligopolists have used to implement coordination and enforcement of market shares.
11. Be able to list and describe several barriers to entry.
12. Know three prominent antitrust laws and their major provisions.
13. Understand the significance of the Herfindahl-Hirshman Index.
14. Know the criteria used by the Justice Department to determine if an antitrust case should be prosecuted.

Using Key Terms

Fill in the puzzle on the opposite page with the appropriate term from the list of Key Terms at the end of the chapter in the text.

Across

1. The number and relative size of firms in an industry.
4. Temporary price reductions designed to alter market shares or drive out competition.
7. Government intervention to prevent the abuse of market power.
8. One way a firm can establish the market price for all firms in the industry.
9. A measure of industry concentration that accounts for the number of firms and the size of each.
11. One of the dominant firms in an oligopoly.
15. Used by a firm to make its product appear different and superior to other products.
16. Drawn as two distinct curves for an oligopoly with a kinked demand curve.
17. Obstacles that help to keep potential competitors out of an industry.
18. A market structure with high barriers to entry, substantial market power, and a few firms.

Down

2. A group of firms with an explicit agreement to fix prices and output shares.
3. Firms produce at the rate of output where $MR = MC$.
5. An imperfectly competitive industry subject to potential entry if prices or profits increase.
6. The study of how decisions are made when strategic interaction exists.
10. The proportion of total industry output produced by the largest firms.
12. Occurs when market power leads to resource misallocation or greater inequity.
13. The percentage of total market output produced by a firm.
14. An explicit agreement among producers regarding the price at which a good is to be sold.

Puzzle 25.1

351

True or False: *Circle your choice and explain why any false statements are incorrect.*

T F 1. Firms are divided into specific market structures based on their ability to earn a profit.

T F 2. In imperfect competition, individual firms do not have direct influence on the market price of a particular product.

T F 3. Firms in an oligopoly market are highly independent because of their relatively small number.

T F 4. When OPEC members set the price of oil they are participating in price-fixing.

T F 5. An attempt by one oligopolist to increase its market share by cutting prices will leave competitors unaffected.

T F 6. The shape of the demand curve facing an oligopolist does not depend on the responses of its rivals to a change in the price of its own output.

T F 7. The reason that changes in marginal cost may have no effect on the output of an oligopoly characterized by a kinked demand curve is that the accompanying marginal revenue curve contains a vertical segment or gap.

T F 8. The kinked demand curve demonstrates that if an oligopolist raises its price, it is likely to lose market share.

T F 9. An increase in the market share of one oligopolist will not necessarily reduce the shares of the remaining oligopolists if the industry is growing.

T F 10. One example of a barrier to entry into an oligopoly market is the control of a distribution process.

Multiple Choice: *Select the correct answer.*

_____ 1. The only market structure in which there is significant interdependence among firms with regard to their pricing and output decisions is:
(a) Monopolistic competition.
(b) Monopoly.
(c) Oligopoly.
(d) Perfect competition.

_____ 2. Which of the following firms has significant market power?
(a) A firm that has a patent on the production of its unique product.
(b) A firm that is the same size as the 1,000 other firms in the industry.
(c) A firm that produces a product with many close substitutes.
(d) A firm that produces in an industry with high economic profits but low barriers to entry.

_____ 3. Which of the following is evidence of the interdependence that characterizes the relationship among oligopolists?
(a) Retaliation.
(b) Price wars.
(c) Gamesmanship.
(d) All of the above.

_____ 4. Characteristics of an oligopolistic market include:
   (a)   Tacit collusion.
   (b)   High barriers to entry.
   (c)   High concentration ratios.
   (d)   All of the above.

_____ 5. A kinked demand curve indicates that rival oligopolists match:
   (a)   All price changes.
   (b)   No price changes.
   (c)   Price reductions but not price increases.
   (d)   Price increases but not price reductions.

_____ 6. The gap in the marginal revenue curve of an oligopolist is caused by:
   (a)   The existence of two alternative demand curves that apply to the oligopolist, depending on whether it raises prices or lowers prices.
   (b)   The failure of the marginal cost curve to intersect the demand curve at the profit-maximizing level.
   (c)   The ability of oligopolists to make above-normal profits if they cooperate with each other.
   (d)   All of the above.

_____ 7. Because of the gap in the marginal revenue curve, when the marginal cost curve rises, the kinked demand curve oligopolist may have an incentive to:
   (a)   Speed up production and lower prices—behavior that leads to greater profits.
   (b)   Maintain both production rates and prices—behavior that leads to lower profits but not necessarily to losses.
   (c)   Lower production rates and maintain prices—actions that raise profits by countering cost increases.
   (d)   Speed up production rates and maintain prices—actions that result in losses.

_____ 8. If an oligopolist is going to change its price or output, its concern is:
   (a)   The response of consumers.
   (b)   The possibility of losing market share.
   (c)   Gamesmanship practiced by its competitors.
   (d)   All of the above are concerns.

_____ 9. If a firm is producing at the kink in its demand curve and increases its price, according to the kinked-demand model:
   (a)   It will lose market share to the firms that do not follow the price increase.
   (b)   It will gain market share.
   (c)   Its market share will not be affected.
   (d)   It will not gain market share but it will definitely increase profits.

_____ 10. Which of the following is an explanation of why oligopolists have an incentive to collude?
   (a)   The demand for each firm's product would be kinked.
   (b)   Each firm would face a perfectly inelastic demand for its product.
   (c)   Each firm would face a relatively inelastic demand for its product rather than a relatively elastic demand when firms raise prices independently.
   (d)   The market demand curve would become perfectly inelastic.

_____ 11. Game theory is:
   (a)   The study of price fixing and collusion.
   (b)   The study of how decisions are made when interdependence between firms exists.
   (c)   An explanation of how oligopolists become monopolists.
   (d)   Only useful in perfectly competitive markets.

_____ 12. Oligopolists will maximize total market profits at the rate of output where:
   (a) $MR = MC$ for the largest firms.
   (b) $MR = MC$ for the average firm.
   (c)   The market's MC equals the market's MR.
   (d) $MR = MC$ for the marginal firm.

_____ 13. Open and explicit agreements concerning pricing and output shares transform an oligopoly into a:
   (a)   Monopoly.
   (b)   Cartel.
   (c)   Differentiated oligopoly.
   (d)   Perfectly competitive firm.

_____ 14. Price leadership:
   (a)   Typically results in greater price stability in oligopolistic markets.
   (b)   Is observed in oligopolistic markets.
   (c)   Permits oligopolistic firms in a given market to coordinate market-wide price changes without formal collusion.
   (d)   All of the above.

_____ 15. For an oligopoly, above-normal profit cannot be maintained in the long run unless:
   (a)   A cartel is formed.
   (b)   Barriers to entry exist.
   (c)   A firm has a high concentration ratio.
   (d)   The market is contestable.

_____ 16. An example of nonprice competition in the computer market is:
   (a)   Advertising.
   (b)   Availability of service on weekends.
   (c)   Providing financing for the purchase of a computer.
   (d)   All of the above.

_____ 17. Barriers to entry into an imperfectly competitive market include:
   (a)   Patents.
   (b)   Control of the distribution process.
   (c)   Government regulation.
   (d)   All of the above.

_____ 18. Market power leads to market failure when it results in:
   (a)   Decreased market output.
   (b)   Increased market prices.
   (c)   Long lasting, above normal economic profits.
   (d)   All of the above.

_____ 19. Which of the following are problems associated with pursuing anti-trust policy based on the behavior of firms rather than the structure of a market?
   (a)   It is more expensive to investigate behavior rather than structure.
   (b)   It is more difficult to prove anti-competitive behavior.
   (c)   The general absence of public awareness and interest in the problem of collusion.
   (d)   All of the above are problems.

_____ 20. Since 1996, anti-trust guidelines adopted by the Justice Department and the Federal Trade Commission have emphasized:
    (a) Consumer welfare.
    (b) The HHI.
    (c) Increased government regulation.
    (d) All of the above.

Problems and Applications

Exercise 1

This exercise shows how to compute concentration ratios and market shares for an industry.

1. Market share is:
    (a) The percentage of total market output produced by the largest firms (usually the four largest).
    (b) The percentage of total market output produced by the largest firm.
    (c) The percentage of total market output produced by a given firm.
    (d) A type of stock issued by the firms in a market.

2. Concentration usually refers to:
    (a) The percentage of total market output produced by the four largest domestic firms.
    (b) The percentage of total market output produced by any four large domestic firms.
    (c) The percentage of total market output produced by a given domestic firm.
    (d) The percentage of total market output produced by the four largest domestic or foreign firms.

3. Table 25.1 gives the sales of the top four firms (A, B, C, D) in a market. Insert the total sales for the top four firms and total sales for the market. Then, using this information, compute the market share for each firm separately, the market share for the "Top four firms," and the market share for "All other firms."

Table 25.1
Sales and market shares of top four firms, by company

Firm	Sales (millions of dollars per year)	Market share
A	$ 60	_____ %
B	40	_____
C	30	_____
D	20	_____
Top four firms	$_____	_____ %
All other firms	50	_____ %
All firms	$_____	100 %

4. T   F   The sum of the market shares of the top four firms is the same as the four-firm concentration ratio.

Exercise 2

This exercise illustrates the differences between using the concentration ratio and the Herfindahl-Hirshman Index to measure market power. It also will help you complete a problem in the text.

Table 25.2 presents the market shares for two separate markets. Each market has only four firms.

Table 25.2
Market shares for calculating concentration ratios and the Herfindahl-Hirshman Index

First market		Second market	
Firm	Market share	Firm	Market share
A	25%	E	97%
B	25%	F	1%
C	25%	G	1%
D	25%	H	1%

1. The four-firm concentration ratio for the first market is _____ and for the second market is _____ .

2. The Herfindahl-Hirshman Index for the first market is _____ and for the second market is _____ .

3. Would you expect the market power exerted in the two markets to be the same? _____ Why or why not? _____
   _____

4. According to the Justice Department guidelines:
   (a) Mergers would be permitted in both markets.
   (b) A merger would be permitted only in the first market.
   (c) A merger would be permitted only in the second market.
   (d) Mergers would not be permitted in either market.

Exercise 3

This exercise reviews costs and revenues and provides further experience with profit maximization.

Figure 25.1 represents cost curves for an oligopolist. Use Figure 25.1 to answer questions 1-4.

Figure 25.1

1.   What is the profit-maximizing rate of output for the oligopolist in Figure 25.1? _____

2.   What price will the oligopolist charge in Figure 25.1? _____

3.   If the MC curve shifts up by a small amount, $4 or less, the profit maximizing oligopolist will (increase; decrease; not change) price because of the gap in the (MR; demand) curve.

4.   The demand curve for the oligopolist is kinked because rival oligopolists will match price (increases; reductions) but not price (increases; reductions).

Exercise 4

The media often provide information about the strategies, both successful and unsuccessful, employed by oligopolists as they attempt to compete in the marketplace. By using one of the articles in the text, this exercise will show you what to look for.

Reread the article in the text entitled "Pop Culture: RC Goes for the Youth Market" and then answer the following questions.

1.   What is the concentration ratio in the U.S. soft drink market? _____

2.   What was the Royal Crown strategy in the 1980s? Which phrase indicates the result? _____
   _____

3.   What is the new Royal Crown strategy? What is their target? _____
   _____

357

4. What barriers to entry exist in the soft drink market? _____

5. Calculate an HHI on the basis of the information in the pie chart in the article._____

6. Would game theory be useful in analyzing behavior in this market? Why? _____

Common Errors

The first statement in each "common error" below is incorrect. Each incorrect statement is followed by a corrected version and an explanation.

1. The concentration ratio accurately measures market power. WRONG!

   The concentration ratio is a rough, simple measure of market power. RIGHT!

   Information on availability of substitutes, the appropriate market, the relative size of firms in the market, and barriers to entry must be known before we can determine whether market power exists. Concentration ratios are usually computed for the nation as a whole, but many industries are characterized by local or regional markets. Also, any given market may produce a variety of different products, each with a unique concentration ratio. The concentration ratio gives no idea of barriers to entry that may exist, nor does it give any idea whether a market contains one dominant firm or several equally large firms.

2. American industry consists mostly of monopolies. WRONG!

   There are only a few monopolies in the U.S. economy. RIGHT!

   The text has shown that many U.S. markets are imperfectly competitive, but concentration ratios of 100 percent are rare. Monopolies are most likely to occur in the utility industries, which are then heavily regulated by government.

3. All large firms have market power. WRONG!

   The largest firms in concentrated markets are *likely* to have market power. RIGHT!

   Control of a market is more important than actual firm size in determining market power. Relative size as measured by concentration is more important than absolute size as measured by sales. For example, while conglomerates may be very large, they may play only small roles in many different markets and have no ability to influence prices in any of them.

4. Oligopolists have unlimited power to raise prices and curtail production to make large profits. WRONG!

   Oligopolists' ability to raise prices is limited by demand and their competitive rivalry. RIGHT!

   The demand for oligopolists' products is limited by foreign competition, availability of substitutes, and potential entry by other firms. Such markets as the railroad-car market, the market for rifles, and the auto market contain only a few large firms, but they are limited by potential competition from other countries or at home.

358

Furthermore, there is no guarantee that oligopolists will cooperate with each other. Oligopolists may use their market power cooperatively through collusion, price leadership, or indirect means of supporting prices above competitive levels. Such cooperative activity *may* lead to profits in the long run as well as in the short run. Changes in demand and costs, however, can force oligopolists to take losses or even to fail. Most importantly, oligopolists may not cooperate with each other. They may conduct price wars and engage in nonprice competition in order to erode each other's market share. Such conduct often leads to instability and substantial losses.

5. Competition between oligopoly firms is the same as competition between perfectly competitive firms. WRONG!

   Unlike perfectly competitive firms, oligopolies often are interdependent in their rivalry. RIGHT!

   When firms have market power, they become aware of their interdependence. The often warlike or conspiratorial conduct—rivalry—that occurs is quite different from the conduct of perfectly competitive firms. Since a single perfectly competitive firm cannot affect market price, firms do not see each other as a threat. As an example, there is certainly no reason for one farmer to engage in a price war with another farmer, since both represent such a small part of the market. In addition, unlike oligopolies, perfectly competitive firms do not work together or collude to fix prices since there are also far too many firms for this to be possible.

•ANSWERS•

Using Key Terms

Across
1. market structure
4. predatory pricing
7. antitrust
8. price leadership
9. Herfindahl-Hirshman Index
11. oligopolist
15. product differentiation
16. marginal revenue
17. barriers to entry
18. oligopoly

Down
2. cartel
3. profit maximization rule
5. contestable market
6. game theory
10. concentration ratio
12. market failure
13. market share
14. price fixing

True or False

1. F   The division is based on market power.
2. F   Firms do have varying degrees of control over the market price in imperfect competition.
3. F   Oligopolies are interdependent.
4. T
5. F   Oligopolists are interdependent, i.e., a change in one firm's price or output will affect its competitors.
6. F   The shape of the demand curve facing an oligopolist does depend on the responses of its rivals to a change in the price of its own output.
7. T
8. T
9. F   Market share is a percentage measure. If one firm's percentage share of the market increases, other firms must experience a reduction in market share.
10. T

Multiple Choice

1. c	5. c	9. a	13. b	17. d
2. a	6. a	10. c	14. d	18. d
3. d	7. b	11. b	15. b	19. d
4. d	8. d	12. c	16. d	20. a

Problems and Applications

Exercise 1

1. c
2. a
3. **Table 25.1 Answer**

Firm	Sales	Market share
A	$ 60	30%
B	40	20
C	30	15
D	20	10
Top four firms	$150	75%
All other firms	50	25%
All firms	$200	100%

4. T

Exercise 2

1. 100 percent; 100 percent
2. 2,500 (= $25^2 + 25^2 + 25^2 + 25^2$); 9,412 (= $97^2 + 1^2 + 1^2 + 1^2$)
3. No. The second market would exhibit much more market power since firm E is the dominant firm and would effectively determine the price. By contrast, market power would be more diffused among the four equally sized firms in the first market.

4. d; Both markets have a Herfindahl-Hirshman Index above 1800.

Exercise 3

1. 76 units
2. $37
3. Not change; *MR*
4. Reductions; increases

Exercise 4

1. The four firm concentration ratio is 92.3%, the sum of the shares of the four largest producers.
2. The strategy was, apparently, not to spend on advertising. The result was ". . . we lost a whole generation of cola drinkers . . . ."
3. Their new strategy is to spend $15 million on advertising, the largest amount in their history, and to toss out a ". . . bunch of beverages targeted toward younger drinkers."
4. The article indicates that Pepsi and Coke ". . . have huge amounts of marketing muscle, financial resources, experience and bottling agreements, . . ." which will deter new entrants.
5. Based on the information in the pie chart, the HHI is 3151.27 ($= 44.1^2 + 31.4^2 + 14.7^2 + 2.1^2$).
6. Very likely, since Coke and Pepsi dominate the soft drink market. There are numerous opportunities for moves and countermoves by these oligopolists, and this is where game theory is very useful.

CHAPTER 26

Monopolistic Competition

Quick Review

- A market characterized as "monopolistic competition" has many firms and each firm has some market power. The firms are relatively independent and the barriers to entry are also characteristically low.

- Concentration ratios in these industries are relatively low and even then the firms must often contend with significant competition from foreign entrants.

- The market power possessed by monopolistically competitive firms is the direct result of product differentiation. Advertising is very important in creating brand loyalty.

- Firms in monopolistic competition use the same profit-maximizing rule ($MC = MR$) as firms in other markets. In the short run firms may earn economic profits, but low barriers to entry permit the entry of new firms with the consequent erosion of those profits. In the long run only normal profits can be earned.

- Because the demand curves of the firms slope downward, the long-run equilibrium will be one in which $P = ATC$, but will occur at a point to the left of the minimum of the ATC curve. Thus there is production inefficiency (since $P >$ minimum ATC) and allocative inefficiency because the wrong mix of output is produced.

- Firms in monopolistic competition spend tremendous amounts on advertising aimed at increasing demand and hopefully reducing the price elasticity of demand for their output. Other forms of nonprice competition are also used.

- The presumption follows that nonprice competition leads to a less desirable use of society's resources.

Learning Objectives

After reading Chapter 26 and doing the following exercises, you should:

1. Be able to describe structural characteristics of monopolistic competition.
2. Know how firms in monopolistic competition achieve their market power.
3. Know why the demand curve faced by the firms in monopolistically competitive markets is downward-sloping.
4. Be able to tell why monopolistically competitive firms use the $MC = MR$ rule in making the production decision.
5. Be able to describe the process by which the economic profits are eroded away by the entry of new firms.
6. Be able to explain why the long-run equilibrium in monopolistic competition suffers from production *and* allocative inefficiency.
7. Understand the difference between price competition and nonprice competition and how it may lead to an undesirable use of resources.

Using Key Terms

Fill in the puzzle on the opposite page with the appropriate term from the list of Key Terms at the end of the chapter in the text.

Across

3. Features that make one product appear different from competing products in the same market.
5. Obstacles that make it difficult or impossible for new firms to enter a market.
6. The ability to alter the market price of a good or service.
7. The choice of the short-run rate of output.
8. The offer of goods at prices equal to their marginal cost.

Down

1. A market in which firms produce a similar product but each maintains some independent control of price.
2. The proportion of total industry output produced by the largest firms.
4. The difference between total revenue and total economic costs.

Puzzle 26.1

True or False: *Circle your choice and explain why any false statements are incorrect.*

T F 1. A monopolistically competitive firm confronts a downward-sloping demand curve and, as a result, has some market power.

T F 2. In monopolistic competition, changes in the output or price of any single firm will have no significant influence on the sales of other firms.

T F 3. In monopolistic competition, each firm competes with other firms offering identical substitutes.

T F 4. When marginal costs rise, monopolistically competitive firms do not change output or price.

T F 5. For a monopolistically competitive firm, low barriers to entry tend to push economic profits toward zero in the long run.

T F 6. As new firms enter a monopolistically competitive industry, the demand curve for individual firms will shift to the right.

T F 7. The monopolistically competitive firm charges prices at the minimum of the long-run average total cost curve in the long run.

T F 8. When compared to a perfectly competitive market, monopolistic competition tends to result in a lower output level and a higher price.

T F 9. Monopolistic competition results in allocative efficiency.

T F 10. Firms in a monopolistically competitive industry tend to advertise to increase brand loyalty and thus sales.

Multiple Choice: *Select the correct answer.*

_____ 1. One of the main differences between oligopoly and monopolistic competition is the:
    (a) Amount of revenue a firm can earn.
    (b) Amount of nonprice competition that occurs.
    (c) Size of the concentration ratio.
    (d) Existence of market power.

_____ 2. One of the main similarities of perfect competition and monopolistic competition is:
    (a) That in the long run, price equals average total cost and marginal revenue equals marginal cost.
    (b) The amount of product differentiation.
    (c) The point on the long-run average total cost curve at which firms maximize profits.
    (d) All of the above.

_____ 3. A major difference between monopoly and monopolistic competition is:
    (a) One maximizes profits by setting *MR* equal to *MC*, and the other does not.
    (b) The number of firms.
    (c) One type of firm has market power, and the other does not.
    (d) One has a downward-sloping demand curve, and the other does not.

_____ 4. In monopolistic competition:
- (a) Firms have market power.
- (b) Entry is easy.
- (c) A firm's demand curve is downward-sloping.
- (d) All of the above.

_____ 5. "Product differentiation" refers to:
- (a) Different prices for the same product in a certain market.
- (b) The selling of identical products in different markets.
- (c) Features that make one product appear different from competing products in the same market.
- (d) The charging of different prices for the same product in different markets.

_____ 6. A monopolistically competitive firm maximizes profits or minimizes losses in the long run by producing where:
- (a) $MR = MC$.
- (b) The demand curve is tangent to the long-run average total cost curve.
- (c) $P = ATC$.
- (d) All of the above.

_____ 7. If more firms enter a monopolistically competitive market, we would expect the demand curves facing existing firms to shift to the:
- (a) Left and become more price inelastic.
- (b) Left and no change in price elasticity.
- (c) Left and become more price elastic.
- (d) Right and no change in price elasticity.

_____ 8. Exit from a market characterized by monopolistic competition:
- (a) Can easily occur if firms are earning economic losses.
- (b) Rarely occurs because each firm possesses significant market power.
- (c) Rarely occurs because of federal regulations controlling the number of firms in the market.
- (d) Rarely occurs because of strong brand name identification.

_____ 9. Entry into a market characterized by monopolistic competition:
- (a) Is rare because firms have market power.
- (b) Is frequent because barriers to entry are low.
- (c) Occurs when a firm's demand is below its long-run average cost curve at all levels of output.
- (d) Results from economies of scale.

_____ 10. Firms in a monopolistically competitive market will:
- (a) Produce efficiently.
- (b) Make zero economic profits in the long run.
- (c) Use the profit-maximizing rule $TC = TR$.
- (d) All of the above.

_____ 11. Compared to the outcome under a marginal cost pricing strategy, a monopolistically competitive firm will produce a:
- (a) Lower output and charge a higher price.
- (b) Greater output and charge a higher price.
- (c) Lower output and charge a lower price.
- (d) Greater output and charge a lower price.

_____ 12. Monopolistically competitive firms are productively inefficient because long-run equilibrium occurs at an output rate where:
(a) MC is greater than MR.
(b) Price is greater than MC.
(c) ATC is greater than the minimum ATC.
(d) Diseconomies of scale exist.

_____ 13. In monopolistic competition there is allocative inefficiency because:
(a) Price is greater than the minimum ATC.
(b) Production is not at the minimum ATC.
(c) Of excess capacity.
(d) Price is greater than MC.

_____ 14. A monopolistically competitive firm can raise its price somewhat without fear of great change in unit sales because of:
(a) Brand loyalty.
(b) Economies of scale.
(c) Perfectly elastic demand.
(d) Large market shares of firms in the market.

_____ 15. Advertising is:
(a) An efficient form of competition.
(b) Less important than price competition in oligopolistic and monopolistic competition.
(c) A major component of competition in perfectly competitive markets.
(d) A form of nonprice competition.

_____ 16. When firms enter a monopolistically competitive industry, _ceteris paribus_, the:
(a) Market price increases.
(b) Market price decreases.
(c) Market price remains unchanged.
(d) Change in market price is impossible to determine.

Select the letter of the diagram representing long-run equilibrium in Figure 26.1 that best matches the type of market named in questions 17-20. Use each diagram *only once*.

Figure 26.1 Long-run cost curves

Firm A

PRICE OR COST

MC
ATC
D
MR

QUANTITY

Firm B

PRICE OR COST

MC
ATC
D = MR

QUANTITY

Firm C

PRICE OR COST

MC
ATC
MR   D

QUANTITY

Firm D

PRICE OR COST

MC
ATC
D
MR

QUANTITY

_____ 17. Perfect competition.

_____ 18. Oligopoly.

_____ 19. Monopolistic competition.

_____ 20. Monopoly.

Problems and Applications

Exercise 1

This exercise contrasts monopoly, oligopoly, monopolistic competition, and competition, and summarizes their differences.

In Table 26.1 select the appropriate answer given in parentheses at the left and fill in the blanks on the right.

Table 26.1
Characteristics of four market structures

	Monopoly	Oligopoly	Monopolistic competition	Competition
Characteristic				
1. How many firms are there? (many, few, one)	_____	_____	_____	_____
2. Product is_____ . (standardized, differentiated, unique)	_____	_____	_____	_____
3. Entry is _____ . (blocked, impeded, easy)	_____	_____	_____	_____
4. Is there market power? (yes, no)	_____	_____	_____	_____
Conduct				
5. Do firms use marginal cost pricing? (yes, no)	_____	_____	_____	_____
6. Is there the possibility of collusion, price leadership, or price wars? (yes, no)	_____	_____	_____	_____
Performance (long run)				
7. Are prices too high? (yes, no)	_____	_____	_____	_____
8. Is market production too low? (yes, no)	_____	_____	_____	_____
9. Is the market efficient? (yes, no)	_____	_____	_____	_____
10. Are profits greater than normal expected in the long run? (yes, no)	_____	_____	_____	_____

370

Exercise 2

This exercise examines the characteristics of monopolistic competition using a graph.

Use Figure 26.2 to answer questions 1-6.

Figure 26.2

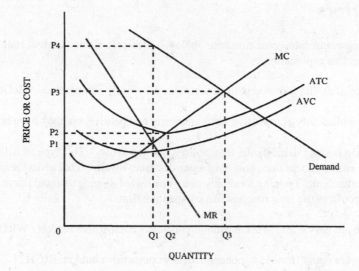

1. The profit-maximizing rate of output for a monopolistically competitive firm occurs where
   _____.

2. According to Figure 26.2, the profit-maximizing rate of output is _____ units and the price is
   _____.

3. Does Figure 26.2 represent a short run or a long run situation? _____

4. This firm is earning a (profit; loss) because at the profit-maximizing output level, the demand
   curve is above the _____ curve.

5. In the long run, the average total cost curve will be tangent to the _____ curve and
   economic profits will be _____.

6. A perfectly competitive firm would maximize profits at an output of _____ and a price of _____.

Exercise 3

This exercise will use one of the articles in the text to show what kind of information to look for to
determine whether a market is characterized by monopolistic competition.

Reread the article entitled "The Cola Wars: It's Not All Taste." Then answer the following questions.

1. Which passages address the market share held by Coke and Pepsi? _____
   _____

2. What form of nonprice competition do the two firms engage in? _____

3. Through their advertising campaigns, Pepsi and Coke hope to establish _____ _____ for each of their products.

4. Which phrase indicates that the advertising is successful? _____
_____

Common Errors

The first statement in each "common error" below is incorrect. Each incorrect statement is followed by a corrected version and an explanation.

1. Monopolies that face competition are monopolistically competitive. WRONG!

   Monopolistically competitive firms are nearly competitive, but they have brand loyalty. RIGHT!

   Do not be misled by the terminology "monopolistic." This type of industry is essentially competitive except that firms have some customer loyalty. That gives them a little ("monopolistic") pricing flexibility and a downward-sloping demand curve. But they still make zero profit in the long run, just like competitive firms.

2. There are only a few firms in a monopolistically competitive market. WRONG!

   There are many firms in a monopolistically competitive market. RIGHT!

   Again, don't let the word "monopolistic" fool you. Firms can easily enter or exit from a monopolistically competitive market. Each firm is likely to have excess capacity—which suggests there may be too many firms in a monopolistically competitive market. The restaurant business is a good example of a monopolistically competitive market.

3. Because price equals average cost in the long run in a monopolistically competitive firm, such firms must be efficient. WRONG!

   Because price equals average cost in the long run in a monopolistically competitive firm, profits are zero in the long run, but the firm is inefficient. RIGHT!

   Long-run profits are normal (zero economic profits) because competition forces prices to equal long-run average total cost. The firm does not reach the *lowest* long-run average total cost level, however, and so it is inefficient. The firm's demand curve touches the long-run average total cost curve, but not at its lowest point.

•ANSWERS•

Using Key Terms

Across
3. product differentiation
5. barriers to entry
6. market power
7. production decision
8. marginal cost pricing

Down

1. monopolistic competition
2. concentration ratio
4. economic profit

True or False

1. T
2. T
3. F   In monopolistic competition, each firm offers slightly different products.
4. F   The *MR* curve for monopolistically competitive firms does not have a vertical segment because there is no significant interdependence between firms. As a consequence, a shift in *MC* will result in an intersection between *MC* and *MR* at a new output level.
5. T
6. F   As new firms enter, individual firms will experience a decrease in the number of customers resulting in a shift in demand to the left.
7. F   A monopolistically competitive firm will charge a price above the minimum *ATC* because of product differentiation.
8. T
9. F   A monopolistically competitive firm will produce less than the allocatively efficient output level because of a downward sloping demand curve facing each firm.
10. T

Multiple Choice

1.	c	5.	c	9.	b	13.	d	17.	b
2.	a	6.	d	10.	b	14.	a	18.	c
3.	b	7.	c	11.	a	15.	d	19.	d
4.	d	8.	a	12.	c	16.	b	20.	a

Problems and Applications

Exercise 1

Table 26.1 Answer

	Monopoly	Oligopoly	Monopolistic competition	Competition
1.	one	few	many	many
2.	unique	standardized or differentiatiated	differentiated	standardized
3.	blocked	impeded	impeded or easy	easy
4.	yes	yes	yes	no
5.	no	no	no	yes
6.	no	yes	no	no
7.	yes	yes	yes	no
8.	yes	yes	yes	no
9.	no	no	no	yes
10.	yes	yes	no	no

Exercise 2

1. $MC = MR$
2. Q_1, P_4
3. Short run
4. Profit; ATC
5. Demand; zero
6. Q_3, P_3

Exercise 3

1. "The Coca-Cola Company produces about 40 percent . . . while Pepsi-Cola produces about 30 percent . . . With nearly 70 percent of the market between them, Pepsi and Coke wage fierce battles for market share."
2. Advertising
3. Brand loyalty
4. "Half of all soft drink consumers profess loyalty to either Coke or Pepsi."

CHAPTER 27

(De)Regulation of Business

Quick Review

- "Market failure" means that the market provides an inadequate output mix. To improve market outcomes where market failure occurs, the government intervenes in several ways.

- In situations of market power, the government has two possible methods of intervention. Antitrust laws address either the structure of the industry or its behavior. Regulation is focused specifically on industry behavior.

- The clearest case for intervention is in "natural monopolies," where a market is best served by a single firm because it alone can capture continuous economies of scale.

- In regulating natural monopolies, regulators may pursue three basic but potentially conflicting goals including price efficiency, production efficiency, and equity.

- Regulation itself may impose significant opportunity costs on the economy. Resources are used in devising and administering regulations. The firms in a regulated market use resources to comply with (or get around) regulations. Efficiency costs that result from bad decisions and incomplete information may worsen the mix of output.

- In recent years, deregulation has occurred in the railroad, telephone service, and airline industries. However, regulations remain in other industries and have even been increased in some industries.

- The question to be answered is, "Do the benefits of regulation exceed the cost of regulation?" In some cases, deregulation seems to have served the consumer well by reducing prices and increasing output.

Learning Objectives

After reading Chapter 27 and doing the following exercises, you should:

1. Know several sources of market failure and be able to identify government intervention techniques.
2. Be able to distinguish social regulation from economic regulation.
3. Be able to describe natural monopoly graphically and verbally.
4. Understand economies of scale.
5. Understand the potential conflict among the goals of price efficiency, production efficiency, and equity.
6. Know the difficulties associated with regulating the price, output, or profits of natural monopolies.
7. Understand the difficulty of devising regulations and why second-best solutions are a realistic goal.
8. Be able to distinguish between administrative, compliance, and efficiency costs of regulation.
9. Know the history of regulation and deregulation in the U.S. economy and be able to cite some recent examples of deregulation.

Using Key Terms

Fill in the puzzle on the opposite page with the appropriate term from the list of Key Terms at the end of the chapter in the text.

Across

3. The "free rider" problem is an issue when dealing with a _____ _____.
5. An industry in which one firm can achieve economies of scale over the entire range of market supply.
10. The use of high prices and profits on one product to subsidize low prices on another product.
11. Obstacles that make it difficult or impossible for new firms to enter a market.
13. An imperfectly competitive industry subject to potential entry if prices or profits increase.
14. Laws to prevent the abuse of market power.

Down

1. Occurs when the market mechanism results in a suboptimal outcome.
2. The decrease in minimum average costs because of an increase in the size of plant and equipment.
3. A form of nonprice competition to make a product appear different from competing products.
4. Government intervention that fails to improve economic outcomes.
6. The doctrine of nonintervention by government.
7. The goods and services that must be given up in order to obtain something else.
8. Equal to total revenue minus total economic cost.
9. The offer of goods at prices equal to their marginal cost.
12. Government intervention to alter the behavior of firms.

Puzzle 27.1

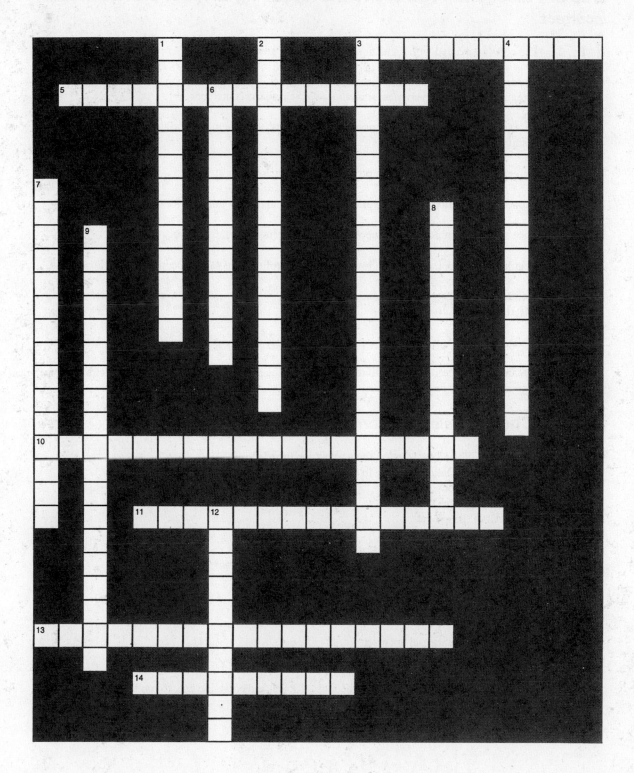

True or False: *Circle your choice and explain why any false statements are incorrect.*

T F 1. The costs associated with regulation are a source of government failure.

T F 2. The argument for regulation is that markets can generate imperfect outcomes, and the argument for deregulation is that government sometimes worsens market outcomes.

T F 3. Deregulation implies that government failure is worse than the market failure that regulation is designed to correct.

T F 4. Unregulated natural monopolies produce optimal rates of output.

T F 5. Economic regulation focuses on prices, production, and the conditions for industry entry or exit.

T F 6. Price regulation of a natural monopoly does not require a subsidy.

T F 7. Regulated monopolies that are allowed a specific profit rate have an incentive to hold down costs.

T F 8. In industries where governments regulate price, individual firms often engage in product differentiation.

T F 9. In the pursuit of profits, unregulated airlines are likely to increase expenditures on airport security.

T F 10. The marginal benefits of regulation should exceed the marginal costs of regulation if additional regulations are to be imposed.

Multiple Choice: *Select the correct answer.*

_____ 1. Which of the following is an example of government failure?
   (a) Over-regulation resulting in wasted resources.
   (b) Public goods.
   (c) Externalities.
   (d) All of the above.

_____ 2. Which of the following is an example of market failure?
   (a) Inequities in the output mix and the distribution of income.
   (b) Natural monopoly.
   (c) Under production, from society's perspective.
   (d) All of the above.

_____ 3. If government failure did not exist:
   (a) Laissez faire would apply to all markets.
   (b) Deregulation would be unnecessary.
   (c) The invisible hand would be the most efficient and equitable way to run the economy.
   (d) All markets would be regulated.

_____ 4. Government can intervene in the structure or behavior of a market. Which of the following correctly distinguishes between antitrust and regulation?
   (a) Antitrust focuses on both, while regulation focuses mostly on behavior.
   (b) Antitrust focuses on both, while regulation focuses mostly on structure.
   (c) Regulation focuses on both, while antitrust focuses mostly on behavior.
   (d) Regulation focuses on both, while antitrust focuses mostly on structure.

_____ 5. Natural monopolies:
   (a) Always face downward-sloping long-run average total cost curves.
   (b) Capture economies of scale over the entire market.
   (c) Incur losses if they produce where price equals marginal cost.
   (d) All of the above.

_____ 6. An unregulated natural monopoly is most likely to:
   (a) Produce a lower output at a higher price than a perfectly competitive market.
   (b) Price its output equal to marginal cost.
   (c) Charge a lower price than if the same product were produced in a competitive market because of the monopoly's greater technical efficiency.
   (d) Take advantage of the concept of marginal cost pricing.

_____ 7. Which of the following problems results from output regulation of a natural monopoly?
   (a) Losses and bankruptcy for the natural monopoly.
   (b) Loss of quality.
   (c) Excess output.
   (d) All of the above.

_____ 8. If the government regulated a natural monopolist to achieve price efficiency without subsidies or price discrimination, the monopolist would:
   (a) Earn economic profits.
   (b) Earn only normal profits.
   (c) Have no incentive to stay in the market.
   (d) Earn less of a profit than before, but still earn a profit.

_____ 9. Which of the following problems results from profit regulation of a natural monopoly?
   (a) Production does not occur at a socially optimal rate.
   (b) The firm has no incentive to strive for efficiency.
   (c) There is an incentive to "pad costs."
   (d) All of the above are problems.

_____ 10. The economic cost for a manufacturer to comply with the clean air law would be:
   (a) The additional money required to buy an automobile with emissions control equipment.
   (b) The resources that were used to produce the emissions control equipment.
   (c) The best alternative goods and services forgone when the emissions control equipment is produced.
   (d) All of the above.

_____ 11. The basic issue in regulatory policy is:
   (a) Whether or not the benefits of government regulation exceed the costs.
   (b) How to achieve second-best solutions in all markets.
   (c) How to eliminate all natural monopolies.
   (d) How to achieve profit regulation in all industries.

12. The case for deregulation of an industry rests on the argument that:
    (a) The cost of market failure exceeds the cost of government failure.
    (b) Regulations are more costly to implement than the market failure that is to be corrected.
    (c) Regulation aids adaptation to market changes in tastes, costs, and technology.
    (d) Antitrust intervention is less costly than regulation.

13. When market outcomes are improved after government regulation is enforced:
    (a) Technical efficiency is being achieved.
    (b) The net effect of government intervention on society in this case has been beneficial.
    (c) Government intervention still may not be justified if the marginal costs of regulation are larger than the marginal benefits.
    (d) All of the above.

14. If a natural monopoly was forced to break up into several small competing firms, economists would expect the:
    (a) Costs of production to decrease because the new firms would be more efficient.
    (b) Price charged by the competing firms to decrease because they would be more efficient.
    (c) Price charged by the competing firms to increase because they would be less efficient.
    (d) Total production in the industry to increase because the new firms would be more efficient.

15. The first major regulatory target in the United States was:
    (a) Airlines.
    (b) Railroads.
    (c) Trucking firms.
    (d) Telephone companies.

16. Deregulation of the railroad industry led to:
    (a) A reduction in rates.
    (b) Improved service.
    (c) A reduction in operating costs.
    (d) All of the above.

17. As a consequence of the deregulation of the telephone industry:
    (a) Many telephone companies have abandoned the market.
    (b) Long-distance phone rates have increased sharply.
    (c) Local telephone rates have risen in the absence of cross-subsidization of local costs from long-distance profits.
    (d) Long-distance users now subsidize local users of phone service to a greater extent than before deregulation.

18. Proponents of the deregulation of the electricity industry argued that deregulation was justified because:
    (a) Other industries had been deregulated.
    (b) Improvements in technology allowed easy transmission of electricity using satellite technology.
    (c) Improvements in technology allowed easy transmission of electricity through the deregulated telephone system.
    (d) Of the development of high-voltage transmission lines.

19. Deregulation of the airline industry has been followed by:
    (a) Lower fares on shorter, less-traveled routes.
    (b) Increased concentration in the airline industry.
    (c) Higher average cost of service by surviving airlines.
    (d) Reduced competition in most airline markets.

_____ 20. The electric utility industry became a target for deregulation when:
  (a)   The cost of constructing nuclear power plants declined.
  (b)   New technology allowed the transmission of power from region to region with insignificant power loss.
  (c)   Local utility companies began behaving like monopolies.
  (d)   All of the above.

Problems and Applications

Exercise 1

This exercise provides practice in identifying market imperfections, finding an appropriate form of government intervention, and recognizing the possible side effects of government intervention.

Table 27.1 lists market imperfections, means for the government to intervene, and some of the side effects of government policy.

Table 27.1
Market imperfections, government interventions, and side effects

Market imperfections	Means of government intervention	Side effects of government policy
I. Externalities	A. Taxes, subsidies, or transfers	1. Inefficiency (unnecessarily high costs)
II. Inequities	B. Regulation of prices, output, or entry	2. Shortages or surpluses
III. Natural monopoly	C. Antitrust activity	3. Lack of quality
IV. Nonexclusive goods	D. Provision of information	4. Inefficient government bureaucracy
V. Market power	E. Production of goods by the government	5. Dynamic inefficiencies
VI. Lack of information about tastes, costs, or prices		
VII. Lack of information about profitability or technology		

1. For each of the situations described in Table 27.2, choose the Roman numeral(s) for each market imperfection that applies, the letter(s) that represent appropriate action by the government, and the number(s) that indicate possible side effects of government involvement.

Table 27.2
Market imperfections and government intervention

Situation	Market imperfection	Government intervention	Possible side effects of government policy
1. Because of severe balance-of-trade deficits, the United States needs to export more goods abroad. If not, foreign exchange markets will be increasingly disrupted. However, many small American companies do not know enough about foreign markets to become exporters of goods and services.	_____	_____	_____
2. It is not economical to have firms compete to provide sewage facilities for residential areas. Each house needs only one set of pipes and it is most efficient to attach all pipes from houses to one major sewer conduit.	_____	_____	_____
3. Many workers at a firm find they are becoming nauseated in the workplace. Futhermore, the cancer rate among the employees appears to be very high. They cannot get management to study the problem because the firm can simply fire them and hire new employees.	_____	_____	_____
4. Farmers are willing to use the latest techniques for growing crops. However, they have difficulty determining what the newest techniques are by themselves and the market does not undertake the continuous research process necessary to develop them.	_____	_____	_____
5. If the farmers do not change continually to the latest disease-resistant seed varieties, it is likely that there will be a disastrous spread of disease that will threaten the economy's food supply. However, new varieties of grain are expensive to develop, and the private market would not undertake the continuous research process necessary to develop them.	_____	_____	_____
6. At the beginning of World War II, the United States found that it was cut off from important suppliers of rubber, sugar, and hemp by the Japanese. The private market had not kept enough inventories of these goods on hand in case of war.	_____	_____	_____
7. The St. Joe Mineral Company dumped taconite tailings filled with asbestos into the Great Lakes. While St. Joe suffered no bad side effects from this activity, many people who used the lakes began to suffer such effects.	_____	_____	_____
8. Many older people are poor and as they age and become weaker are beset by various problems and cannot take care of themselves adequately. Private charities do not do enough to maintain a standard of care that society as a whole considers desirable.	_____	_____	_____
9. It is very costly to run electrical lines into a house; thus, it is not economical to put more than one set of electric lines into a home. Electrical services are most economically provided by only one firm.	_____	_____	_____
10. General Electric and Westinghouse decided to coordinate their activities and conspired to set the price of electronic equipment on which they were bidding.	_____	_____	_____

Exercise 2

This exercise emphasizes the characteristics of a natural monopoly using a graph.

Use Figure 27.1 to answer questions 1-6.

Figure 27.1

1. Label the ATC curve, the MC curve, the MR curve, and the demand curve in Figure 27.1.

2. What is the profit-maximizing price and output level for the unregulated natural monopolist in Figure 27.1? _____

3. At the unregulated output level, the natural monopolist (will; will not) earn an economic profit.

4. Regulation designed to achieve price efficiency would result in a price of _____ and an output level of _____.

5. At the output level in question 4, the natural monopoly will earn a (profit; loss) because ATC is (greater; less) than the price.

6. Profit regulation for the natural monopoly would result in a price of _____ and an output level of _____.

Exercise 3

This exercise focuses on the costs of government regulation.

Reread the In the News article "FCC Seeking More Money to Enforce New Cable Rules" in the text.

1. Which passage indicates the dollar cost of new regulation in the cable TV market? _____
    _____

2. Which passage indicates the anticipated savings to cable TV customers because of new regulation?
    _____

3.   T   F   Compliance with government regulations results in both monetary costs and
                  opportunity costs for regulated firms.

Common Errors

The first statement in each "common error" below is incorrect. Each incorrect statement is followed by a corrected version and an explanation.

1.   Once regulations are in place and enforced, the cost to society is zero. WRONG!

     Regulations impose costs of their own. RIGHT!

     Many people believe that government regulation of business solves the problems, but do not consider whether the regulations themselves cause other problems. It costs society a great deal in terms of opportunity costs to devise, administer, and comply with regulations. In addition, once a regulation is in place, it is difficult to remove because bureaucratic and political machinery works slowly.

2.   Competition will solve the problems of a natural monopoly. WRONG!

     If average total costs continue to decline as the rate of production increases, a single producer (natural monopoly) is the desired market structure in terms of lowest costs. RIGHT!

     A natural monopoly is a unique situation in which a number of smaller, competitive firms will experience higher costs than a single firm. In this case, competition would result in higher costs and possibly higher prices for consumers.

3.   Government regulation of prices, profits or output will solve the problem of a natural monopoly. WRONG!

     When the government regulates prices, profits or output, other problems emerge. RIGHT!

     Regulation of a natural monopoly provides a challenge for economists as well as public officials. Seemingly obvious solutions such as profit regulation may cause firms to pad costs or operate inefficiently. Output regulation may cause firms to provide minimal service or inferior products. Prices set at marginal costs require subsidies to the natural monopoly.

•ANSWERS•

Using Key Terms

Across
    3.   public good
    5.   natural monopoly
    10. cross subsidization
    11. barriers to entry
    13. contestable market
    14. antitrust

Down

1. market failure
2. economies of scale
3. product differentiation
4. government failure
6. laissez faire
7. opportunity cost
8. economic profit
9. marginal cost pricing
12. regulation

True or False

1. T
2. T
3. T
4. F Unregulated natural monopolies tend to produce less than optimal levels of output.
5. T
6. F Price regulation occurs where MC = demand, which is below the firm's ATC, making a subsidy necessary.
7. F When a firm is allowed a specific profit rate, it has no incentive to keep costs in check.
8. T
9. F Airport security is a public good so deregulated airlines are likely to reduce expenditures on airport security.
10. T

Multiple Choice

1. a	5. d	9. d	13. c	17. c
2. d	6. a	10. c	14. c	18. d
3. b	7. b	11. a	15. b	19. b
4. a	8. c	12. b	16. d	20. b

Problems and Applications

Exercise 1

1. **Table 27.2 Answer**

Situation	Market imperfections	Government interventions	Possible side effects of government policy
1.	VI, VII	D	1, 4
2.	III, V	B or E	1, 2, 3, 4, 5
3.	I, IV	B, D	1, 2, 3, 4, 5
4.	VI, VII	D	1, 4, 5
5.	I, III, IV, VI, VII	A, D, E	1, 3, 4, 5
6.	I, IV	A, E	2, 4, 5
7.	I	A or B	1, 2, 4, 5
8.	II, IV	A	1, 4, 5
9.	III, V	B	1, 2, 3, 4, 5
10.	V	C	1, 2, 4, 5

Exercise 2

1. **Figure 27.1 Answer**

2. P_1; Q_1
3. Will
4. P_3; Q_3
5. Loss; greater
6. P_2; Q_2

Exercise 3

1. "... the FCC wants to charge the nation's cable TV operators $16 million ..."
2. "... projected to save cable subscribers as much as $1.5 billion a year."
3. T

CHAPTER 28
Environmental Protection

Quick Review

- Nearly everyone is concerned about the environment and agrees that we ought to protect it. Air, water, and solid waste pollution result in both social and economic costs.

- External costs are the costs of a market transaction borne by a third party. Externalities create a divergence between social costs and private costs and lead to suboptimal market outcomes. In the case of externalities such as pollution, too much of the polluting good is produced.

- Most of the current pollution could be eliminated with known and available technology, but businesses and consumers are influenced by market incentives.

- Businesses are always attempting to maximize profits. In making the efficiency decision the firm chooses the least cost method of production.

- The existence of external costs means that a firm is able to avoid part of the costs of production by pushing some of the costs onto a third party. In this case, a private firm will not maximize social welfare and market failure will occur.

- To correct this failure the government can intervene by altering market incentives or bypassing the market and using direct controls.

- Market-based options to reduce pollution include emissions charges, higher user fees, "green" taxes, and pollution fines.

- Tradable pollution permits provide incentives for new, more cost-efficient technologies to be developed. Those with the highest marginal costs of pollution reduction purchase the right to pollute from those with the lowest marginal costs. As a result, the total resource cost of reducing pollution decreases.

- The direct-regulation (command and control) approach specifies mandatory pollution reductions *and* the specific technologies for achieving them.

- The optimal rate of pollution occurs when the marginal costs of cleaning up the environment are equal to the value of the marginal benefits from the cleanup.

Learning Objectives

After reading Chapter 28 and doing the following exercises, you should:

1. Know the principal types and sources of pollution.
2. Understand how to apply the notion of opportunity cost to the pollution problem.
3. Understand how market forces influence production decisions.
4. Be able to distinguish between private costs and social costs.
5. Understand the term "externality," and how externalities arise.
6. Be able to show how taxes, emission charges, marketable pollution rights, and effluent charges can be used to control pollution.
7. Be able to show how regulation can be used to control pollution.
8. Understand the rationale for pollution credit markets.
9. Understand how the optimal rate of pollution is determined and know why it is *not* zero.
10. Understand the international dimensions of the pollution problem.

Using Key Terms

Fill in the puzzle on the opposite page with the appropriate term from the list of Key Terms at the end of the chapter in the text.

Across
1. A fee imposed on polluters based on the quantity of pollution.
5. Occurs when government intervention fails to improve economic outcomes.
9. The most desired goods and services that are given up in order to obtain something else.
10. The cost of a market activity borne by a third party is referred to as _____ _____.

Down
2. Occurs when the marginal social benefit of pollution control equals its marginal social cost.
3. The total costs of all resources used in an economic activity.
4. The choice of a short-run rate of output using existing plant and equipment.
6. The choice of a production process that minimizes costs for any rate of output.
7. Occurs when the market mechanism results in a suboptimal outcome.
8. The resource costs borne by the specific producer.

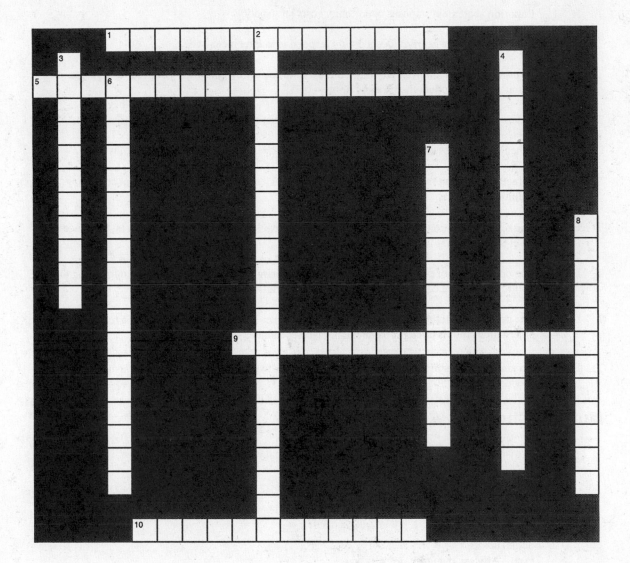

True or False: *Circle your choice and explain why any false statements are incorrect.*

T   F   1.   Pollution abatement imposes opportunity costs on society.

T   F   2.   Pollution occurs when producers do *not* respond to market incentives.

T   F   3.   Firms that are able to push part of their costs onto society by polluting will produce a greater output of their product than society desires.

T   F   4.   Externalities are a measure of the divergence between social costs and private costs.

T   F   5.   When externalities exist, firms will not allocate their resources to maximize social welfare.

T   F   6.   Direct government regulation is generally more efficient than market incentives in correcting pollution problems.

T   F   7.   Marketable pollution permits rely on government regulation, not market incentives, to reduce the level of pollution.

T   F   8.   The optimal rate of pollution is attained when the marginal benefits received from lowering the pollution level are equal to the marginal costs that must be incurred to achieve it.

T   F   9.   The problem of pollution applies to market economies where the market fails as a result of externalities, but is not a problem in command economies without markets.

T   F   10.   An emission fee shifts marginal private costs closer to marginal social costs by raising the costs of production.

Multiple Choice: *Select the correct answer.*

_____   1.   In making the production decision, polluting firms equate marginal:
   (a)   Social cost with marginal social benefits.
   (b)   Revenue and private marginal costs.
   (c)   Social cost and marginal revenue.
   (d)   Private costs and marginal social costs.

_____   2.   Social costs:
   (a)   Are less than private costs.
   (b)   Include private costs.
   (c)   Are unrelated to private costs.
   (d)   Are always borne by the producer.

_____   3.   When social costs and private costs of consumption and production diverge, then inevitably:
   (a)   Producers have an incentive to produce too little.
   (b)   Consumers have an incentive to consume too little.
   (c)   Both producers and consumers have an incentive to produce and consume too much.
   (d)   External costs are zero.

_____ 4. When external costs result from the production of some good, the output level of that good tends to be:
  (a) Larger than is desirable.
  (b) Smaller than is desirable.
  (c) Neither too small nor too large.
  (d) Too small if the private costs exceed the external costs.

_____ 5. The market will overproduce goods that have external costs because:
  (a) Producers experience lower costs than society.
  (b) Producers experience higher costs than society.
  (c) The government is not able to produce these goods.
  (d) Producers cannot keep these goods from consumers who do not pay so they have to produce greater amounts.

_____ 6. A firm that dumps its waste products into our waterways will:
  (a) Pay the full cost of production.
  (b) Incur more than the full cost of production.
  (c) Sell its product at a lower price than if it cleaned up its wastes.
  (d) Cause the firm to internalize more of its costs.

_____ 7. Other things being equal, if a perfectly competitive firm is forced to switch to a more expensive, nonpolluting production process:
  (a) The average cost curve will shift downward.
  (b) The profit-maximizing level of output will be increased.
  (c) The marginal cost curve will shift downward or to the right.
  (d) Total profits will decrease.

_____ 8. When firms are allowed to pollute the environment without bearing the costs of polluting, then:
  (a) Their marginal cost curve is too low.
  (b) Their average variable cost curve is too low.
  (c) Their average total cost curve is too low.
  (d) All of the above.

_____ 9. Solution to the pollution-abatement problem involves:
  (a) Eliminating the divergence between private costs and social costs.
  (b) Compelling firms to consider all costs resulting from their production.
  (c) Forcing polluters to pay all social costs.
  (d) Doing all of the above.

_____ 10. If emission charges were affixed to all production and consumption activities:
  (a) The relative price of highly polluting activities would increase.
  (b) People would stop producing and consuming.
  (c) Pollution would be eliminated.
  (d) There would be no redistribution of income.

_____ 11. The purpose of an emission charge is to:
  (a) Increase the difference between social and private costs.
  (b) Externalize the costs of pollution.
  (c) Reduce the socially optimal rate of output.
  (d) Force polluters to consider externalities as a cost of production.

_____ 12. From an economic standpoint, the principal advantage of tradable pollution permits is their incentive to:
   (a)   Reduce, but not eliminate, the level of pollution.
   (b)   Minimize the cost of pollution control.
   (c)   Increase government control over pollution.
   (d)   Completely eliminate pollution.

_____ 13. The 1990 Clean Air Act relied on which of the following strategies to clean up the environment?
   (a)   Command-and-control approach to regulation.
   (b)   Marketable pollution permits.
   (c)   Subsidizing new pollution-control technologies.
   (d)   All of the above.

_____ 14. When there are external costs of production, then the social optimum occurs where marginal revenue equals:
   (a)   Private marginal cost.
   (b)   Social marginal cost.
   (c)   The minimum of the average cost curve.
   (d)   Social marginal benefit.

_____ 15. An optimal amount of pollution can be described as:
   (a)   The minimal amount technically possible.
   (b)   The amount that would result when polluting firms spend revenues on pollution-control equipment until they earn only normal profits.
   (c)   The amount for which a $1 increase in pollution-control expenditures creates $1 in additional social welfare.
   (d)   Zero.

_____ 16. A 5-cent container deposit on bottles:
   (a)   Decreases the price of recycled materials and thus encourages their use.
   (b)   Increases the price of recycled materials and thus discourages their use.
   (c)   Has no impact on the price of recycled materials.
   (d)   Increases the price of containers that do not use recycled materials.

_____ 17. The pursuit of a pollution-free environment is:
   (a)   The morally correct strategy and costs should not be a consideration.
   (b)   The economically correct strategy as long as benefits accrue to society.
   (c)   The economically correct strategy.
   (d)   Probably not in society's best interest, in view of the extremely high opportunity costs.

_____ 18. In cost-benefit analysis, the government should intervene as long as:
   (a)   Government corrects market failures without incurring resources costs.
   (b)   The value of government failure exceeds the value of market failure.
   (c)   Government's improvement of market outcomes exceeds costs of government intervention.
   (d)   Government corrects market failures in spite of government failure.

_____ 19. The costs of pollution control will:
   (a)   Always be borne entirely by the polluting producer.
   (b)   Always be passed on completely to the consumer.
   (c)   Be distributed between producer and consumer depending on factors like the price elasticity of demand.
   (d)   Be borne entirely by the taxpayers in the United States.

_____ 20. When human lives are involved, a cost-benefit ratio:
   (a)   Should have no bearing on decision making.
   (b)   Must be considered because it provides a measure of the opportunity costs of government policies.
   (c)   Is useless because human lives cannot be measured in dollars and cents.
   (d)   Is an indication that a policy should be implemented if it is a very high value.

Problems and Applications

Exercise 1

This exercise shows how to compute the optimal rate of pollution and will help with a problem in the text.

Table 28.1 indicates various levels of pollution that might be experienced in a lake near your home. It also contains information concerning the value of damages imposed on society by the pollution and the cost to society of cleaning the lake to particular levels. For example, the lake could be made pollution-free with an expenditure of $280,000. The question is: "Is it worth it?" Complete questions 1-7 to find out.

Table 28.1
Annual value of damages associated with
polluted water and costs of reducing pollution

(1) Quantity of pollution (units of waste material per 100 cubic feet of water)	(2) Monetary value of damages (thousands of dollars)	(3) Marginal benefits of pollution abatement (thousands of dollars)	(4) Costs of treating polluted water (thousands of dollars)	(5) Marginal cost of pollution abatement (thousands of dollars)
6	$140	$ ---	$ 0	$ ---
5	100	40	5	5
4	70	_____	15	_____
3	45	_____	30	_____
2	25	_____	50	_____
1	10	_____	100	_____
0	0	_____	280	_____

1. Assume that without any controls, polluters will annually impose $140,000 of damages on the lake's users by generating 6 units of waste for every 100 cubic feet of water. To clean out the sixth unit of pollutants (that is, lower the quantity of pollution from 6 units to 5) costs $5,000. The value of the benefits gained is $40,000. Complete the rest of column 3.

2. Complete column 5 in Table 28.1 in the same way. The first calculation has been done for you.

3. Should the annual level of pollution be reduced from 6 units to 5? _____

4. Which of the following reasons explains why annual pollution should (or should not) be reduced from 6 to 5 units of pollution?
   (a)   The optimal rate of pollution has been reached.
   (b)   The marginal social benefits exceed the marginal social cost from reducing the pollution.
   (c)   The marginal social costs exceed the marginal social benefits from reducing the pollution.

5. Should pollution be reduced annually from 5 units to 4? _____

6. What is the optimal rate of pollution? _____

7. Which of the following is true concerning the lake?
   (a) The optimal rate of pollution has been reached when the lake is totally free of pollution.
   (b) The marginal social costs incurred in eliminating all pollution would exceed the marginal social benefits achieved.
   (c) The marginal social costs incurred in eliminating all pollution would be less than the marginal social benefits achieved.
   (d) Pollution should be eliminated as long as the monetary value of the damages caused by pollution exceeds the costs of treating the polluted water.

Exercise 2

This exercise shows how externalities affect third parties. This exercise will help you complete the problems in the text.

A chemical plant and a plastics factory are located adjacent to the same stream. The chemical plant is located upstream. The downstream plastics factory requires pure water for its production process. Its basic supply is the stream that runs past both firms.

Figure 28.1
Markets for plastics and chemicals

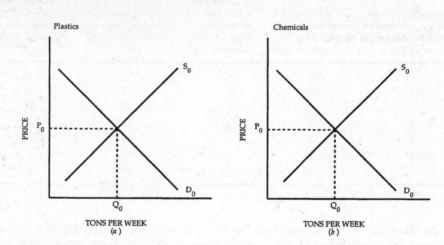

In Figure 28.1, diagrams a and b, S_0 and D_0 represent the supply and demand for plastics and chemicals, respectively. Assume that the economy is initially competitive and resources are allocated efficiently. Equilibrium price and quantity are P_0 and Q_0 in each case. But then the chemical producer decides to dump waste products into the stream rather than dispose of them with the costly process that had been used.

1. In Figure 28.1 diagram b, draw in a new supply curve for chemicals after the dumping in the stream begins. Label it S_1. (*Hint:* There are many ways to draw the curve.)

2. The pollution from the chemical plant forces the plastics manufacturer to use a costly water-purifying system. Draw a new supply curve for plastics in Figure 28.1 diagram a. Label it S_1. (There are many ways to draw this curve correctly.)

3. The effect of the decision to pollute on the quantity of chemicals sold is the same as if:
   (a) A new, improved technology were discovered.
   (b) Wages to its labor force were reduced.
   (c) The Social Security tax on employers had been abolished.
   (d) All of the above were the case.

4. As a result of the chemical plant's polluting activities:
   (a) The price of chemicals has risen.
   (b) The price of chemicals has fallen.
   (c) The price of plastics has not changed.
   (d) None of the above is the case.

5. As a result of the chemical plant's activities:
   (a) More chemicals are produced and sold than society desires.
   (b) More labor is used to produce chemicals than society desires.
   (c) More capital inputs are used to produce chemicals than society desires.
   (d) All of the above are the case.

6. The effect of the chemical firm's pollution is to:
   (a) Raise the price of plastics and reduce the quantity sold.
   (b) Lower the price of plastics and increase the quantity sold.
   (c) Raise the price of plastics and increase the quantity sold.
   (d) Do none of the above.

7. The impact of the pollution on the plastics industry in this example is, *ceteris paribus*, to:
   (a) Reduce the output of plastics below the level that society desires.
   (b) Reduce the employment possibilities in the plastics industry.
   (c) Raise the price of products made with plastics.
   (d) All of the above.

Exercise 3

This exercise shows the difference between private marginal costs and social marginal costs.

1. An iron-producing firm mines iron ore. Assume the iron ore industry is competitive. Table 28.2 depicts the private costs and social costs of the firm's iron production at each daily production rate. Complete Table 28.2.

Table 28.2 Costs of producing iron

Production rate (tons per day)	Total private cost (dollars per day)	Private marginal cost (dollars per ton)	Total social cost (dollars per day)	Social marginal cost (dollars per ton)
0	$ 0	$ ---	$ 0	$ ---
1	40	_____	80	_____
2	90	_____	170	_____
3	150	_____	270	_____
4	220	_____	380	_____
5	300	_____	500	_____
6	390	_____	630	_____
7	490	_____	770	_____
8	600	_____	920	_____
9	720	_____	1,080	_____
10	850	_____	1,250	_____
11	990	_____	1,430	_____
12	1,140	_____	1,620	_____

2. In Figure 28.2, the price of the iron in the competitive market is $140 per ton. Draw the private marginal cost curve and label it *PMC*. Draw the social marginal cost curve and label it *SMC*. Label the demand curve "Demand."

Figure 28.2

3. What is the profit-maximizing production rate for the firm if it considers only its private costs?
   (a) 5 tons per day.
   (b) 7 tons per day.
   (c) 9 tons per day.
   (d) 11 tons per day.

4. What is the profit-maximizing production rate if the firm is required to pay all social costs?
   (a) 5 tons per day.
   (b) 7 tons per day.
   (c) 9 tons per day.
   (d) 11 tons per day.

5. How much should the pollution (emission) fee be in order to induce the iron-producing firm to produce the socially optimal rate of output?
   (a) $4 per ton.
   (b) $40 per ton.
   (c) $100 per ton.
   (d) $50 per ton.

Exercise 4

The effects of pollution have become an increasingly important topic in the media. This exercise will use one of the articles in the text to show the kind of information to look for to identify the effects of pollution.

Reread the *In the News* article entitled "Dirty Air Can Shorten Your Life." Then answer the following questions.

1. What are the three general sources of pollution mentioned in the article? _____
    _____

2. What phrase tells you that EPA standards do not guarantee healthy air to breathe? _____
    _____

3. How is the author implicitly measuring the cost of pollution in affected areas? _____
    _____

4. What phrase indicates that the effects of breathing polluted air are like those associated with
    smoking cigarettes? _____

5. The effect of new and tougher standards on the polluting industries by the monitoring agency
    would cause the *MC* and *ATC* curves to shift (upward; downward).

Common Errors

The first statement in each "common error" below is incorrect. Each incorrect statement is followed by a corrected version and an explanation.

1. We should eliminate all pollution. WRONG!

    There is an optimal rate at which pollution can take place given the limited resources of our economy. RIGHT!

    Eliminating pollution involves some significant costs. Would it be practical to make sure that every cigarette butt on campus was picked up—even those that might have been flipped into the bushes? No, because the additional costs necessary to achieve a 100 percent pollution-free environment would exceed the additional benefits of doing so. We stop short of that 100 percent pollution-free level—at the point where the marginal social benefits equal the marginal social costs. It would be inefficient to do otherwise.

2. If business firms have a social conscience, they won't pollute. WRONG!

    Even if business firms have a social conscience, there will still be pollution. RIGHT!

    Firms produce goods and services to make profits. In so doing, they serve the rest of society by providing the goods and services society wants and jobs for millions of workers in the process. To avoid polluting, the firms would have to raise their own costs beyond what society could support, and firms would close down or never exist.

•ANSWERS•

Using Key Terms

Across
1. emission charge
5. government failure
9. opportunity cost
10. external cost

Down
2. optimal rate of pollution
3. social costs
4. production decision
6. efficiency decision
7. market failure
8. private costs

True or False

1. T
2. F   Pollution is the result of rational responses by producers to market incentives (i.e., private costs).
3. T
4. T
5. T
6. F   Market incentives are typically more efficient than direct government regulation.
7. F   Pollution permits rely on market incentives.
8. T
9. F   Pollution also occurs as a result of government failure when government planners place a low priority on environmental quality.
10. T

Multiple Choice

1.	b	5.	a	9.	d	13.	a	17.	d
2.	b	6.	c	10.	a	14.	b	18.	c
3.	c	7.	d	11.	d	15.	c	19.	c
4.	a	8.	d	12.	b	16.	a	20.	b

Problems and Applications

Exercise 1

1. See Table 28.1 Answer, column 3

Table 28.1 Answer

Quantity of pollution	(3) Marginal benefits	(5) Marginal cost
6	$ ---	$ ---
5	40	5
4	30	10
3	25	15
2	20	20
1	15	50
0	10	180

2. See Table 28.1 Answer, column 5
3. Yes, because the marginal benefits are worth $40,000 annually, while the marginal costs are only $5,000 annually.
4. b
5. Yes
6. When pollution has been reduced to 2 units per 100 cubic feet of water annually
7. b

Exercise 2

1. See Figure 28.1 Answer, diagram b, line S_1.

Figure 28.1 Answer

2. See Figure 28.1 Answer, diagram a, line S_1.

3. d   4. b   5. d   6. a   7. d

Exercise 3

1. **Table 28.2 Answer**

Production rate	Private marginal cost	Social marginal cost
0	$ ---	$ ---
1	40	80
2	50	90
3	60	100
4	70	110
5	80	120
6	90	130
7	100	140
8	110	150
9	120	160
10	130	170
11	140	180
12	150	190

2. **Figure 28.2 Answer**

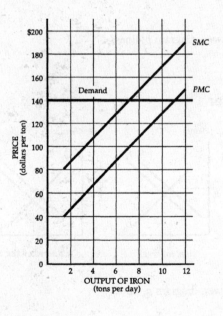

3. d   4. b   5. b

Exercise 4

1. Large particles, fine particles, gases
2. "This form of pollution is killing citizens even in areas that meet Environmental Protection Agency air quality standards. . ."
3. By estimating the probability of premature death due to breathing polluted air.
4. ". . . run a risk of premature death about one-sixth as great as if they had been smoking for 25 years."
5. Upward

CHAPTER 29
The Farm Problem

Quick Review

- There are 2 million farmers in the United States and even though some farms are very large, no one farmer has market power. As a result, the farming industry has many of the characteristics of a perfectly competitive market.

- Barriers to entry into the farming industry are low so anytime farmers are earning an economic profit new farmers are attracted to the market. This pushes long-run economic profit to zero.

- On the demand side, both price and income elasticities make it difficult for farmers. The price elasticity of agricultural goods is low because people only eat so much food regardless of a price decrease. Productivity advances, which are welcome in most other markets, result in much lower prices and farm incomes because of this low price elasticity of demand. A low income elasticity (low sensitivity of the demand for agricultural goods to changes in income) causes domestic demand to grow slowly even when the economy is growing.

- In addition, short-run price fluctuations because of supply changes are an issue for farmers. Sudden droughts, freezes, or blights shift the supply curve which, in turn, affects price. Time lags between when production decisions are made and when the harvest occurs also contribute to price changes.

- After World War II ended, demand for U.S. farm goods on the part of European countries decreased. At the same time, restrictions on international trade reduced demand while new technology caused an increase in supply for the agricultural industry. The result was a huge decrease in the price of farm goods.

- The U.S. government responded to the crisis with several programs, and assistance for farmers still exists today. Price supports are used to raise and stabilize farm prices, but the down side is that this creates a market surplus for the industry.

- Cost subsidies and supply restrictions are also used to increase farm prices, and direct income support aids farmers but does not change market price or output.

- Farm prices were severely impacted in the 1980s because of increased fuel and fertilizer costs and rising interest rates, which reduced farm profits. The export of farm goods also decreased because the strength of the dollar made U.S. agricultural goods too expensive on the world market.

- Recently the government has taken steps to deregulate the farming industry. However, the Asian Crisis in 1997 and the economic slowdown in 2001 caused farmers to demand and get more government assistance. Essentially, U.S. farmers now expect the government to come to their aid, which creates a situation of moral hazard.

Learning Objectives

After reading Chapter 29 and doing the following exercises, you should:

1. Know the dimensions and nature of the farm problem.
2. Understand the role of income and price elasticities in the farm problem.
3. Be able to relate the farm problem to forces on both the supply side and demand side of the market.
4. Understand the impact of supply- and demand-induced changes in prices of inputs on farm decision-making and profits.
5. Be able to describe several types of farm policies and their effects on the farming economy.
6. Be able to describe the causes and dimensions of the two great farm depressions.
7. Understand the direction and rationale of the efforts to deregulate farming.

Using Key Terms

Fill in the puzzle on the opposite page with the appropriate term from the list of Key Terms at the end of the chapter in the text.

Across

2. Total revenue minus total economic costs.
6. Percentage change in quantity demanded divided by the percentage change in price.
9. The ability to change the market price of a good or service.
10. The implicit price paid by the government for surplus crops taken as collateral.
11. Land withdrawn from farm production in an effort to increase crop prices.
12. Income transfer paid to farmers for the difference between target and market prices.

Down

1. Percentage change in quantity demanded divided by percentage change in income.
3. The relative price of farm products in the period 1910-1914.
4. An incentive to engage in undesirable behavior.
5. Obstacles that make it difficult or impossible for new producers to enter a market.
7. The amount by which the quantity supplied exceeds the quantity demanded at a given price.
8. Total revenue minus total cost.

Puzzle 29.1

True or False: *Circle your choice and explain why any false statements are incorrect.*

T   F   1.   Because the average corn farmer produces over 100,000 bushels of corn, that farmer has significant market power.

T   F   2.   Agricultural price-supports lead farmers to produce more goods than consumers want.

T   F   3.   When prices for farm commodities rise, total revenue will increase because the market demand for farm commodities is price inelastic.

T   F   4.   The demand for farmland reflects the present and future income-generating potential of the land.

T   F   5.   Price supports have lowered the price of farm products, increased consumption, and reduced production.

T   F   6.   Counter-cyclical payments are designed to establish the same ratio of farm to nonfarm income as would parity prices.

T   F   7.   Direct income payments to farmers are less efficient at raising farm incomes than are price-support programs.

T   F   8.   When a large crop is produced by American farmers farm prices will decrease because the price elasticity for agricultural products is low.

T   F   9.   The Farm Security Act of 2001 increased farm subsidies and created new subsidies for previously unsubsidized farm products.

T   F   10.   When the government continually bails out farmers during economic crises, rather than relying on the farmers themselves to manage their risks, the government has created a "moral hazard."

Multiple Choice: *Select the correct answer.*

_____ 1.   If an agricultural market is perfectly competitive, then:
   (a)   A farmer is a price taker.
   (b)   A farmer uses price discrimination.
   (c)   The market demand curve is perfectly elastic.
   (d)   Each firm's demand curve is perfectly inelastic.

_____ 2.   The Farm Security Act of 2001 created new subsidies for:
   (a)   Sugar growers.
   (b)   Hog operators.
   (c)   Horse breeders.
   (d)   All of the above.

_____ 3.   Which of the following would result from a price-support program when the support price is set above the equilibrium price?
   (a)   The price paid by consumers would be higher.
   (b)   The consumption of the product would be reduced.
   (c)   Output would increase, *ceteris paribus*.
   (d)   All of the above would result.

4. When government subsidizes the purchase of irrigation water by farmers, the result is:
   (a) Higher marginal costs of production.
   (b) Lower fixed costs to farmers.
   (c) Increased output because marginal costs are lower.
   (d) Higher fixed costs to farmers.

5. Which of the following programs will raise farm incomes without generating market distortions?
   (a) Set-aside programs.
   (b) Direct income-support programs.
   (c) Import restrictions.
   (d) All of the above.

6. The primary intent of the 1996 Freedom to Farm Act was to:
   (a) Make farmers more dependent on market forces.
   (b) Increase prices paid to farmers.
   (c) Increase set-aside acreage.
   (d) All of the above.

7. Which of the following is consistent with farming as a competitive market?
   (a) A small number of firms.
   (b) Marginal revenue lower than price for each firm.
   (c) Exit of small firms when profits are high for large firms.
   (d) Zero economic profit in the long run.

8. When effective price floors are set for an agricultural market, the quantity demanded will be:
   (a) Less than the equilibrium quantity, and price will be greater than the equilibrium price.
   (b) Less than the equilibrium quantity, and price will be less than the equilibrium price.
   (c) Greater than the equilibrium quantity, and price will be greater than the equilibrium price.
   (d) Greater than the equilibrium quantity, and price will be less than the equilibrium price.

9. The surplus induced by farm price-support programs can be eliminated by all of the following *except*:
   (a) Export sales.
   (b) Reduced demand.
   (c) Government purchases and stockpiling.
   (d) Supply restrictions.

10. What impact did the "Asian crisis" have on U.S. agriculture beginning in 1997?
    (a) Decreased farm exports to Asia.
    (b) A decrease in grain prices.
    (c) A decrease in employment in the U.S. farm equipment industry.
    (d) All of the above.

11. Which of the following is *not* generally a characteristic of agriculture?
    (a) Ease of entry and exit.
    (b) Market power.
    (c) Homogeneous products.
    (d) Artificial restraints on prices.

12. Individual farmers view the demand curve they face for agricultural commodities as very price elastic, and they are:
    (a) Correct even though the market demand curve tends to be quite inelastic.
    (b) Correct, and the market demand curve is quite elastic as well.
    (c) Incorrect because the market demand curve tends to be price inelastic.
    (d) Incorrect because price and quantity demanded are inversely related in the product market.

_____ 13. Which of the following characterizes the price and income elasticities for farm products?
- (a) When prices fall, consumers respond by buying a great deal more; when income increases, consumers respond by buying less.
- (b) When prices and income fall, consumers respond by buying less.
- (c) When prices fall, farmers get less revenue; when income rises, consumers do not change purchases much.
- (d) All of the above.

_____ 14. The government creates a "moral hazard" when it:
- (a) Encourages the type of behavior that leads to an undesirable allocation of resources.
- (b) Ignores the plight of a group suffering economic depravation, e.g., farmers during the third farm depression.
- (c) Passes laws it knows can't be enforced.
- (d) Doesn't provide the same level of moral leadership that it expects from U.S. citizens.

_____ 15. If the price of corn falls by 25 percent on world markets, causing American corn consumption to increase by 5 percent, _ceteris paribus_, the absolute value of the price elasticity of demand for corn in the United States would be:
- (a) 0.25.
- (b) 0.5.
- (c) 5.0.
- (d) 0.20.

_____ 16. If the price elasticity of corn is 0.3 and the price of corn falls by 10 percent, the income from corn for farmers will:
- (a) Increase as quantity demanded increases.
- (b) Decrease as quantity demanded increases.
- (c) Increase as quantity demanded decreases.
- (d) Decrease as quantity demanded decreases.

_____ 17. _Ceteris paribus_, when interest rates fall, land values:
- (a) Increase because the profitability of land decreases.
- (b) Increase because the profitability of land increases.
- (c) Decrease because the profitability of land decreases.
- (d) Decrease because the profitability of land increases.

_____ 18. If the market price of wheat is below the government's "loan rate":
- (a) The Commodity Credit Corporation lends the farmer an amount equal to the loan rate times the farmer's wheat output and takes the farmer's wheat crop as full payment of the loan.
- (b) The wheat farmer defaults on the loan but keeps the crop; the CCC keeps the money.
- (c) The wheat farmer, in effect, "buys" the crop from the CCC.
- (d) All of the above.

_____ 19. An advantage of set-aside programs over price-support programs is that they:
- (a) Reduce the price of agricultural goods.
- (b) Transfer more income to farmers.
- (c) Raise the price of agricultural production but do not lead to a surplus of output.
- (d) Affect the demand side as well as the supply side of the farm problem.

_____ 20. Which of the following agricultural programs reduces agricultural output, rather than increasing it?
   (a)   Direct income-support programs.
   (b)   Farm cost subsidies.
   (c)   Marketing orders.
   (d)   Export sales.

Problems and Applications

Exercise 1

This exercise shows the impact of farm subsidies on the market and consumers.

Figure 29.1 represents the agricultural market. Use this figure to answer questions 1-6.

Figure 29.1

1.   Without government intervention, the price of farm goods is determined by the intersection of
_____.

2.   The equilibrium price is _____ and farmers supply farm goods equal to _____.

3.   Individual farmers are price (makers; takers) and will always produce the level of output where price equals _____.

4.   Government price supports would (increase; decrease) the price of farm goods and cause price to move to _____.

5.   At the new price farmers would supply farm goods equal to _____.

6.   The price support caused a (shortage; surplus) of output in the agricultural market equal to the distance _____.

409

Exercise 2

Articles about agriculture often provide information about shortages or surpluses. This exercise will use one of the articles in the textbook to show the kind of information to look for to determine whether shortages or surpluses exist.

Reread the *In the News* article entitled "EU Farm Subsidies." Then answer the following questions.

1. The article indicates there are:
   (a)   Shortages.
   (b)   Surpluses.

2. Which passage in the article indicates the existence of the shortage or surplus? _____
   _____

3. Which diagram in Figure 29.2 best represents the shortage or surplus mentioned in the article?
   _____

Figure 29.2
Shortages or surpluses

4. What phrase indicates the impact of the farm subsidies on consumers? _____
   _____

Common Errors

The first statement in each "common error" below is incorrect. Each incorrect statement is followed by a corrected version and an explanation.

1. Advances in farm productivity should be accompanied by improved profitability. WRONG!

   Competition translates improved productivity into lower prices, which can cause lower profitability. RIGHT!

   The spectacular increases in farm productivity that have occurred in the past decades have resulted in lower prices and lower incomes. Increases in supply coupled with price-inelastic and slow-growing demand have lowered rather than raised net farm income. Yet competition forces the adoption of the newest techniques of farming.

2. When there is a bumper crop, farm incomes will increase. WRONG!

   When there is a bumper crop, farm incomes are likely to decrease. RIGHT!

Because the demand for farm goods is price inelastic, a large percentage increase in output will cause an even larger percentage reduction in the price of farm goods.

•ANSWERS•

Using Key Terms

Across

2. economic profit
6. price elasticity of demand
9. market power
10. loan rate
11. acreage set-aside
12. counter-cyclical payment

Down

1. income elasticity of demand
3. parity
4. moral hazard
5. barriers to entry
7. market surplus
8. profit

True or False

1. F   Even though 100,000 bushels of corn is a large amount, that amount is insignificant relative to the total market output. As a result, the individual farmer has zero market power.
2. T
3. T
4. T
5. F   Price supports have raised the price of farm products, reduced consumption, and encouraged production.
6. F   Counter-cyclical payments are payments made to farmers to make up the difference between target and market prices. Target prices may or may not be designed to reach parity.
7. F   Direct income payments are more efficient because they do not cause market distortions, e.g., surpluses.
8. T
9. T
10. T

Multiple Choice

1.	a	5.	b	9.	b	13.	c	17.	b
2.	d	6.	a	10.	d	14.	a	18.	a
3.	d	7.	d	11.	b	15.	d	19.	c
4.	c	8.	a	12.	a	16.	b	20.	c

Problems and Applications

Exercise 1

1. Market supply and market demand
2. P_1; Q_1
3. Takers; MC
4. Increase; P_2
5. Q_3
6. Surplus; $Q_3 - Q_2$

Exercise 2

1. b
2. ". . . member governments also agree to purchase any surplus production."
3. Diagram b (surplus)
4. "All this protection costs the average EU consumer over $200 a year."

PART 11 Factor Markets: Basic Theory

CHAPTER 30

The Labor Market

Quick Review

- The motivation to work comes from a variety of social, psychological, and economic forces. The need to have income to purchase desired goods and services is, of course, very important. Working imposes opportunity costs on the worker because leisure time must be given up when one chooses to work.

- An increase in the wage rate motivates people to work more initially and the individual's supply curve of labor slopes upward to the right. At a point, higher wages allow people to work fewer hours and still earn the same income. When the income effects become greater than the substitution effects, the labor supply curve bends backward.

- The demand for labor is derived from the demand for the goods and services that the labor produces. The quantity of labor demanded will increase as the wage rate decreases. The marginal physical product (MPP) of labor is the change in total output because of an additional worker. The demand curve for labor is the marginal revenue product (MRP) curve; it combines the productivity of labor with the price of the output. The law of diminishing returns affects both MPP and MRP.

- The hiring decision requires that managers consider the contribution of labor to the firm's revenues (called its marginal revenue product) and what it costs to hire the labor. The marginal revenue product thus sets an upper limit to the wage that will be paid to labor. Labor should be hired until the marginal revenue product declines to the level of the wage rate. Increases in the productivity of labor and increases in the market price of the output will shift the demand for labor (MRP curve) to the right.

- The market equilibrium wage is determined by the intersection of the market supply and market demand curves. A minimum wage is set above the market equilibrium wage and causes the quantity of labor supplied to exceed the quantity of labor demanded.

- When choosing amongst alternative production processes (the efficiency decision), a producer must compare input costs and then choose the least-cost method of production. The most cost effective input is the one that produces the most output per dollar spent, not necessarily the cheapest one.

- It is sometimes difficult to determine the wages of certain individuals because their marginal revenue product is so difficult to calculate. In this situation opportunity wages, custom, power, tradition, and the like are used to determine the wage.

Learning Objectives

After reading Chapter 30 and doing the following exercises, you should:

1. Understand the labor-supply curve and its nonprice determinants.
2. Be able to apply the law of diminishing marginal utility to the labor market.
3. Know how people determine the number of hours they want to work.
4. Be able to explain the shape of the labor-supply curve using the income and substitution effects of wages.
5. Know how to calculate the elasticity of the market supply of labor.
6. Understand why the demand for factors of production is derived from the demand for goods and services.
7. Be able to derive the marginal revenue product curve and know why it slopes downward.
8. Understand how market supply and market demand interact to determine market wage rates when their nonprice determinants change.
9. Understand cost efficiency and how the efficiency decision is made.
10. Know that the "opportunity wage" reflects a worker's productivity in his or her best alternative employment, *ceteris paribus*.

Using Key Terms

Fill in the puzzle on the opposite page with the appropriate term from the list of Key Terms at the end of the chapter in the text.

Across

1. The choice of a production process for any given rate of output.
8. Determined by the intersection of the market supply and market demand for labor.
14. The percentage change in quantity of labor supplied divided by the percentage change in wage rate.
15. The willingness and ability to work specific amounts of time at alternative wage rates.
16. A specific combination of resources used to produce a good or service.

Down

2. The quantity of resources purchased by a firm depends on the firm's expected sales and output.
3. An increased wage rate causes people to work more hours.
4. The relocation of production to foreign countries.
5. The MPP of labor declines as the quantity of labor employed increases.
6. The change in total output because of one additional unit of input.
7. An increased wage rate allows people to reduce the hours worked without losing income.
9. The change in total revenue because of one additional unit of input.
10. The total quantity of labor that workers are willing and able to supply at alternative wage rates.
11. The MPP of an input divided by its price.
12. The highest wage an individual would earn in his or her best alternative job.
13. The quantity of labor employers are willing and able to hire at alternative wage rates.

Puzzle 30.1

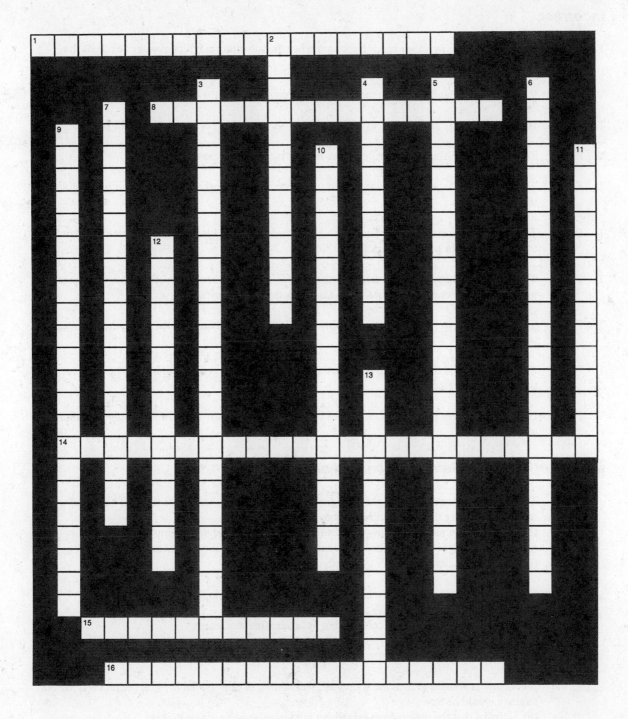

True or False: *Circle your choice and explain why any false statements are incorrect.*

T   F   1.   The supply curve for labor bends backward when the substitution effect of wages exceeds the income effect of wages.

T   F   2.   For wages to be higher without sacrificing jobs, productivity must decrease.

T   F   3.   Higher wage rates are required to compensate for the increasing opportunity cost of labor.

T   F   4.   The value of additional income decreases as total income increases.

T   F   5.   The demand for labor is downward sloping because as more workers are hired their productivity increases.

T   F   6.   The concept of derived demand means that the demand for bricklayers, for example, is determined by the demand for new brick houses.

T   F   7.   The law of diminishing returns suggests that the fewer the number of workers employed, the more total output they can produce in a given time period, *ceteris paribus*.

T   F   8.   The intersection of the labor market supply and market demand curves establishes the minimum wage.

T   F   9.   The labor demand curve is equivalent to the marginal physical product multiplied by the price of the product being produced.

T   F   10.   If salary caps were placed on CEO wages below their opportunity wage, there would be a shortage of CEOs.

Multiple Choice: *Select the correct answer.*

_____ 1.   The number of hours that a worker is willing to work is determined by the tradeoff between:
(a)   Decreasing marginal utility for both income and leisure.
(b)   Increasing marginal utility for leisure and decreasing marginal utility for income.
(c)   Increasing total utility for leisure and decreasing total utility for income.
(d)   Increasing marginal utility for both income and leisure.

_____ 2.   One reason why an individual's labor supply curve is upward sloping is because of the:
(a)   Alternative jobs available to a worker.
(b)   Increasing opportunity cost of labor as leisure time decreases.
(c)   Discrimination faced by some workers.
(d)   Increasing satisfaction from working as a worker becomes more skilled.

_____ 3.   If consumers wanted to increase wages and the number of jobs available for apple pickers, the best strategy would be to:
(a)   Insist that the government establish a minimum wage for apple pickers.
(b)   Boycott apples until wages increased.
(c)   Buy more apples.
(d)   Insist that the sellers raise the price of apples.

_____ 4. An upward-sloping labor-supply curve illustrates, *ceteris paribus*, that:
   (a) The supply of labor and the wage rate are inversely related.
   (b) The quantity supplied of labor and the hours of work per week are directly related.
   (c) The quantity supplied of labor and the hours of work per week are inversely related.
   (d) A greater quantity of labor would be supplied at higher wage rates.

_____ 5. The elasticity of labor supply does *not* depend on:
   (a) The demand for labor.
   (b) Income and wealth.
   (c) The prices of consumer goods.
   (d) Expectations for income or consumption.

_____ 6. If household income and wealth increases over time, the supply of labor will:
   (a) Shift to the left.
   (b) Shift to the right.
   (c) Move up the curve to the right.
   (d) Move down the curve to the left.

_____ 7. Determinants of the market supply of labor include:
   (a) Tastes.
   (b) Income and wealth.
   (c) Expectations.
   (d) All of the above.

_____ 8. A competitive firm should continue to hire workers until the:
   (a) *MRP* is equal to demand.
   (b) *MPP* is equal to the number of workers hired.
   (c) *MRP* is equal to the market wage rate.
   (d) *MRP* is equal to zero.

_____ 9. If Kendra's income effect outweighs her substitution effect, her labor supply curve will:
   (a) Appear horizontal.
   (b) Slope upward.
   (c) Bend backward.
   (d) Appear vertical.

_____ 10. Which of the following is true about the equilibrium market wage?
   (a) All workers are satisfied with the wage.
   (b) All employers are satisfied with the wage.
   (c) There is no unemployment in this market at the equilibrium wage.
   (d) All of the above are correct.

_____ 11. At the market equilibrium wage:
   (a) *MRP* = wage rate.
   (b) There is neither a surplus nor a shortage of labor.
   (c) The market demand curve for labor intersects the market supply curve of labor.
   (d) All of the above.

_____ 12. The cost efficiency of labor is equal to:
   (a) The marginal cost of output.
   (b) The *MPP* of labor times the wage rate.
   (c) The *MPP* of labor divided by the wage rate.
   (d) The *MRP* of labor divided by the unit price of labor.

_____ 13. In order to calculate the marginal revenue product of labor, we need to know:
    (a)   The change in total output and the change in quantity of labor.
    (b)   The marginal physical product of labor and the unit price of the product.
    (c)   The marginal revenue and the total amount of the product produced.
    (d)   The marginal revenue and the cost of the factor input.

_____ 14. The diminishing returns to a factor may be due to:
    (a)   The declining utility of a good as we consume more of it.
    (b)   Crowding or overuse of other factors as production is increased.
    (c)   The decline in the demand curve for a product.
    (d)   The decline in the marginal revenue curve for a product.

_____ 15. The efficiency decision involves choosing the input combination or process that:
    (a)   Produces the greatest output.
    (b)   Results in the lowest output per dollar of input.
    (c)   Results in a given rate of output for the least cost.
    (d)   Has the lowest ratio of _MPP_ to input.

_____ 16. The marginal revenue product curve and marginal physical product curve have similar shapes:
    (a)   Because marginal revenue product depends on marginal physical product.
    (b)   Because the product demand curve slopes downward in accordance with the law of diminishing returns.
    (c)   Because the law of demand and the law of diminishing returns are due to the same economic behavior.
    (d)   For all of the above reasons.

_____ 17. Employment will definitely rise when:
    (a)   Productivity and wages rise.
    (b)   Productivity rises and wages fall.
    (c)   Productivity falls and wages rise.
    (d)   Productivity and wages fall.

_____ 18. A change in wages causes a:
    (a)   Shift in the marginal revenue product curve for labor.
    (b)   Shift in the marginal physical product curve for labor.
    (c)   Shift in the derived demand curve for labor.
    (d)   Movement along the labor-demand curve.

_____ 19. When the minimum wage is raised in a competitive market, _ceteris paribus_:
    (a)   All workers are better off.
    (b)   All workers are worse off.
    (c)   Some workers are better off and some are worse off.
    (d)   Workers are not affected by a minimum wage increase, only by decreases.

_____ 20. "Opportunity wage" is defined as:
    (a)   The highest wage an individual would earn in his or her best alternative employment.
    (b)   The value of goods or services that an individual can purchase with the income earned by working 1 hour.
    (c)   The income equivalent of a volunteer worker.
    (d)   The income a worker loses when he or she quits a job.

Problems and Applications

Exercise 1

This exercise shows how to determine the supply of labor. It provides practice in graphing labor supply and examines backward-bending supply curves, the substitution effect, and the income effect.

Suppose you came to school without any means of support and your advisor suggests that you take a job at the school. Your only task is to correct true-false examinations (the professors give you all of the answers to the exams), add up the scores, and calculate each student's grade. You can work as many hours as you wish because opportunities are plentiful.

Drawing Labor-Supply Curves

If the work were offered to you on a volunteer basis, you would not work at all. But at $2 an hour you might work 1 hour per day—just to see how well your classmates are doing. Only at $4 an hour would it be worthwhile to work many hours—perhaps 4 hours per day. At $8 an hour you would work 6 hours per day and at $16 an hour you would make it a full-time job of 8 hours per day. But at $32 an hour you would decide to spend more time at leisure and work only 6 hours per day.

1. Fill in column 2 of Table 30.1, your labor-supply schedule, using the information in the paragraph above.

Table 30.1
Supply of labor

(1) Hourly wage (dollars per hour)	(2) Work effort (hours worked per day)	(3) Elasticity of supply
$ 0	_____	—
2	_____	_____
4	_____	_____
8	_____	_____
16	_____	_____
32	_____	_____

2. Graph the labor-supply curve in Figure 30.1. First label the axes for the graph and then draw the curve and label it. (The curve should pass through point *A*.)

Figure 30.1

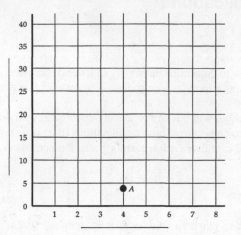

Backward-Bending Supply Curves

3. On the backward-bending segment of a supply curve, wage and quantity supplied are:
   (a) Directly (positively) related.
   (b) Inversely related.
   (c) Related by a horizontal line.
   (d) Related by a vertical line.

4. Which of the following circumstances might explain a backward-bending supply curve such as the one you have drawn in Figure 30.1?
   (a) You want to make a certain amount of income, and you want to spend the rest of your time sleeping and watching videos.
   (b) Because of the increased income you receive from an increase in your wage, you can increase your leisure without losing any income.
   (c) The marginal utility of each extra dollar falls as income rises.
   (d) All of the above might explain such a curve.

Substitution and Income Effects

5. An increase in wage rates:
   (a) Definitely increases hours worked through both the substitution and income effects.
   (b) Tends to increase hours worked through the substitution effect but may tend to decrease hours worked through the income effect.
   (c) Tends to increase hours worked through the substitution effect but definitely decreases hours worked through the income effect.
   (d) Tends to decrease hours worked through the substitution effect and may increase hours worked through the income effect.

6. On the backward-bending portion of the supply curve:
   (a) The income effect is greater than the substitution effect.
   (b) The substitution effect overpowers the income effect.
   (c) Both effects tend to decrease the quantity of labor supplied as a result of a wage increase.

7. In column 3 of Table 30.1, compute the elasticity of supply between each successive wage rate. Use the midpoint formula from the text.

Exercise 2

This exercise illustrates the relationship between marginal physical product and marginal revenue product for a company producing bottled water.

1. T F The marginal physical product (*MPP*) measures the change in total output that occurs when one additional worker is hired.

2. Which of the following formulas would provide a correct calculation of the marginal physical product?
   (a) Quantity ÷ labor
   (b) Change in quantity ÷ labor
   (c) Change in quantity ÷ change in labor
   (d) Change in total revenue ÷ change in labor

3. Calculate total revenue, marginal revenue product, and marginal physical product for Table 30.2.

Table 30.2
Marginal physical product and marginal revenue product

(1)	(2)	(3)	(4)	(5)	(6)
Labor (workers per hour)	Quantity produced (gallons per hour)	Price (dollars per gallon)	Total revenue (dollars per hour)	Marginal revenue product (dollars per worker)	Marginal physical product (gallons per worker)
0	0	$1	_____	_____	_____
1	15	1	_____	_____	_____
2	27	1	_____	_____	_____
3	36	1	_____	_____	_____
4	42	1	_____	_____	_____
5	45	1	_____	_____	_____
6	46	1	_____	_____	_____

4. The law of diminishing returns implies that:
   (a) The marginal revenue declines as additional labor is employed in a given production process.
   (b) The marginal revenue product declines as additional labor is employed in a given production process.
   (c) The marginal physical product of labor increases as additional labor is employed in a given production process.
   (d) None of the above.

5. T F There are diminishing returns to labor with increased production in Table 30.2.

Exercise 3

This exercise provides experience in computing and graphing derived demand as well as determining the number of workers to hire.

1. You are the producer of a protein bar called EnerG, which sells for $1 per bar. You must pay $6 an hour for labor. Complete Table 30.3.

Table 30.3 EnerG production, by labor hours

(1) Wage (dollars per hour)	(2) Labor (workers per hour)	(3) Quantity produced (bars per hour)	(4) Price (dollars per bar)	(5) Total revenue (dollars per bar)	(6) Marginal revenue product (dollars per worker)
$6	0	0	$1	$_____	$ _____
6	1	15	1	_____	_____
6	2	27	1	_____	_____
6	3	36	1	_____	_____
6	4	42	1	_____	_____
6	5	45	1	_____	_____
6	6	46	1	_____	_____

2. T   F   The demand curve for EnerG workers is found by plotting the marginal revenue product curve.

3. In Figure 30.2 draw the demand curve for labor from Table 30.3. Label it demand or *MRP*.

Figure 30.2

4. Draw a straight line at a wage of $6 in Figure 30.2 and label it wage rate.

5. How many workers are you willing to hire to produce EnerG bars? _____

6. How many EnerG bars will be produced per hour? _____

Exercise 4

This exercise examines the impact of a minimum wage on a labor market.

Figure 30.3

1. Figure 30.3 shows the labor market for unskilled workers. The equilibrium wage rate occurs at _____ per hour and at a quantity of _____ workers.

2. Now assume that the minimum wage is set at $8.00 per hour. The result of this government intervention is to create a (shortage; surplus) of labor.

3. At the new minimum wage, _____ workers keep their jobs and _____ workers are unemployed.

4. An increase in labor productivity in Figure 30.3 would cause the labor (supply, demand) curve to shift to the (left; right).

Common Errors

The first statement in each "common error" below is incorrect. Each incorrect statement is followed by a corrected version and an explanation.

1. The labor-supply curve is the same as the supply curve of the products that labor produces. WRONG!

   The labor-supply curve is a supply curve in a factor market, whereas a product supply curve applies to a product market. RIGHT!

   Supply curves in different markets are not the same curves, although they may look the same. The chief difference is found on the axes, as shown in Table 30.4.

Table 30.4
Axes of labor-supply and product-supply curves

Axis	Labor-supply curve	Product supply curve
x-axis	Labor services in a given time period	Output in a given time period
y-axis	Wage for labor	Price of a product

2. Workers demand jobs. WRONG!

   Employers demand labor services and workers (employees) supply them. RIGHT!

   Demand refers to what a buyer is willing and able to buy. Certainly workers are not seeking to pay their employers. Rather, the workers are trying to find someone who is willing and able to pay them for their labor.

3. Employers employ those factors that are least expensive. WRONG!

   Employers want to employ those factors that are most cost-effective. RIGHT!

   If a factor is cheap, there may be a reason for it. It may not last long, may not work correctly, or may require heavier use of other factors of production—for example, maintenance workers. The marginal productivity of the cheap factor may therefore be low. An apparently more expensive factor might perform its proper function well and even save on the costs of other factors. The marginal productivity of the more expensive input would more than make up for its higher cost. Businesses would choose the more expensive factor of production.

4. Marginal revenue product is the same as marginal revenue. WRONG!

   The marginal revenue product curve applies to the factor market, while the marginal revenue curve applies to the product market. RIGHT!

   The formula for marginal revenue product is

$$\frac{\text{Change in total revenue}}{\text{Change in quantity of input}}$$

while that for marginal revenue is

$$\frac{\text{Change in total revenue}}{\text{Change in quantity of output}}$$

Marginal revenue shows changes in total revenue as a result of increased output and therefore is appropriate in analyzing what happens in the product market.

Marginal revenue product shows how total revenue changes as a result of the increased use of a factor and therefore is appropriate in analyzing what happens in the factor market. Both curves are derived from the demand curve in the product market. However, in order to find marginal revenue product, it is necessary also to know the relationship between the quantity of input and quantity of output. That is why the marginal physical product becomes important.

5. The law of diminishing returns means that average total costs will rise as a firm expands. WRONG!

    The law of diminishing returns applies only to changes in the use of one factor while all others remain constant. RIGHT!

    If a firm could expand all factors of production proportionately, there might be no decline in productivity at all, and thus no increase in average total cost. If the firm could do so without affecting factor prices, there would then be no change in unit costs either. The law of diminishing returns applies to changes of only one factor or group of factors, *ceteris paribus* (all other factors being held constant).

•ANSWERS•

Using Key Terms

Across

1. efficiency decision
8. equilibrium wage
14. elasticity of labor supply
15. labor supply
16. production process

Down

2. derived demand
3. substitution effect of wages
4. outsourcing
5. law of diminishing returns
6. marginal physical product
7. income effect of wages
9. marginal revenue product
10. market supply of labor
11. cost efficiency
12. opportunity wage
13. demand for labor

True or False

1. F   The supply curve for labor bends backward when the income effect of wages exceeds the substitution effect of wages.
2. F   For wages to be higher without sacrificing jobs, productivity must increase.
3. T
4. T
5. F   The demand for labor is downward sloping due to diminishing marginal productivity caused by the fact that the amount of capital and space available to each worker decreases as more workers are hired.
6. T
7. F   When fewer workers are hired total output is typically lower. It is also usually true, however, that when fewer workers are hired the *MPP* of the last worker increases.
8. F   The intersection of supply and demand establishes the equilibrium wage. The minimum wage is typically set above the equilibrium wage by the government.
9. T
10. T

Multiple Choice

1.	b	5.	a	9.	c	13.	b	17.	b
2.	b	6.	a	10.	c	14.	b	18.	d
3.	c	7.	d	11.	d	15.	c	19.	c
4.	d	8.	c	12.	c	16.	a	20.	a

Problems and Applications

Exercise 1

1. See Table 30.1 Answer, column 2.

Table 30.1 Answer

(1) Hourly wage (dollars per hour)	(2) Work effort (hours worked per day)	(3) Elasticity of supply
$ 0	0	---
2	1	1.0
4	4	1.8
8	6	0.6
16	8	0.429
32	6	-0.429

2. **Figure 30.1 Answer**

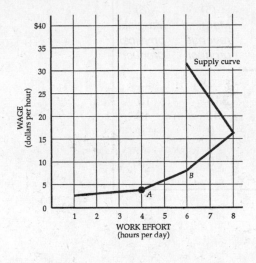

3. b   4. d   5. b   6. a

7. See Table 30.1 Answer, column 3. The formula for the elasticity of labor supply is

$$\frac{\text{Percentage change in quantity of labor supplied}}{\text{Percentage change in wage rate}}$$

The elasticity of labor supply can be estimated (just as the elasticity of demand was estimated) by using the following midpoint formula:

$$\frac{(L_2 - L_1) \div [1/2 \times (L_2 + L_1)]}{(W_2 - W_1) \div [1/2 \times (W_2 + W_1)]} = \frac{(6 - 8) \div [(1/2 \times (6 - 8)]}{(32 - 16) \div [(1/2 \times (32 - 16)]} = \frac{-.286}{.667}$$

In the formula, L_1 is the amount of labor offered at the wage W_1 in period 1 and L_2 is the amount of labor offered at the wage W_2 in period 2. (*Note:* Elasticity is negative only on the backward-bending part of the supply curve.)

Exercise 2

1. T
2. c

3. **Table 30.2 Answer**

(1) Labor	(4) Total revenue	(5) Marginal revenue product	(6) Marginal physical product
0	----	----	----
1	$15	$15	15
2	27	12	12
3	36	9	9
4	42	6	6
5	45	3	3
6	46	1	1

4. b
5. T

Exercise 3

1. **Table 30.3 Answer**

(2) Labor	(5) Total revenue	(6) Marginal revenue product
0	$ 0	$ ----
1	15	15
2	27	12
3	36	9
4	42	6
5	45	3
6	46	1

2. T

3. **Figure 30.2 Answer**

4. See Figure 30.2 Answer.
5. 4 workers
6. 42 bars

Exercise 4

1. $7.00; 1000
2. Surplus
3. 980, 40
4. Demand; right

CHAPTER 31

Labor Unions

Quick Review

- The outcomes in the labor market, including the wage rate and the level of employment, can be distorted by market power on either the supply or demand side. Where the labor market is segmented by geographical, occupational, or industrial boundaries, market power may exist.

- Unions typically negotiate over a large number of objectives, but the most important is usually the wage rate. Unions tend to reduce the number of people they permit to be employed and to bargain for higher wages than would occur if the labor market were competitive. Union decisions are based on the collective interests of the members.

- The labor demand curve is downward sloping, which means that additional labor can only be sold at a lower wage rate. The marginal wage is the change in total wages that results from employment of an extra unit of labor, and it lies below the labor demand curve.

- Unions establish the level of employment where the labor supply curve and the marginal wage rate are equated. The union wage is determined by the labor demand curve at the desired employment level.

- It is also possible for the firm to have market power such as a monopsonist or oligopolist. In this case, the more labor an employer seeks, the higher the wages will have to be. And when wages are raised for any worker, they must be raised for everyone. The marginal factor cost is therefore higher than the market wage rate.

- Monopsonists will attempt to equate marginal factor cost with marginal revenue product and then determine the wage rate from the labor supply curve. They will end up paying less than the competitive wage rate.

- In bilateral monopolies, where power exists on both sides of the labor market, unions and employers engage in collective bargaining to negotiate a final settlement.

- There is general agreement that unions have raised relative wages. Organized labor is also considered to be a potent political force. The impact of unions on prices and productivity is debated and appears to be complex.

Learning Objectives

After reading Chapter 31 and doing the following exercises, you should:

1. Understand the characteristics that are used to define the boundaries of labor markets.
2. Be able to demonstrate the meaning of the equilibrium wage rate.
3. Be able to describe the various types of labor buyers and suppliers.
4. Be familiar with the history of labor unions and their role in the economy.
5. Be able to define, compute, and graph the marginal wage curve and the demand curve for labor.
6. Be able to determine the optimal level of employment from a union point of view.
7. Know how to measure union power using the unionization ratio.
8. Be able to define, compute, and graph the marginal factor cost of labor and the supply curve of labor.
9. Be able to describe the monopsonist's desired equilibrium.
10. Understand how wages are determined in a market characterized by bilateral monopoly.
11. Be able to discuss the impact of unions in the U.S. economy.

Using Key Terms

Fill in the puzzle on the opposite page with the appropriate term from the list of Key Terms at the end of the chapter in the text.

Across
2. The change in total wages paid because of a one-unit increase in the quantity of labor employed.
5. A market with only one buyer and one seller.
10. The change in total costs because of a one-unit increase in the quantity of a factor employed.
11. A workplace in which all workers must join the union within 30 days after being employed.
12. The willingness and ability to work specific amounts of time at alternative wage rates.

Down
1. The quantity of labor employers are willing and able to hire at alternative wages.
2. The change in total revenue because of an additional unit of input.
3. Direct negotiations between employers and unions to determine labor market outcomes.
4. Output per unit of input.
6. The wage rate at which the quantity of labor supplied equals the quantity of labor demanded.
7. The percentage of the labor force belonging to a union.
8. The ability to alter the market price of a good or service.
9. A market in which there is only one buyer.

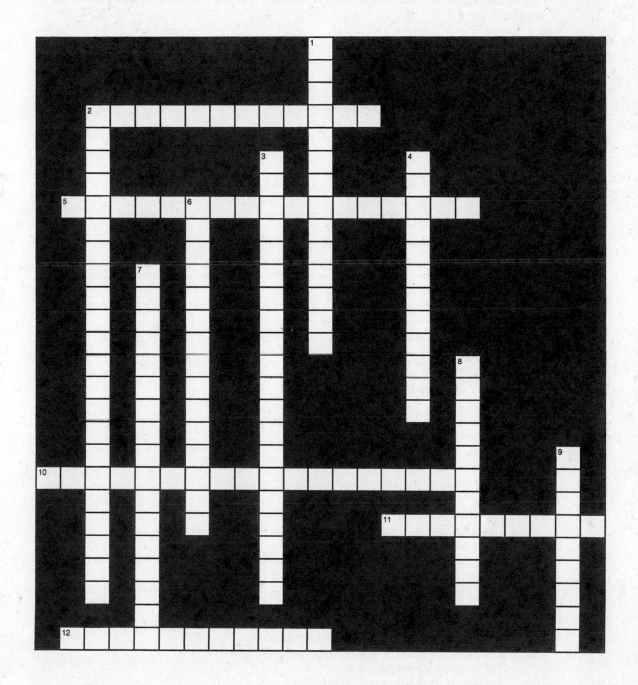

True or False: *Circle your choice and explain why any false statements are incorrect.*

T F 1. The equilibrium wage rate is the rate at which the quantity of labor demanded equals the quantity supplied.

T F 2. When determining the optimum level of employment, monopsonists will equate the marginal wage and the marginal revenue product.

T F 3. When determining the optimum level of employment, monopolists in the labor market will equate the marginal wage and the labor supply curve.

T F 4. The marginal wage curve lies below the labor-demand curve because all worker's wages are lowered when one more worker is hired.

T F 5. Unions do not need to control the labor supply in order to have market power.

T F 6. A craft union is a labor organization that represents workers in a particular industry.

T F 7. Union membership in the United States has risen steadily since the 1950s.

T F 8. A monopsony employer seeks to establish a wage rate that is lower than competitive standards.

T F 9. The collective bargaining process results in prices above the marginal revenue product curve.

T F 10. Unions have been successful in establishing minimum wage laws, work and safety rules, and retirement benefits.

Multiple Choice: *Select the correct answer.*

_____ 1. Typical goals of a labor union in the United States include:
   (a) Job security.
   (b) Wages.
   (c) Fringe benefits.
   (d) All of the above.

_____ 2. The reason that a union may worry about having too many members is that:
   (a) The union faces a downward-sloping marginal revenue product curve.
   (b) It may be unable to control all of its members.
   (c) It may not be able to reach optimal employment, at which the marginal labor cost curve intersects the demand curve.
   (d) All of the above.

_____ 3. Total wages paid to labor are maximized when workers are hired up to the point where:
   (a) The marginal wage is equal to the market wage.
   (b) The demand for labor is equal to the marginal factor cost.
   (c) The marginal wage equals zero.
   (d) The market wage equals the marginal factor cost.

_____ 4. Unions must distinguish between the marginal wage and the market wage, but nonunion workers generally do *not* because:
  (a) The demand curve for labor from the union point of view slopes downward.
  (b) For a nonunion worker who has no market power, the demand curve appears flat.
  (c) For a nonunion worker who has no market power, the demand curve is the same as the marginal wage curve.
  (d) All of the above.

_____ 5. From a union's perspective, the optimal level of employment is determined by the intersection of the:
  (a) Labor-demand curve and the labor-supply curve.
  (b) Marginal wage curve and the labor-supply curve.
  (c) Labor-demand curve and the marginal wage curve.
  (d) Labor-demand curve and the marginal factor cost curve.

_____ 6. Assume a firm hires 10 workers at a wage rate of $15 per hour, but in order to hire the eleventh worker wages must fall to $14 per hour. What is the marginal wage of the eleventh worker?
  (a) $154 per hour.
  (b) $14 per hour.
  (c) $4 per hour.
  (d) $-1 per hour.

_____ 7. To be successful in changing wage rates and employment conditions, labor unions need to have control over only:
  (a) Their own members.
  (b) The supply of labor to the market.
  (c) The *MRP* of employers.
  (d) The production decision of employers.

_____ 8. An industrial union:
  (a) Exerts market power by controlling the demand for labor in a particular industry.
  (b) Exerts market power by controlling the supply of labor to a particular firm.
  (c) Is an organization of workers with a particular skill.
  (d) Is an organization of workers in a particular industry.

_____ 9. At a union-imposed level of employment:
  (a) Employment is lower than at the competitive equilibrium.
  (b) The marginal wage is negative.
  (c) Employment and wages are both at the maximum possible levels.
  (d) Employment would not be increased by reducing the wage rate.

_____ 10. A monopsonist must pay a higher wage rate to hire additional workers because as a single:
  (a) Seller in the market, it has market power.
  (b) Buyer in the market, it faces an upward-sloping supply curve for labor.
  (c) Seller in the market, it does not have to compete with other firms for customers.
  (d) Buyer in the market, it faces a flat supply curve for labor.

_____ 11. The difference between a competitive labor market and a monopsonistic labor market is that the:
  (a) Monopsony will attempt to charge a higher wage than will be charged in a competitive market, *ceteris paribus*.
  (b) Monopsony will hire less labor than will be hired in a competitive market, *ceteris paribus*.
  (c) Shape of the marginal revenue product curve of a monopsony will differ from that of a competitive market.
  (d) All of the above.

_____ 12. The marginal factor cost for labor is the:
  (a) Net cost to a monopsonist of hiring an additional unit of labor.
  (b) Net gain to a monopolist seller of labor if an additional unit of labor is hired.
  (c) Demand for labor.
  (d) Supply of labor.

_____ 13. A monopsonist pays $15 per hour for 10 workers. In order to hire an eleventh worker, the monopsonist must increase the wage rate to $16 per hour. What is the marginal factor cost of labor with eleven workers?
  (a) $176 per hour.
  (b) $26 per hour.
  (c) $16 per hour.
  (d) $15 per hour.

_____ 14. A profit-maximizing monopsonist will hire workers to the point where the marginal factor cost curve intersects the:
  (a) Marginal wage curve.
  (b) Equilibrium wage.
  (c) Marginal revenue product curve.
  (d) Labor-supply curve.

_____ 15. The buyer's profit-maximizing level of input use occurs at:
  (a) Marginal wage = marginal factor cost.
  (b) MRP = marginal wage.
  (c) Marginal wage = zero.
  (d) MRP = marginal factor cost.

_____ 16. A workplace that requires workers to become a member within thirty days of being hired by a firm is:
  (a) A craft union.
  (b) An industrial union.
  (c) A union shop.
  (d) The AFL-CIO.

_____ 17. Which of the following correctly assesses the impact of unions in the U.S. economy?
  (a) Unions have been successful in redistributing some income from nonunion to union workers.
  (b) Union work rules have contributed to inflation because productivity increases have generally exceeded wage increases.
  (c) The political power of unions has grown because the unionization ratio has grown at the same rate as the labor force.
  (d) Most of the rise in labor's share of total income is due to unionization.

_____ 18. The trend in the U.S. toward the merger of unions is driven by the labor movement's desire to:
  (a) Increase representation.
  (b) Increase financial support.
  (c) Enhance their political power.
  (d) All of the above.

_____ 19. In a bilateral monopoly, wages and employment are determined by:
  (a) Negotiation.
  (b) The intersection of market supply and demand.
  (c) The intersection of marginal cost and marginal revenue product.
  (d) The intersection of marginal wage and market demand.

_____ 20. Which of the following is true concerning union work rules?
   (a)   They are designed to maximize the level of employment at any given rate of output.
   (b)   They tend to reduce labor turnover.
   (c)   They may make workers more willing to learn new tasks.
   (d)   All of the above.

Problems and Applications

Exercise 1

This exercise provides practice in calculating the marginal factor cost of labor (marginal wage) and the marginal revenue product of labor for a monopsony situation.

1. Suppose the data in Table 31.1 represent the wages, number of workers, and the price that you face when producing different amounts of Roaring Ripple, a new soft drink. Complete Table 31.1.

Table 31.1
Labor market with variable wage

(1)	(2)	(3)	(4)	(5)	(6)	(7)	(8)
					MFC		MRP
				TC	(dollars	TR	(dollars
Labor	Wage	Ripple	Price	(dollars	per	(dollars	per
(workers	(dollars	(quarts	(dollars	per hour)	worker)	per hour)	worker)
per hour)	per hour)	per hour)	per quart)	(1) x (2)	(ΔTC/ΔL)	(3) x (4)	(ΔTR/ΔL)
0	$1	0	$1	$ _____	$ ___	$ _____	$ ___
1	2	15	1	_____	_____	_____	_____
2	7	27	1	_____	_____	_____	_____
3	9	36	1	_____	_____	_____	_____

2. The amount of Roaring Ripple you will produce to maximize your profits is _____ ; the wage you will pay your workers is _____ ; the marginal cost of labor will be _____ ; the number of employees you will hire will be _____ .

3. T   F   For each new worker you hire, you must raise wages for all of the workers together, which means that the marginal cost of labor is different from the supply curve of labor.

4. T   F   The wage at which the marginal cost of labor curve intersects the marginal revenue product curve is the equilibrium wage rate.

Exercise 2

The differences in labor goals are the focus of this exercise.

Suppose that the supply and demand schedules in Table 31.2 apply to a particular labor market.

Table 31.2
Labor supply and demand

Wage rate (dollars per hour)	$14	13	12	11	10	9	8	7	6	5
Quantity of labor demanded (workers per hour)	0	1	2	3	4	5	6	7	8	9
Total wage bill (dollars per hour)	—	—	—	—	—	—	—	—	—	—
Marginal wage (dollars per worker)	—	—	—	—	—	—	—	—	—	—

Wage rate (dollars per hour)	$3	4	5	6	7
Quantity of labor supplied (workers per hour)	1	3	5	7	9
Total wage (dollars per hour)	—	—	—	—	—
Marginal factor cost (dollars per worker)	—	—	—	—	—

Figure 31.1

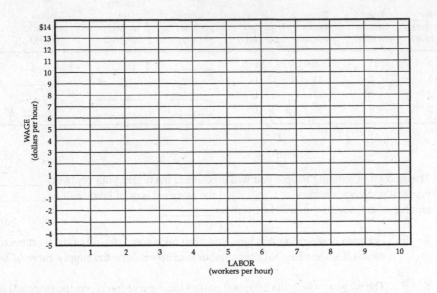

1. Compute the marginal wage and the marginal factor cost in the space provided in Table 31.2.

2. Graph the labor demand curve, the labor supply curve, marginal wage, and marginal factor cost in Figure 31.1.

3. The amount of labor hired in a competitive market would be _____ workers at a wage of _____ per hour.

4. The amount of labor that a union would want hired if it acted as a monopolist would be _____ workers at a wage of _____ per hour.

5. Suppose a union asks each member to contribute a certain percentage of income to the union. Therefore, when the wage bill is maximized the union maximizes the dues it receives. The amount of labor that would maximize union dues would be _____ workers at a wage of _____ per hour.

6. Suppose the union wishes to maximize the number of employees that it has so that it can become a political force at the ballot box. The maximum amount of labor that such a union would be able to recruit would be _____ workers at a wage of _____ per hour.

7. The amount of labor hired by a monopsonist would be _____ workers at a wage of _____ per hour.

The following are the names of some of the labor market situations described in the questions above:

    A.   Competition (question 3)
    B.   Union monopolist (question 4)
    C.   Monopsony (question 7)

8. Each of the labor market situations listed above will result in a different wage-labor combination. Use the corresponding letter to label each wage-labor outcome in Figure 31.1.

9. Rank the above list of labor markets in order with respect to wage rates and then rank them with respect to total employment.

Table 31.3

Rank	Wage (highest to lowest)	Rank	Amount of labor (lowest to highest)
1. _____		1. _____	
2. _____		2. _____	
3. _____		3. _____	

10. T F Market power, regardless of whether it is possessed by the buyer or the supplier, results in output equal to or lower than in a competitive labor market.

11. T F Market power, regardless of whether it is possessed by the buyer or the supplier, results in wage rates higher than those in a competitive labor market.

Exercise 3

Reread the *In the News* article titled "A Win for the Graduate(s)." Then answer the following questions.

1. Before the decision in the article, private universities had _____ power in the labor market for their own graduate students.

2. Now that graduate students are allowed to unionize, salaries should (increase; decrease; remain the same).

3. For a monopsonist, the marginal factor cost is (greater; less) than the wage rate because additional workers can be hired only if the wage rate for all workers (increases; decreases).

4. A monopsonist hires (more; fewer) workers at a (higher; lower) wage rate than would occur in a competitive market.

Common Errors

The first statement in each "common error" below is incorrect. Each incorrect statement is followed by a corrected version and an explanation.

1. The marginal cost of labor curve is the same as the marginal cost curve, and therefore it is also the supply curve for a firm. WRONG!

   The marginal cost of labor curve is derived from the supply of labor and is applicable only to the labor market, not to the product market. RIGHT!

   The marginal cost of labor is given by the formula

$$\frac{\text{Change in total wage cost}}{\text{Change in quantity of labor}}$$

   while the marginal cost curve is given by

$$\frac{\text{Change in total wage cost}}{\text{Change in quantity of product}}$$

   While the marginal cost of labor applies only to labor costs in the labor market, the marginal cost curve applies to all costs in the product market.

2. In bilateral monopoly, the optimal level of employment occurs where the marginal cost of labor curve intersects the marginal wage curve. WRONG!

   In bilateral monopoly, it is possible to determine the limits between which the labor employment and wage levels will fall but not the precise optimal levels. RIGHT!

   The buyer wishes to buy labor at the point where the marginal cost of labor curve intersects the labor-demand curve. Only through negotiation can a compromise be worked out. The final outcome reflects the relative market power of supplier and buyer.

3. Powerful unions can get whatever wage they want. WRONG!

   Powerful unions are limited by the demand for labor. RIGHT!

   If unions make and receive exorbitant wage demands, they may find the union membership dwindling as more employees are laid off. Frequently, unions moderate wage demands in order to prevent employers from going out of business, foreign competition from undercutting prices, and non-unionized workers from becoming attractive to employers. All of these considerations reflect the law of demand.

•ANSWERS•

Using Key Terms

Across

2. marginal wage
5. bilateral monopoly
10. marginal factor cost
11. union shop
12. labor supply

Down

1. demand for labor
2. marginal revenue product
3. collective bargaining
4. productivity
6. equilibrium wage
7. unionization ratio
8. market power
9. monopsony

True or False

1. T
2. F   Monopsonists will equate marginal factor cost and marginal revenue product.
3. T
4. T
5. F   To maintain higher than equilibrium wages labor supply must be reduced.
6. F   A craft union represents workers with specific skills.
7. F   The unionization rate in the United States has been in steady decline for more than 40 years.
8. T
9. F   The marginal revenue curve sets an upper limit for wages because it measures the value of each worker to the firm.
10. T

Multiple Choice

1. d	5. b	9. a	13. b	17. a
2. a	6. c	10. b	14. c	18. d
3. c	7. b	11. b	15. d	19. a
4. d	8. d	12. a	16. c	20. d

Problems and Applications

Exercise 1

1. **Table 31.1 Answer**

(1) Labor	(2) Wage	(5) TC	(6) MFC	(7) TR	(8) MRP
0	$1	$ 0	$ ---	$ 0	$ ---
1	2	2	2	15	15
2	7	14	12	27	12
3	9	27	13	36	9

2. 27 quarts per hour; $7 per hour; $12 per hour; 2 employees per hour
3. T
4. F

Exercise 2

1. **Table 31.2 Answer**

Wage rate (dollars per hour)	$14	13	12	11	10	9	8	7	6	5
Quantity of labor demanded (workers per hour)	0	1	2	3	4	5	6	7	8	9
Total wage bill (dollars per hour)	0	13	24	33	40	45	48	49	48	45
Marginal wage (dollars per worker)	—	13	11	9	7	5	3	1	-1	-3

Wage rate (dollars per hour)	$3	4	5	6	7
Quantity of labor supplied (workers per hour)	1	3	5	7	9
Total wage (dollars per hour)	$3	12	25	42	63
Marginal factor cost (dollars per worker)	3	4.5	6.5	8.5	10.5

2. **Figure 31.1 Answer**

Note: When demand falls below the price at which workers are willing and able to work, there can be no greater employment. So the dues-maximizing and wage bill-maximizing unions will push employment to the competitive level. However, more inelastic demand can mean that wage bill-maximizing unions would produce less than the competitive level at a higher wage.

3. 7 (Labor supply and labor demand intersect at 7.5 workers.); between $6 and $7
4. 5; $9.00
5. 7; $6.50. The wage bill is maximized where the marginal wage intersects the *x*-axis. But the equilibrium amount of labor, where labor supply equals labor demand, tells us the maximum number of workers which could be hired.
6. 7; $6.50
7. 6; $5.50; Remember that a monopsonist forces the wage down to the supply curve from which the wage is read.
8. See the letters marking the points in Figure 31.1 Answer

9. **Table 31.3 Answer**

	Wage		Amount of labor
Rank	(highest to lowest)	Rank	(lowest to highest)
1.	Union monopolist	1.	Union monopolist
2.	Competition	2.	Monopsony
3.	Monopsony	3.	Competition

10. T
11. F   Monopsony results in a lower price than the competitive price.

443

Exercise 3

1. Monopsony
2. Increase
3. Greater; increases
4. Fewer; lower

CHAPTER 32

Financial Markets

Quick Review

- Financial markets assist the economy in its search for the optimal mix of output by helping to mobilize savings, manage risk, and signal desired resource allocations.

- Financial markets bring together those who wish to save more than they spend (the savers) and those who wish to spend more than they save (the borrowers). This is vital to the process of "spreading the risk" of failure over a large number of individuals.

- Three distinct financial markets, the stock market, the bond market, and the futures market, aid in financial intermediation through which risk spreading occurs. Financial intermediaries also reduce the costs of information and search, and in doing so, they make the financial markets more efficient.

- Financial intermediaries discount future dollars by the opportunity cost of money or the market interest rate. Higher interest rates and a longer time until future payment will cause a decrease in the present discounted value of a future payment. Risk also has an impact on the expected value of future payments.

- The stock market allows firms to raise capital by selling ownership in the corporation. Changing expectations regarding the future profitability of particular corporations and the future course of the economy are important determinants of the price of a stock.

- Debt instruments, called bonds, are bought and sold in the bond market. Each bond is essentially an IOU which states the principal amount, interest, and terms on which the debt must be repaid. While the initial purchasers lend directly to the borrower, the bonds are also traded in a secondary market. Bond yields are inversely related to bond prices.

- Changes in investors' expectations concerning future interest rates and the borrowers' potential ability to pay interest and repay principal will affect the supply and demand for bonds.

- Venture capitalists provide initial funding for entrepreneurial ventures. If the project is a success, they reap profits; if not, they experience losses.

Learning Objectives

After reading Chapter 32 and doing the following exercises, you should:

1. Understand the primary function of financial markets.
2. Understand how financial markets increase efficiency.
3. Know what present discounted value means and how to calculate it.
4. Know that risk has an impact on the expected value of future payments.
5. Understand how companies raise funds through the stock market and the bond market.
6. Know some of the determinants of the demand for and supply of stocks and bonds, and know how changes in those determinants affect stock and bond prices.
7. Be able to explain why bond yields are inversely related to bond prices.
8. Understand the role of venture capitalists.

Using Key Terms

Fill in the puzzle on the opposite page with the appropriate term from the list of Key Terms at the end of the chapter in the text.

Across

2. The probable value of a future payment, including the risk of nonpayment.
6. A limited liability form of business.
7. An IOU issued by corporations and government agencies.
9. Amount of corporate profit paid out for each share of stock.
11. The ability of an asset to be converted to cash.
12. The rate of return on a bond.
14. An increase in the market value of an asset.
15. The first sale to the general public of stock in a corporation.
16. The price of a stock share divided by earnings per share.

Down

1. The interest rate set for a bond at the time of issuance is the _____ rate.
3. The value today of future payments, adjusted for interest accrual.
4. An institution that brings savers and dissavers together.
5. Failure to make scheduled payments of interest or principal on a bond.
6. Shares of ownership in a corporation.
8. Corporate profits not paid out in dividends.
10. The difference in rates of return on risky and safe investments.
13. The face value of a bond.

Puzzle 32.1

True or False: *Circle your choice and explain why any false statements are incorrect.*

T F   1.   Financial intermediaries change the mix of output by transferring purchasing power from dissavers to savers.

T F   2.   If the opportunity cost of money was zero, the expected value of future dollars would be equal to their present value.

T F   3.   A risk premium compensates people who invest in risky ventures that succeed.

T F   4.   One reason present dollars are worth more than future dollars is that income-earning investment opportunities exist.

T F   5.   The present discounted value of a future payment will decrease when interest rates increase.

T F   6.   Stock prices will increase, *ceteris paribus*, when the prevailing interest rate increases.

T F   7.   When a corporation issues a bond, it is borrowing funds.

T F   8.   External shocks to the stock market have little impact on stock prices since investors look at the long run when investing.

T F   9.   The present value of a future payment is discounted by potential interest accumulation.

T F 10. As bond prices increase, bond yields also increase.

Multiple Choice: *Select the correct answer.*

_____ 1. The function of financial intermediaries is to transfer purchasing power from:
     (a)   Dissavers to consumers.
     (b)   Savers to dissavers.
     (c)   Consumers to savers.
     (d)   Dissavers to savers.

_____ 2. Financial intermediaries:
     (a)   Reduce search and information costs for savers and investors.
     (b)   Transfer purchasing power from spenders to savers.
     (c)   Concentrate investment risk.
     (d)   Do all of the above.

_____ 3. Present dollars are worth more than future dollars because:
     (a)   Income-earning investment opportunities exist.
     (b)   There is always a chance that you may not receive the future dollars.
     (c)   Of the opportunity cost of money.
     (d)   All of the above.

_____ 4. The supply of loanable funds is influenced by:
     (a)   The desire for loanable funds.
     (b)   The expected rate of return.
     (c)   Interest rates.
     (d)   All of the above.

_____ 5. Higher interest rates:
  (a) Reflect a higher opportunity cost of money.
  (b) Raise the future value of current dollars.
  (c) Lower the present value of future payments.
  (d) All of the above.

_____ 6. The present discounted value of a future payment will increase when the:
  (a) Risk of non-payment decreases.
  (b) Interest rate increases.
  (c) Future payment is further into the future.
  (d) Opportunity cost of money decreases.

_____ 7. The possibility of non-payment is taken into account in the calculation of the:
  (a) Present discounted value.
  (b) Future discounted value.
  (c) Expected value.
  (d) Profits.

_____ 8. The term "expected value" refers to the:
  (a) Future value of a current payment.
  (b) Present value of a future payment.
  (c) Probable value of a future payment.
  (d) Difference in the rates of return on risky and safe investments.

_____ 9. Suppose Bill has a 40 percent chance of not collecting $5,000 in 4 years. If the interest rate is 12 percent, the expected value of the future payment is closest to:
  (a) $1,907.
  (b) $3,000.
  (c) $3,178.
  (d) $4,721.

_____ 10. A motivation for holding stocks is:
  (a) To receive interest payments on the firm's debt.
  (b) To receive potential capital gains.
  (c) To have a direct role in the operation of the corporation.
  (d) All of the above.

_____ 11. The purpose of an initial public offering is to:
  (a) Raise funds for investment and growth by selling shares of the company to the public.
  (b) Change the membership of the Board of Directors.
  (c) Borrow funds for investment and growth.
  (d) See if there is a demand for a company's new product.

_____ 12. Which of the following determines the price of a stock?
  (a) The amount of stock that people are willing and able to purchase.
  (b) The amount of stock that people offer for sale.
  (c) Expectations of future earnings.
  (d) All of the above.

_____ 13. The price of a stock will increase, *ceteris paribus*, when:
   (a) When there is a shortage of the stock at the current price.
   (b) The demand for the stock increases.
   (c) The supply of the stock decreases.
   (d) All of the above.

_____ 14. The expected rate of return for an IPO must take into consideration the:
   (a) Risk factor.
   (b) Time value of money.
   (c) Interest rate.
   (d) All of the above.

_____ 15. You purchase shares in Acme Gadget Company for $20 per share. The company believes there is a 20 percent chance they will fail to earn a discounted future profit of $1.85. The expected rate of return is closest to:
   (a) 2.7 percent.
   (b) 7.4 percent.
   (c) 5.0 percent.
   (d) 2.2 percent.

_____ 16. When investors expect greater future profits from a company, the:
   (a) Demand for the company's bonds increases.
   (b) Price of the company's bonds increases.
   (c) Yield on the company's bonds decreases.
   (d) All of the above occur.

_____ 17. The higher the expected return, or the _____ the cost of funds, the _____ will be the amount of loanable funds demanded.
   (a) Lower; greater.
   (b) Lower; lower.
   (c) Greater; greater.
   (d) Greater; lower.

_____ 18. The present value of $100,000 to be received every year for 3 years when the discount rate is 10 percent is:
   (a) $300,000.
   (b) $248,685.
   (c) $133,100.
   (d) $330,000.

_____ 19. As the interest rate increases, the opportunity cost of money:
   (a) Increases for both lender and borrower.
   (b) Increases for the borrower but not the lender.
   (c) Decreases for both lender and borrower.
   (d) Decreases for the borrower but not the lender.

_____ 20. As the interest rate increases, *ceteris paribus*, the tradeoff between present and future consumption:
   (a) Is not affected.
   (b) Encourages present consumption.
   (c) Changes in favor of future consumption.
   (d) Makes it less appealing to sacrifice present consumption.

Problems and Applications

Exercise 1

This exercise shows how to compute the present discounted value of an investment. It also shows how important the interest rate and length of time until payment are in the present value calculation.

1. Suppose you own 1,000 acres of forest land. Next year you could have the trees cut down for lumber and receive $1,320,000 (after taxes and all other expenses). The interest rate is 10 percent. Find the present discounted value of your 1,000 acres of forest land. _____

2. Suppose interest rates rose to 20 percent. What would the present discounted value of cutting down the forest for lumber be at the 20 percent interest rate if the cost and profit were the same as at 10 percent? _____

3. Suppose interest rates are at the original 10 percent. What would the present discounted value of cutting down the forest for lumber be if you had to wait two years to receive $1,320,000? _____

4. T F When the interest rate rises, the present value of an investment rises.

5. T F The longer one has to wait for a future payment, the less present value it has.

Exercise 2

This exercise uses the loanable funds market to determine the market interest rate and investment.

1. The supply and demand of loanable funds are shown in Figure 32.1. If the supply of loanable funds is S_1, then the equilibrium interest rate is _____ percent.

Figure 32.1
Investment demand, and the supply of loanable funds

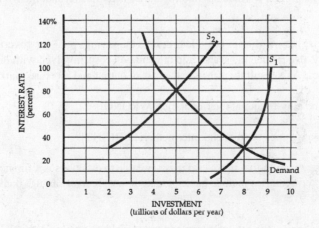

INVESTMENT
(trillions of dollars per year)

2. At the equilibrium interest rate, the level of investment would equal $_____ trillion.

3. If the supply of loanable funds shifts to S_2, this represents a(an) (increase; decrease) in loanable funds.

4. The equilibrium interest rate would (increase; decrease) to _____ percent and the level of investment would (increase; decrease) to $_____ trillion.

5. One reason for the shift in loanable funds in Figure 31.1 might be the (increase; decrease) in savings by consumers.

Exercise 3

The media often carry information about the amount of money won in lotteries. The reality is often different than what is reported.

Reread the section in the text titled "Time Value of Money" about the MegaMillions lottery winners. Then answer the following questions.

1. What was the advertised amount of the payoff from the winning lottery? _____

2. When discounted at 4.47%, what was the present value of the payout? _____

3. What would happen to the present value of the payout if it were discounted at an interest rate greater than 4.47%? _____

4. How many total payments was the winner of the lottery to receive? _____

5. If the payoff was made in ten annual installments instead of the number above, what would have happened to the present value of the winnings? _____

Common Errors

The first statement in each "common error" below is incorrect. Each incorrect statement is followed by a corrected version and an explanation.

1. The primary function of financial intermediaries is to provide checking accounts for customers. WRONG!

   The primary function of financial intermediaries is to transfer income from savers to spenders. RIGHT!

   Financial intermediaries provide access to the savings pool for government and the business sector. They also reduce the search and information costs involved with lending and investment opportunities. As a result they change the mix of output and increase market efficiency.

2. Banks are the only financial intermediaries. WRONG!

   There are many types of financial intermediaries. RIGHT!

   Any organization that makes savings available to dissavers is a financial intermediary. Financial intermediaries include banks, credit unions, federal savings banks, and insurance companies.

3. As bond prices rise, the rate of return or current yield also rises. WRONG!

   As bond prices rise, the rate of return or current yield falls. RIGHT!

452

The rate of interest earned on a bond, or the coupon rate, is stated on the bond certificate and does not change. The current yield represents the rate of return on a bond. It is calculated as the annual interest payment divided by the bond price. The price of a bond in the secondary bond market varies based on changes in expectations and opportunity cost. If the annual interest payment stays constant and the bond price increases, the rate of return or current yield falls.

•ANSWERS•

Using Key Terms

Across

2. expected value
6. corporation
7. bond
9. dividend
11. liquidity
12. current yield
14. capital gain
15. initial public offering
16. price earnings ratio

Down

1. coupon
3. present discounted value
4. financial intermediary
5. default
6. corporate stock
8. retained earnings
10. risk premium
13. par value

True or False

1. F Financial intermediaries change the mix of output by transferring purchasing power from savers to dissavers.
2. F The expected value calculation takes into account the possibility of not getting the future payment. Whenever this is a possibility, future dollars will be worth less than current dollars.
3. T
4. T
5. T
6. F Stock prices will decrease when the prevailing interest rate increases because the opportunity cost of holding stocks will increase, making stocks a less desirable investment option (i.e., the demand for stocks will decrease).
7. T
8. F External shocks, such as a war, can and do have an impact on stock prices by affecting confidence and future expectations.
9. T
10. F Bond prices and yields move in opposite directions.

Multiple Choice

1. b	5. d	9. a	13. d	17. a
2. a	6. d	10. b	14. d	18. b
3. d	7. c	11. a	15. b	19. a
4. c	8. c	12. d	16. d	20. c

Problems and Applications

Exercise 1

1. $\$1,320,000 \div (1.10)^1 = \$1,200,000$
2. $\$1,320,000 \div (1.20)^1 = \$1,100,000$
3. $\$1,320,000 \div (1.10)^2 = \$1,090,909$
4. F
5. T

Exercise 2

1. 30 percent
2. $8 trillion
3. Decrease
4. Increase; 80 percent; decrease; $5 trillion
5. Decrease

Exercise 3

1. The advertised amount was $294 million.
2. $168 million.
3. If discounted at more than 4.47%, the present discounted value would be less than $168 million.
4. The text says that the $294 million was payable in 26 annual installments.
5. Ten annual installments would increase the present discounted value.

CHAPTER 33

Taxes: Equity vs. Efficiency

Quick Review

- The distribution of income is a major concern of public policy because income determines, to a large extent, who receives the goods and services in our society. Income is a flow and is measured over time; wealth is a stock of purchasing power and is measured at a point in time.

- The size distribution of income concentrates on the way income is distributed among income-receiving units, such as households. The Lorenz curve is a graph that compares the actual distribution of income to a distribution of income in which everyone receives the same income.

- The distribution of income in the United States is definitely not equal across all groups. The top 20 percent of households receives almost half of all income.

- Taxes are used to transfer command of resources from the private sector to the public sector and to redistribute income from the rich to the poor. The impact of taxes on the economy is not always easy to determine, and there appears to be a tradeoff between society's goals of equity and efficiency.

- Provisions in the tax law, called "loopholes," allow individuals to reduce the amount of income subject to tax. The loopholes also result in horizontal and vertical inequities. Economists use the nominal tax rate and the effective tax rate to analyze the tax system.

- The Tax Reform Act of 1986 closed loopholes, reduced marginal tax rates, reduced the number of tax brackets, increased the tax burden of corporations relative to individuals, and provided tax relief for the poor. The revisions in 1990 and 1993 added a fourth bracket, a new marginal tax rate and a surcharge.

- The Bush tax cuts of 2001 reduced marginal tax rates and also created tax incentives for education, marriage, and saving.

- State and local governments raise money through sales and property taxes. Both are regressive because low-income families spend a greater percentage of their income on housing and basic consumption goods than do high-income families. The payroll tax is also regressive.

- Tax incidence refers to the actual burden of the tax. Many argue that the burden of a payroll tax falls to the employees because employers reduce wages to compensate for their share of the tax.

- Income is distributed unequally in the United States. Some believe more should be transferred from those with higher incomes to those with lower incomes. Others argue that such a redistribution of income would damage the incentives to produce.

- There is debate about replacing the current tax structure with a flat tax. This would simplify the tax system, but it would also reduce the government's ability to alter the mix of output.

Learning Objectives

After reading Chapter 33 and doing the following exercises, you should:

1. Be able to distinguish between wealth and income.
2. Understand the size distribution of income and be able to interpret a Lorenz curve.
3. Be aware of the impact of taxes and transfers on the distribution of income.
4. Understand the principles of horizontal and vertical equity.
5. Be able to distinguish the marginal, nominal, and effective tax rates.
6. Understand the impact of tax "loopholes."
7. Be able to distinguish arguments for equality from arguments for equity.
8. Know the major reforms in the Tax Reform Act of 1986 and the changes in 1990, 1993, and 2001.
9. Be able to distinguish among progressive, regressive, and proportional taxes.
10. Recognize that the most serious potential cost of greater equality would be damaged incentives.
11. Be aware of the arguments for and against the proposed "flat tax."

Using Key Terms

Fill in the puzzle on the opposite page with the appropriate term from the list of Key Terms at the end of the chapter in the text.

Across
4. The percentage change in the quantity supplied divided by the percentage change in tax rates.
7. A tax system in which tax rates rise as incomes rise.
14. Taxes paid divided by total income.
15. Taxes paid divided by taxable income.
16. The proportion of total income received by a particular group.
17. The change in total revenue associated with one additional unit of input.
20. The idea that people with higher incomes should pay more taxes.
21. A tax system in which tax rates fall as incomes rise.

Down
1. The tax rate imposed on the last dollar of income.
2. The way total personal income is divided among households.
3. People with equal incomes should pay equal taxes.
5. Distribution of the real burden of a tax.
6. A graph that contrasts complete equality with the actual distribution of income.
7. Income received by households before taxes.
8. Goods and services received directly, without payment in a market transaction.
9. A mathematical summary of inequality based on the Lorenz curve.
10. A situation in which the market mechanism prevents optimal outcomes.
11. A situation in which government intervention fails to improve market outcomes.
12. A single-rate tax system.
13. Payments to individuals for which no current goods or services are exchanged.
18. The amount of income directly subject to nominal tax rates.
19. The market value of assets.

Puzzle 33.1

True or False: *Circle your choice and explain why any false statements are incorrect.*

T F 1. Marginal tax rates must increase as income increases for a tax to be progressive, *ceteris paribus*.

T F 2. When people believe that the market's answer to the FOR WHOM question is suboptimal, taxes can be used as a policy lever to address the problem.

T F 3. A flat tax rate would take the same dollar amount from each taxpayer.

T F 4. The efficiency issue in taxation refers to the negative impact of higher marginal tax rates on the incentive to produce and work.

T F 5. Fewer workers are employed and the net wage is reduced when a payroll tax is imposed.

T F 6. The nominal tax rate refers to the taxes actually paid as a percentage of total income.

T F 7. Greater income equality has only positive impacts on an economy.

T F 8. The Tax Relief Act of 2001 reduced the marginal tax rates, which was intended to increase the incentive to work and produce.

T F 9. The federal income tax is a proportional tax.

T F 10. Government failure results when government intervention fails to improve market outcomes.

Multiple Choice: *Select the correct answer.*

_____ 1. The distribution of income is basically the answer to the:
(a) WHAT question for society.
(b) HOW question for society.
(c) FOR WHOM question for society.
(d) WHEN question for society.

_____ 2. Which of the following typically functions as a regressive tax?
(a) A sales tax.
(b) A property tax.
(c) The Social Security tax.
(d) All of the above.

_____ 3. When people believe that the market's answer to the FOR WHOM question is suboptimal:
(a) Market failure exists.
(b) Taxes can be used as a policy to address the problem.
(c) The government has an obligation to change the market outcome.
(d) All of the above are correct.

_____ 4. Suppose that in 2001, Ms. Gonzales had a taxable income of $100,000. Assume that the marginal tax rates are 10% of the first $10,000, 20% of the income in excess of $10,000 up to $60,000, and 30% of any income over $60,000. Ms. Gonzales' tax bill was:
(a) $23,000.
(b) $18,000.
(c) $10,000.
(d) $30,000.

_____ 5. If income is distributed unequally, the:
    (a)   Lorenz curve would be a straight line.
    (b)   Line of equality sags below the Lorenz curve.
    (c)   Lorenz curve sags below the line of equality.
    (d)   Gini coefficient is less than zero.

_____ 6. The U.S. tax system results in a slight reduction in inequality of after-tax income because:
    (a)   Of the progressive nature of state and local taxes.
    (b)   Of the progressive nature of the federal income tax.
    (c)   The rich have fewer available loopholes than the poor.
    (d)   The poor receive such generous welfare benefits.

_____ 7. Government attempts to create a more equitable income distribution by increasing marginal tax rates may:
    (a)   Reduce output.
    (b)   Increase unemployment.
    (c)   Reduce government tax receipts.
    (d)   All of the above.

_____ 8. The argument _in favor_ of greater equality of income distribution in the United States hinges on:
    (a)   The idea that greater equality does not affect incentives.
    (b)   The idea that low-income earners would be more willing and able participants in the economy if income were distributed more equally.
    (c)   The idea that those with high incomes wield greater political power and strengthen the democratic process.
    (d)   All of the above.

_____ 9. In making comparisons of income among countries, care must be exercised because:
    (a)   In poor countries much of what is produced does not pass through markets and thus does not get counted in the nation's income.
    (b)   In countries such as Sweden and Great Britain, the government provides more goods and services directly than in the United States.
    (c)   In-kind benefits should be included in real income in all countries.
    (d)   All of the above are true.

_____ 10. The tax elasticity of labor supply measures the:
    (a)   Response of workers to a change in the tax rate.
    (b)   Response of workers to a change in prices.
    (c)   Change in the amount of taxes workers must pay when tax rates change.
    (d)   Response of employers to a change in the tax rate.

Use the following information to answer questions 11-12. The tax schedule is hypothetical to keep the calculations simple.

Suppose an individual has total income of $150,000, has taxable income of $100,000, and pays taxes of $10,000.

_____ 11. This individual's _____ tax rate is 6.7 percent.
    (a)   Effective.
    (b)   Nominal.
    (c)   Marginal.
    (d)   Incidence.

459

_____ 12. This individual's _____ tax rate is 10 percent.
    (a)   Marginal.
    (b)   Effective.
    (c)   Nominal.
    (d)   Incidence.

_____ 13. The principle of taxation that says people with equal incomes should pay equal taxes is called:
    (a)   Vertical equity.
    (b)   Horizontal equity.
    (c)   Progressive.
    (d)   Regressive.

_____ 14. Transfer payments are an appropriate mechanism for correcting:
    (a)   Market power.
    (b)   Government failure.
    (c)   Natural monopoly.
    (d)   Inequity.

_____ 15. Food stamps, public housing, and subsidized public education are examples of:
    (a)   Free goods.
    (b)   "In-kind" benefits or income.
    (c)   Tax expenditures.
    (d)   Money incomes.

_____ 16. If the tax elasticity of supply is negative 0.7 and tax rates increase by 21 percent, the quantity of labor supplied would:
    (a)   Increase by 14.7 percent.
    (b)   Decrease by 14.7 percent.
    (c)   Increase by 30 percent.
    (d)   Decrease by 30 percent.

_____ 17. The flat tax:
    (a)   Reduces the government's ability to alter the mix of output.
    (b)   Encourages economic activity through deductions and credits.
    (c)   Includes many tax brackets.
    (d)   All of the above.

_____ 18. The major source of revenue for state governments is:
    (a)   Property taxes.
    (b)   State lotteries.
    (c)   Income taxes.
    (d)   Sales taxes.

_____ 19. A tax is progressive if it takes a:
    (a)   Larger number of dollars as income rises.
    (b)   Larger number of dollars as income falls.
    (c)   Smaller fraction of income as income falls.
    (d)   Smaller fraction of income as income rises.

_____ 20. New loopholes in the personal income tax law tend to:
    (a)   Make the system more regressive.
    (b)   Increase horizontal equity.
    (c)   Increase the tax base.
    (d)   All of the above.

Problems and Applications

Exercise 1

This exercise will help you understand the Lorenz curve.

1. Complete column 3 in Table 33.1 using the data from column 2. Then draw a Lorenz curve based on column 3 in Figure 33.1.

Table 33.1
Size distribution of personal income, by household income group

(1) Quintile of income recipients (households)	(2) Percent of total household income received	(3) Percent of income received (cumulative)
Lowest fifth	3.8%	_____%
Second fifth	9.6	_____
Third fifth	16.0	_____
Fourth fifth	24.2	_____
Highest fifth	46.3	_____

Figure 33.1
Lorenz curve

2. According to the information given in Table 33.1, income was distributed (equally; unequally).

3. Draw the line of absolute equality in Figure 33.1 and label it. Shade in the area between the Lorenz curve and the line of equality. The shaded area is a measure of the degree of _____.

461

4. In Figure 33.1 draw a second Lorenz curve that indicates the distribution of wealth for the same year. Use the hypothetical data from Table 33.2. Calculate column 3 first.

Table 33.2
Size distribution of wealth, by wealth-holding group

(1) Quintile of wealth owners	(2) Wealth owned	(3) Wealth owned (cumulative)
Lowest fifth	0.5%	_____ %
Second fifth	5.0	_____
Third fifth	12.0	_____
Fourth fifth	20.0	_____
Highest fifth	62.5	_____

5. Although the data in Table 33.2 are hypothetical, they do actually indicate the direction of inequality of wealth ownership relative to the distribution of income. Wealth is (more, less) equally distributed than income.

Exercise 2

This exercise shows the impact of a change in tax policy on vertical and horizontal equity.

For the 2001 tax year the federal tax liability for single individuals in the country of Utopia was computed on the basis of the schedule shown in Table 33.3.

Table 33.3
2001 Tax table

If your taxable income Is above:	But below:	Then your tax is:
$11,650	$13,920	$1,297.70 + 18% of anything over $11,650
13,920	16,190	1,706.30 + 20% of anything over $13,920
16,190	19,640	2,160.30 + 23% of anything over $16,190

For the 2002 tax year the corresponding federal tax liability for single individuals in the country of Utopia was computed with the schedule found in Table 33.4.

Table 33.4
2002 Tax table

If your taxable income Is above:	But below:	Then your tax is:
$ 1,800	$16,800	$ 198.00 + 15% of anything over $ 1,800
16,800	27,000	2,448.00 + 28% of anything over $16,800

1. What was the marginal tax rate for a single taxpayer with a taxable income of $17,000 in 2001? _____ In 2002? _____ On the basis of this information, does it appear that the tax reform for this country increased work incentives for single taxpayers with a taxable income of $17,000? _____

2. For the three taxpayers listed in Table 33.5, compute the taxable income, taxes in the years 2001 and 2002, and the difference in taxes for the two years.

Table 33.5
Taxable income and tax computations

Taxpayer	Gross income	Exemptions and deductions	Taxable income	2001 Tax	2002 Tax	Difference
1	$30,000	$18,000	$ _____	$ _____	$ _____	$ _____
2	30,000	13,000	_____	_____	_____	_____
3	50,000	38,000	_____	_____	_____	_____

3. On the basis of Table 33.5 did the tax reform package lower taxes for single taxpayers in the taxable income range of $12,000 to $17,000? _____

4. In Table 33.6 rank each taxpayer on the basis of the effective tax rate. Then complete the table by filling in the nominal, effective, and marginal tax rates for each taxpayer.

Table 33.6
Rankings for 2002

Rank	Taxpayer	Nominal tax rate	Effective tax rate	Marginal tax rate
1	_____ (highest)	_____ %	_____ %	_____ %
2	_____ (middle)	_____	_____	_____
3	_____ (lowest)	_____	_____	_____

5. How should horizontal equity be determined?
    (a) The two taxpayers with the same nominal incomes should be compared for their marginal tax rates.
    (b) The two taxpayers with the same nominal incomes should be compared for their effective tax rates.
    (c) The effective tax rate of the taxpayer with the highest nominal income should be compared with the effective tax rates of taxpayers with lower nominal incomes.
    (d) The marginal tax rate of the taxpayer with the highest nominal income should be compared with the marginal tax rates of taxpayers with lower nominal incomes.

6. How should vertical equity be determined?
    (a) The two taxpayers with the same nominal incomes should be compared for their marginal tax rates.
    (b) The two taxpayers with the same nominal incomes should be compared for their effective tax rates.
    (c) The effective tax rates of the taxpayer with the highest nominal income should be compared with the effective tax rates of taxpayers with lower nominal incomes.
    (d) The marginal tax rate of the taxpayer with the highest nominal income should be compared with the marginal tax rates of taxpayers with lower nominal incomes.

7. T F For single taxpayers with taxable incomes between $12,000 and $17,000, the tax-reform package reduced vertical equity from 2001 to 2002. (See last column in Table 33.5)

Exercise 3

Around April 15 of every year many articles appear which discuss changes in the tax laws from the previous year. This exercise will use one of the cartoons in the text to show the kind of information to look for to identify and classify changes in the tax system.

Look at the cartoon in the section titled "The Benefits of Greater Equality" in the text. Then answer the following questions.

1. What word indicates a change in policy has occurred or has been proposed?_____

2. What three words indicate a change in horizontal or vertical equity resulting from the change?
   _____

3. The change in equity indicated in the article concerns:
   (a) Vertical equity.
   (b) Horizontal equity.

Common Errors

The first statement in each "common error" below is incorrect. Each incorrect statement is followed by a corrected version and an explanation.

1. Income and wealth are the same thing. WRONG!

   Income and wealth mean distinctly different things. RIGHT!

   The distinction between income and wealth is critical to sound economic analysis. Income is a flow and has a time dimension. For example, one states one's income in dollars *per year*. Wealth is a stock and is measured at a point in time; for example, you may say you have $5,000 in your savings account *today*. Some people with apparently great wealth may have very little income, as in the case of someone who owns land known to contain oil. On the other hand, someone who has much income may have little wealth; some famous entertainers earn large incomes, save little (accumulate no wealth), and wind up in bankruptcy. Of course, wealth and income may go hand in hand: the incomes of some oil magnates flow *from* their wealth. But clearly the two terms imply different things about one's economic well-being and command over goods and services.

2. Equity and equality of income distribution mean the same thing. WRONG!

   Equity and equality of income distribution mean different things. RIGHT!

   Many arguments over the division of the income pie, whether at the national level, the corporate level, or the university level, are laced with the terms "equity" and "equality" used interchangeably. They are *not* interchangeable. Equality of income distribution means that each person has an equal share. Equity of income distribution implies something about fairness.

•ANSWERS•

Using Key Terms

Across

4. tax elasticity of supply
7. progressive tax
14. effective tax rate
15. nominal tax rate
16. income share
17. marginal revenue product
20. vertical equity
21. regressive tax

Down

1. marginal tax rate
2. size distribution of income
3. horizontal equity
5. tax incidence
6. Lorenz curve
7. personal income
8. in-kind income
9. Gini coefficient
10. market failure
11. government failure
12. flat tax
13. income transfers
18. tax base
19. wealth

True or False

1. T
2. T
3. F   A flat tax takes the same percentage of income from each taxpayer.
4. T
5. T
6. F   The nominal tax rate refers to the taxes actually paid as a percentage of taxable income.
7. F   Greater income equality can have negative impacts on work incentives and efficiency.
8. T
9. F   The federal income tax is a progressive tax.
10. T

Multiple Choice

1. c	5. c	9. d	13. b	17. a
2. d	6. b	10. a	14. d	18. d
3. d	7. d	11. a	15. b	19. c
4. a	8. b	12. c	16. b	20. a

Problems and Applications

Exercise 1

1. **Table 33.1 Answer**

(1) Quintile of income recipients (households)	(3) Percent of income received (cumulative)
Lowest fifth	3.8%
Second fifth	13.4
Third fifth	29.4
Fourth fifth	53.6
Highest fifth	99.9

Figure 33.1 Answer

2. Unequally
3. Inequality; See line of absolute equality and shaded area in Figure 33.1.

4. **Table 33.2 Answer**

(1) Quintile of wealth owners	(3) Wealth owned (cumulative)
Lowest fifth	0.5%
Second fifth	5.5
Third fifth	17.5
Fourth fifth	37.5
Highest fifth	100.0

5. Less

Exercise 2

1. 23 percent for 2001 (the percentage used in the formula is the marginal tax rate); 28 percent for 2002; no

2. **Table 33.5 Answer**

Taxpayer	Taxable income	2001 Tax	2002 Tax	Difference
1	$12,000	$1,360.70	$1,728	$367.30
2	17,000	2,346.60	2,504	157.40
3	12,000	1,360.70	1,728	367.30

3. No

4. **Table 33.6 Answer**

Rank	Taxpayer	Nominal tax rate	Effective tax rate	Marginal tax rate
1	2	14.7% (=2,504/17,000)	8.4% (=2,504/30,000)	28%
2	1	14.4% (=1,728/12,000)	5.8% (=1,728/30,000)	15
3	3	14.4% (=1,728/12,000)	3.5% (=1,728/50,000)	15

5. b
6. c
7. T   The difference in total taxes paid was greater at a $12,000 taxable income than it was at a $17,000 taxable income, as shown in the last column of Table 33.5 Answer.

Exercise 3

1. "it," when referring to some generic policy that has changed
2. "favors the rich"
3. a

CHAPTER 34

Transfer Payments: Welfare and Social Security

Quick Review

- Approximately half of every U.S. tax dollar is spent on income transfers, payments for which no current goods or services are exchanged. Most of the transfer payments received by poor families are in the form of "in-kind" transfers such as food stamps, medical aid, and housing assistance. Other transfer payments, such as Social Security, are cash transfers.

- Welfare programs are means-tested and require some type of income eligibility test, while social insurance programs offer event-conditioned benefits. They insure people against events such as old age or unemployment.

- All income transfers result in a redistribution of income, but not all income transfers go to the poor.

- Welfare benefits perpetuate dependence, since they do not increase human capital or job opportunities, and welfare benefits may *worsen* the poverty problem by discouraging recipients from working. Because of how welfare benefits are calculated, a person might be worse off if he or she enters into the labor market.

- Modifications of existing programs have taken this into account by adjusting the marginal tax rate on earned income. The basic problem is that low marginal tax rates encourage more work effort, but make more people eligible for welfare. High marginal tax rates discourage work effort, but make fewer people eligible for welfare.

- The Social Security program faces the same work disincentives as the welfare program. The program provides income for older people who do not work, but it imposes high marginal tax rates on those who do work. Because of the way the program is designed, people retire earlier than they would otherwise. The result is a decrease in total output for the economy.

- The economic issue with Social Security has to do with costs versus benefits. If the work test was eliminated, the economic cost of the Social Security program could be reduced. This would do away with the work disincentive and total output would increase. Others say Social Security should operate like a private retirement plan where people make a contribution to their own pension plan.

Learning Objectives

After reading Chapter 34 and doing the following exercises, you should:

1. Know the impact of transfer payments in the United States.
2. Be able to distinguish between cash transfers and "in-kind" transfers.
3. Understand the role of human capital and derived demand in the poverty dilemma.
4. Know what the basic government welfare programs are, which level of government administers them, and who is eligible for the various programs.
5. Be able to describe the work disincentive that results from the welfare program and Social Security.
6. Understand how welfare eligibility changes as income increases.
7. Be able to describe how a welfare recipient's real income changes as money income increases.
8. Know some of the recent initiatives to reform the welfare system and Social Security.

Using Key Terms

Fill in the puzzle on the opposite page with the appropriate term from the list of Key Terms at the end of the chapter in the text.

Across

1. The income level at which welfare eligibility ceases.
10. The percentage of income transfers that goes to the intended recipients and purposes.
11. An incentive to engage in undesirable behavior.
12. Payment to individuals for which no good or service is exchanged.
13. Means-tested income transfer programs.
14. The percentage of base wages paid out in benefits is the _____ _____ rate.

Down

2. The _____ _____ _____ _____ is the percentage of the working-age population working or seeking employment.
3. Income transfers of direct cash payments.
4. The tax rate imposed on the last dollar of income.
5. Direct transfers of goods and services rather than cash.
6. Occurs when the market mechanism results in a suboptimal outcome.
7. The willingness and ability to work specific amounts of time at alternative wage rates.
8. The shortfall between actual income and the poverty threshold.
9. _____ _____ programs provide event-conditioned income transfers.
10. The percentage change in quantity of labor supplied divided by the percentage change in tax rates is the _____ _____ of labor supply.

Puzzle 34.1

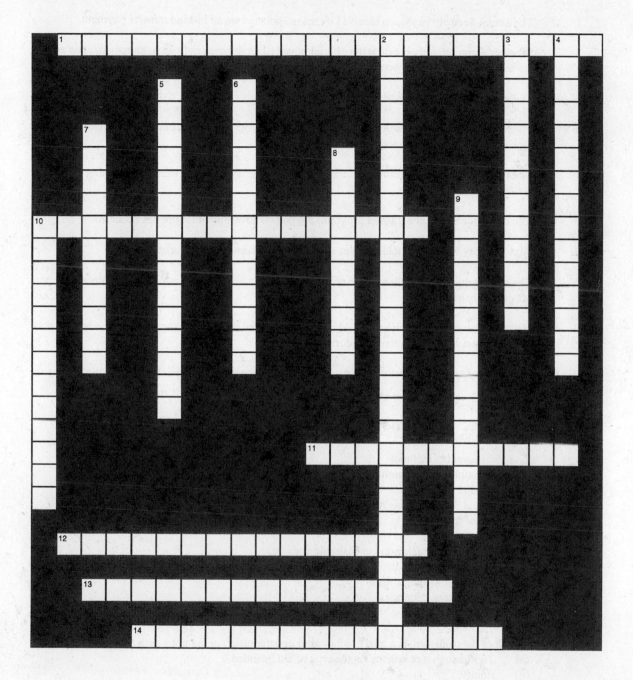

471

True or False: *Circle your choice and explain why any false statements are incorrect.*

T F 1. The Social Security payments received by retired persons are an in-kind transfer payment.

T F 2. Whether a given family is below the official poverty line depends only on its money income and the number of family members.

T F 3. The availability of welfare benefits shifts the labor supply curve to the right.

T F 4. The higher the marginal tax rate of any given welfare program, the greater the damage to the work incentives of recipients, *ceteris paribus*.

T F 5. The break-even level of income is the amount of income a person can earn before losing all welfare benefits.

T F 6. The existence of income transfer programs suggests a government failure has occurred.

T F 7. Almost every U.S. household receives some form of income transfer payments.

T F 8. The impact on labor supply because of a decrease in the marginal tax rate does not depend on the tax elasticity of supply.

T F 9. If welfare benefits for each household in poverty equaled the poverty gap, people who are not poor would have a strong incentive to become poor.

T F 10. The primary economic cost of the Social Security program is the financial cost of administering the program.

Multiple Choice: *Select the correct answer.*

_____ 1. Transfer payments include:
   (a) Unemployment benefits for the unemployed.
   (b) In-kind transfers.
   (c) Social Security benefits.
   (d) All of the above.

_____ 2. Increased income transfers are undesirable because:
   (a) They create dependency.
   (b) Work disincentives result.
   (c) Total output decreases.
   (d) All of the above.

_____ 3. Which of the following is a goal of an in-kind transfer program but not a cash transfer program?
   (a) To insure that recipients get the type of aid intended.
   (b) Equity.
   (c) To change the market's answer to the WHO question.
   (d) All of the above are correct.

_____ 4. Medicaid and food stamps are received by:
   (a) Anyone who applies.
   (b) Only the elderly.
   (c) Only the poor.
   (d) Mostly upper income households in the U.S. due to inequities in the system.

_____ 5. Social insurance programs:
   (a)   Are event conditional.
   (b)   Insure people against specific problems, e.g., unemployment.
   (c)   Are not welfare programs.
   (d)   All of the above are correct.

_____ 6. Income-transfer programs can:
   (a)   Change the answer to the WHAT to produce question.
   (b)   Change the answer to the FOR WHOM to produce question.
   (c)   Result in reduced output.
   (d)   All of the above are correct.

_____ 7. If welfare benefits for each household in poverty equaled the poverty gap:
   (a)   The effective marginal tax rate for welfare recipients would be 100 percent.
   (b)   People who are not poor would have a strong incentive to become poor.
   (c)   Poverty would be eliminated.
   (d)   All of the above would occur.

_____ 8. Suppose a poverty program provides a basic benefit of $3,000, and a marginal tax rate of 0.50. The break-even level of income is:
   (a) $6,000.
   (b) $1,500.
   (c) $4,500.
   (d) $9,000.

_____ 9. The official poverty index is based on:
   (a)   Family size.
   (b)   Cash income.
   (c)   Age of the household head.
   (d)   All of the above.

_____ 10. A good reason for excluding in-kind transfers from income calculations is:
   (a)   That the more poor there are, the more jobs there will be for bureaucrats.
   (b)   That people would be forced above the poverty line by consuming things like medical services.
   (c)   That it is impossible to place a value on most of the services provided.
   (d)   All of the above.

Use the following welfare benefit formula to answer the following questions.
Welfare Benefit = Maximum benefit - 0.60 [Wages - (work expenses + child care costs)]

_____ 11. Based on the information given above, the marginal tax rate is:
   (a)   Zero percent.
   (b)   0.40 percent.
   (c)   0.60 percent.
   (d)   100 percent.

_____ 12. Suppose that Mr. Henry works 1,200 hours per year at a wage of $8 per hour, has child care expenses of $1,600 per year and work expenses of $1,400. If Mr. Henry's state has a maximum welfare benefit of $8,000 per year, based on the welfare formula given above, Mr. Henry's welfare benefit will be:
   (a)   Zero. His income has exceeded the limit.
   (b) $4,040.
   (c) $1,400.
   (d) $6,600.

_____ 13. Social security benefits paid by the federal government:
   (a) Are income transfers financed by taxes on workers and employers.
   (b) Are classified as in-kind benefits.
   (c) Have no effect on the decision regarding for whom output is to be produced.
   (d) All of the above.

_____ 14. Which of the following programs does *not* provide in-kind benefits?
   (a) The food stamp program.
   (b) The housing assistance program.
   (c) Temporary Aid to Needy Families (TANF).
   (d) Medicaid.

_____ 15. When authorities choose to "disregard" income earned by welfare recipients, they are:
   (a) Intentionally helping the welfare recipient cheat.
   (b) Attempting to improve work incentives.
   (c) Looking out for their own jobs because the more income they disregard, the more poor there will be.
   (d) Being arbitrary in their administration of the program.

_____ 16. Higher marginal tax rates in welfare programs will:
   (a) Decrease the incentive to work.
   (b) Decrease total welfare costs.
   (c) Reduce the number of people on welfare.
   (d) Do all of the above.

_____ 17. The Social Security program tends to:
   (a) Increase work incentives for both older and younger workers.
   (b) Increase work incentives for older workers but not younger workers.
   (c) Decrease work incentives for both older and younger workers.
   (d) Decrease work incentives for older workers but not younger workers.

_____ 18. If the Social Security program is privatized:
   (a) Work disincentives for younger workers will be reduced.
   (b) Income inequalities would increase.
   (c) Another kind of public transfer program may have to be implemented for those elderly who made bad investments.
   (d) All of the above could occur.

_____ 19. The primary economic cost of the Social Security program is the:
   (a) Financial cost of administering the program.
   (b) Reduction in total output the program causes because of work disincentives.
   (c) Redistribution of income from younger to older workers.
   (d) Benefits paid.

_____ 20. The primary benefit of the Social Security program is the:
   (a) Increased work incentives for older workers.
   (b) More equitable distribution of income that results.
   (c) Jobs created by the additional spending.
   (d) All of the above are benefits.

Problems and Applications

Exercise 1

This exercise examines welfare benefits and the marginal tax rate on benefits.

Assume the welfare benefit is calculated as:

Benefit = maximum benefit - wages

1. Every additional dollar of wages (increases; reduces) welfare benefits by the same amount.

2. T   F   In this case there is a disincentive to work because the marginal tax rate is 100 percent.

3. Now assume the welfare benefit formula changes to:

    Benefit = maximum benefit - 0.4(wages)

    What is the marginal tax rate? _____

4. A decrease in the marginal tax rate will encourage (more; less) work effort and make (more; fewer) people eligible for welfare.

5. Use the formula in question 3. Assume the maximum benefit is $12,000. If a welfare recipient earns $5,000 in a part-time job, his or her total income will be _____.

6. The breakeven level of income is the amount of income a person can earn before losing (some; all) welfare benefits.

7. The breakeven level of income in question 5 is _____.

Exercise 2

This exercise focuses on the Social Security program.

1. The Social Security program is a _____ transfer program because it sends checks to recipients.

2. T   F   The primary economic cost of the Social Security program is benefits it pays to retired workers.

3. Assume a person is entitled to a maximum award of $12,000 in Social Security benefits. But this person continues to work upon reaching retirement age and earns $10,000 per year. Given the following benefit formula:

    Benefit amount = maximum award - 0.60(wage - $6000)

    What is the Social Security benefit for this individual? _____

4. What is the total income for this individual? _____

Common Errors

The first statement in each "common error" below is incorrect. Each incorrect statement is followed by a corrected version and an explanation.

1. The federal government runs the welfare system. WRONG!

   The welfare system consists of programs administered by federal, state, and local governments. RIGHT!

   It's true that the federal government is heavily involved in the welfare system, but state and local governments are involved as well. As a matter of fact, the benefits that a poor person may receive vary from state to state. The differentials in benefits have been the reason for the migration of some poor people from low-benefit states to high-benefit states. The federal government is trying to reduce its role in this area, however.

2. Welfare recipients are typically minority families headed by able-bodied males. WRONG!

   There is no average welfare recipient. RIGHT!

   The stereotype of the welfare recipient seems firmly entrenched in the minds of American taxpayers. The poor are a very heterogeneous group, however, with many more whites than minority-group members. Most work when they can find employment. Some work all year long and are still poor.

•ANSWERS•

Using Key Terms

Across
1. breakeven level of income
10. target efficiency
11. moral hazard
12. transfer payment
13. welfare programs
14. wage replacement

Down
2. labor-force participation rate
3. cash transfers
4. marginal tax rate
5. in-kind transfers
6. market failure
7. labor supply
8. poverty gap
9. social insurance
10. tax elasticity

True or False

1. F They are a cash transfer payment.
2. T
3. F The availability of welfare benefits reduces the incentive to work, thus shifting the labor supply curve to the left.
4. T
5. T
6. F The existence of income transfer programs suggests that market failure has occurred. The program is intended to help correct the market failure.
7. T
8. F Whether a person chooses to work more hours due to a decrease in the marginal tax rate depends to a large extent on the tax elasticity of supply.
9. T
10. F The primary economic cost of the Social Security program is the reduction in total output the program causes because of work disincentives.

Multiple Choice

1. d	5. d	9. d	13. a	17. c
2. d	6. d	10. b	14. c	18. d
3. a	7. d	11. c	15. b	19. b
4. c	8. a	12. b	16. d	20. b

Problems and Applications

Exercise 1

1. Reduces
2. T
3. 40 percent
4. More, more
5. $15,000 [$12,000 - 0.4($5,000) = $12,000 - $2000 = $10,000 $10,000 + $5,000 = $15,000]
6. All
7. $12,000 ÷ 0.4 = $30,000

Exercise 2

1. Cash
2. F The primary economic cost is the decrease in total output because workers retire early.
3. $12,000 - 0.6($10,000 - $6000) = $12,000 - 0.6($4000) = $12,000 - $2400 = $9600
4. $10,000 + $9600 = $19,600

PART 13   International Economics

CHAPTER 35

International Trade

Quick Review

- The trade balance for any country is the difference between its exports and imports. Since the mid-1970s, the United States has experienced a trade deficit.

- Without trade, each country's consumption possibilities are limited to its production possibilities. With trade, a country may concentrate its resources on the goods it produces relatively efficiently. Trade allows for specialization and increases total world output. For each country, consumption possibilities will exceed production possibilities.

- For trade to be mutually beneficial, each country must exploit its comparative advantage. Comparative advantage is based on relative efficiency in production. If Country A produces a specific good, and in doing so gives up less in terms of other goods than Country B gives up to produce the same good, then Country A has a comparative advantage. Comparative advantage relies on a comparison of relative opportunity costs.

- For trade to be mutually beneficial, the terms of trade—the rate at which one good is exchanged for another—must lie between the opportunity costs for each of the individual countries. The closer the terms of trade are to the slope of a country's production-possibilities curve, the fewer benefits it receives, and vice versa.

- Not everyone benefits from trade. Those involved in import competing industries will object to trade because they may lose jobs to foreign producers. Other arguments against free trade include concerns about national security, dumping, and protection of infant industries. Those engaged in export industries will favor trade because jobs and profits are likely to increase.

- There are several different types of trade barriers. An embargo prohibits the trade of certain goods. Tariffs discourage imports by making the goods more expensive. Quotas set a limit on the quantity of a particular good that may be imported. Nontariff barriers can also restrict trade.

- The World Trade Organization (WTO) polices world trade and looks for trade agreement violations. Regional pacts, such as NAFTA and the EU, are designed to reduce trade barriers.

Learning Objectives

After reading Chapter 35 and doing the following exercises, you should:

1. Know the basic facts about U.S. trade patterns.
2. Understand the macroeconomic impact of international trade.
3. Understand why specialization and trade increase both production possibilities and consumption possibilities.
4. Be able to explain comparative advantage using opportunity costs.
5. Know how to determine the limits to the terms of trade.
6. Be able to calculate the gains from specialization and trade at given terms of trade.
7. Be able to show how trade allows a country to consume beyond its production-possibilities curve.
8. Recognize the sources of pressure that result in restricted trade.
9. Know some of the arguments used by those wishing to restrict trade.
10. Be able to discuss tariff and nontariff barriers to trade.
11. Be able to discuss the reasons for the rise of regional trading arrangements.

Using Key Terms

Fill in the puzzle on the opposite page with the appropriate term from the list of Key Terms at the end of the chapter in the text.

Across

2. Alternative combinations of goods and services that can be produced with available resources and technology.
3. Alternative combinations of goods and services that a country can consume.
5. The ability to produce a good at a lower opportunity cost than another country.
9. A negative trade balance.
11. The sale of goods in export markets at prices below domestic prices.
13. A limit on the quantity of a good that may be imported.
14. The most desired goods and services that are foregone in order to obtain something else.
15. A tax imposed on imported goods.
16. The amount of good A given up for good B in trade.

Down

1. An agreement to reduce the volume of trade in a specific good.
4. Determined by the intersection of market demand and market supply.
6. The ability of a country to produce a good with fewer resources than other countries.
7. A prohibition on exports or imports.
8. The amount by which exports exceed imports.
10. Goods and services sold to foreign buyers.
12. Goods and services purchased from foreign sources.

True or False: *Circle your choice and explain why any false statements are incorrect.*

T   F   1.   The United States buys large quantities of goods and services from other countries but foreign countries buy very few of our goods and services.

T   F   2.   Workers in an exporting industry have an incentive to lobby for restrictions on trade.

T   F   3.   The United States relies less on foreign trade, as measured by the ratio of exports to GDP, than most other nations.

T   F   4.   Comparative advantage refers to the ability to produce output with fewer resources than any other country.

T   F   5.   If one country has a comparative advantage in producing one of two goods, the other country must have a comparative advantage in the other good.

T   F   6.   It is impossible for a country to consume a mix of goods and services beyond its production-possibilities curve.

T   F   7.   The terms at which countries will trade one good for another will occur between their respective domestic opportunity costs.

T   F   8.   Everybody wins when countries specialize and trade.

T   F   9.   From the consumer's point of view, quotas have the potential to inflict more damage than do tariffs because additional imports are not available at any price.

T   F   10.   Tariffs and quotas raise the price of imported goods to consumers.

Multiple Choice: *Select the correct answer.*

_____   1.   Suppose the production of 1 ton of steel in the United States requires the same amount of resources as the production of 100 metric tons of wheat. In Canada, 2 tons of steel requires the same amount of resources as 200 metric tons of wheat. This means that:
   (a)   Neither country has a comparative advantage.
   (b)   Canada has the comparative advantage in steel.
   (c)   The United States has an absolute advantage in steel.
   (d)   The United States has the comparative advantage in steel.

_____   2.   In Germany, suppose 6 cameras or 4 bicycles can be produced with 1 unit of labor. In Japan, suppose 9 cameras or 5 bicycles can be produced with 1 unit of labor. Therefore:
   (a)   Japan has an absolute advantage in the production of both goods.
   (b)   Japan has a comparative advantage in the production of both goods.
   (c)   Germany has a comparative advantage in the production of cameras.
   (d)   Japan has a comparative advantage in the production of bicycles.

_____   3.   If a country is completely self-reliant in producing goods for its own consumption needs, then:
   (a)   It is consuming more than it could with trade.
   (b)   Its consumption possibilities will equal its production possibilities.
   (c)   It is promoting specialization.
   (d)   It will achieve a higher standard of living by exporting.

_____ 4. The expansion of world output as a result of trade is mainly due to the effects of:
  (a) Higher trade barriers.
  (b) Improved terms of trade.
  (c) Specialization according to comparative advantage.
  (d) Specialization according to absolute advantage.

_____ 5. When one country can produce a given amount of a good using fewer inputs than any other country:
  (a) It has an absolute advantage in producing the good.
  (b) It has a comparative advantage in producing the good.
  (c) Specialization will definitely increase worldwide consumption possibilities.
  (d) All of the above.

_____ 6. "Terms of trade" refers to:
  (a) The opportunity costs incurred in trade.
  (b) The rate at which goods are exchanged.
  (c) The degree to which one country has an absolute advantage.
  (d) Which country pays the transportation costs when trade occurs.

_____ 7. To say that a country has a comparative advantage in the production of wine is to say that:
  (a) It can produce wine with fewer resources than any other country can.
  (b) Its opportunity cost of producing wine is greater than any other country's.
  (c) Its opportunity cost of producing wine is lower than any other country's.
  (d) The relative price of wine is higher in that country than in any other.

_____ 8. America's tariffs on foreign goods result in:
  (a) Lower domestic prices than those that would prevail in their absence.
  (b) A stimulus to efficient American firms that are not protected.
  (c) Higher employment and output in protected industries than would otherwise be the case.
  (d) A more efficient allocation of resources than would occur in their absence.

_____ 9. A principal objective of GATT is to:
  (a) Reduce barriers to trade.
  (b) Settle domestic tax disputes internationally.
  (c) Equalize income tax structures in various countries.
  (d) Protect domestic producers from foreign competition.

_____ 10. World output of goods and services increases with specialization because:
  (a) The world's resources are being used more efficiently.
  (b) Each country's production possibilities curve is shifted outward.
  (c) Each country's workers are able to produce more than they could before specialization.
  (d) All of the above are correct.

_____ 11. Suppose the production of 12 tons of copper in the United States requires the same amount of resources as the production of 1 ton of aluminum. In Mexico, 12 tons of copper requires the same amount of resources as 2 tons of aluminum. This means that:
  (a) Mexico has an absolute advantage in producing copper.
  (b) The United States has a comparative advantage in producing copper.
  (c) The United States has an absolute advantage in producing aluminum.
  (d) All of the above.

Suppose the production possibilities of Japan and the U.S. are given in Table 35.1. Use Table 35.1 to answer questions 12 and 13.

Table 35.1
Output per worker day in the United States and Japan

Country	TV sets (per day)	Bicycles (per day)
Japan	2	10
United States	1	8

_____ 12. Which of the following statements is true?
- (a) The United States has an absolute advantage in the production of bicycles.
- (b) Japan has an absolute advantage in the production of bicycles only.
- (c) Japan has an absolute advantage in the production of TV sets only.
- (d) Japan has an absolute advantage in the production of both bicycles and TV sets.

_____ 13. Suppose the terms of trade are established in such a way that 1 TV set equals 5 bicycles. Which of the following statements would be true?
- (a) These terms of trade provide gains for the United States, but Japan is worse off.
- (b) These terms of trade provide gains for Japan, but the United States is worse off.
- (c) These terms of trade provide gains for the United States, and Japan is no worse off.
- (d) These terms of trade provide gains for Japan, and the United States is no worse off.

_____ 14. As a result of specialization and trade, total world output of goods and services:
- (a) Decreases along with consumption levels.
- (b) Increases along with consumption levels.
- (c) Decreases, but consumption levels increase.
- (d) Increases, but consumption levels decrease.

_____ 15. "Dumping" is said to occur when:
- (a) Foreign producers sell more of a particular good in the United States than domestic producers sell.
- (b) Foreign producers sell their goods in the United States at prices lower than the U.S. average cost of production.
- (c) Foreign producers sell their goods in the United States at prices lower than those prevailing in their own countries.
- (d) The foreign countries have trade surpluses and the United States has a trade deficit.

_____ 16. What should happen to the equilibrium price and quantity in a market as a result of a tariff on imports?
- (a) Equilibrium price and quantity should both go up.
- (b) Equilibrium price should go up, and equilibrium quantity should go down.
- (c) Equilibrium price should go down, and equilibrium quantity should go up.
- (d) Equilibrium price and quantity should both go down.

_____ 17. With regard to international trade, the market mechanism:
- (a) Provides a profit incentive to producers who specialize in the goods and services for which a comparative advantage exists.
- (b) Provides a profit incentive to producers who trade in the goods and services for which a comparative advantage exists.
- (c) Determines the terms of trade.
- (d) Does all of the above.

_____ 18. International trade:
   (a)   Lowers prices to consumers.
   (b)   Alters the mix of domestic production.
   (c)   Redistributes income toward export industries.
   (d)   All of the above.

_____ 19. Suppose that Brazil has a comparative advantage in coffee and Mexico has a comparative advantage in tomatoes. Which of the following groups would be worse off if these two countries specialize and trade?
   (a)   Brazilian tomato producers.
   (b)   Brazilian coffee producers.
   (c)   Mexican tomato producers.
   (d)   Everyone is better off when specialization and trade take place.

_____ 20. If we add together all the gains from specialization and trade and then subtract all the losses, the net result would be:
   (a)   Zero; the gains and losses would cancel out.
   (b)   Positive; a net gain for the world and each country.
   (c)   Negative; a net loss for the world and each country.
   (d)   Impossible to tell; the net result could be zero, positive, or negative.

Problems and Applications

Exercise 1

This exercise shows how trade leads to gains by all trading partners through specialization and comparative advantage.

Suppose that Japan has 20 laborers in total and that the United States has 40 laborers. Suppose their production possibilities are given in Table 35.2. (*Be careful:* The table tells you that a worker in Japan can produce 2 TV sets per day *or* 10 bicycles per day, *not* two TV sets *and* 10 bicycles!)

Table 35.2
Output per worker day in the United States and Japan

Country	TV sets (per day)	Bicycles (per day)
Japan	2	10
United States	1	8

1.   Draw the production possibilities curves for each country in Figure 35.1. Assume constant costs of production.

Figure 35.1

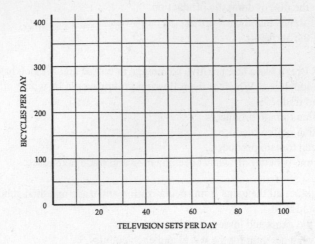

2. Suppose that before trade, Japan uses 12 laborers to produce bicycles and 8 laborers to produce television sets; suppose also that in the United States 20 workers produce bicycles and 20 produce television sets. Complete Table 35.3.

Table 35.3
Output produced and consumed without trade

Country	TV sets (per day)	Bicycles (per day)
Japan	_____	_____
United States	_____	_____
Total	_____	_____

3. Before trade, the total output of television sets is _____ ; of bicycles, _____ .

4. What is the opportunity cost of 1 television set in Japan? _____ In the United States? _____

5. What is the opportunity cost of 1 bicycle in Japan? _____ In the United States? _____

6. If Japan and the United States specialize according to their respective comparative advantages, Japan will produce _____ and the United States will produce _____ . They will do so because the opportunity cost of bicycles in terms of television sets is (lower; higher) in the United States than in Japan, and the opportunity cost of television sets in terms of bicycles is (lower; higher) in Japan than in the United States.

7. After specialization, the total output of television sets is _____ and the total output of bicycles is _____ . (*Hint:* Assume 20 Japanese produce only TV sets, and 40 Americans produce only bicycles.)

8. This output represents an increase of _____ bicycles and _____ television sets over the pre-specialization output. (*Hint:* Compare answers to questions 3 and 7.)

Exercise 2

This exercise will help you understand how the terms of trade are determined. Refer to Exercise 1 for the data.

If Japan and the United States are to benefit from the increased production, trade must take place. The Japanese will be willing to trade television sets for bicycles as long as they get back more bicycles than they could get in their own country.

1. The terms of trade will be between 1 television set equals _____ bicycles and 1 television set equals _____ bicycles.

2. If the terms of trade were 4 bicycles equals one television set:
    (a) Neither country would buy bicycles, but both would buy TV sets.
    (b) Neither country would buy TV sets, but both would buy bicycles.
    (c) Both countries would buy bicycles and TV sets.

3. Suppose that the two countries agree that the terms of trade will be 6 bicycles equals 1 television set. Let Japan export 20 television sets per day to the United States. Complete Table 35.4. Assume that Japan produces 40 television sets per day and the United States produces 320 bicycles.

Table 35.4
Consumption combination after trade

Country	TV sets (per day)	Bicycles (per day)
Japan	_____	_____
United States	_____	_____
Total	40	320

4. As a result of specialization and trade, the United States has the same quantity of television sets and _____ more bicycles per day. (Compare Tables 35.3 and 35.4.)

5. As a result of specialization and trade, Japan has the same number of bicycles and _____ more television sets per day.

Now suppose that at the exchange rate of 6 bicycles to 1 TV set, Japan would like to export 10 TV sets and import 60 bicycles per day. Suppose also that the United States desires to export 90 bicycles and import 15 television sets per day.

6. At these terms of trade there is a (shortage; surplus) of television sets.

7. At these terms of trade there is a (shortage; surplus) of bicycles.

8. Which of the following terms of trade would be more likely to result from this situation?
    (a) 5 bicycles equal 1 television set.
    (b) 6 bicycles equal 1 television set.
    (c) 7 bicycles equal 1 television set.

Exercise 3

When protection is provided to producers of a particular product, consumers of that product are harmed because they must pay higher prices than in the absence of protection. In addition, the effects of the protection in one market spill over into related factor and product markets, thus distorting both production and consumption patterns. This exercise will help you to discover how this occurs.

Reread the *In the News* article entitled "Some See Bush Sheltering Sugar for Votes," and then answer the following questions.

1. What was the U.S. sugar price versus the world sugar price? _____
    _____

2. If the U.S. sugar quota was abolished, which of the following would most likely occur for the price of sugar in the United States, *ceteris paribus*?
    (a)   The price would rise.
    (b)   The price would fall.
    (c)   The price would stay the same.

3. If the sugar quota was abolished, what would you predict to happen to the number of sugar producers in the United States?_____

4. Who is opposed to the sugar quota and why? _____
    _____

5. If the U.S. sugar quota was abolished, what would you predict to happen to the marginal revenue product of labor and the level of employment in the Australian sugar industry, *ceteris paribus*?_____

Common Errors

The first statement in each "common error" below is incorrect. Each incorrect statement is followed by a corrected version and an explanation.

1. A country must have an *absolute advantage* in order to gain from trade with another country. WRONG!

    A country must have a *comparative advantage* in order to gain from trade with another country. RIGHT!

    Mutually advantageous trade requires only that the opportunity costs of producing goods differ between the two countries, *ceteris paribus*. Another way of stating this is that the production possibilities curves of the two countries must have different slopes. The two circumstances noted above are indicated in Figure 35.2 below.

Figure 35.2

In diagram (a), in which country B has an absolute advantage over country A, the production possibilities curves have the same slope; thus mutually advantageous trade *is not* possible. In diagram (b), each country has a comparative advantage because the production possibilities curves of the two countries have different slopes; thus mutually advantageous trade *is* possible.

2.   Foreign trade costs a country jobs. WRONG!

Although jobs may be lost, new ones may be created by the opportunities opened up with trade. RIGHT!

    When countries specialize and trade according to the law of comparative advantage, some particular workers and firms may be hurt by imports, but the economy as a whole may gain from trade. More output per resource input will be attainable.

3.   A country is well off only as long as it exports more than it imports. WRONG!

Countries may, at times, be well off when they experience a trade surplus; they may also be well off when they have a trade deficit. RIGHT!

    Both trade deficits and trade surpluses can be problems if either situation persists for a long period of time. Trade surpluses mean that a country is giving more of its limited, precious resources in trade than it is acquiring from other countries. The currencies of deficit countries tend to depreciate, which means they will be unable to buy as many foreign goods with a unit of currency.

4.   Countries tend to enter into trade to get things they cannot produce themselves. WRONG!

Countries very often trade for things they could produce themselves. RIGHT!

    Be careful! Countries often trade for things they could produce themselves because the relative costs of domestic production would be prohibitive. Take baskets as an example. Producers in the U.S. could certainly produce baskets if they really wanted to. The technique is not difficult to learn and the materials are abundant. But baskets do not lend themselves to machine production, and hand labor is expensive here. The cost in terms of goods forgone would be tremendous. (So would the price of the baskets.) The United States is better off specializing in something such as computers, where it has a comparative advantage and trading for baskets, where it clearly does not have a comparative advantage.

489

5. The effects of protection affect only workers in the protected industry and the domestic consumers of the protected commodity. WRONG!

The effects of protection spread to many other markets both here and abroad as producers and consumers adjust their production and consumption patterns. RIGHT!

Protection and output changes in any market are bound to set off additional changes in related markets. Higher prices for a protected product lead consumers to seek out substitutes with lower prices. This should increase the demand for the substitute and set off a host of other changes in related input and product markets. Similarly, if the protected commodity is used as an input, an increase in its price will lead to a search for substitutes with lower prices and have consequent impacts on related markets. In the case of sugar, corn based high-fructose corn syrup has replaced sugar to such an extent that corn growers, fearing a reduction in the demand for their output, now lobby their congressional delegations to maintain the sugar quota! Similar impacts can be expected in the markets of foreign producers.

•ANSWERS•

Using Key Terms

Across
2. production possibilities
3. consumption possibilities
5. comparative advantage
9. trade deficit
11. dumping
13. quota
14. opportunity cost
15. tariff
16. terms of trade

Down
1. voluntary restraint agreement
4. equilibrium price
6. absolute advantage
7. embargo
8. trade surplus
10. exports
12. imports

True or False

1. F   Approximately 10 percent of U.S. GDP is exported. In dollar terms, the U.S. is the world's largest exporter of goods and services.
2. F   Workers in an exporting industry typically benefit from trade so they would not lobby for trade restrictions.
3. T
4. F   Comparative advantage refers to the ability to produce output at a smaller opportunity cost than another country, i.e., giving up fewer alternative goods and services.
5. T

6. F   With specialization and free trade it is possible for a country to consume a mix of goods and services beyond its production possibilities curve although it is never possible for a country to produce beyond its production possibilities curve.
7. T
8. F   Although countries as a whole benefit from specialization and free trade, there are always individuals and groups that may lose, e.g., import-competing firms.
9. T
10. T

Multiple Choice

1.	a	5.	a	9.	a	13.	c	17.	d
2.	a	6.	b	10.	a	14.	b	18.	d
3.	b	7.	c	11.	b	15.	c	19.	a
4.	c	8.	c	12.	d	16.	b	20.	b

Problems and Applications

Exercise 1

1. **Figure 35.1 Answer**

2. **Table 35.3 Answer**

Country	TV sets	Bicycles
Japan	16	120
United States	20	160
Total	36	280

3. 36; 280
4. 5 bicycles; 8 bicycles
5. 1/5 television set; 1/8 television set
6. Television sets; bicycles; lower; lower
7. 40; 320
8. 40; 4

Exercise 2

1. 5; 8
2. a
3. **Table 35.4 Answer**

Country	TV sets	Bicycles
Japan	20	120
United States	20	200
Total	40	320

4. 40
5. 4
6. Shortage; The Japanese wish to export fewer (10) TV sets than Americans want to import (15).
7. Surplus; The Americans wish to export more (90) bicycles than the Japanese want to import (60).
8. c; The shortage of TV sets will cause their price to increase.

Exercise 3

1. The U.S. sugar price was 21.4 cents per pound and the world sugar price was 7.5 cents per pound.
2. b; The market should reach equilibrium between the world price and the protected U.S. price.
3. The number of producers should decrease because the absence of protection should cause economic losses in the U.S. sugar industry.
4. The Grocery Manufacturers of America are opposed. They believe the decision is politically motivated. In addition the users of sugar, such as candymakers and consumers, are likely to be opposed because the quota forces them to pay higher prices for sugar. Australian sugar producers are also adversely affected.
5. Their marginal product should increase as the world price of sugar rises, and the level of employment should increase.

CHAPTER 36

International Finance

Quick Review

- All of the trade between nations must somehow be financed. Since each country has its own money and in order to facilitate trade, markets for foreign exchange have developed.

- When goods are traded between countries, there is an exchange of currency. The exchange rate is the price of one currency in terms of another currency.

- A currency will appreciate or depreciate in value based on the supply and demand for the currency. Factors that shift the foreign exchange supply or demand include changes in relative incomes, relative prices, and interest rates.

- If a nation's currency appreciates, its goods become more expensive for foreigners and it exports less, *ceteris paribus*. The opposite is true if the currency depreciates.

- The balance of payments is an accounting statement of a country's international economic transactions. It is composed of the capital-account balance and the current-account balance.

- Countries resist exchange rate movements because any change in the exchange rate automatically alters the price of all exports and imports. These changes complicate the conduct of domestic monetary and fiscal policy.

- Under a fixed exchange rate system, the value of a currency does not change because of shifts in the supply or demand for the foreign exchange. In this case balance of payments deficits or surpluses occur because of the excess demand or excess supply of foreign exchange.

- To maintain fixed rates, governments must intervene. Intervention requires a country to accumulate reserves (foreign currencies, gold, etc.) sometimes and to release reserves at other times.

- A flexible exchange rate system does not require government intervention because the exchange rate automatically adjusts to the equilibrium rate. But a totally flexible system can result in many changes. To avoid this problem a system of "managed rates" has evolved in which governments still intervene, but now with the idea of reducing, rather than eliminating, fluctuations.

Learning Objectives

After reading Chapter 36 and doing the following exercises, you should:

1. Understand that an exchange rate is the price of a currency.
2. Know the forces that operate on the demand side of the foreign exchange market.
3. Know the forces that operate on the supply side of the foreign exchange market.
4. Understand how supply and demand interact to determine the equilibrium exchange rate.
5. Understand the essential aspects of balance-of-payments accounting.
6. Be able to demonstrate graphically the forces that cause a currency to appreciate or depreciate.
7. Understand why there is resistance to exchange-rate changes.
8. Be able to describe several exchange-rate systems and their consequences.
9. Understand the macroeconomic and microeconomic consequences of exchange-rate movements.
10. Be able to describe a balance-of-payments problem.
11. Be aware of the recent history of currency bailouts.

Using Key Terms

Fill in the puzzle on the opposite page with the appropriate term from the list of Key Terms at the end of the chapter in the text.

Across

2. Places where foreign currencies are bought and sold.
4. The amount by which the quantity demanded exceeds the quantity supplied.
6. A system in which governments intervene in foreign-exchange markets to limit exchange-rate fluctuations.
8. Stocks of gold held by a government to purchase foreign exchange.
9. A rise in the price of a currency relative to another.
10. The price of one currency in terms of another currency.
11. A fall in the price of one currency relative to another.
13. A mechanism for fixing the exchange rate.
14. The price at which the quantity demanded equals the quantity supplied.
15. An excess demand for domestic currency at current exchange rates.

Down

1. An excess demand for foreign currency at current exchange rates.
2. Holdings of foreign exchange by official government agencies.
3. Floating exchange rates.
5. A summary record of a country's international economic transactions.
7. An abrupt depreciation of a currency whose value was fixed or managed by the government.
12. A situation in which the value of imports exceeds the value of exports.

Puzzle 36.1

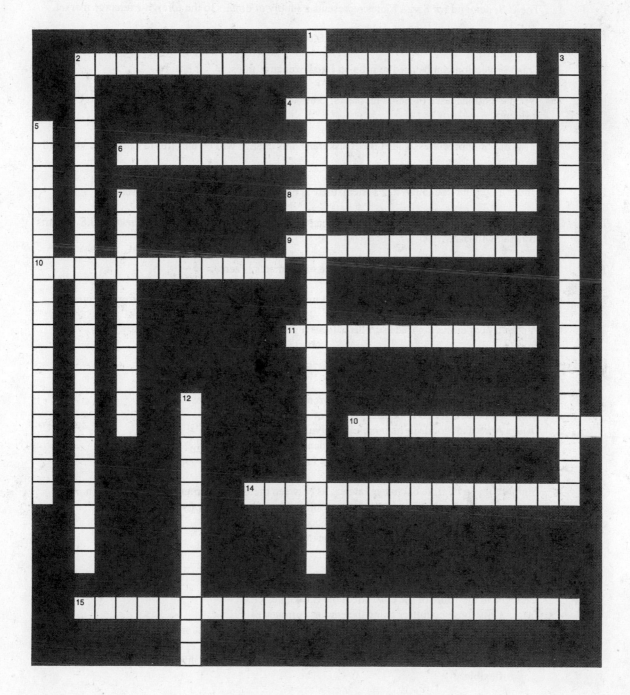

495

True or False: *Circle your choice and explain why any false statements are incorrect.*

T   F   1.   The U.S. demand for Swiss francs represents a supply of dollars to the foreign-exchange market.

T   F   2.   Increased foreign travel by Americans tends to cause the dollar to appreciate, *ceteris paribus.*

T   F   3.   Trade protection can be used to prop up fixed exchange rates.

T   F   4.   When the dollar price of Euros increases, German machinery becomes more expensive to U.S. residents.

T   F   5.   If the dollar appreciates against the Swiss franc, this change will be harmful to California vineyard owners.

T   F   6.   Under a flexible-exchange-rate system, there is no need for foreign-exchange reserves.

T   F   7.   If the U.S. price level rises more rapidly than the Japanese price level, *ceteris paribus,* U.S. exports to Japan will rise.

T   F   8.   When exchange rates are fixed, the balance of payments is zero.

T   F   9.   If there is a deficit in the capital account, it must be offset by a surplus in the current account.

T   F   10.   A country experiencing trade surpluses faces higher foreign debt and interest costs.

Multiple Choice: *Select the correct answer.*

_____   1.   An increase in the dollar price of other currencies will tend to cause:
(a)   American goods to be cheaper for foreigners.
(b)   American goods to be more expensive for foreigners.
(c)   Foreign goods to be cheaper to residents of the United States.
(d)   Foreign goods to be more expensive to residents of foreign countries.

_____   2.   Suppose that a flexible exchange rate exists between the U.S. dollar and the Japanese yen. An increase in the supply of yen (a rightward shift in the supply curve of yen) will tend to:
(a)   Increase U.S. imports of Japanese goods.
(b)   Push the U.S. balance of trade in the direction of a surplus.
(c)   Lower the yen price of the dollar.
(d)   Raise the dollar price of the yen.

_____   3.   Changes in the value of the euro affect the economies of:
(a)   Only those countries using the euro as currency.
(b)   All European countries but there would no significant impact on countries outside Europe.
(c)   Potentially the entire world.
(d)   There would be no significant impact on any economies as long as exchange rates are flexible.

_____   4.   If the exchange rate between U.S. dollars and Japanese yen changes from $1 = 100 yen to $1 = 90 yen:
(a)   All Japanese producers and consumers will lose.
(b)   U.S. auto producers and autoworkers will lose.
(c)   U.S. consumers of Japanese TV sets will gain.
(d)   Japanese tourists to the U.S. will gain.

_____ 5. A country will experience a reduction in its balance-of-payments deficit, *ceteris paribus*, if:
   (a) Its level of GDP rises relative to foreign levels of GDP.
   (b) Its prices fall relative to foreign price levels, *ceteris paribus*.
   (c) The domestic price of the foreign currency falls.
   (d) It lowers its tariffs.

_____ 6. A result of the Asian Crisis of 1997-98 was:
   (a) A general increase in the value of the U.S. dollar in relation to Southeast Asian currencies.
   (b) A major decrease in the level of U.S. exports to Southeast Asia.
   (c) Political unrest in many Southeast Asian countries.
   (d) All of the above.

_____ 7. Greater volatility of floating exchange rates results in:
   (a) Greater costs because of uncertainty.
   (b) Balance-of-payments instability.
   (c) Smaller market shortages and surpluses of currencies.
   (d) Depletion of foreign reserves.

_____ 8. Which of the following changes will tend to cause a shift in the domestic demand curve for foreign currencies?
   (a) Changes in domestic incomes, *ceteris paribus*.
   (b) Changes in domestic prices of goods, *ceteris paribus*.
   (c) Changes in consumer taste for foreign goods, *ceteris paribus*.
   (d) All of the above.

_____ 9. An increase in the U.S. trade deficit could be caused by:
   (a) A depreciation of the dollar in terms of other currencies.
   (b) An appreciation of the dollar in terms of other currencies.
   (c) The imposition of a tariff on imported goods.
   (d) An increase in the capital-account deficit.

_____ 10. In a floating-exchange-rate system, the capital-account balance equals:
   (a) The negative of the current-account balance.
   (b) Foreign purchases of U.S. assets minus U.S. purchases of foreign assets.
   (c) The balance of payments minus the sum of the trade balance, the services balance, and unilateral transfers.
   (d) All of the above.

_____ 11. American citizens planning a vacation abroad would welcome:
   (a) Appreciation of the dollar.
   (b) Depreciation of the dollar.
   (c) Devaluation of the dollar.
   (d) Evaluation of the dollar.

_____ 12. A change in the exchange rate for a country's currency alters the prices of:
   (a) Exports only.
   (b) Imports only.
   (c) Both exports and imports.
   (d) Only domestic goods and services.

_____ 13. In a floating exchange-rate regime, the overall "balance" of the balance of payments must be:
   (a) Equal to zero.
   (b) Positive if exports of goods and services exceed imports of goods and services.
   (c) Positive if the capital account is in surplus.
   (d) Negative if the current account is in deficit.

14. When exchange rates are flexible, they are:
    (a) Determined by proclamation of the monetary authorities of a country.
    (b) Determined by the relative levels of gold reserves.
    (c) Permitted to vary with changes in supply and demand in the foreign exchange market.
    (d) Determined by the provisions of the Bretton Woods agreement.

15. If the U.S. dollar depreciates, the United States should experience, in the long run, a:
    (a) Lower inflation rate.
    (b) Smaller deficit on the U.S. trade balance.
    (c) Larger deficit on the U.S. current account.
    (d) Larger deficit on the U.S. capital account.

16. The major drawback to a system of managed exchange rates is that:
    (a) A country's efforts to manage exchange-rate movements may arouse suspicion and retaliation.
    (b) A country's efforts to affect changes in exchange rates are almost totally ineffective.
    (c) Government efforts to alter exchange rates usually result in violent disruptions of the domestic economy.
    (d) It requires enormous gold reserves.

17. If French speculators believed the yen was going to appreciate against the dollar, they would:
    (a) Purchase euros.
    (b) Purchase dollars.
    (c) Purchase yen.
    (d) Sell yen.

18. Suppose that at the prevailing yen-dollar exchange rate, there is an excess demand for yen. To prevent the dollar from depreciating, the United States might:
    (a) Raise taxes.
    (b) Reduce government spending.
    (c) Raise interest rates.
    (d) Do all of the above.

19. A currency bailout:
    (a) Occurs when an economy is lent money in order to increase or maintain the value of its currency.
    (b) Can help avoid a "domino effect" of depreciating currencies in other economies.
    (c) Can be ultimately self-defeating because it saves the country receiving the bailout from implementing politically unpopular domestic policies which could have prevented the problem in the first place.
    (d) All of the above are correct.

20. The capital account includes:
    (a) Trade in goods.
    (b) Foreign purchases of U.S. assets.
    (c) Unilateral transfers.
    (d) Trade in services.

Problems and Applications

Exercise 1

This exercise provides practice in determining exchange rates.

1. Table 36.1 depicts the hypothetical demand for and supply of British pounds in terms of U.S. dollars. Use the information in Table 36.1 to plot the demand and supply of British pounds at the exchange rates indicated in Figure 36.1. Then answer questions 2-4.

Table 36.1
Monthly demand for and supply of British pounds in the United States

Dollars per British pound	Quantity demanded	Quantity supplied
4.50	100	700
4.00	200	600
3.50	300	500
3.00	400	400
2.50	500	300
2.00	600	200
1.50	700	100

Figure 36.1
Demand and supply curves for pounds

2. What is the equilibrium rate of exchange? _____

3. At a price of $2 per pound there would be excess:
   (a) Demand, and the exchange rate for pounds would rise.
   (b) Demand, and the exchange rate for pounds would fall.
   (c) Supply, and the exchange rate would rise.
   (d) Supply, and the exchange rate would fall.

499

4. Suppose that Americans suddenly increased their demand for British exports. The dollar price of pounds would (rise; fall).

5. T F Whenever one currency depreciates, another currency must appreciate.

6. As a result of the increased demand for British exports, the pound price of the dollar would (rise; fall).

Exercise 2

This exercise shows why one currency appreciates when another currency depreciates. It also shows why the demand for dollars represents the supply of other currencies, while the supply of dollars represents the demand for other currencies in the foreign-exchange markets. In learning these things, you will get practice in making calculations with exchange rates.

1. Table 36.2 includes the sources of demand and supply of dollars. In the first column, check off the items that are the source of the demand for dollars. In the second column, check off the items that are the source of the supply of dollars. (*Hint*: There are two kinds of speculators—those who think the dollar will rise and those who think it will fall. You must sort the two types of speculators to determine which type will supply dollars and which will demand dollars.)

Table 36.2
Sources of supply and demand for dollars and pounds

	(1) Demand for $	(2) Supply of $	(3) Demand for £	(4) Supply of £
Foreign demand for American exports	___	___	___	___
Foreign demand for American investments	___	___	___	___
Speculation that the dollar will appreciate	___	___	___	___
American demand for imports	___	___	___	___
American demand for investments in foreign countries	___	___	___	___
Speculation that the dollar will depreciate	___	___	___	___

2. If we assume there are just two currencies in the world, the dollar ($) and the pound (£), then the items in Table 36.2 also account for the supply and demand for the pound. Once again, place checks in the appropriate blanks of Table 36.2 to indicate which items will constitute the demand for pounds and which items will constitute the supply of pounds.

3. T F In a two-country world the sources of demand for dollars are the same as the sources of the supply of the pound, and the sources of the supply of dollars are the same as the sources of the demand for pounds.

4. T F The sources of demand for dollars are the same as the sources of supply for all other currencies in terms of dollars. The sources of supply of dollars are the same as the sources of demand for all other currencies in terms of dollars.

5. Let's return to our assumption that there are only two countries. Use your observations in the previous two questions and your knowledge of converting one currency into another to find the quantities of dollars supplied (column 3) and quantities of dollars demanded (column 6) in Table 36.3. Use the information in Table 36.3, which is the same as the data we used in Exercise 1 above, to compute the supply and demand for pounds.

Table 36.3
Supply and demand for dollars ($) and pounds (£)

(1) Price of a £ ($ / £)	(2) Quantity of £ demanded	(3) Quantity of $ supplied	(4) Price of a $ (£ / $)	(5) Quantity of £ supplied	(6) Quantity of $ demanded
4.50	100	_____	_____	700	_____
4.00	200	_____	_____	600	_____
3.50	300	_____	_____	500	_____
3.00	400	_____	_____	400	_____
2.50	500	_____	_____	300	_____
2.00	600	_____	_____	200	_____
1.50	700	_____	_____	100	_____

6. Complete column 4 of Table 36.3 by converting the price of pounds (£) in terms of dollars ($) in column 1 to the price of dollars in terms of pounds. (*Hint*: They are reciprocals of each other. Remember that to find the price of any good or currency, that good or currency appears in the denominator!)

7. From the data on the demand for the dollar (columns 4 and 6 of Table 36.3), draw the demand curve for the dollar in Figure 36.2. From the data on the supply of the dollar (columns 3 and 4 of Table 36.3), draw the supply curve for the dollar in Figure 36.2.

Figure 36.2
Demand and supply of dollars

8. The equilibrium value of the dollar is _____ , and the equilibrium quantity of dollars is _____ .

9. When you multiply the equilibrium quantity of dollars by the equilibrium exchange rate for the dollar in terms of pounds (£), you find the quantity of pounds is _____. When you find the reciprocal of the equilibrium exchange rate for the dollar, you find the exchange rate for pounds is _____ .

10. T F When you multiply the equilibrium quantity of dollars by the equilibrium exchange rate for the dollar in terms of pounds (£), you have calculated the equilibrium quantity of pounds. (Compare your answer to question 9 in this exercise with your answer to question 2, Exercise 1 above.)

11. T   F   The equilibrium exchange rate for the dollar equals the equilibrium exchange rate for the pound.

Exercise 3

The media often feature articles about international financial issues.

Read the article entitled "Nobel Prize Was Nobler in October." Then answer the following questions.

1. According to the article, what was the dollar value of the Nobel Prize at the time it was announced? _____

2. How much was it worth two months later? _____

3. Why did the value change so much? _____

Common Errors

The first statement in each "common error" below is incorrect. Each incorrect statement is followed by a corrected version and an explanation.

1. The price of a dollar in terms of yen is the number of dollars per yen. WRONG!

    The price of a dollar in terms of yen is the number of yen per dollar. RIGHT!

    This mistake can cost a bundle if you are in a foreign country and don't know how to distinguish the price of a dollar from the price of the other currency. In Japan you don't want to give $100 for a single yen note when you should be receiving 100 yen for $1! Remember that the item for which you want a price must appear in the denominator of the price. For example, the price of tomatoes is the number of dollars divided by the number of tomatoes that are purchased. Similarly, the price of a yen is the number of dollars divided by the number of yen that are purchased. The price of a dollar is the number of yen divided by the number of dollars that are purchased.

2. The supply and demand for dollars in the foreign-exchange market is the same thing as the supply and demand for money (dollars) targeted by the Fed. WRONG!

    The supply and demand for dollars in the foreign-exchange market is a totally different concept from the supply and demand for money. RIGHT!

    Remember that the price of money was the interest rate when we were focusing on the supply and demand for money. In the foreign-exchange market the price is the exchange rate, not the interest rate. Furthermore, the supply and demand for money (dollars), which is the focus of the Fed, occurs geographically within the United States. The foreign-exchange market occurs between countries—literally on the phone lines between banks of different countries. We can visualize the foreign-exchange market as an area totally outside of borders in which money temporarily enters for the purpose of being exchanged. While domestic monetary policies may influence the amount of money going into the foreign-exchange market, the link is often indirect. In fact, when the Fed tightens monetary policy to reduce the supply of dollars, the foreign-exchange market may see an *increase* in the supply of dollars as foreigners seek the higher interest rates from a tighter U.S. monetary policy.

3. A country is well off if its currency appreciates steadily over a long period of time. WRONG!

   Both appreciating currencies and depreciating currencies create problems. RIGHT!

   Be careful! There are problems associated with steadily appreciating currencies *and* with steadily depreciating currencies. People sometimes view a depreciating currency as a source of national shame and dislike the higher cost (and inflation) associated with higher prices of foreign goods. However, depreciation may make a country's exports more competitive, may lead to more jobs, and may help correct a trade deficit. By contrast, a country with an appreciating currency develops employment problems and a loss of competitiveness against other countries, even if it has more buying power as a result of its stronger currency.

4. When countries have trade deficits, money really flows out. When they have surpluses, money really flows in. WRONG!

   Money is not physically sent in most transactions, but the claim to ownership is. RIGHT!

   Most foreign trade is transacted by check and is just a "flow" of bookkeeping entries. Thus, it is the claim to ownership that flows, not the money. When countries run trade deficits, their trading partners add to their claims against them. For countries with a trade surplus, the reverse is true.

5. There are balance-of-payments surpluses and deficits under floating exchange rates. WRONG!

   The balance of payments is always zero under floating exchange rates. RIGHT!

   Under fixed exchange rates, the government must balance surpluses and deficits on the balance of payments with changes in reserves. With floating exchange rates, there is no reserve currency and any transfers abroad by the government are simply classified as unilateral transfers and are included in the current account. By definition, the current account and the capital account balance each other under a floating exchange-rate system.

•ANSWERS•

Using Key Terms

Across
2. foreign-exchange markets
4. market shortage
6. managed exchange rates
8. gold reserves
9. appreciation
10. exchange rate
11. depreciation
13. gold standard
14. equilibrium price
15. balance-of-payments surplus

Down

1. balance-of-payments deficit
2. foreign-exchange reserves
3. flexible exchange rate
5. balance of payments
7. devaluation
12. trade deficit

True or False

1. T
2. F   Increased foreign travel by Americans tends to increase the demand for foreign currency, thus increasing the supply of U.S. dollars and reducing the value of the dollar.
3. T
4. T
5. T
6. T
7. F   U.S. goods will be relatively more expensive to Japan, thus reducing exports.
8. F   Fixed exchange rates tend to cause balance-of-payments deficits and surpluses because they cause shortages and surpluses of currencies.
9. T
10. F   A country experiencing trade deficits will have higher foreign debt and interest rates because that country will have to borrow to finance the additional goods and services it is consuming over what it is producing.

Multiple Choice

1. a	5. b	9. b	13. a	17. c
2. a	6. d	10. d	14. c	18. d
3. c	7. a	11. a	15. b	19. d
4. d	8. d	12. c	16. a	20. b

Problems and Applications

Exercise 1

1. **Figure 36.1 Answer**

2. $3 per British pound   3. a   4. rise   5. T   6. fall

Exercise 2

1. and 2.   **Table 36.2 Answer**

	(1) Demand for $	(2) Supply of $	(3) Demand for £	(4) Supply of £
Foreign demand for American exports	X	—	—	X
Foreign demand for American investments	X	—	—	X
Speculation that the dollar will appreciate	X	—	—	X
American demand for imports	—	X	X	—
American demand for investments in foreign countries	—	X	X	—
Speculation that the dollar will depreciate	—	X	X	—

3. T
4. T
5. and 6.   **Table 36.3 Answer**

Price of a £ ($ / £) (1)		Quantity of £ demanded (2)		Quantity of $ supplied (3)	Price of a $ (£ / $) (4)	Quantity of £ supplied (5)	Quantity of $ demanded (6)
4.50	x	100	=	450	0.222 = 1/4.50	700	3,150
4.00	x	200	=	800	0.25 = 1/4	600	2,400
3.50	x	300	=	1,050	0.29 = 1/3.50	500	1,750
3.00	x	400	=	1,200	0.33 = 1/3	400	1,200
2.50	x	500	=	1,250	0.40 = 1/2.50	300	750
2.00	x	600	=	1,200	0.50 = 1/2	200	400
1.50	x	700	=	1,050	0.67 = 1/1.50	100	150

7.   **Figure 36.2 Answer**

505

8. 1/3 £ per dollar; $1,200
9. 400 (= 1,200 x 1/3); $3 per pound [= 1 ÷ (1/3)]
10. T
11. F   The equilibrium exchange rate for the dollar equals the *reciprocal* of the equilibrium exchange rate for the pound.

Exercise 3

1. $1.2 million
2. $958,000
3. The Swedish krona depreciated, which caused the value of the prize to decrease.